Dear ...

for you

I really can't thank you enough. It's been a real pleasure, and I will miss you!

♡ Laura

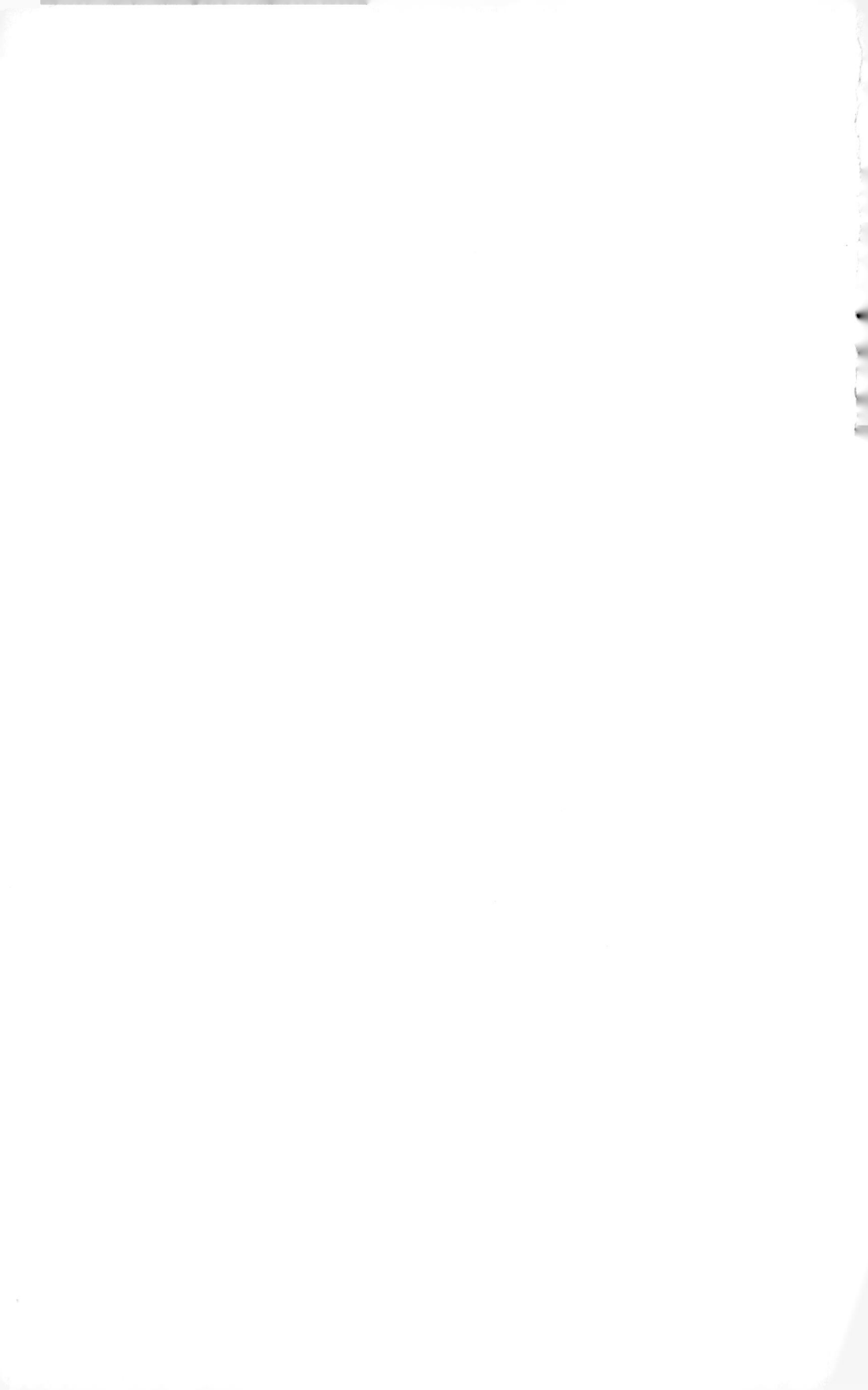

Catholic Gentry in English Society

Coughton Court from the West, Coughton Court, The Throckmorton Collection (The National Trust), by John Hammond.

Catholic Gentry in English Society
The Throckmortons of Coughton from Reformation to Emancipation

Edited by

PETER MARSHALL AND GEOFFREY SCOTT

ASHGATE

© Peter Marshall, Geoffrey Scott and the contributors 2009

All rights reserved. No part of this publication may be reproduced, stored in a retrieval system or transmitted in any form or by any means, electronic, mechanical, photocopying, recording or otherwise without the prior permission of the publisher.

Peter Marshall and Geoffrey Scott have asserted their moral right under the Copyright, Designs and Patents Act, 1988, to be identified as the editors of this work.

Published by
Ashgate Publishing Limited
Wey Court East
Union Road
Farnham
Surrey, GU9 7PT
England

Ashgate Publishing Company
Suite 420
101 Cherry Street
Burlington
VT 05401-4405
USA

www.ashgate.com

British Library Cataloguing in Publication Data
Catholic Gentry in English Society : the Throckmortons of Coughton from Reformation to Emancipation. – (Catholic Christendom, 1300–1700)
  1. Throckmorton (Family) 2. Throckmorton (Family) – Political activity
3. Aristocracy (Social class) – England – Biography 4. Catholics – England
– Political activity – History 5. Religion and politics – England – History
  I. Marshall, Peter II. Scott, Geoffrey
305.5'2'088282

Library of Congress Cataloging-in-Publication Data
Catholic Gentry in English Society : Throckmortons of Coughton from Reformation to Emancipation / [edited by] Peter Marshall and Geoffrey Scott.
    p. cm. — (Catholic Christendom, 1300–1700)
  Includes index.
  ISBN 978-0-7546-6432-1 (hardcover : alk. paper) 1. Throckmorton family.
2. Catholics—England—Biography. 3. Gentry—England—Biography.
4. Coughton Court (England)—Biography. 5. Coughton Court (England)
—History. 6. England—Biography. 7. England—Social life and customs.
8. England—Social conditions.
  I. Marshall, Peter, 1964– II. Scott, Geoffrey, OSB.

CT787.T48M37 2008
941—dc22
                                                                        2008055070

ISBN 978-0-7546-6432-1

Mixed Sources
Product group from well-managed
forests and other controlled sources
www.fsc.org Cert no. SGS-COC-2482
© 1996 Forest Stewardship Council
FSC

Printed and bound in Great Britain by
TJ International Ltd, Padstow, Cornwall

Contents

Series Editor's Preface		vii
List of Figures		ix
Notes on Contributors		xi
Foreword by David Starkey		xiii
Acknowledgements		xv
Abbreviations and Notes		xvii
1	Introduction: The Catholic Gentry in English Society *Peter Marshall and Geoffrey Scott*	1
2	Crisis of Allegiance: George Throckmorton and Henry Tudor *Peter Marshall*	31
3	Reputation, Credit and Patronage: Throckmorton Men and Women, *c.*1560–1620 *Susan Cogan*	69
4	Coughton and the Gunpowder Plot *Michael Hodgetts*	93
5	Agnes Throckmorton: A Jacobean Recusant Widow *Jan Broadway*	123
6	Stratagems for Survival: Sir Robert and Sir Francis Throckmorton, 1640–1660 *Malcolm Wanklyn*	143
7	The Throckmortons at Home and Abroad, 1680–1800 *Geoffrey Scott*	171
8	An English Catholic Traveller: Sir John Courtenay Throckmorton and the Continent, 1792–1793 *Michael Mullett*	213

| 9 | The Throckmortons Come of Age: Political and Social Alignments, 1826–1862
Alban Hood | 247 |

Appendix: Genealogical Tables 269
Index 273

Series Editor's Preface

The still-usual emphasis on medieval (or Catholic) and reformation (or Protestant) religious history has meant neglect of the middle ground, both chronological and ideological. As a result, continuities between the middle ages and early modern Europe have been overlooked in favor of emphasis on radical discontinuities. Further, especially in the later period, the identification of 'reformation' with various kinds of Protestantism means that the vitality and creativity of the established church, whether in its Roman or local manifestations, has been left out of account. In the last few years, an upsurge of interest in the history of traditional (or catholic) religion makes these inadequacies in received scholarship even more glaring and in need of systematic correction. The series will attempt this by covering all varieties of religious behavior, broadly interpreted, not just (or even especially) traditional institutional and doctrinal church history. It will to the maximum degree possible be interdisciplinary, comparative and global, as well as non-confessional. The goal is to understand religion, primarily of the 'Catholic' variety, as a broadly human phenomenon, rather than as a privileged mode of access to superhuman realms, even implicitly.

The period covered, 1300–1700, embraces the moment which saw an almost complete transformation of the place of religion in the life of Europeans, whether considered as a system of beliefs, as an institution, or as a set of social and cultural practices. In 1300, vast numbers of Europeans, from the pope down, fully expected Jesus's return and the beginning of His reign on earth. By 1700, very few Europeans, of whatever level of education, would have subscribed to such chiliastic beliefs. Pierre Bayle's notorious sarcasms about signs and portents are not idiosyncratic. Likewise, in 1300 the vast majority of Europeans probably regarded the pope as their spiritual head; the institution he headed was probably the most tightly integrated and effective bureaucracy in Europe. Most Europeans were at least nominally Christian, and the pope had at least nominal knowledge of that fact. The papacy, as an institution, played a central role in high politics, and the clergy in general formed an integral part of most governments, whether central or local. By 1700, Europe was divided into a myriad of different religious allegiances, and even those areas officially subordinate to the pope were both more nominally Catholic in belief (despite colossal efforts at imposing uniformity) and also in allegiance than they had been four hundred years earlier. The pope had become only one political factor, and not one of the first rank. The clergy, for its part, had virtually disappeared from secular governments as well as losing much of its local authority. The stage was set for the Enlightenment.

Thomas F. Mayer,
Augustana College

List of Figures

Frontispiece: Coughton Court from the West, Coughton Court, The Throckmorton Collection (The National Trust), by John Hammond. ii
1.1 Weston Underwood, *c.*1826, lithograph at Coughton Court, courtesy of The Throckmorton Estates, Coughton Court. 8
2.1 The Denny Dole Gate, Coughton Court, courtesy of The National Trust. 55
2.2 Katherine, wife of Sir George Throckmorton, *c.*1489–1552, Coughton Court, courtesy of The National Trust. 64
6.1 Ambrose Throckmorton, Coughton Court, courtesy of The National Trust. 158
7.1 Buckland House, engraving of *c.*1827, courtesy of Douai Abbey Library. 174
7.2 Late seventeenth-century Flemish Mass cabinet, Coughton Court, courtesy of The National Trust. 177
7.3 'Child Robin', later Sir Robert Throckmorton, fourth baronet, Coughton Court, courtesy of The National Trust. 186
7.4a Abbess Frances Anne Throckmorton, by Nicolas de Largillière, Coughton Court, courtesy of The National Trust. 196
7.4b Abbess Elizabeth Throckmorton, by Largillière, courtesy of National Gallery of Art, Washington DC. 196
7.4c Sir Robert Throckmorton, fourth baronet, by Largillière, Coughton Court, courtesy of The National Trust. 196
7.4d Sister Frances Wollascott, by Largillière, courtesy of the Art Gallery of South Australia, Adelaide. 196
7.5 Robert Throckmorton (1750–79), by Pompeo Batoni, Coughton Court, courtesy of The National Trust. 197
7.6 Anna Maria Throckmorton (née Paston) (*c.*1732–99), Coughton Court, courtesy of The National Trust. 203
7.7 Sir John Courtenay Throckmorton (1753–1819), fifth baronet, by Thomas Phillips, Coughton Court, courtesy of The National Trust. 210
9.1 Sir Robert George Throckmorton, eighth baronet (1800–62), Coughton Court, courtesy of The National Trust. 254

Notes on Contributors

Jan Broadway is technical director of the Centre for Editing Lives and Letters at Queen Mary, University of London. She is the author of 'No historie so meete': Gentry culture and the development of local history in Elizabethan and early Stuart England (2006) and is currently working on a biography of Sir William Dugdale (1605–86).

Susan Cogan is a doctoral candidate in history at the University of Colorado, Boulder, and is completing a thesis on patronage and clientage among Catholic families in the Midlands in the later sixteenth and seventeenth centuries.

Michael Hodgetts is editor of *Midland Catholic History* and of the publications of the Archdiocese of Birmingham Historical Commission. He was formerly editor of *Recusant History* and of the Records and Monographs series of the Catholic Record Society.

Alban Hood OSB is novice master at Douai Abbey and a member of the English Benedictine History Commission. He was awarded his doctorate in history from the University of Liverpool for a thesis on the English Benedictines in the early nineteenth century. He is a contributor to the *ODNB* and to various journals, including *Recusant History*.

Peter Marshall is Professor of Early Modern Religious and Cultural History at the University of Warwick. His books include *Reformation England, 1480–1642* (2003) and *Mother Leakey and the Bishop: A Ghost Story* (2007).

Michael Mullett is Professor Emeritus of History at the University of Lancaster. His many publications include *Catholics in Britain and Ireland, 1558–1829* (1998) and *The Catholic Reformation* (1999).

Geoffrey Scott OSB is abbot of Douai Abbey, president of the Catholic Archives Society, vice president of the Catholic Record Society, and the author of a number of works on eighteenth-century English Catholicism.

Malcolm Wanklyn is Emeritus Professor of Regional History at the University of Wolverhampton. He is currently working on a history of the counties of the Severn Valley (with Kevin Down) and on a database of Midlands Catholics who fought for the king in the First Civil War.

Foreword

David Starkey

Certain families serve as 'the abstracts and brief chronicles' of our broader history. They are not necessarily the most wealthy or powerful, but they are among the most interesting. One such is the Throckmortons of Coughton in Warwickshire. The Throckmortons – the name originally meant 'Town by the Frog Marsh' in Anglo-Saxon – first acquired Coughton in 1409 as the result of a fortunate marriage. Six hundred years later, the Throckmortons live at Coughton still. This book is the story of the family, and, through them, of England.

But 2009 is not only the 600th anniversary of Throckmortons at Coughton; it is also the 500th of the accession of Henry VIII. The head of the family of the day – Sir George – was a favourite of the king and dedicated the great gatehouse at Coughton to him. But he dabbled, almost fatally, in opposition to the Divorce and the Reformation. And where George led, most of his descendants followed – and more boldly.

The result is a paradox. Coughton Court, which attracts thousands of tourists each year, seems to tell its visitors a story of stability and continuity, of the survival and social tenacity of the English landed elites in their rural heartlands. But it should also put the visitor in mind of the deep ideological fractures and contested loyalties that have riven our country's past since Henry VIII and the Reformation. When most of the English ceased being Catholics, the Throckmortons in the main line refused to follow. Instead, they became Roman Catholics or papists: designations at times virtually synonymous with traitor. Like many other Catholic families, the Throckmortons protested against the taint of treason and often sought to become paragons of 'Catholic loyalism'.

But for Catholics, then as arguably now, loyalism has its limits – as it did for the Throckmortons. Even the most casual visitor to Coughton Court will come away remembering that the house and family were deeply implicated in the murderous Gunpowder Plot of 1605; they may even have learned about the 'Throckmorton Plot' of 1583, when Francis, a son of the judge Sir John Throckmorton, was executed for conspiring to assassinate Queen Elizabeth I and put Mary Queen of Scots on the throne. Subsequent Catholic Throckmortons were more circumspect, though this did not shield their estates from sequestration during the Civil War and interregnum; nor their chapel on the east side of the main courtyard at Coughton from the destructive attentions of a Protestant mob in the aftermath of the Revolution of 1688.

By the beginning of the nineteenth century, English (as opposed to Irish) Catholicism was diminishing in its 'otherness'. The Catholic Emancipation Act of 1829 gave papists civil rights and, two years later, Sir Robert Throckmorton was elected as the first English Catholic MP since the seventeenth century. Nevertheless, far into the nineteenth century and beyond – despite the best efforts of families like the Throckmortons – Catholicism retained its exotic, mildly dangerous flavour for most upright Englishmen.

But to label the Throckmortons as a purely 'Catholic' family is to obscure the extent to which the Reformation cut like a knife through the tissues and sinews of the English body politic. For the Throckmortons were divided rather than repulsed by the advent of Protestantism. One important scion, Nicholas, the son of Coughton's rebuilder, Sir George Throckmorton, chose the other path: he was favoured by the Protestant administration of Edward VI. In 1554 he was acquitted – in an astonishing cause célèbre – of treason for complicity in the Wyatt rebellion against the Catholic Mary Tudor, and under Queen Elizabeth he rose to become Chief Butler and Chamberlain of the Exchequer. His daughter, Bess Throckmorton, was a lady-in-waiting to Elizabeth I and wife of the favourite, Sir Walter Ralegh. In Tudor England, leading dissidents were rarely more than a twig or two in the family tree from the heart of the establishment.

Throckmorton is a name that not only weaves its way through English history, nationally as well as locally; it also made its mark on the emergent history of the United States through the Throckmortons who went forth to Roanoke, Virginia and Ellington, Connecticut and multiplied greatly there.

But activity is meaningless without records. Fortunately, the Throckmorton family archive, now split between the Warwickshire Record Office and the Shakespeare Birthplace Trust, is superb. It is fitting that in this anniversary year Peter Marshall, Geoffrey Scott and their team of British and American collaborators have drawn on this material not only to illuminate the history of a remarkable dynasty, but also to raise important questions about the relationship of England's longest-standing religious minority to the mainstream of political and cultural life. Throughout the period between Reformation and Emancipation, 'Catholic gentry' were not merely *in* English society, but through their political and social manoeuvres and negotiations made a notable contribution to its distinctive texture and contours. A history of England with the Catholics left out, or confined to a footnote or an appendix, may be a neater and more comfortable national narrative. But the messy story of conflict, compromise, collaboration and confrontation, which the Throckmorton family and its presence at Coughton exemplifies, is both a more authentic and, ultimately, a more compelling one.

Acknowledgements

The editors have accumulated a litany of debts in the course of compiling this volume. The contribution of Henry Mayr-Harting was critical in getting the book off the ground in its planning stages, and he has maintained a kindly interest in it since. We are similarly grateful to David Starkey, both for recognising the historical importance of the Throckmorton family and for generously agreeing to contribute a foreword. The interest and encouragement expressed by Patrick Collinson, Thomas Freeman, Michael Questier, John Tobias and Chris Warwick has also been much appreciated. We speak for the contributors as a whole in thanking the staff of the Warwickshire Record Office and the Shakespeare Centre Library in Stratford for their efficient and cheerful custodianship of the Throckmorton Papers, and for much help in facilitating access to them. Thanks are due also to John Sharp, Birmingham archdiocesan archivist, and Nicholas Schofield of the Westminster archdiocesan archives, as well as to Peter Huestis of the National Gallery of Art, Washington DC, Tracey Dall of the Art Gallery of South Australia, Adelaide and the staffs of the Berkshire Record Office and British Library. At Coughton Court, Jon Payne and other staff of the Throckmorton estates have been invariably helpful. Charlotte Humphrey's work in cataloguing books and family papers has proved invaluable, as has the willing assistance provided by The National Trust's managerial team, especially Lucy Reid and Linda Martin. We are grateful in addition to Michael Winwood, who drew up the genealogical tables. Mention must also be made of Patrick Tansey, parish priest of Buckland and Faringdon, and of the support offered, in various ways, by Ali, Isabel, Maria and Catherine Marshall. Finally, we wish to record our warm gratitude to Clare McLaren-Throckmorton, current head of the Throckmorton family and chatelaine of Coughton Court, for her generosity in contributing to the costs of the illustrations.

Clare's energy and enthusiasm have from the outset been driving forces behind this project, and without them it would undoubtedly have stalled. This book is for her, and in memory of Andrew.

Abbreviations and Notes

APC	*Acts of the Privy Council of England 1542–1628*, ed. J.R. Dasent et al. (46 vols, London, 1890–1964)
BL	British Library, London
CRS	Catholic Record Society
CSPD	*Calendar of State Papers, Domestic Series*: *of the reigns of Edward VI, Mary, Elizabeth, 1547–1625*, ed. R. Lemon and M.A.E. Green (12 vols, London, 1856–72; *of the reign of Charles I 1625–1649*, ed. J. Bruce, W.D. Hamilton and S.C. Lomas (23 vols, London, 1858–97); *of the reign of Charles II 1660–1685*, ed. M.A.E. Green, F.H.B. Daniell and F. Bickley (28 vols, London, 1860–1939); *of the reign of James II 1685–1689*, ed. E.K. Timings (3 vols, London, 1960–72)
HMC	Historical Manuscripts Commission
ODNB	*Oxford Dictionary of National Biography*, Online Edition
SCLA	Shakespeare Centre Library and Archive, Stratford-upon-Avon
TNA	The National Archive, London
VCH	*The Victoria History of the Counties of England*
WDA	Westminster Diocesan Archives, London
WRO	Warwickshire Record office, Warwick

In citations from primary documents from before 1752, all dates are Old Style, though the year has been taken to begin on 1 January.

CHAPTER 1

Introduction: The Catholic Gentry in English Society

Peter Marshall and Geoffrey Scott

Early modern Catholic history has begun to come in from the cold. Recounting the vicissitudes of the Catholic community was once regarded as a distinctly specialist historical project, marginal, if not unconnected to the main themes of England's social, cultural and political development. Catholic history was largely left to the Catholics themselves, and the emphases of the account were what one would expect from a self-conscious minority, deeply aware – well into the twentieth century – of its peculiar status within the nation. Catholic history was 'recusant history', a story of resistance and refusal, of separation and survival. Its principal focus was the clerical mission, beginning in the 1570s and punctuated by persecution and martyrdom, by confinement in the prisons of the Elizabethan and Stuart state, or in the priest-holes of sympathetic manor houses. The Catholic laity, particularly the gentry, were not marginalised from this account, but the emphasis was ever on their separateness, on their being identified and fined for the statutory offence of recusancy, and on the inward-looking practice of a faith in which, as Lord Vaux claimed when presented for not attending church in Bedfordshire in 1581, the gentry manor house might be 'a parish by itself'.[1] The study of post-Reformation Catholicism took a major step forward in 1975, when John Bossy published his *The English Catholic Community 1570–1850*. This ambitious synoptic account brought scholarly rigour to its subject, eschewing the hagiographical tone of some earlier studies, and presented Catholicism as (sociologically speaking) a species of non-conformity. But Bossy's was an avowedly internalist study, concerned with 'the body of Catholics as a social whole and in relation to itself'; his subject was the society of Catholics, rather than Catholics in society.[2]

---

[1] John Bossy, 'The Character of Elizabethan Catholicism', in Trevor Aston (ed.), *Crisis in Europe 1560–1660* (London, 1965), p. 225.

[2] John Bossy, *The English Catholic Community 1570–1850* (London, 1975), quote at p. 5. It should be noted, however, that 'papists in society' was a major theme (the longest index entry) of an unjustly neglected study appearing about the same time as Bossy: J.C.H.

Within the last decade or so, however, a growing body of work has brought about a significant realignment, encouraging us to consider both the variety of ways in which Catholics were integrated into mainstream society and the extent to which Catholicism itself should remain integral to the master narrative of national history throughout this period. Much of this work has taken as its focus the remarkable potency of anti-Catholicism for forging identity, or creating division, within English society as a whole.[3] But other studies have invited a reconsideration of the social and political significance of Catholicism by advocating a reassessment of the term itself.

In particular, it has become clear that the words Catholicism and recusancy should not be regarded as interchangeable. Recusancy was a legal category, imposed on a certain group of dissenters by the state – those identified as refusing to attend Protestant services as required by law – but not all Catholics were recusants. That there were those after 1559 who can meaningfully be described as Catholics within the fold of the Church of England has long been recognised, and was widely commented on at the time. True Protestants disdained these 'Church papists', and the Roman Catholic clergy stigmatised them as 'schismatics', but they were a significant (in some eyes, alarmingly significant) social group. An older view that Church papistry was a transitional phenomenon of the first half of Elizabeth I's reign has been persuasively revised in recent years. It is now apparent that the boundary between strict recusancy and conformity, or occasional conformity, remained porous throughout the course of the seventeenth century. Individuals moved in and out of recusancy at certain points in the life cycle, or in response to the intensity of state repression; Catholic families might be divided between recusant and conformist branches, or the split might be evident within the household itself, with (typically) a conforming husband married to a recusant wife.[4] Catholics

---

Aveling, *The Handle and the Axe: The Catholic Recusants in England from Reformation to Emancipation* (London, 1976).

[3] Peter Lake, 'Anti-Popery: the Structure of a Prejudice', in Richard Cust and Ann Hughes (eds), *The English Civil War* (London, 1997), pp. 181–210; Alexandra Walsham, '"The Fatall Vesper": Providentialism and Anti-Popery in Late Jacobean London', *Past and Present*, 144 (1994): 36–87; Arthur Marotti (ed.), *Catholicism and Anti-Catholicism in Early Modern English Texts* (Basingstoke, 1999); Linda Colley, *Britons: Forging the Nation, 1707–1837* (New Haven and London, 1992); Colin Haydon, *Anti-Catholicism in Eighteenth-century England, c. 1714–80* (Manchester, 1993).

[4] Alexandra Walsham, *Church Papists: Catholicism, Conformity and Confessional Polemic in Early Modern England* (Woodbridge, 1993); W.J. Sheils, 'Household, Age, and Gender among Jacobean Yorkshire Recusants', in Marie Rowlands (ed.), *Catholics of Parish and Town 1558–1778*, CRS Monograph, 5 (1999), pp. 131–52. See also his 'Catholics and their Neighbours in a Rural Community: Egton Chapelry 1590–1780', *Northern History*, 25 (1998): 109–33. Michael Questier, 'The Politics of Religious Conformity and the Accession of

were thus often the outsiders within, a situation which might, depending on circumstance, ameliorate neighbourly relations, or might serve to heighten fears and anxieties within the majority Protestant community.

A growing interest in Church popery has been accompanied in the past few years by a noticeable shift of attention towards the phenomenon of popular and plebeian Catholicism. When William Trimble published in 1964 a book on the Catholic laity in Elizabethan England, his subject matter was in fact almost entirely the gentry. Bossy sought 'to keep a balance between the gentry and the rest of the community', but in recent years, and for some good and understandable reasons, the balance has started to tilt towards the latter.[5] Paradoxically, however, as historians of early modern Catholicism have begun to shift their gaze downwards, there has been a noticeable revival of interest in landed families within the historical profession more broadly. Scholars have been fruitfully examining such themes as marriage strategy and kinship networks, estate management and expansion, the exercise of patronage, patterns of consumption and expenditure, cultural interests, concepts of honour and ideological commitments among the gentry. As a result, our understanding of early modern English society, at both local and national level, has been much enhanced.[6] But, with some exceptions, the social, cultural and political worlds of English Catholic gentry families have not been a discernible focus of this work.[7] The only significant recent book-length study is Michael

---

James I', *Historical Research*, 71 (1998): 14–30; Questier, 'Conformity, Catholicism and the Law', in Peter Lake and Michael Questier (eds), *Conformity and Orthodoxy in the English Church, c. 1560–1660* (Woodbridge, 2000), pp. 237–61.

[5] William R. Trimble, *The Catholic Laity in Elizabethan England, 1558–1603* (Cambridge, MA, 1964); Bossy, *English Catholic Community*, p. 6. The most important recent works on popular Catholicism are Rowlands, *Parish and Town*; Sheils, 'Catholics and their Neighbours'; Alison Shell, *Oral Culture and Catholicism in Early Modern England* (Cambridge, 2007).

[6] As representative of a larger literature, see Felicity Heal and Clive Holmes, *The Gentry in England and Wales 1500–1700* (Stanford, 1994); Jacqueline Eales, *Puritans and Roundheads: The Harleys of Brampton Bryan and the Outbreak of the English Civil War* (Cambridge, 1990); Susan Whyman, *Sociability and Power in Late-Stuart England: The Cultural Worlds of the Verneys 1660–1720* (Oxford, 1999); John Broad, *Transforming English Rural Society: The Verneys and the Claydons, 1600–1820* (Cambridge, 2004); Jan Broadway, *'No Historie so Meete': Gentry Culture and the Development of Local History in Elizabethan and early Stuart England* (Manchester, 2006); Stephen K. Roberts, 'Patronage, Office and Family in Early Modern Wales: The Carnes of Nash Manor and Ewenni in the Seventeenth Century', *Welsh History Review*, 23 (2006): 25–49.

[7] See, however, Sandeep Kaushik, 'Resistance, Loyalty and Recusant Politics: Sir Thomas Tresham and the Elizabethan State', *Midland History*, 21 (1996): 37–72; Richard Cust, 'Catholicism, Antiquarianism and Gentry Honour: the Writings of Sir. Thomas Shirley', *Midland History*, 23 (1998): 40–70; Margaret Sena, 'William Blundell and the Networks of Catholic Dissent in Post-Reformation England', in Alexandra Shepard, Alexandra and

Questier's important analysis of the 'entourage' centred on the Browne family, Viscounts Montague, of Cowdray and Battle in Sussex. Questier incisively opens up the theme which Bossy had avoided, 'the interaction of the Catholic community with the outside world', while at the same time demonstrating the vital importance of Catholic kinship networks.[8] But the aristocratic Brownes were hardly archetypal of Catholic landowners as a group, and further studies are needed if we are to understand how, in a new and changing historiographical landscape, the elites of the Catholic community stand in relation to the social topography around them.

This volume is intended as a fresh tributary to this productive confluence of historical themes. It takes as a case-study the experiences of a single Catholic gentry family, and examines them from a variety of perspectives over the course of a long early modern period, from *c*.1530 to 1860. The chronology here is thus considerably broader than Questier's (1550–1640) and, while it follows Bossy's lead in tracing the story through emancipation to the restoration of the Catholic hierarchy in England, it implicitly challenges the latter's emphatic denial that 'the proper place to begin a history of the English Catholic community [is] the reign of Henry VIII'. Bossy's view was that orthodox religion of the early sixteenth century 'is so far a different thing from the history of English Catholicism that anyone who tries to conflate the two is in trouble'.[9] It is not part of the agenda here – far from it – to assert an unproblematic continuity across the Reformation divide. In parallel with Bossy, a 1976 study, by the former Benedictine Hugh Aveling, warned its readers against 'the grand and moving vision' of a post-Reformation Catholicism which was 'a direct prolongation into the modern world of late medieval English religion, continuing its characteristic temper and virtues' – a vision which could move 'even a complete outsider' when he or she visited 'such old Catholic mansions as Coughton Court'.[10] Nonetheless, it is the contention here that following the choices and experiences of an individual family from before the break with Rome has the potential to enhance our understanding of

---

Phil Withington (eds), *Communities in Early Modern England: Networks, Place, Rhetoric* (Manchester, 2000), pp. 54–75; Pauline Croft, 'The Catholic Gentry, the Earl of Salisbury and the Baronets of 1611', in Lake and Questier, *Conformity and Orthodoxy*, pp. 262–81; Sarah Bastow, 'The Catholic Gentry and the Catholic Community in the City of York, 1536–1642: the focus of a Catholic country?' *York Historian*, 18 (2001): 13–22; Jan Broadway, '"To Equall their Virtues": Thomas Habington, Recusancy and the Gentry of Early Stuart Worcestershire', *Midland History*, 29 (2004):1–24.

[8] Michael C. Questier, *Catholicism and Community in Early Modern England: Politics, Aristocratic Patronage and Religion, c. 1550–1640* (Cambridge, 2006), quote at p. 3.

[9] Bossy, *English Catholic Community*, p. 4.

[10] Aveling, *Handle and the Axe*, p. 18.

how the Catholic community took shape, and of why it took the shapes that it did.

A question immediately presents itself. Why *this* gentry family? What is special about the Throckmortons of Coughton? Their claim to historical attention is not self-evident, and indeed has not always been recognised. Bossy takes no notice of any individual member of the family before the late eighteenth century, and 'Throckmorton' does not even appear in Aveling's list of 42 leading Catholic families of the seventeenth century, a catalogue evincing a 'magnificence and solidity about the roll of names'.[11] Only a couple of family members in the direct line appear in the *Oxford Dictionary of National Biography (ODNB)*. Previous scholarship has not entirely passed the Throckmortons by. The fortuitous survival of a seventeenth-century steward's account book prompted the antiquarian Etwell Barnard to publish a study of one head of the family, Sir Francis Throckmorton, in 1944 (reassessed in Malcolm Wanklyn's chapter). And another fortunate archival survival (a sixteenth-century diary; discussed below), coupled with the fact that one of the Throckmorton women married Sir Walter Raleigh, led a more renowned twentieth-century historian, A.L. Rowse, to produce his book, *Ralegh and the Throckmortons*, in 1962.[12] A family history of any sort requires an archive, and the Throckmortons possess a good one. The family's papers were preserved at the ancestral seat at Coughton in Warwickshire until they were transferred in recent times to the County Record Office and the Shakespeare Library in Stratford.[13]

But it is one feature of the family's early modern history in particular which has periodically grabbed the attention of historians. From an early date the Throckmortons were, in Felicity Heal's phrase, 'that ideologically divided family'.[14] The head of the family in the 1530s, Sir George Throckmorton, had to decide whether or not to accept Henry VIII's break with Rome, and chose to conform, just (his travails are the subject of Peter Marshall's chapter). His sons, however, took divergent paths, and Protestant and Catholic branches of the family were founded. One of Sir George's grandsons was Job Throckmorton, the Puritan activist and part-author of the scurrilously anti-episcopal Marprelate Tracts; another was Francis Throckmorton, a Catholic conspirator who gave his name to one of the more serious plots

---

[11] Bossy, *English Catholic Community*, p. 340; Aveling, *Handle and the Axe*, p. 141.

[12] Ettwell Barnard, *A Seventeenth-Century Country Gentleman: Sir Francis Throckmorton 1640–1680* (Cambridge, 1944); A.L. Rowse, *Ralegh and the Throckmortons* (London, 1962).

[13] The bulk of the papers are in WRO (classmark CR 1998); deeds and court rolls relating to particular estates are in SCLA (classmark DR 5). Some materials of interest (particularly relating to the nineteenth century) remain at the house itself.

[14] Felicity Heal, *Reformation in Britain and Ireland* (Oxford, 2003), p. 241.

against Elizabeth I.[15] To Rowse it seemed that there was 'something in the family temperament – its extremism. With the Throckmortons it was either one thing or the other: either wholly Catholic, involved in recusancy, exile, sometimes treason, or else left-wing Protestant, militant and aggressive ... No middle course was good enough for them.'[16] Patrick Collinson once termed the Throckmortons 'a family of slightly unstable extremists', and David Starkey has referred to a 'family gallery of heroes and traitors (which is which, of course, depends on your point of view)'.[17]

All of this sounds as if the Throckmortons should be regarded as a remarkably untypical gentry family, which in some respects they were. 'Typicality' may in any case be something of a historical chimera: English gentry families, like Tolstoy's unhappy families, often conducted their business in their own distinctive ways. But if we substitute for all-embracing typicality an ability to focus discussion on a range of broader representative themes, then the Throckmortons have much to recommend them. The fact of their ideological fracture was not unique, or even unusual in sixteenth- and seventeenth-century England: many convinced Catholics had conformist or even whole-heartedly Protestant kinsfolk.[18] The extended family, it deserves to be more widely recognised, may thus be a prime location from which to study inter-confessional relations in this period. In other ways, too, the Throckmortons serve as an effective window onto the relationship between the Catholic community and wider society. Despite their persistent adherence to Catholicism over several centuries in the main line, in no sense did the Throckmortons inhabit a 'recusant bubble', even if their role as managers of substantial estates, and leading members of 'county society' in Warwickshire, Worcestershire and Buckinghamshire, had allowed them so to do. Members of the Coughton branch of the family were periodically involved in politics on the national stage, from Sir George Throckmorton's resistance to the break with Rome in the 1530s to Sir John Courtenay Throckmorton's involvement in the emancipation campaigns of

---

[15] Leland H. Carlson, *Martin Marprelate, Gentleman: Master Job Throkmorton Laid Open in his Colors* (San Marino, CA, 1981), modified by Patrick Collinson, 'Throckmorton, Job (1545–1601)', *ODNB*. The fullest and most recent study of the Throckmorton Plot is John Bossy, *Under the Molehill: An Elizabethan Spy Story* (New Haven and London, 2001).

[16] Rowse, *Ralegh and the Throckmortons*, p. 20.

[17] Patrick Collinson, *The Elizabethan Puritan Movement* (London, 1967), p. 306; David Starkey, *Elizabeth: Apprenticeship* (London, 2000), p. 245.

[18] For example, the questionnaires or *responsa* of students entering the Catholic colleges at Valladolid and Rome in the late sixteenth and early seventeenth centuries show a remarkable number with family members who were either 'schismatics' or 'heretics': Michael C. Questier, 'Clerical Recruitment, Conversion and Rome c. 1580–1625', in Claire Cross (ed.), *Patronage and Recruitment in the Tudor and Early Stuart Church* (York, 1996), pp. 76–94.

the late eighteenth century, and Robert George Throckmorton's election as the first English Catholic MP in 1831. As a gentry family that remained politically and socially significant from the sixteenth century through to the nineteenth, the Throckmortons provide a golden opportunity to track the fortunes of lay Catholic elites in a changing world.

A brief overview of the history of the Throckmorton family will serve to underline some of the key themes which the subsequent chapters in this volume explore in more detail. The Throckmortons, or Throgmortons (this and other variants are common up to the eighteenth century), originated from Fladbury in Worcestershire, but a fortunate marriage in 1409 led to the acquisition of the manor of Coughton in Warwickshire. They prospered in the fifteenth century as clients of the earls of Warwick, and intermarried with other Midlands gentry families – one of these marriages brought into their hands the Buckinghamshire estate of Weston Underwood, which was to be a second and sometimes principal residence for the family over several succeeding centuries (Figure 1.1).

Throughout the fifteenth century, the family was purchasing land, and by the time of Robert Throckmorton (Sir George Throckmorton's father) the principal focus of their economic and social interests had shifted from Worcestershire to Warwickshire, and a major rebuilding of the house at Coughton was undertaken. The Throckmortons proved themselves adept at navigating the treacherous shoals of fifteenth-century politics, and were in favour with both Lancastrian and Yorkist kings. Robert Throckmorton was knighted by Henry VII in 1494 (the first of the family to be so honoured by the Crown) and received other tokens of royal favour in exchange for conspicuous loyalism to the new dynasty.[19]

If the fifteenth-century Throckmortons were politically and economically astute, they seem to have been more than ordinarily engaged in the practice of their religion. In addition to the chantry foundations and gifts to religious houses that were the conventional status markers of the late medieval gentry, several members of the family seem to have collected vernacular religious texts. One surviving manuscript, which may have belonged to Thomas Throckmorton (d. 1414) or John Throckmorton (d. 1445), prescribes a pious daily regimen for a layman – the medievalist W.A. Pantin characterises its owner as 'particularly literate and devout'.[20]

---

[19] Christine Carpenter, 'Throgmorton family (per. 1409–1518)', *ODNB*; *VCH Warwickshire*, vol. 3, pp. 74–86.

[20] William A. Pantin, 'Instructions for a Devout and Literate Layman. [Throckmorton Muniments, 76]', in J.J.G. Alexander and M.T. Gibson (eds), *Medieval Learning and Literature: Essays presented to Richard William Hunt* (Oxford, 1976), pp. 398–422; Mary C. Erler, *Women, Reading and Piety in Late Medieval England* (Cambridge, 2002), pp. 111–15.

Figure 1.1 Weston Underwood, c.1826, lithograph at Coughton Court.

As Peter Marshall demonstrates in Chapter 2, Sir Robert Throckmorton's piety too was notably expressive and intense. There is a research topic waiting to be explored here: whether across the country as a whole any broad connections can be established between gentry families which were Catholic after 1558, and the patterns of religion practised by their fifteenth- and early sixteenth-century ancestors.

The Reformation split the Throckmorton family just as it split the nation. Sir George Throckmorton opposed Henry VIII's religious and marital policies, and was lucky to escape with his head (see Chapter 2). His eldest son and heir, Robert Throckmorton, was, like his father, a conservative in religion, but four of his brothers, Kenelm, Clement, Nicholas and George can be described as Protestants by Edward VI's reign. Of these, Clement was the most 'forward', a friend of the Marian martyr Thomas Hawkes, and of the Protestant firebrand, Edward Underhill. In Elizabeth's reign he helped administer funds to 'preachers of the gospel in Warwickshire' via a patent secured by the Earl of Leicester.[21] Nicholas Throckmorton, however, was the most eminent of the clan. Favoured by the Protestant regime of Edward VI, Nicholas rose under Elizabeth to become Chief Butler and Chamberlain to the Exchequer and, more importantly, a leading diplomat in France and Scotland, handling delicate negotiations with Mary Queen of Scots. Nicholas was suspected in Mary's reign of complicity in Wyatt's rebellion, and was spectacularly acquitted at his treason trial in 1554, where he persuaded the jury that his actions did not come under the compass of the relevant law.[22]

Tudor religious policy required choices: those choices divided families and none perhaps more so than the Throckmortons. When, in 1564, Elizabeth's Privy Council instructed the bishops to survey the attitudes of justices of the peace, classifying them as 'favourers', 'adversaries' or 'indifferent' towards 'true religion', the returns for Warwickshire found Throckmortons listed under all three headings.[23] Yet the family's experiences suggest that, for the mid-Tudor decades at least, there was no necessary direct connection between religious affiliation on the one hand, and political loyalty and Crown service on the other. Sir George Throckmorton reconciled his Catholic beliefs with sterling service to the Edwardian state. A sixteenth-century family tradition, which may be well founded, maintained that it was four of the Throckmorton brothers,

---

[21] Collinson, 'Throckmorton, Job'; P.W. Hasler (ed.), *The House of Commons, 1558–1603* (3 vols, London, 1981), vol. 3, p. 491.

[22] *House of Commons, 1558–1603*, vol. 3, pp. 497–9.

[23] Mary Bateson (ed.), 'A Collection of Original Letters from the Bishops to the Privy Council, 1564', in *Camden Miscellany, Vol. 9* (Camden Society, ns, 53, London, 1895), pp. 7–8.

including Nicholas, who were first to send news of Edward VI's death to his sister, Mary (though she is supposed to have responded that 'If Robert had beene there, she durst / Have gag'd her life, and hazarded the happ').[24] Robert (who was knighted before September 1553) served Mary as Sheriff of Warwickshire and Constable of Warwick Castle, and sat as a knight of the shire in three Marian parliaments.[25] As a refuser of the Act of Supremacy, his eventual political eclipse in the next reign was perhaps inevitable (he was removed from the commission of the peace in 1570), though it was neither immediate nor seen at the time as predictable. As Queen Mary lay dying in November 1558, the Spanish ambassador, the Count of Feria, wrote home (wrongly, as it turned out) that Robert Throckmorton was one of the group of courtiers and politicians with whom the Lady Elizabeth was 'on very good terms', and could be expected to hold office in the next reign.[26] Openly Catholic Throckmortons sat in the parliaments of 1559 (Robert's son, Thomas, and his cousin, Simon), and of 1563 (his brother, Anthony).[27]

The career of another of Robert's brothers, John Throckmorton, exemplifies the confessional untidiness of the early Elizabethan decades. Rowse regarded him as 'a life-long Catholic', while his biography in the *History of Parliament* paints him as 'an opportunist of no deep convictions either in religion or politics'.[28] Neither description is wholly adequate. In Edward's reign, John was closely associated with the regime of the Duke of Northumberland, receiving considerable patronage and appointment to the post of attorney to the Council in the Marches of Wales. Upon the death of Edward VI (according to the later testimony of William Cecil) it was John Throckmorton who drafted the proclamation declaring Jane Grey as Queen, though his conscience was reportedly 'troubled therewith.' Yet this substantial *faux pas* did not prevent his acquisition of favour from Mary, to whose cause he soon adhered. He sat in four out of five Marian parliaments, and was created Recorder of Coventry, Justice of Chester, and Master of the Court of Requests. In 1558, he was one of the witnesses of Mary's will. Yet his career suffered no setback with the accession of Elizabeth – he was knighted by the new queen, and rose by 1565 to become vice president of the Council in Wales, having served

---

[24] *The Legend of Sir Nicholas Throckmorton*, ed. J.G. Nichols (London, 1874), p. 29.

[25] S.T. Bindoff (ed.), *The House of Commons, 1509–1558* (3 vols, London, 1982), vol. 3, p. 460–61.

[26] *House of Commons, 1558–1603*, vol. 3, p. 500; David Loades, *Mary Tudor: The Tragical History of the First Queen of England* (London, 2006), p. 201.

[27] *House of Commons, 1558–1603*, vol. 3, pp. 489, 499, 500.

[28] Rowse, *Ralegh and the Throckmortons*, p. 25; *House of Commons, 1558–1603*, vol. 3, p. 495.

along the way as one of the commissioners enforcing the new religious settlement in the recalcitrant diocese of Chester. In 1579, he was disgraced, fined, and imprisoned (dying shortly afterwards). This was for corruption and maladministration, not (overtly, at least) for recusancy or political disaffection. Throughout his life, Sir John was a conformist member of the Church of England. Yet at the same time, there is little doubt that he was in a meaningful sense a Catholic. His sons were certainly raised in that religion: one of them (Thomas) was a prominent exile; another (Francis) a conspirator and condemned traitor; a third (Edward) a saintly seminarian who was received into the Society of Jesus on his deathbed in Rome in 1582. The impressive alabaster tomb of Sir John and his wife in Coughton parish church, dating from 1580, records his service to Queen Mary 'of happie memorie', and carries the (by this date) highly provocative inscription 'On whose soules God take mercy', an invocation of intercessory prayer.[29] It is a striking illustration of the power wielded by Catholic gentry in their localities that they could oblige Protestant congregations to worship in the presence of such overtly Catholic formulae.[30]

Sir John Throckmorton, in short, was a Church papist, or occasional conformist. His *CV* reinforces the insight that recusancy and Church papistry were not so much alternative as complementary patterns of Catholic gentry behaviour, and that the practice of the latter did not bar one from participation in political life (indeed, that was rather the point). Even the most devout and orthodox among the Catholic clergy were sometimes inclined to be forgiving about this. The hagiographical 'Life of Brother Edward Throgmorton', composed either by Robert Southwell or by the Jesuit rector of the English College in Rome, Alfonso Agazzari, conceded that Edward's father 'yielded to the time, and lived for a long period in schism, cut off from the perfect unity of the Church'. But despite this, 'still in heart and will he retained an inclination to the piety and devotion in which he had been educated', and he was so far from being a persecutor that missionary priests 'thought themselves nowhere safer than under the shadow of his roof and the protection of his patronage and authority.'[31]

---

[29] Rowse, *Ralegh and the Throckmortons*, pp. 25, 45–6; *House of Commons, 1509–1558*, vol. 3, pp. 455–6; A.G. Dickens, *Reformation Studies* (London, 1982), p. 359; Alison Plowden, 'Throckmorton, Francis (1554–1584)', *ODNB*; *Records of the English Province of the Society of Jesus*, ed. Henry Foley (7 vols, London, 1875–83), vol. 4, pp. 288 ff; *VCH Warwickshire*, vol. 3, p. 85.

[30] For other examples, see Peter Marshall, *Beliefs and the Dead in Reformation England* (Oxford, 2002), pp. 176–7.

[31] Foley, *Society of Jesus*, vol. 4, p. 291. There is some confusion to clear up here. The 'Life' (p. 290) presents Edward's father as 'Sir N. Throgmorton, Knight, President or Chief Justice of the Principality of Wales', which Foley understood as Nicholas, being followed in

An impulse towards a stricter practice of the faith is found on the part of Sir John's nephew, Thomas Throckmorton, heir to the Coughton estate after Sir Robert's death in 1581, a figure who (like his brother-in-law, Sir Thomas Tresham) seems to represent the recusant tradition in its purest form. Thomas was repeatedly fined for refusal to attend church, and in the 1580s and 90s spent extended periods imprisoned in Banbury Castle.[32] In 1596, Thomas commissioned the extraordinary *Tabula Eliensis*, which still hangs at Coughton. This large painted cloth (9 by 7 feet) is a pair with an Elizabethan copy of the medieval *Tabula* from Ely, which portrays the East Anglian cathedral church, along with the arms of the knights stationed there by William I, the pedigrees of the abbots, bishops, deans of Ely, and of the kings and queens of England. But the Coughton copy adds to this depiction, in seven grouped columns, the heraldic arms of all the gentlemen 'committed prisoners for recusancye to ye palace of Ely', to the castle of Broughton in Oxfordshire and to Banbury Castle between 1590 and 1596, including of course Thomas Throckmorton himself. The *Tabula* is simultaneously a defiant martyrology and a graphic assertion of fidelity to the Crown and ancient Church. As Richard Cust has noted, an almost obsessive concern with heraldry, lineage and pedigree, and with traditions of service, is characteristic of the Catholic gentry in this period, and perhaps served as psychological compensation for their exclusion from county office-holding, an important source of gentry honour.[33]

Thomas Throckmorton's sufferings were real enough, but in the end he was, as it were, only a weekend martyr. Despite the cumulative fines, he remained one of the wealthiest Midlands Catholics, his income assessed at £666 13s 4d in 1586. During his periods of imprisonment, in 1593 and again in 1597, he was granted temporary release to attend to lawsuits, and was let out again during a period of ill-health.[34] Nor did Thomas establish a lasting pattern of pristine recusancy within the Throckmorton main line. As Jan Broadway shows in her chapter, Thomas's son and heir, John, seems to have been a church papist or occasional conformist, and his son, Robert, was twice married to the daughters of church papist families.

---

this by other authorities such as Walsham, *Church Papists*, p. 83. But it is clear from internal and external evidence that John is meant. See *The First and Second Diaries of the English College, Douay*, ed. Thomas F. Knox (London, 1878), p. 333. The uncle with whom Edward is said to have lodged as a boy ('Life', p. 294) is almost certainly Robert Throckmorton of Coughton; there appears to have been a chaplain saying mass in the house in the later 1570s.

[32] *House of Commons, 1558–1603*, vol. 3, pp. 500–501.

[33] John M. Robinson, *Heraldry at Coughton Court* (Alcester, 1996), pp. 18–20; Cust, 'Writings of Thomas Shirley', *passim*.

[34] Trimble, *Catholic Laity*, pp. 155, 157–8, 199, 237–8.

Maintaining Catholicism and maintaining the wealth, power and status of the family were always potentially at odds with each other. For Catholics, the usual hazards to the integrity of a gentry estate, such as times of minority and wardship, were magnified, as various predatory forces sensed an opportunity to exploit the legal disabilities of papists.[35] Some channels of prestige and influence – such as the universities or local Crown office – were closed to Catholics, and there is little doubt that despite their continuing social clout, the fortunes of the Throckmorton family declined relatively between the mid-sixteenth and mid-seventeenth centuries. Marriage was the principal gentry strategy for survival and expansion, and the Throckmortons, like most Catholic dynasties, tended to marry into other papist families. The dense network of Throckmorton connections around the Gunpowder Plot in 1605 (nearly all the principal plotters were related to them by blood or marriage) vividly illustrates the cumulative effect of this strategy. Yet as Michael Hodgetts's analysis of this network in Chapter 4 demonstrates, the pattern of intermarriage among Catholic families extended outwards into church papist and even Protestant circles, prompting his suggestion, for example, that some Midlands Catholics had expectations of preferential treatment at the hands of the Protestant sheriff, Sir Richard Verney. Further, as Susan Cogan demonstrates in her chapter, Catholics like the Throckmortons were not barred from all channels of non-Catholic patronage, and their approach to the business of getting and keeping economic and social 'capital' can look distinctly similar to that of their Protestant neighbours.

The quality of day-to-day relations with those neighbours is an intriguing topic. Modern scholarship is increasingly coming to the paradoxical conclusion that early modern English society was at once fervently anti-Catholic and at the same time often surprisingly tolerant on a practical and neighbourly level.[36] The Throckmortons, of course, had close kin who were Protestants, and here some insight is supplied by a remarkable source: the diary (covering the years 1578–95 and 1609–13) of Arthur Throckmorton, son of Elizabeth's adviser, Sir Nicholas Throckmorton, and first cousin to the recusant Thomas Throckmorton and nephew of the church papist, Sir John.[37]

---

[35] See Jan Broadway's and Malcolm Wanklyn's chapters in this volume.

[36] See, for example, Anthony Milton, 'A Qualified Intolerance: the Limits and Ambiguities of Early Stuart Anti-Catholicism', in Arthur Marotti (ed.), *Catholicism and Anti-Catholicism in Early Modern English Texts* (Basingstoke, 1999), pp. 85–115; Alexandra Walsham, *Charitable Hatred: Tolerance and Intolerance in England 1500–1700* (Manchester, 2006), esp. pp. 269–80.

[37] The diary is in Canterbury, Canterbury Cathedral Archives, MS U. 85, Box 38, I–III, and provides the core source material for Rowse, *Ralegh and the Throckmortons*.

Arthur's diary makes it clear that he had not broken ties with his Catholic cousins. He stayed with Thomas Throckmorton at Coughton and Weston Underwood, and he was on particularly good terms with Sir John, for whom he interceded at his time of trouble in 1579. He seems too to have liked Sir John's son Francis, executed for his part in the 'Throckmorton Plot', and he continued afterwards to receive news of one of Francis's brothers in exile. But Arthur was not in any sense 'soft' on Catholics, and he seems to have held the conventional anti-papist attitudes of an educated Englishman of his day. Nor were family relations impervious to political winds. As Sheriff of Northamptonshire, Arthur was involved in searching the houses and seizing the goods of suspects in the aftermath of the Gunpowder Plot. Some of these, like Muriel Throckmorton, Lady Tresham, were his relations, and were aggrieved by his actions. Arthur wrote gratefully to Robert Cecil that 'it is no small comfort to understand how gracious a construction, in the midst of the outcries of my unkind kindred, you pronounced of my carriage.'[38]

During an earlier crisis, the Spanish invasion scare of 1599, Arthur had similarly been active in searching recusant houses and confiscating papist books. He also advised the government that those needing to be disarmed included not just professed recusants, but conformists whose wives refused to go to church, while the male spouses reckoned to preserve 'their livings and their liberties by their feigned faiths. Such have a common saying that the unbelieving husband shall be saved by the believing wife: of which sort there are many here and of no mean estate.'[39] Throckmorton's jaundiced comment highlights an important theme (addressed in this volume by Susan Cogan and Jan Broadway): the prominence of women in English Catholic activism and the prevalence of Protestant concerns about that influence.[40] Southwell's life of Edward Throckmorton attributed the youth's constancy in the faith to the influence of his mother (Margaret Puttenham), who, unlike her husband, 'never swerved in the least from the moment that heresy invaded the kingdom'.[41] Another Margaret Throckmorton, daughter of Sir Thomas Throckmorton of Tortworth, a Protestant cadet branch, was committed by the Council to the custody of the Dean of Gloucester in 1593 as 'a verie obstinate Recusant'. Her

---

[38] Rowse, *Ralegh and the Throckmortons*, pp. 71, 74, 78, 83, 96, 252–3. In 1610, however, Arthur showed himself notably reluctant to certify the list of recusants in Northants refusing the oath of allegiance: ibid., pp. 298–9.

[39] Ibid., p. 213.

[40] Marie Rowlands, 'Recusant Women 1560–1640', in Mary Prior (ed.), *Women in English Society 1500–1800* (London, 1985), pp. 154–80; Frances Dolan, *Whores of Babylon: Catholicism, Gender, and Seventeenth-Century Print Culture* (Ithaca, 1999).

[41] Foley, *Society of Jesus*, vol. 4, p. 291.

mother was the root of the problem, 'noted to have done muche harme by pervertinge of some of her children and divers of her familie in matter of religion'.[42] Here the spiritual relationship between husband and wife seems to have been antagonistic, rather than collusive. But either way, a gendered politics of religion within the household seems to represent a fundamental point of difference between the world of the Catholic gentry and that of their Protestant counterparts.

Another important point of difference concerns the physical dimensions of that world. In an unjustly neglected essay, Caroline Hibbard has pointed to what was perhaps, in social and political terms, the most distinctive feature of early modern English Catholicism: 'no other English group has been tied by an umbilical cord to the continent of Europe for over 200 years'. Ultimately, she suggests, 'the friendly, familiar face of English Catholicism' could not completely be separated from 'the spectre of international Catholicism'.[43] The Throckmortons exemplify the importance of this theme, and illustrate the complex interplay between the two 'faces' of English Catholicism over the longest possible stretch of time. Sir George Throckmorton's brother Michael was already an ideological Catholic exile in the reigns of Henry VIII and Edward VI, disowned (at least outwardly) by his loyalist relatives at home. In the next generation, Sir Robert Throckmorton maintained discreet contacts with the exiles' seminary at Douai, sending a servant there in 1575.[44] The international contacts of the family were both cause and consequence of the Throckmorton Plot of 1583, Francis and his brother Thomas going abroad at some point before their father's death in 1579 and making contact with the hot political Catholic exiles in the Low Countries. After Francis's arrest, his brothers George and Thomas escaped overseas to begin a lifetime of exile and plotting. The latter, often operating under the codename Barasino, was a thorn in the side of the government for years to come. He was also an active player in the internecine disputes of the Catholic exile community, closely allied (despite his brother Edward's exemplary affiliation with the Society) with the anti-Jesuit faction headed by Charles Paget and Thomas Morgan.[45]

Not all the Throckmortons in exile were rootless adventurers and plotters. John and Agnes's eldest daughter, Margaret, became in 1611 a professed sister of the Augustinian convent of St Monica's in Louvain,

[42] *APC 1592–1593*, pp. 279–80.

[43] Caroline Hibbard, 'Early Stuart Catholicism: Revisions and Re-Revisions', *Journal of Modern History*, 52 (1980), 29–30.

[44] Knox (ed.) *Douay Diaries*, pp. 98, 101, 102.

[45] Plowden, 'Throckmorton, Francis'. See also Leo Hicks, *An Elizabethan Problem: Some Aspects of the Careers of Two Exile-Adventurers* (London, 1964).

probably as a result of the influence of her mother's sister, who was already a nun there.[46] In due course Margaret became prioress of the house, the first of many Throckmorton daughters to take the veil on the continent over the course of the following century. Meanwhile, a grandson of Sir George Throckmorton, William Gifford, had entered the Benedictine Order after a scholarly career spanning the colleges of Rome, Douai and Rheims.[47] In 1623, Gifford was appointed Archbishop of Rheims, the most distinguished of all French bishoprics. Like his cousin Thomas Throckmorton before him, Gifford was closely linked to the pro-French, anti-Spanish and anti-Jesuit faction within English Catholicism – a political pattern of allegiance that was to prove remarkably enduring in the Throckmorton family.

Within England, the Throckmorton family of the mid-seventeenth century continued a pattern of modulation between disobedience and compliance that may have been characteristic of the Catholic gentry as a whole. During the Civil War and Interregnum, the Throckmortons adopted, for reasons of self-preservation, a policy of outward political and religious conformity, whilst continuing to adhere to the practice of the Catholic faith, albeit within a domestic setting. If, as Malcolm Wanklyn argues in Chapter 6, the Throckmortons were recusants but not recusant delinquents, then their natural attraction to royalism was deliberately concealed, in Francis Throckmorton's case, behind the shield of a Puritan guardian. External pressures to conform aided the process by which English Catholicism found itself retreating into the private domestic sphere, becoming increasingly quietist and separatist. Thus, the evidence of the mid-seventeenth-century Throckmortons, whose 'strategy for survival' balanced public conformity with the Catholic household's private celebration of fasts and feasts, seems to support Bossy's case for a religious group evolving towards a Catholic nonconformity and breaking free of any continuity with the medieval past and Tudor 'survivalism'. Christopher Haigh, on the other hand, has argued that such 'Protestant Papists' – with their continuous religious beliefs sometimes hidden, but at other times publicly and nostalgically shared with co-religionists at, for instance, pilgrimage sites like Holywell – were the representatives of a continuous religious tradition extending back into the medieval period.[48] Walsham has suggested that 'conformity was not always a transient or protracted stage in an uncomfortable inner struggle towards recusancy; it

---

[46] See Jan Broadway's chapter in this volume.

[47] Michael E. Williams, 'Gifford, William (1557/8–1629)', *ODNB*.

[48] Christopher Haigh, 'The Continuity of Catholicism in the English Reformation', in Haigh (ed.), *The English Reformation Revised* (Cambridge, 1987), pp. 176–208; Haigh, *English Reformations: Religion, Politics, and Society under the Tudors* (Oxford, 1993), pp. 259–60.

was as often the final outcome of that struggle itself'; if so, this provides the key to unlock some of those ambivalences which haunt the Throckmortons' later history and make it such an interesting family.[49] The persistent traces of Church papistry among the Throckmortons renders obsolete Rowse's facile statement that 'no middle course was good enough for them'.

Despite having to cope with personal difficulties – such as Sir Francis's poor health, the break-up of his marriage, and his premature death in 1680, not to mention the renewed persecution and flight of Catholics sparked off by the Popish Plot – the Throckmortons retained a prominent role as leading gentry within the Catholic community at a time when that body had reached the nadir of its fortunes. This decline, Bossy believed, was due principally to lack of episcopal leadership and to divisions among the clergy caused by conflict over the question of a proposed oath of allegiance to the government. As laity who for some time had developed the stratagem of *quieta non movere* (do not move settled things), the Throckmortons were largely unaffected by such internecine disputes. Their chaplains remained firmly under the family's control, and the paucity of information about them during this shadowy period adds credence to the view that they kept their heads down. The family would have remembered with dismay its provocative chaplain, the priest Johnson, a loose cannon whose obstructionism in 1625 brought about his own imprisonment and that of his patroness, Lady Mary Throckmorton, by admitting that he had lived for four years with her at Weston.[50] In this so-called time of transition, on the eve of the accession of the Catholic King James II (1685–88), when Catholics were to nudge closer towards assimilation into English society, the family was buoyant; it had preserved its estates, wealth and status. Furthermore, its earlier benefactions and residencies overseas suggest well-established religious and cultural links with European Catholic networks which were themselves participating in a religious revival. In this continental dimension, the Throckmortons saw themselves as partners rather than merely exiles. Meanwhile, in the battle for the leadership of the English Catholic community, wealth, status and, above all, education were never to allow the Throckmorton family to lag behind. Its members were to kick the trend, as clerical influence over the English Catholic Church increased over the following century, and as growing independent, more plebeian congregations replaced rural gentry chaplaincies as the nodal points of Catholic life.

---

[49] Walsham, *Church Papists*, p. 95. Cf. Aveling, *Handle and the Axe*, p. 162: 'It was the Church-papists who saved the Catholic community.'

[50] Bossy, *English Catholic Community*, pp. 282–5; Martin J. Havran, *The Catholics in Caroline England* (London, 1962), p. 106.

Under James II, the Throckmortons, like many other Catholic families, rose in importance through the extension of royal patronage deliberately exercised to favour Catholics in local and national politics. Sir Robert, the third baronet, thus became a Deputy Lieutenant of Buckinghamshire, a Justice of the Peace for Worcestershire and a Captain of a military troop in the fateful year of 1688. That separatism of the Catholic body from general society, which Bossy associated with the gentry and aristocracy, was at this time hardly manifest. Thus, the chapel which Sir Robert built at Coughton in 1687, and which was to be destroyed by a Protestant mob from Alcester the following year, must have been strikingly large. Though still attached to the house, it seems less a domestic chapel and more of a parish church, for it encompassed the entire east wing of the Court. It was being completed moreover at the same time as Sir Robert was paying for the melting down and recasting of peals of bells in the Anglican parish churches at Weston and Coughton. In the summer of 1687, the baronet welcomed the only Catholic bishop in England, John Leyburn, to confirm crowds of the local faithful at Weston, an indication of how important this centre was held to be in the eyes of the Catholic community as a whole. Sir Robert gave obsessive attention between 1686 and 1692 to stocking his moats and 'pools' at Weston and Coughton with carp and tench. Whether this reveals his attachment to an alternate Catholic calendar of fasts and feasts, and to the custom of Friday abstinence with its implied consciousness of a superior purity, cannot be known for certain. Perhaps he just enjoyed fishing.[51]

The English Catholic gentry in the long eighteenth century are generally deemed not to have had to cope with the challenges faced by their forbears in the extreme political and religious conditions of the previous century. Nevertheless, from around 1714, they are usually seen as experiencing a slow decline in their social position – retreating as backwoodsmen or vainly battling against the tide by striving to preserve their hold over native Catholicism through sustaining or creating households of the faith comprising their own tenants. These centres, which remained separate from establishment Christianity and free of any effective episcopal jurisdiction, and where chaplains were hired or fired at will, became, in effect, separatist nonconformist churches. Reasons for the declining status of Catholic elites have been suggested: on top of suspicions of Jacobitism, the continuing presence of penal legislation and the imposition of discriminatory taxation,

---

[51] Aveling, *Handle and the Axe*, p. 227; *CSPD, 1687–1689*, nos 787, 1356, 1669; Bossy, *English Catholic Community*, pp. 71, 108–10; WRO, CR 1998/CD/Drawer 3/8, Memorandums of Sir Robert Throckmorton, Bart, 1682–1701; J.A. Hilton et al. (eds), *Bishop Leyburn's Confirmation Register of 1687* (Wigan, 1997), pp. 9–11: 126 persons were confirmed at Weston and at the Earl of Peterborough's house at Drayton.

the eighteenth century brought large-scale apostasy, Anglican conformity, economic pressures of various kinds and a lack of male heirs. Though they were not immune to any of these misfortunes, the Throckmortons kicked the trend and survived. They were increasingly marked out as 'progressive' Catholics, and how they became so demands some examination.[52]

Without any doubt, the Throckmortons followed the separatist trend which distanced them from the contemporary Anglican establishment as well as from Catholic clerical authority. They took Catholic brides without exception, sent their children to Catholic schools, and remained on the margins of national and local politics. As non-jurors, they registered their estates in 1715 and entered the lists of papists in the 1767 House of Lords Returns. References to their religious faith are significantly few and far between in the 1730s correspondence of the court gossip, Mary Pendarves, with Lady Catherine Throckmorton, 'dearest Collyflower', who was the granddaughter of the fifth Viscount Montague and who moved effortlessly around fashionable spas like Bath and Scarborough. Catherine was deeply in love with the fourth baronet, 'so different from the generality of the world ... (and) the most amicable of mankind', whose 'generosity to Bath hospital cuts a fine figure in the newspapers'. For Pendarves, her friend's Catholicism was little more than an endearing eccentricity, and she joked inoffensively about the practice of confession and 'the punishment of telling your beads'. Badges of minority status remained in place throughout the century. Anna Maria Throckmorton, for instance, reported from her home in Bath in the 1770s that some newcomers were 'Cats. (Catholics), & I believe Card Players' and that 'we have a strict Lent in all Places, except the North'.[53] Bossy makes a great deal of the compilation of Catholic registers as a defining moment of Catholic gentry congregationalism, since they record the process of separation from Anglican dominance through critical rites of passage. He notes the enduring tradition among Catholics of marriage rituals being 'entrenched in the domestic environment'. The early

---

[52] Aveling, *Handle and the Axe*, pp. 250, 253, 262–5; Bossy, *English Catholic Community*, pp. 71, 74, 108.

[53] *The English Catholic Nonjurors of 1715*, ed. Edgar E. Estcourt and John Orlebar Payne (London, 1885), pp. 3, 14, 216, 279, 291, with estates and land held in trust in Berkshire, Buckinghamshire, Oxfordshire, Shropshire, Warwickshire and Worcestershire valued at nearly £5,000. WRO, CR 1998/Box 72/D/Folder 49, nos 18, 19, 38, 40, 41 and 49/1 (15 June 1714, Lawyer Nathaniel Pigott's advice to Sir Robert Throckmorton on landed property of Catholics); *Returns of Papists 1767, Volume 2*, ed. E.S. Worrall, CRS Occasional Publications, 2 (1989), pp. 163–4 (Buckland, 42 papists, the majority being members of the Throckmorton household); p. 74 (Weston, 173 papists, of whom 20 were Throckmorton servants); p. 107 (Chaddesley Corbett including Harvington, 85 papists); p. 108 (Coughton, 75 papists). Geoffrey Scott, *Gothic Rage Undone. English Monks in the Age of Enlightenment* (Bath, 1992), p. 112.

date of entries in the Throckmorton registers, with frequent inclusion of family names and servants, suggests a secure and recognisable congregation had formed by 1710, although the Coughton congregation seems only to have stabilised from 1744. Throckmorton marriages were celebrated 'before a numerous assembly', and we might note, by way of exception, the entry for the marriage of William Throckmorton, a Protestant relation, married in the chapel in January 1714. Only much later, however, did the separation of the Catholic community extend to its dead; that is, sometime after 1791, and in the case of the Throckmortons, not until the creation of the separate Catholic churchyards attached to the new neo-Gothic churches at Buckland and Coughton in 1848 and 1853 respectively.[54]

Congregationalism within the Catholic community itself was a feature of the eighteenth century, a time when central clerical control through the Vicars Apostolic was weak, and when religious networks tended to be established horizontally rather than vertically by way of kinship affiliations and loyalty to certain religious orders which were not territorially subject to local bishops. Thus, the Throckmortons' preferred choices as chaplains were monks, who acted independently of the Vicars Apostolic. During the internal Catholic debates, over political loyalty to the state and the degree of acceptable Roman control, known as the 'Cisalpine stirs', Sir John resolutely supported the monk Cuthbert Wilks, son of the Coughton agent, against the papalist Vicars Apostolic.[55] On occasions of clerical unemployment, the vicars were, up to a point, deferential to Throckmortons who acted as patrons to clerical livings. Thus, Bishop Stonor 'recommended' Sir Robert appoint nominated secular priests to Harvington in 1722 and 1742, noting that 'when anyone shall be sent, even for a time, he immediately upon notice acquaint Sir Rob. Throckmorton, upon whose good will depends the Gentleman's holding his Congregation or living there: but no more'.[56] There was nonetheless a long war over rival jurisdictions between the Throckmorton baronets and the Vicars Apostolic: the battles between Sir John Courtenay Throckmorton and Bishops John Milner and John Douglass in the 1790s centred on the baronet's protection of the radical priest, Joseph Berington. Sir John complained that if earlier bishops had behaved in the same way towards the gentry, 'maintenance would have been withdrawn, because it cannot be expected for us to maintain priests

---

[54] Bossy, *English Catholic Community*, pp. 132–6, 140, 143–4; *The Catholic Registers of Weston Underwood, in the County of Buckingham*, ed. Frederick Arthur Crisp (privately printed, 1887), p. 1; Birmingham Diocesan Archives, Coughton Register.

[55] Geoffrey Scott, 'Dom Joseph Cuthbert Wilks [1748–1829] and English Benedictine Involvement in the Cisalpine Stirs', *Recusant History*, 23 (1997): 318–40.

[56] Birmingham Diocesan Archives, Z3/4/85/A3, Z5/3/27/6/3; Michael Hodgetts, 'Priests at Harvington, 1660–1690', *Worcestershire Recusant*, 16 (December 1970), 13.

at our expense if they are liable to be suspended ... and are subject to the will and pleasure of an Apostolic Vicar'. Douglass believed Sir John was 'the *first* who takes that revenge of us Vicars Apostolic', meaning that although Berington's faculties at Buckland were not renewed by Douglass, Sir John snubbed the bishop and continued to maintain the troublesome priest.[57] The conflict was still smouldering half a century later when, as Alban Hood notes in his chapter, Bishop Bernard Ullathorne crossed swords with the eighth baronet. By then, however, the bishops enjoyed considerably enhanced status and the future lay with them.

The pamphlet war in the early 1790s between Sir John Courtenay Throckmorton and Bishop John Milner which culminated in the latter's emphatic *The divine right of episcopacy*[58] was part of the lengthy and immensely complex struggle for the soul of English Catholicism waged between leading Catholic Cisalpine laymen like the Throckmortons and the bishops.[59] The fashionable Cisalpine ideals of the day suggested that bishops should be elected by the laity, approved by the papacy and appointed by the Protestant government. These preoccupations soon broadened out to embrace the issue of the extent of the pope's own authority and power, an indication of how a state of affairs produced by the period's confusion of political ideology, ecclesiastical debate and civil unrest was fraught with supreme ironies. For the Throckmortons, the basic irony was that their time-honoured preference in favour of separateness was ultimately their first step towards achieving Catholic integration into the English establishment. The usual story of eighteenth-century English Catholicism describes everything in terms of England itself: how a persecuted minority sect took advantage of expanding toleration and dawning enlightenment within eighteenth-century English society to seek greater civil, religious and political rights. Such is the measured march described in most histories of eighteenth-century English Catholicism towards the liberties enshrined in the Catholic Relief Acts of 1778 and 1791, and to the practical freedom provided by the 1829 Emancipation Act. The Throckmortons were to be heavily involved in the struggle for such liberties; their early progressive and patriotic values, enhanced by their education in classical public virtues, made them natural Whigs at the century's end.

---

[57] Bernard Ward, *The Dawn of the Catholic Revival in England 1781–1803* (2 vols, London, 1909), vol. 1, pp. 47, 112, 227, 229; Eamon Duffy, 'Ecclesiastical Democracy Detected: III, 1796–1803', *Recusant History*, 13 (1975), 124, 135.

[58] John Milner, *The divine right of episcopacy addressed to the Catholic laity of England, in answer to the layman's second letter to the Catholic clergy of England; with remarks on the oaths of supremacy and allegiance* (London, 1791) was a response to Sir John Courtenay's *A second letter addressed to the Catholic clergy of England on the appointment of bishops* (London, 1791).

[59] See the chapters by Geoffrey Scott and Michael Mullett in this volume.

Yet this concentration on England ignores the strong currents of contemporary Gallican theory, which seem to have penetrated the family and influenced Sir John Courtenay Throckmorton in particular. We should recognise that Cisalpinism in England was not necessarily entirely native but, courtesy of a family like the Throckmortons, could be directly coloured by the state of French ecclesiastical and political affairs. Much of Sir John's youth had been spent in France and Italy before he returned to Weston in 1778 and joined the Cisalpine Catholic Committee in 1782, aged only 29. In the aftermath of the registration of the 1682 Four Gallican Articles, no serious visitor to France would have been unaware of a patriotic neo-Gallicanism which gripped Church and state and asserted the authority of the monarchy and episcopate above the papacy. Jansenist and Gallican manuals in French were carried back home by Throckmorton travellers, among them the classic exposition of Gallicanism by Jacques and Pierre Dupuy first published in 1639.[60] Of significance too is the fact that the family's favourite female religious order, the Augustinian canonesses in Paris, in which a number of Throckmortons were professed, was, unusually for a 'monastic' order, directly under the jurisdiction of the local bishop. If the *approchement* with English politics and society which the family had developed over at least a century had always had a Gallican flavour, this became much more obvious from the 1780s, when, for the first time, it was possible openly to promote Anglo-Gallicanism as a Catholic ideology of collaboration with the government as a means of securing further liberty for Catholics.

The Throckmortons' advocacy of political Gallicanism led them towards what might best be termed Catholic Whiggery, defined as a liberal support for political, social and religious reform, but always within a framework of respect for constitutional forms. In a way, Sir John Courtenay is more accurately defined as a Catholic Whig rather than as an English Cisalpine. Through his collaboration with Joseph Berington, a Catholic Whig ideology was developed which underpinned the strategy of the Catholic Committee (1782) and the more progressive Cisalpine Club (1793), in which Sir John was a leading member. It seems likely that Berington's views significantly matured, even mellowed, thanks to the influence on him of Sir John. Berington's gloomy work, *The State and Behaviour of English Catholics*, noted decay all around, a Catholic gentry with a 'mind peculiarly narrowed' by a 'foreign education', and 'the diminution of piety and of honest virtue which now prevails, is, in my opinion, but

---

[60] WRO, CR 1998/LCB/62, Buckland library catalogue, *Traité des Droits d l'Eglise Gallicane*, no author or publication date. Despite Bossy's assertion, *English Catholic Community*, p. 290, that French Jansenist authors had little impact in England, the Throckmorton library was stuffed with Jansenist works in French.

poorly compensated by the tinsel acquirements of a more political life'. He was speaking here of the qualified measure of emancipation given to Catholics by the 1778 Relief Act. Berington re-published in 1785 the most popular exposition of Anglo-Gallicanism, *Roman-Catholick Principles in reference to God and the King*, first published in 1680 (though Berington substituted *Country* for *King*). The pamphlet contained the principal points of doctrine of the Catholic Church, so its slant was not particularly French, but in its condemnation of the deposition of kings, murder of Protestants and foreign invasion, it assured the English that Catholics were no foreign political threat. Its political and ecclesiastical agenda – the work insisted papal supremacy was purely spiritual – was adopted by the Catholic Committee in its struggle with parliament for further Catholic relief. Not only had Sir John, a leading campaigner for the 1778 and 1791 Catholic Relief Acts, been educated in Gallican attitudes on the continent, he had probably learned by rote from this very Gallican catechism as a teenager.[61]

Sir John remained a political Gallican and a Whig despite the effects of the French Revolution. His pamphlet of 1806 clearly reveals his political colours. In this work, where he praised 'the beauty of the British constitution', he campaigned against the handling of Irish Catholics, who were treated as 'a subservient sect', and aligned himself with Henry Grattan, their chief spokesman. Sir John switched his Cisalpine campaign from England to Ireland since, because of its Catholic majority, the grant of further emancipation was more likely to be given there. Ireland also appeared to him paradigmatically Gallican; it boasted a strong nationalist faith, and its bishops possessed full jurisdiction. Yet, in the opinion of many at the time, the British Crown should be allowed to exercise a veto over their appointment. Here, in Ireland, the papal power was moderated, and Sir John invoked the 1801 Concordat between Napoleon and Pius VII to demonstrate how the English Crown might appoint, and the Pope confirm, new bishops who would be paid salaries by the government. For Sir John, the Concordat gave Gallicanism a new lease of life following the Revolution's destruction of the Church of the *ancien régime*.

For all his political liberalism, and despite his setbacks, Sir John remained a staunch Catholic. Surrounded by friends, colleagues and

---

[61] Joseph Berington, *The State and Behaviour of English Catholics* (London, 1780), pp. 116, 120, 124–5, and *Reflections addressed to the rev. John Hawkins. To which is added, an exposition of Roman Catholic principles in reference to God and the country* (Birmingham, 1785), pp. viii, ix, 92–5, compare the fate of Huguenots in Gallican France to Catholics in Anglican England. John Kirk (ed.), *Roman-Catholick Principles in reference to God and the King* (London, 1815), pp. 7, 9, 10, 12, 18, 44–7, 51, 53 and esp. 94, where Sir John noted in 1791 that the 'Principles' were annexed to the *Catholic Christian's Manual* (London 1766), and later *Manuals*.

relatives who had apostatised from the Catholic Church in order to enter the English establishment and enjoy its benefits, he entertained no doubts about the strength of the arguments for the continuity of the religious tradition to which he adhered: 'We are not sectaries, We went out from no church ... We stedfastly adhered to the ancient faith, and have continued to adhere to it, when all human motives have ceased to operate, and when the most powerful incentives, the love of wealth, of power, and of ease solicited a change.'[62]

The successes achieved by individual English Catholics in the eighteenth century, in science and the arts, were usually accomplished, according to the traditional view, against all the odds and despite society's resistance to their religious beliefs. The Throckmortons, especially Sir John, seem, however, never to have been sidelined in this way, attaining success only in adversity. They were confident socially and politically, at home and abroad, even if they did not enjoy full political rights and religious freedom in England. Geoffrey Scott has pointed out the galaxy of artists among whom Sir John moved in the British School at Rome, and his interest in French architecture might have influenced the classicism of the 1791 chapel at Coughton. The correspondence of Sir John's grandfather indicates how insistent he was to employ the polymath monk, Augustine Walker (1721–94), as Sir John's tutor. The chapters by Michael Mullett and Alban Hood demonstrate how Sir John and the baronets who succeeded him continued to be fascinated by invention and improvement, contributing in their characteristic Whig manner to the progress of the nation. Sir James Graham (1792–1861), the devout evangelical and Whig politician, had in his early life been keenly interested in agriculture. He recounted meeting Sir John Courtenay near Buckland, and admitted it was the baronet who first interested him in agricultural improvement. Perhaps the influence was more pervasive than this, for Graham later became Peel's Home Secretary and favoured the Irish Catholics through supporting the Irish Maynooth Grant in 1845, a means by which he hoped to gain the Church's support for order in that country.[63]

If a stance of political Gallicanism contributed to Throckmorton attempts to achieve more integration into English society towards the end

---

[62] Sir John Throckmorton, Bart., *Considerations arising from the debates in Parliament on the Petition of the Irish Catholics* (London, 1806), pp. 1, 2, 8, 16, 26, 148, 150–51.

[63] Scott, *Gothic Rage*, pp. 23, 75, 122, 155–8, 161, 163–6, 169, 187; Geoffrey Scott, 'A Monk's View of the Durham Coal Industry in 1750', *Northern Catholic History*, 15 (Spring 1982): 3–12. Walker was also tutor to the traveller, Henry Swinburne, and responsible for the Latin inscription on the plinth of the Warwick Vase offered to the British Museum by Sir William Hamilton: Ian Jenkins and Kim Sloan, *Vases and Volcanoes: Sir William Hamilton and his Collection* (London, 1996), pp. 220–21; John Towers Ward, *Sir James Graham* (London, 1967), p. 16.

of the eighteenth century, some aspects of ecclesiastical Gallicanism also seem to have been adopted as a means of securing more firmly the place of the English Catholic Church within the nation and of strengthening its internal unity. Differences between the small and marginal English Catholic community and the hugely prestigious Gallican Church across the Channel were, of course, vast. England was a missionary country; its Vicars Apostolic, with limited powers and subject to the Congregation of Propaganda Fide in Rome, were hardly the equivalents of the grand prelates of the *ancien régime*. With no vast reservoirs of ecclesiastical wealth and patronage to tap (as had the leading Catholic laity in France), the English Catholic aristocracy and gentry endeavoured to keep faith communities alive, rather than finding themselves in a position to exploit the affluence of any English First Estate. The eighteenth-century French Church experienced a revival of its ancient Gallican rites, while Catholic chapels in England struggled to celebrate the liturgy of the Council of Trent. All this being said, there was, however, some common ground, and in the absence of a national hierarchy with full jurisdictional rights, it fell to some of the lay leaders of the English Catholic body – the Throckmortons among them – to devise a Gallican template with which they aimed to assure English Catholicism's future. A foundation had already been laid: suggestions that the Gallican and Anglican churches, as national bodies, had much in common, including reservations about papal interference, had surfaced in the early eighteenth century, and the various protestations and oaths of allegiance composed by the Cisalpines were the final stage in the search for a Catholic *modus vivendi* with the Protestant state which went back to the Appellant controversy of the early seventeenth century.[64]

A first letter to the clergy on the appointment of bishops (1790) was written, significantly, by 'a layman', in fact Sir John, taking on himself the role of leading and educating the clergy. This pamphlet provides a good example of a striking feature of the English Catholic laity's self-appointed leadership in the Cisalpine stirs, for their spokesmen were determined to seek support for their position from public opinion through the press, and through depositing key documents of the controversy in national institutions such as the British Museum. The last two decades of the century were thus remarkable for the numbers of publications written and funded by the laity. Sir John himself paid for the publication of his two *Letters*, having a run of 1,000 printed of the first and advertising it in the national press. He distributed his second *Letter*, not only to his own party, but also to the episcopal opposition, to Anglican bishops and

---

[64] Jacques Gres-Gayer, *Paris-Cantorbéry (1717–1720). Le Dossier d'un Premier Oecuménisme* (Paris, 1989); Bossy, *English Catholic Community*, ch. 2; Ward, *Dawn of the Catholic Revival*, vol. 2, Appendix E.

politicians, to the English colleges abroad and to Ireland. In the first *Letter* he remarked on the prevalence of Gallican customs operating in other countries: 'in almost all of them the Civil Magistrate interferes with the appointment of the Ministers of the Gospel'. Although he was grateful that Catholicism was not 'the established religion' of England and that the civil power did not interfere with the English Catholic Church, he was insistent that the rules of 'primitive purity' ought to be adhered to, *viz.* that bishops should be elected by clergy and people and not appointed by the Pope. He noted that the decrees of the Council of Trent, which gave 'too great power' to the Roman Pontiff, had never been adopted in France or England. In his longer second *Letter* on the appointment of bishops (1791), Sir John stressed the importance for English Catholics of the 1774 Quebec Act, passed to facilitate the taking of the oath of allegiance to the English Crown by the French Catholic minority in Canada, and a prototype for the Catholic Relief Act of 1778. Both *Lettters* are heavily dependent on Gallican works, including the *Ius Ecclesiasticum* of Zeger Bernhard van Espen (1646–1728) and the *Discours sur les Libertés de l'Eglise Gallicane* of Claude Fleury (1640–1723). In 1793, two years after Sir John had helped bring about the second Catholic Relief Act, his protégé, Joseph Berington, heaped fulsome praise on his efforts. Sir John was an English patriot, 'a *gentleman* of large fortune, and of amiable manners, a *man* of great mental endowments, a *scholar* deeply read, a *citizen* devoted to his country, a *christian* in practice as well as theory, a *Catholic* enlightened in his belief and sincere in his conviction.'[65]

One enduring aspect of Anglo-Gallicanism among the Cisalpines was the support for a vernacular liturgy, not only to help the laity participate more fully in the Church's worship, but also to bring English Catholics closer to the Church of England. Gregory Gregson, the monk chaplain at Weston, published his *Devout Miscellany* in 1790, a text which was roundly condemned by the ecclesiastical authorities for not bearing an official *imprimatur* and on account of its recourse to the Book of Common

---

[65] *The Correspondence of James Peter Coghlan (1731–1800)*, ed. Frans Blom, Jos Blom, Frans Korsten and Geoffrey Scott (Woodbridge, 2007), Letter 133. A Layman, *A letter addressed to the Catholic clergy of England on the appointment of bishops* (1790), pp.1–2, 9, 11, 15; Throckmorton, *A second letter*, pp. xxvii–xxviii, xc–xci, 16, 62, 112–13. Van Espen, whose Gallican and Jansenist sympathies caused his books to be added to the Index, was a favourite with English Gallicans and liberals: Joseph P. Chinnici, *The English Catholic Enlightenment: John Lingard and the Cisalpine Movement 1780–1850* (Shepherdstown, 1980), pp. 31, 35, 58–9; Joseph Berington, *The memoirs of Gregorio Panzani: giving an account of his agency in England, in the years 1634, 1635, 1636* (Birmingham, 1793), pp. xxii, xxiii, 408, 428.

Prayer.⁶⁶ Gregson's book was intended for Catholic chapels, and in the peculiar circumstances in which Catholics found themselves in late eighteenth-century England, lay trusteeship of urban chapels is perhaps the closest approximation that the laity of the time came to their confrères in France, who sometimes held benefices and enjoyed the right of provision to them. Bossy, unaware of Gallican parallels, has rightly, however, compared this Catholic trusteeship to 'nonconformist congregationalism' and has shown Sir John to have been a trustee of the Warwick Street chapel in London. But a Throckmorton role as quasi-trustee can be discerned earlier, for instance, in Mrs Anna Maria Throckmorton's name on the subscription list of 1777 for the new Benedictine chapel in Bath. More intriguing, because of its late date and its rural setting, is the establishment in 1841 of the Kemerton mission in the Cotswolds, noted by Alban Hood, which was a late example of the collaboration of lay trustees from the well-known Catholic families of Throckmorton, Eyston, Canning and Handford.⁶⁷

The French Revolution profoundly affected liberal Catholic sentiment in England. As an example of the march of democracy it was initially welcomed by Sir John Throckmorton and his Whig allies, Charles Butler, Edmund Burke and Charles James Fox. But, as Michael Mullett demonstrates in Chapter 8, Sir John was dismayed to watch the extreme form it began to adopt in the early 1790s. The Revolution's violence ended for the moment any hopes of further Catholic Relief, even though this was promised by the 1801 Irish Act of Union, and it certainly dashed any hopes of Catholic bishops in England being elected by the faithful or appointed by the Crown. Sir John does not seem to have given any help to refugee English religious communities expelled from France, or to have befriended any of the numerous Gallican émigré clergy. Both these groups threatened 'the balance established by the (1791) Relief Act' and might, in the eyes of some Cisalpines, provide a means of extending the powers of the Vicars Apostolic at the cost of lay control over the English Catholic Church. In fact, the English Vicars Apostolic were to have their authority challenged by some of the grander Gallican prelates exiled in England. By the time the Revolution fizzled out, Old Gallicanism was 'passé', despite the protests of a small group of émigré clergy known as the Blanchardists. It was the new

---

⁶⁶ [Gregory Gregson], *The devout miscellany, or the Sunday's companion to the holy mass and vespers; containing the morning and evening service of the Roman Catholic church; the collects, epistles, gospels, &c.* (Leicester, 1790); Lille, Nord, 18 H 36, 16 January, 3 July 1791; Clifton Diocesan Archives, 1791 vol. 6, 1792 vols 32, 33; Scott, *Gothic Rage*, p. 141.

⁶⁷ Bossy, *English Catholic Community*, pp. 337–8, 340, 348, 350–51; Lille, Archives du Nord, 18 H 31, 14 March 1777.

Gallican model established by the 1801 Concordat, with its recognition of some papal control over episcopal appointments, that Sir John seemed to favour by the time of his 1806 pamphlet on Ireland.[68]

Sir John's last years saw him less interested in Church affairs, perhaps because of the drubbing his ideals had received from the Revolution, but he continued to support learning. The Cisalpine Charles Butler dedicated his 1807 book on the history of revolutions to Sir John, noting the latter's attachment to Charles James Fox's political principles and conduct: 'All his friends are sensible of his high esteem of you. I myself heard that great man say, he scarcely knew a person from whom it was less safe to differ than Sir John Throckmorton.' Sir John died in 1819, the year that John Lingard's *History of England* appeared, and which has been taken as the terminal date for English Cisalpinism.[69] Joseph Berington followed him, dying in 1827, and theological debate within the family became quiescent. The Catholic Emancipation Act became law in 1829, and the later baronets showed more interest in politics and science than in Church affairs.

Indicative of the passing of the Cisalpine moment within the Throckmorton family, if not within English Catholicism more generally, was the 1840 appointment of Daniel Rock (1799–1871) as chaplain at Buckland to Sir Robert George Throckmorton. Rock remained at Buckland until 1854, and must have decisively influenced the baronet. Roman trained, with a serious interest in and deep fidelity to English ecclesiastical and liturgical traditions, Rock guided Augustus Welby Pugin amongst others. He was at the same time firmly committed to the restoration of the Catholic hierarchy in England, an event which came in 1850. As a representative of that period (1800–50) which Bossy described as 'a golden age of the English mission', Rock was multi-faceted, Goth and Roman, liberal and ultramontane, as ultimately was the Throckmorton family itself. His liturgical and architectural influences can be seen in the new Throckmorton churches at Buckland, Coughton, and Studley, all built by Charles Hansom. At Buckland he penned two of his most influential works, which hint at the incipient ultramontane regeneration of English Catholicism. In his answer of 1844 to Lord John Manners, a member of the Young England group, which provided proof of papal supremacy in the early Irish Church, Rock launched into an extravagant eulogy of papalist triumphalism: 'this Irish Church has ever held ... that

---

[68] Dominic Aidan Bellenger, *The French Exiled Clergy in the British Isles after 1789* (Bath, 1990), pp. 6, 12–13, 28, 47, 49, 52, 58, 61, 262 (Jean de la Breque, exiled Gallican priest, signed Weston register, 1808).

[69] Charles Butler, *A connected series of notes on the chief revolutions of the principal states which composed the empire of Charlemagne* (London, 1807), p. v. His *Horae Biblicae* (London, 1807) was also dedicated to Sir John: Chinnici, *Enlightenment*, p. 134.

very same religious belief taught by the now reigning Pope Gregory XVI, and professed by the millions of Christians throughout the world keeping communion with him, and willingly yielding him spiritual obedience as successor to St. Peter, and sole head on earth of Christ's Church.' More influential still was his *The Church of our Fathers*, a massive survey on the Sarum Rite and its development published in 1849–53. As evidence for his claim that the hood on the medieval cope was pointed, Rock used 'the beautiful English cope made of purple velvet ... of about the end of the fifteenth century, which belongs to Sir Robert Throckmorton, Bart., and is now lying outspread before me'. The Cisalpine Throckmortons would have been proud, as Oxford Movement liturgiologists were, of this evocation of native Christian worship; Sarum was perhaps, after all, the closest English approximation to the Gallican rite. But for Rock, Anglo-Saxon Christians were the direct predecessors of mid-nineteenth century English Catholics, and both professed their loyalty to the Pope, whose authority was absolute.[70]

Sir Robert George succeeded to the baronetcy in 1840, the year Rock was appointed chaplain at Buckland. His marriage to Elizabeth Acton in 1829 was a crucial means by which the Throckmortons were reconnected to European Catholic networks. This time, however, there was a particular emphasis given to the family's respect for the papacy, helped without doubt by the presence in the curia of Cardinal Januarius Acton, Sir Robert's brother-in-law. In April 1857, Sir Robert, Lady Throckmorton and her cousin John, the future First Lord Acton (1834–1902), knelt in succession before Pius IX, 'a very pleasing old man ... rather large and unworldly', and the most ultramontane of popes. He kindly allowed them to shake his hand rather than 'kiss his red-shoed foot', and then he raised them up. What old Sir John Courtenay Throckmorton – he who had earlier referred to the Pope as 'a foreign prelate', and had refused to have an audience with him whilst in Rome – would have made of this obsequious grovelling, can only be surmised. The times, however, had changed, and the nineteenth-century Throckmortons were again enthusiastic to swim with the tide of a transformed European Catholicism. But the family's style and story never became monochrome, no more than did the character of English Catholicism

---

[70] Judith F. Champ, 'Goths and Romans: Daniel Rock, Augustus Welby Pugin, and Nineteenth-Century English Worship', in R.N. Swanson (ed.), *Continuity and Change in Christian Worship*, Studies in Church History, 35 (Woodbridge, 1999), pp. 289–319; Bossy, *English Catholic Community*, p. 322; Daniel Rock, *Did the Early Church in Ireland acknowledge the Pope's Supremacy? Answered, in a Letter to Lord John Manners* (London, 1844), p. 6; Rock, *The Church of Our Fathers*, ed. G.W. Hart and W.H. Frere (4 vols, London 1905), vol. 2, pp. 29, 30, 35, 208, 209 (although the present privately printed guide-book to Coughton Court (Norwich, 2002), p. 17 ascribes this cope to the work of Queen Katherine of Aragon and her ladies-in-waiting).

itself. John Acton, the figure onto whom the liberal mantle of the family was to fall and who was to become a scholarly historian of national and European eminence, left the papal throne room showing considerably less intoxicated enthusiasm for the Holy Father and rather more reserve: 'My impression is not of any ability and he seems less banally good-natured, than his smiling pictures represent him to be'.[71] The ambivalent currents within English Catholicism which the Throckmortons had exemplified over several centuries – the impulse to be at once thoroughly English and loyally Roman, to be integrated into the social and cultural mainstream, and yet to assert a conspicuous non-conformism – would flow on from the nineteenth century and into modern times.

---

[71] WRO, CR 1998/CD/Drawer 5/9, Journal entry, 18 April 1857; Roland Hill, *Lord Acton* (New Haven and London, 2000), p. 79, suggests Lady Throckmorton was Sir Robert's wife, but she had died in 1850. It was more likely to have been one of Sir Robert's daughters, Mary Elizabeth (1832–1919) or Elizabeth Laura (1844–1927).

CHAPTER 2

Crisis of Allegiance: George Throckmorton and Henry Tudor

Peter Marshall

The origins of the long recusant tradition of the Throckmorton family are generally traced to the notable figure of Sir George Throckmorton, who inherited the estates from his father Sir Robert in 1518 and died (having substantially consolidated them) in 1552. Remembered locally as the builder of, in William Dugdale's phrase, 'that stately Castle-like Gatehouse of free-stone' at Coughton, he has the reputation of a 'staunch Catholic', who consistently resisted all the changes of the early Reformation.[1]

George was an almost exact contemporary of Henry Tudor, scion of another gentry family, though one that had done rather better for itself over the course of the fifteenth century, seizing control of the English Crown in 1485. Henry's resolutions, first to disencumber himself of his wife, Katherine of Aragon, and then to repudiate the spiritual authority of the Pope, set off seismic changes in English religion, politics and society. They also presented his subjects with an unprecedented dilemma of loyalty, and precipitated permanent divisions in English religious culture. Sir George Thockmorton's responses to these remarkable events provide an illuminating case-study in elite resistance and acquiescence, though not because his behaviour can be considered 'typical'. In fact, Sir George dared to go much further than almost anyone else among the religiously conservative gentry in the early 1530s in his opposition to Henry VIII's break with Rome and concurrent casting aside of Queen Katherine. He provides one of the few documented cases when a subject told Henry to his face why the country considered his actions to be misguided, and he was incarcerated for political disaffection on more than one occasion. Yet in the end, Throckmorton kept his head, in more senses than one. Rarely, for one who had defied and displeased Henry VIII, he outlasted his royal master, and he lived to see his own children prosper. His career thus brings into focus the limits of loyalty and dissent in Henrician politics, and the

---

[1] William Dugdale, *The Antiquities of Warwickshire* (London, 1656), p. 561; Jennifer Loach, 'Throckmorton , Sir George (*c.*1489–1552)', rev. J.S. Block, *ODNB*. There is a useful short biography by S.M. Thorpe, in S.T. Bindoff (ed.), *The House of Commons, 1509–1558* (3 vols, London, 1982), vol. 3, pp. 450–55 [hereafter *HOC*].

extent to which lay 'Catholic' identity was being refashioned during these years.

Sir George Throckmorton's early life was (relatively) unremarkable for one of his status in that age. Born in or before 1489, his father Sir Robert had done well under the regime of Henry VII, and was able in 1501 to arrange an advantageous marriage for his eldest son with Katherine Vaux, heiress of one of Henry's trusted associates, Sir Nicholas Vaux.[2] That marriage proved fruitful, to put it mildly, producing 19 children, including seven sons who lived to adulthood, born between c.1510 and 1533: Robert, Kenelm, Clement, Nicholas, John, Anthony and George. In 1505 Sir Robert sent his son to the Middle Temple for some education in the ways of the law, a useful accoutrement for a landowner in a litigious age. Subsequently, George made some progress at court, becoming an esquire of the body by 1511, and in 1516 a knight, by which time he had served the king in the French war of 1513. Royal favour was shown in a slew of appointments to stewardships of royal estates and keepership of royal parks in Warwickshire and Worcestershire. As part of the compact of patronage and good lordship binding the landed gentry to the Crown, Sir George played an expected role in local administration. From 1510 he served regularly as a Justice of the Peace for Warwickshire, and in 1526–27 was sheriff for Warwickshire and Leicestershire, after being considered for the office the previous year. He also acted as a subsidy commissioner for the counties in which he held influence: Worcestershire, Warwickshire and Buckinghamshire.[3] One incident stands out from Sir George's years of young adulthood, indicative of a boldness of purpose manifest in his later career: in 1518 he was given a royal pardon for the killing of William Porter, serjeant at arms, in Foster Lane, Aldersgate. Apparently, Porter had approached Throckmorton 'maliciously', and the latter had struck out 'through fear of death and for the salvation of his own life'.[4]

George Throckmorton grew to adulthood in a world where the traditional verities of the Catholic faith were not seriously questioned. There might have been pockets of Lollard heretics in Coventry, but their opinions impinged little if at all on the rural stretches of Worcestershire

---

[2] On Robert's career, see Christine Carpenter, 'Throgmorton family (*per.* 1409–1518)', *ODNB*.

[3] *HOC*, p. 451; *Letters and Papers, Foreign and Domestic, of the Reign of Henry VIII*, ed. J.S. Brewer, J. Gairdner, and R.H. Brodie (21 vols, London 1862–1910) [hereafter, *LP* and cited by vol., part and item number], 5 (i): 924 (12), 1083 (4); 1 (ii): 2137 (10), p. 1545; 2 (i): 2735, p. 1460; 3 (ii): p. 1364; 4 (i): p. 235, 1795; 4 (ii): 2672.

[4] *LP*, 2 (ii): 3922; WRO, CR 1998/Box 64/7.

and Warwickshire where the Throckmortons had their estates.[5] Catholic devotion in this world was customary and habitual, and could easily become an occasion for conspicuous consumption or a mark of social status. But there are indications that the young Throckmorton heir was raised in a household that was more than merely conventionally pious. In 1491, the infant George, with his parents Robert and Katherine, received letters admitting him to the confraternity of the Abbey of Evesham, a means of securing spiritual benefits such as post-mortem commemoration by formal association with a religious community.[6] Sir Robert was also received into the confraternity of the Augustinian Canons at the order's Chapter of 1506, and he and his wife were for many years among the 'chief benefactors' of the guild of the Holy Cross in Stratford-upon-Avon.[7]

In 1518, Sir Robert Throckmorton made an infinitely more dramatic gesture of pious commitment, the decision to undertake a pilgrimage to the Holy Land. This was an unusual, though by no means unprecedented action on the part of an early Tudor gentleman. A fellow courtier and councillor of Henry VII, Richard Guildford, had died in Jerusalem in 1506, and it is conceivable that Guildford's pilgrimage, or the printed account of it by his chaplain, inspired Robert's decision to follow the same course.[8] The will which Robert made before his departure on the Feast of Sts Philip and Jacob (1 May) 1518 is a striking testimony to the depth and richness of late medieval belief in purgatory and the cult of the saints.[9] Robert requested masses for his soul from the Benedictine monks of Evesham and the Augustinian canons of Studley, from the Franciscan friars at Warwick, Oxford and Cambridge, from the Dominicans in the two university towns and prayers from the poor in the almshouse he had established at

---

[5] See *Lollards of Coventry, 1486–1522*, trans and ed. Shannon McSheffrey and Norman Tanner, Camden Soc. 5th ser., p. 23 (Cambridge, 2003).

[6] WRO, CR 1998/Box 52. For the principles and attitudes underlying confraternity, see Robert N. Swanson, 'Mendicants and Confraternity in Late Medieval England', in James G. Clark (ed.), *The Religious Orders in Pre-Reformation England* (Woodbridge, 2002), pp. 121–41.

[7] *Chapters of the Augustinian Canons*, ed. H.E. Salter, Oxford Historical Society, 74 (1920) and Canterbury and York Society, 29 (1921–22), p. 126; *The Register of the Guild of the Holy Cross*, ed. Mairi Macdonald, Dugdale Society, 42 (2007), pp. 364, 382, 461, 467. There is evidence that Sir Robert's notable piety was a Throckmorton family trait earlier in the fifteenth century: Mary C. Erler, *Women, Reading and Piety in Late Medieval England* (Cambridge, 2002), pp. 112–14.

[8] *The Pylgrymage of Sir Richard Guylforde to the Holy Land, AD 1506*, ed. Henry Ellis, Camden Society, 51 (1851). There may have been a kinship connection. Guildford's second wife, like Robert's daughter-in-law, was a member of the Vaux family: Sean Cunningham, 'Guildford, Sir Richard (*c.*1450–1506)', *ODNB*.

[9] WRO, CR 1998/Box 73/2, an Elizabethan copy. The original is in TNA, Prob 11/20, and granted probate on 9 November 1520.

Worcester. Furthermore, various lands were put into enfeoffment to pay for a perpetual chantry to be established in the north aisle of the parish church at Coughton. The chapel there was to be called the Trinity Chapel, and the priest, the Trinity priest, who was also to keep a school 'and teache grammer freely to all my tenantes children'.

Historians disagree about the level of emotional investment the late medieval gentry typically had in the institution of the parish church.[10] But Robert Throckmorton's detail of prescription for the parish church of St Peter, Coughton, is remarkable and conspicuous, perhaps not surprisingly as the church lay a (literal) stone's throw from his manor house, and had been extensively rebuilt at Sir Robert's initiative during his lifetime. The east window in the chancel was to be glazed 'at my coste and charge' and to depict Doomsday. The east window in the north aisle was to be of the seven sacraments, and in the south aisle, of the seven works of mercy. There was also a series of bequests for the gilding and painting of new images for the church, with precise locations specified: statues of the Virgin and the Archangel Gabriel in a juxtaposition representing the Annunciation; statues of the other archangels, Michael and Raphael; an image of the Trinity. Unsurprisingly, Robert wished to be buried at Coughton 'under the tombe in the myddes of the churche, if it happen me to die within this realme of Englande'. As it turned out, the large tomb-chest in the nave was to lie empty until appropriated by a later Sir Robert Throckmorton in the eighteenth century. Robert died at Rome on his way to Jerusalem in the late summer of 1518.[11]

The chief secular beneficiary of Sir Robert's will was, of course, his 'well beloved sonne and heir', George. Along with his responsibilities as a landowner, Sir George inherited his father's deep commitment to the beliefs and traditions of the Catholic faith.[12] But the world that had engendered those traditions was changing. Even as Robert Throckmorton lay dying in the English Hospice in Rome, Pope Leo X was ordering his legate in Germany to secure the recantation or arrest of the recalcitrant friar, Martin Luther.

---

[10] Contrast Colin Richmond, 'Religion and the Fifteenth-Century English Gentleman', in R.B. Dobson (ed.), *The Church, Politics and Patronage in the Fifteenth Century* (Gloucester, 1984), and Richmond, 'The English Gentry and Religion, c. 1500', in Christopher Harper-Bill (ed.), *Religious Belief and Ecclesiastical Careers in Late Medieval England* (Woodbridge, 1991) with Eamon Duffy, *The Stripping of the Altars: Traditional Religion in England 1400–1580* (New Haven and London, 1992), pp. 121–3, 132–3.

[11] A hasty codicil to Robert's will was written there on 10 August 1518: WRO, CR 1998/Box 73/2.

[12] In the 1520s, for example, he was a member of the guild of St Anne at Knowle: Michael Wood, *In Search of Shakespeare* (London, 2003), p. 21.

Lutheranism had rooted itself in England by the early 1520s, but at first seemed to represent little serious threat to the old order. The earliest English 'evangelicals' were London merchants or university clergymen without social or political clout. The moving force in the campaign to contain heresy (though he had other and more pressing demands on his time) was the king's chief minister, Cardinal Thomas Wolsey. The cardinal was the lodestar of English politics, his palace at Hampton Court a centre of patronage and influence to rival the royal court itself, and ambitious young men gravitated to his service. One of these was the common lawyer, Thomas Cromwell, and another was George Throckmorton. The point of entry may have been Throckmorton's paternal uncle, William, who as a master in chancery worked for Wolsey. Sir George's most discernible role in Wolsey's service in the later 1520s is as a facilitator of the cardinal's flagship policy of educational reform through the disendowment of small decayed monasteries.[13]

Those in the cardinal's favour could expect rewards. In April 1528, Throckmorton wrote requesting promotion to the offices of the recently deceased Sir Giles Greville, and in July he did the same in respect of the late Sir William Compton. He particularly wanted the shrievality of Worcester and the post of *custos rotulorum* for Warwickshire, as well as the stewardship of the see of Worcester and the under-treasurership of England. With a characteristic sense of family honour, he noted that 'my anncestors have in tyme past been under tresorors and stewards to the bisshopes'. Remembering that the cardinal had always offered to help him, he promised in return to be a benefactor to the new college Wolsey was building in Oxford.[14] The under-treasurership went elsewhere, but Throckmorton received the stewardship of Worcester and was placed on the sheriff roll for the county, also acquiring from the Crown at this time a couple of valuable wardships.[15]

In 1529, Throckmorton exercised his local muscle on the cardinal's behalf in a dispute over the headquarters, or preceptory, in the West Midlands of the Order of St John of Jerusalem, at Balsall in Warwickshire. The outgoing Prior of the order in England, Thomas Docwra, had made a

---

[13] *LP*, 4 ii): 4136, 4261, 4734; 4 (iii): 6263. William Throckmorton was in May 1528 identified as the recipient for secret information in Wolsey's campaign against illegal enclosures. Ironically, his nephew himself was an encloser of heath and parkland in the vicinity of Coughton: *The Domesday of Inclosures 1517–1518*, ed. I.S. Leadham (2 vols, London, 1897), vol. 2, pp. 450, 662. It may have been as a result of these activities that Sir George first appears in Wolsey's orbit in July 1524, charged to come before the council and pay whatever fine the cardinal might impose: *LP*, 4 (i): 521.

[14] TNA, SP 1/49, fol. 91r (*LP*, 4 (ii): 4483); *LP*, 4 (ii): 4136, 4734. Sir George's great-grandfather, Sir John Throckmorton, had held the post of under-treasurer: *HOC*, p. 451.

[15] Ibid.; *LP*, 4 (ii): 4914; 4 (iii): 5508, 5815 (8), 6135 (17).

long lease of the preceptory to a kinsman, Martin Docwra, which the new prior, William Weston, disputed. Wolsey ordered Throckmorton to take possession until right in the case could be determined. When he arrived with his retinue to do so, Docwra and his men (whom Throckmorton later alleged to be criminals from the sanctuary at Knowle) resisted, and were evicted by force. The result was a Star Chamber case, alongside a long-running dispute in chancery, in which both sides accused the other of riot and affray. The Throckmorton interest in Balsall was a long-standing one: Sir Robert had leased the preceptory in 1495, and had been involved in a ferocious dispute over it with members of the order in 1503. But Sir George was evidently on good terms with Prior Weston and other knights of the order. His intimacy with Weston's nephew, Thomas Dingley, was later to have significant consequences, as we shall see.[16] Throckmorton seems also to have been on good terms with another of Wolsey's men-of-business, Thomas Cromwell, who handled the arrangements for a projected sale and exchange of lands between Throckmorton and Wolsey in the latter half of 1528. Cromwell was Sir George's 'assuryd frende', to whom Throckmorton sent gifts of £20 and of a greyhound, hoping that 'ye wyll see me no loser'.[17]

In 1528, Wolsey was still the nation's political colossus. By the autumn of 1529, he was a rapidly sinking ship, holed below the waterline by the looming iceberg of the king's 'Great Matter' – his desire to secure an annulment of his marriage – which Wolsey's diplomacy and legal manoeuvring over the past two and a half years had signally failed to produce. Disgraced and stripped of his offices, Wolsey also came under attack in the new parliament of November 1529. Though later to be known as 'the Reformation Parliament', this assembly was called into being principally to underline the attack on the fallen minister, blasted as 'the great wether' in an opening speech by the new Lord Chancellor, Thomas More.[18] On 1 December 1529, 44 articles against Wolsey were presented in the Lords. The 42nd of these charged him with short-cutting legal procedures by issuing a Chancery injunction to Martin Docwra to avoid possession of Balsall, in favour of Sir George Throckmorton.[19] But other than this tarring of the cardinal with his name, Throckmorton does not seem to have been entangled in Wolsey's fall. Like Cromwell, he managed to negotiate political passage away from the disgraced favourite. Both men in fact were sitting as members of the new parliament, Cromwell

---

[16] Gregory O'Malley, *The Knights Hospitaller of the English Langue 1460–1565* (Oxford, 2005), pp. 152, 156–7, 188–96.
[17] TNA, SP 1/49, fols 131r–v (*LP*, 4 (ii): 4543); *LP*, 4 (ii): 4628, 4917, 5024.
[18] Jennifer Loach, *Parliament under the Tudors* (Oxford, 1991), p. 61.
[19] *LP*, 4 (iii): 6075.

as a burgess for Taunton, and Throckmorton as one of the knights of the shire for Warwickshire. In July 1530, Throckmorton was appointed to the commission making inquisition into Wolsey's goods in Warwickshire.[20]

Cromwell meanwhile was starting to emerge as the new power to be reckoned with. Already in November 1529, a correspondent had heard 'comfortable tydynges that you be in favour hilie with the Kynges grace', and by the end of 1530 he was a member of the royal council, and a leading proponent of new, more radical ways to solve the king's Great Matter.[21] There are some indications that relations with Throckmorton continued for a while to be friendly. By 1532, Sir George's son Kenelm may have entered Cromwell's service. But matters became strained over the case of Sir William Spenser, sheriff of Northamptonshire who died in June of that year. Spenser's brothers-in-law, Edmund and Richard Knightley, colluded with the widow to defraud the king of his rights to wardship of the heir, empanelling a local jury to swear that Spenser held no land by 'knight service'. The case was heard in the Exchequer, where the Crown initially lost its case. Throckmorton (a kinsman of the Knightleys) had become involved in the local handling of the case by the new sheriff, and Cromwell suspected him of complicity, or at least lack of assiduity. Sir George wrote with injured protestations that 'what I have don ever for the best yt ys ever torned to the worsse'. When names of prospective new sheriffs for each county were drawn up in November, Throckmorton's was pointedly not on the list for Warwickshire (although he had earlier hinted he would be willing to serve). Cromwell's close ally and Speaker of the Commons, Sir Thomas Audley, wrote on 4 November that 'it is thought that Mr Throgmorton is not so hearty in Warwickshire as he might be'. Henry VIII's title to the Spenser lands was still a hot issue in the Midlands early the next year, with Lady Spenser spreading rumours the king's agents were seeking to rob her of her jointure. Sir Anthony Cope complained to Cromwell in February 1533 that it grieved him to find the king had 'so fewe frendes and so faynte in his right' within the counties of Warwick and Northampton. Furthermore, he alleged, 'Mr. Throkmorton shewed me not long agoon that he wold assist me to the best he cold and that he hath so promised the kinges councell. Nevertheless, secretly he workith the contrary.' Cope recommended that both Throckmorton and Sir William Parr be summoned for an interview with the king and be given a direct

---

[20] *LP*, 4 (iii): 6516. *HOC*, p. 452, notes that Throckmorton may have sat in a previous parliament, as the names of Warwickshire knights for the earlier Henrician parliaments are unknown.

[21] Howard Leithead, 'Cromwell, Thomas, earl of Essex (*b.* in or before 1485, *d.* 1540)', *ODNB*.

mandate for advancing the royal interest in the matter so that 'they can not for shame but faithfully cleave there to'.²²

Sir George had, then, within a couple of years of his entry into parliament, acquired a reputation for unreliability in the eyes of the government. But this went much further than the affairs of the gentry in Warwickshire and Northamptonshire. Already in 1530, Throckmorton was known in some quarters as an opponent of the king's proceedings over the divorce. In April, the vice-chancellor of Cambridge, William Buckmaster, complained to a correspondent that the university's determination in favour of the divorce had cost him a benefice: 'there hath one fallen in Mr Throkmorton's gift, which he hath faithfully promised unto me many a time, but now his mind is turned and alienate from me.²³ Sir George's attitude to the government's key policies went beyond passive disapproval. He used his position in parliament to speak against, and attempt to block, the government's legislative programme. He also held a series of clandestine meetings with other opponents of anti-papal measures. He was, in short, one of the most vocal and visible of dissidents in the political nation Henry Tudor was determined to bend to his will.

We know about Sir George's activities in the early 1530s as a result of a confession produced several years later, in October 1537. (We will return to the circumstances of its composition in due course).²⁴ By his own account, Throckmorton was one of a group of members who dined together regularly at the Queen's Head tavern, and there 'had many communications concerning the parliament matters'. It included Sir William Essex, Sir William Barantyne, Sir John Gifford, Sir Marmaduke Constable and 'divers others'. As parliamentary matters arose, 'so we did commune of them, and every man showed his mind'. Before doing so, they were careful to send the servants out of the room, as 'we thought it not convenient that they should hear us speak of such matters'.

By the time parliament reconvened after its Easter break in 1532, Throckmorton had acquired a reputation as a principled opponent of royal policy, and significant figures of like mind had started to seek him out. The first to do so was William Peto, a Franciscan Observant friar of

---

²² TNA, SP 1/68, fol. 48r (*LP*, 5: 527: misdated to 1531); *LP*, 5: 1051, 1518; TNA, SP 1/74, fol. 132r (*LP*, 6: 128); *Life and Letters of Thomas Cromwell*, ed. R.B. Merriman (2 vols, Oxford, 1902), vol. 1, pp. 348–9. Cf. J.J. Scarisbrick, 'Religion and Politics in Northamptonshire in the Reign of Henry VIII', *Northamptonshire Past and Present*, 5 (1974): 85–90.

²³ Gilbert Burnet, *History of the Reformation of the Church of England* (7 vols, Oxford, 1865), vol. 6, p. 34. Confusingly, Dugdale, *Antiquities*, p. 457 does record Buckmaster's institution to Barcheston on 23 April 1530 at Throckmorton's presentation.

²⁴ The document is TNA, SP 1/125, fols 247–56 (*LP*, 12 (ii): 952), printed in John Guy, *The Public Career of Sir Thomas More* (New Haven and London, 1980), pp. 207–12.

Greenwich, who was also a first cousin of Sir George, his mother Goditha having been a sister of Sir Robert Throckmorton.[25] Peto was to prove over many years an aggravating thorn in the regime's side. In 1533, he fled to Antwerp, and spent the next 20 years conspiring against the Reformation in England.[26] Before this, on Easter Sunday 1532, Peto preached a fiery sermon denouncing the divorce in the presence of Henry himself, and gave the king more of his mind in a private interview to which Henry subsequently summoned him. Shortly after, Peto sent for Throckmorton to come speak to him, 'then being [incarcerated?] in a tower in Lambeth over the gate'. Peto supplied Throckmorton with a medley of arguments against the king's divorce, arguments he said he had delivered to the king's face. Chief among these was that the logic of Henry's case required a consummation of the marriage between Katherine and Prince Arthur, whereas Katherine, 'so virtuous a woman', had sworn to the contrary. In conclusion, Peto urged Throckmorton to stick to his course in parliament 'as I would have my soul saved'.

Not long after the reassembly of parliament, a still more illustrious opponent of royal policy expressed a wish to meet with Sir George. This was Sir Thomas More, shortly to resign his post as Lord Chancellor. Throckmorton had come to his attention 'after I had reasoned to [i.e. spoken against] the bill of Appeals', and More sent word for him to come speak with him 'in a little chamber within the Parliament chamber'.[27] The Lord Chancellor's words were coded, but clear enough in their meaning: 'I am very glad to hear the good report that goeth of you, and that ye be so good a catholic man as ye be; and if ye do continue in the same way that ye began and be not afraid to say your conscience, ye shall deserve great reward of God and thanks of the king's grace at length.' Sir George was flattered, both by the attention and the words of praise, and in consequence took himself to another illustrious partisan of Queen Katherine, Bishop John Fisher of Rochester. They met several times over the following months, and discussed the Acts of Appeals, Annates and Supremacy, as well as the authority of the Pope. At their last meeting, Fisher gave Throckmorton a copy of a book he had written concerning 'the authority that our Lord gave to Peter above the other disciples'. He

---

[25] Jan Broadway, 'Peyto family (*per.* 1487–1658)', *ODNB*.

[26] Peter Marshall, *Religious Identities in Henry VIII's England* (Aldershot, 2006), pp. 230, 247–8.

[27] As Guy has shown, the bill against which Throckmorton spoke could not have been the Act of Appeals, which was passed in 1533 after More's resignation; most likely it was the bill Cromwell introduced for a parliamentary Submission of the Clergy – either Sir George's memory was at fault, or he used 'bill of Appeals' in a loose descriptive way: Guy, *Public Career*, pp. 198–9.

also advised him to seek the counsel of another leading conservative cleric, Dr Nicholas Wilson. Throckmorton met with Wilson several times at the church of St Thomas the Apostle, and was shown more books in support of papal supremacy. Both Fisher and Wilson offered pragmatic advice: 'if I did think in my conscience that my speaking could do no good, that then I might hold my peace and not offend'. But he received a different message from a fourth recalcitrant cleric he met with about this time. This was Richard Reynolds, a monk of the Bridgettine house of Syon in Middlesex, whose fathers were much in demand as confessors to the great and good. Throckmorton made his confession, 'and showed him my conscience in all these causes'. In return, he was given uncompromising advice: his stand was an encouragement to many others in the house to keep in the right way, and he should 'stick to the same to the death'. If he did not, he 'should surely be damned', and would be in a very heavy case at the day of judgement 'if I did speak or do any thing in the Parliament house contrary to my conscience for fear of any earthly power'. Not surprisingly, perhaps, in May 1535 Reynolds himself gave his life for the cause.[28]

Throckmorton's testimony about his attitudes and activities in 1532–33 has earned him a place in most standard histories of the Henrician Reformation, and has also provided fuel for theories about the nature and extent of systematic opposition to royal policy. Sir Geoffrey Elton, in particular, found here evidence of an 'organized opposition group' with the figure of Thomas More at its centre, a group which had managed to recruit a member of parliament, 'instructed him in parliamentary tactics and the arguments to be used, and used his freedom of speech in the Commons to gain a hearing for the opposition point of view'. Throckmorton himself was 'a political innocent', a useful tool 'who could be threatened with hellfire first and flattered by a kind word from the lord chancellor after'.[29]

But this account is overly conspiratorial, and gives far too little credit to the pluck and initiative of Sir George Throckmorton himself. After all, Throckmorton was already active and recognised as an opponent of royal policy when he came to the attention of Peto and More, and (apparently on his own initiative) he sought the advice of Fisher and Reynolds about a course of action on which he was already firmly embarked. Admittedly, Fisher directed him on to Wilson for further stiffening of his resolve. But Wilson, like the bishop of Rochester, offered very different tactical advice

---

[28] David Knowles, *The Religious Orders in England: III The Tudor Age* (Cambridge, 1959), pp. 216–18.

[29] G.R. Elton, 'Sir Thomas More and the Opposition to Henry VIII', in R.S. Sylvester and G.P. Marc'hadour (eds), *Essential Articles for the Study of Thomas More* (Hamden, CT, 1977), pp. 87–8. See also J.S. Block, *Factional Politics and the English Reformation 1520–1540* (London, 1993), pp. 46–8; John Guy, *Tudor England* (Oxford, 1988), p. 125.

from Reynolds's, which hardly suggests a coherent pulling of strings by a tightly organised 'faction'. The members of the commons who dined together at the Queen's Head were doubtless in the main like-minded conservatives who disliked the drift of legislative policy. But this does not make them a hard-core of plotters, for all that the servants were sent away when matters of high policy were discussed. As Throckmorton himself later observed, if they had been about some nefarious business, 'few men would think that place to be meet'. Throckmorton, in other words, was a highly principled country gentleman, who in public was pushing the boundaries of admissible dissent, and in private was going some way beyond them. He had important links to a loose network of Queen Katherine's supporters, but it stretches the evidence to see him as the leg-man of a close-knit cabal, co-ordinating opposition in parliament and among the clergy. Naturally, Sir George would hardly have readily admitted to performing this role were he doing so, but the known facts reinforce rather than contradict the impression that satisfaction of his own conscience was the prevailing concern.[30]

Throckmorton's stance in parliament did not just bring him to the notice of other political malcontents; it also focused on him the attention of the king himself, and as a result of his activities in the 1532 session, Throckmorton was summoned to an interview with Henry and Cromwell. This may not have gone entirely as the king intended. In a fascinating exchange, which has intrigued biographers, Throckmorton put to Henry directly a compelling reason why he should not marry Anne Boleyn. Throckmorton had been told by Friar Peto that it was believed the king had had intercourse both with Anne's mother and her sister, and Peto had informed the king so to his face. Throckmorton now repeated the tactic: 'I told your grace I feared if ye did marry Queen Anne, your conscience would be more troubled at length, for that it is thought ye have meddled with the mother and the sister.' Henry's response to this (whether muted or animated) was simply to assert, 'never with the mother', leaving Cromwell to jump in with 'nor never with the sister neither, and therefore put that out of your mind'.[31]

The incident is revealing of the limits of political expression in early Tudor England. There was no recognised right to 'freedom of speech', even in parliament, but the king was apparently prepared to tolerate an

---

[30] For scepticism about Sir George's putative role in an organised oppositional faction, see Greg Walker, *Persuasive Fictions: Faction, Faith and Political Culture in the Reign of Henry VIII* (Aldershot, 1996), pp. 4–10; G.W. Bernard, *The King's Reformation: Henry VIII and the Remaking of the English Church* (New Haven and London, 2005), pp. 114–15, 210–12.

[31] Guy, *Public Career*, pp. 207–8.

extraordinary level of frankness on matters touching his conscience. It has recently been argued, however, that it is highly unlikely Throckmorton ever spoke such provocative words to the king.[32] In 1537, he was charged with having told Sir Thomas Dingley that he had done so, and he admitted repeating the story to Sir Thomas Englefield, Sir William Essex and Sir William Barantyne. But he had done so, he now admitted, 'upon a proud and vainglorious mind, as who saith they that I did tell it to should note me to be a man that durst speak for the common wealth and never for untruth in thought, word or deed.'[33] Yet somehow the notion that Sir George was a braggart who had invented an audacious personal admonition of Henry Tudor in order to puff himself up in the eyes of fellow conservatives does not quite ring true. The emphasis in the interrogatories of 1537 was on from whom he had heard such a report about the king, to whom he had repeated it, whether he had considered the implications of telling the tale to men likely to travel overseas and whether he thinks 'it were expedient for the quiete of a common weale, that a kinges subiectes be broughte to suche an opinion of their prince'. The interrogatories were not predicated on the contention that no such words had passed between Sir George and the king, and neither did Sir George in his confession explicitly deny that they had.[34]

As a result of his known intransigence, Throckmorton was clearly a marked man – his name heads a list drawn up by Cromwell in early 1533 of MPs thought to be opposed to the crucial Act of Appeals.[35] But he was not a condemned man, and he worked hard over the next couple of years to demonstrate his loyalty and trustworthiness. He had an opportunity to do so in May 1533 when he was summoned to be a servitor at the coronation of Anne Boleyn.[36] With parliament prorogued in the spring of 1533, Throckmorton returned to the country. Here he continued to perform his duties as a JP, including, ironically enough, the policing of political dissent. In early October, along with the Abbot of Kenilworth and other justices, Throckmorton examined the case of Richard Panemore, who was so exercised by Hugh Latimer's heretical preaching against

---

[32] Bernard, *King's Reformation*, pp. 211–12. J.A. Froude, *The Divorce of Catherine of Aragon* (London, 1891), p. 59, dismissed the suggestion that Mary Boleyn had been Henry's mistress as resting on 'the version of a confessed boaster'. Nonetheless, the emperor was being informed in February 1533 that there was a closer affinity between Henry and Anne Boleyn than between Henry and Katherine 'in consequence of his previous connection with her sister': *LP*, 6: 134.

[33] Guy, *Public Career*, p. 208.

[34] TNA, SP 1/125, fols 211r–v (*LP*, 12 (ii): 953).

[35] Bernard, *King's Reformation*, p. 211; *LP*, 9: 1077 (misdated to 1535).

[36] *LP*, 6: 562 (i).

images and fasting, with, as he thought, the licence both of the king and the Archbishop of Canterbury, that in front of drinking companions he declared himself ready to 'die as St Thomas of Canterbury did, in a rightful quarrel'.[37]

Sir George himself had no intention of dying in such a quarrel, and wrote to Cromwell on 29 October assuring him that with parliament out of session he would not come up to London, but would instead take the minister's advice 'to lyve at home, serve God, and medyll little ... ye shall see I wyll performe all promesys made with you'.[38] In fact, as Throckmorton devoted himself to the perennial preoccupation of the early Tudor gentleman, the consolidation of family estates, he was regularly in need of Cromwell's good will and patronage. Over the course of 1534–35, we find Sir George writing to the minister asking him to intercede with the Duke of Norfolk over lands in Solihull; offering him first refusal of the manor of Tattenhoe, Buckinghamshire; following a request to arbitrate a dispute of the abbot of Leicester's; currying favour in a dispute over the farm of a parsonage for himself; begging the wardship of his daughter's fiancé, should his father happen to die, and requesting Cromwell to advance the marital prospects of his son, Kenelm.[39] At the same time, Throckmorton continued to perform the duties of a royal servant, producing upon request in January 1534 a certificate of the state of the woods in the king's park of Haseley (of which he was bailiff and keeper), and serving as a commissioner for the new clerical tax of tenths of spiritualities in January 1535.[40]

A political chill, however, remained. In a letter of 8 January 1535 to the courtier Sir Francis Bryan he complained that he had heard that 'the kynges grace shuld be in displeasure wythe me. And that I shuld be greatly hyndred to hym, by whom I know not.' He asked Bryan to intercede so that he could personally defend himself from his calumniators. Indeed, the king himself had 'promysed me at the last prorogation whan I toke my leve that he wold be good and gracious lorde unto me, and what reporte so ever shuld be made hereafter of me, I shuld come to myn Awnser.'[41] This apparent pledge of royal fair dealing, putting aside 'all matters paste ... without dyspleasure', must have been made at the close of the parliamentary session in December 1534, a session which formally enacted the Royal Supremacy over the Church, but whose most contentious business may

---

[37] *LP*, 6: 1255.
[38] TNA, SP 1/80, fol. 47r (*LP*, 6: 1365).
[39] *LP*, 6: 838, 1004; 8: 229.
[40] *LP*, 7: 46; 8: 149 (62).
[41] TNA, SP 1/89, fol. 14r (*LP*, 8: 26). Throckmorton's son Nicholas would later marry Bryan's niece, Anne Carew: Stephen Alford, *Kingship and Politics in the Reign of Edward VI* (Cambridge, 2002), p. 152.

have been the passing of a new Treasons Act, creating a statutory offence of treason by words alone. Robert Fisher, MP for Rochester, told his brother the bishop that 'there was never such a sticking at the passing of any Act in the Lower House', and it is possible that Throckmorton was again one of the stickers.[42] Royal displeasure was still being directed at Throckmorton via Cromwell in September 1535, when Sir George had to defend himself against charges of failing to attend upon the king during his royal progress through the Midlands earlier that summer. Throckmorton protested that 'I was not within [50] myles of his Grace all the while he lay in these parts'; he had spent much of the year in Buckinghamshire since 'great part of my house here [at Coughton] is taken downe'. Relations with Cromwell frayed again over Throckmorton's blocking of the legal manoeuvres of the minister's client, Peter Irlam, vicar of Aston Cantlow in Warwickshire, a man who in Sir George's opinion was a vexatious litigant: he 'hath in maner undone the holl parish where he is curate and hath arrested the most parte of theym with ... citations'.[43] Whether Throckmorton sat again in the short-lived parliament of June–July 1536 is not known; the king's general desire was for members of the previous parliament to return, but as a known trouble-maker, Sir George may have been encouraged to stay away.[44]

If a test of loyalty was required, it was not long in coming, for the whole country was put to it in the autumn of 1536, when rebellion on an unprecedented scale erupted in the north of England, first in Lincolnshire, and then across Yorkshire and other northern shires. In the event, neither the Lincolnshire Rising nor the Pilgrimage of Grace was put down by force of arms, but the king's initial instinct was to raise and lead an army to crush the rebels, and letters were soon sent out commanding notables to join the royal muster at Ampthill in Bedfordshire. Throckmorton was required to bring with him 200 men from Warwickshire (the largest contingent expected from the county); in the event he brought 300. The Ampthill forces were dispersed after news of the collapse of the Lincolnshire revolt in mid-October, and the Throckmorton contingent was sent home, but Henry soon began to gather a new army to muster at Northampton, and Throckmorton was one of those charged to be ready to attend 'in readiness with horse and harness'. The king wanted another 100 men sent north to Lincoln, and Throckmorton despatched them, under the command of one of his sons.[45]

[42] *LP*, 8: 856 (2), 858.
[43] TNA, SP 1/97, fol. 55r (*LP*, 9: 488).
[44] *HOC*, p. 453.
[45] *LP*, 9: 580 (p. 233), 906, 1406. On the musters of 1536, see Richard Hoyle, *The Pilgrimage of Grace* (Oxford, 2001), pp. 170, 173, 283–6.

During the development of this, the greatest crisis of Henry VIII's reign, Sir George was apparently the complete loyalist. But at the end of 1536, he was suddenly arrested and placed in the Tower. The cause of this was noted in a newsletter to the Calais governor Lord Lisle from his man of business John Husee: 'for reading and copying with publishing abroad of news'. Hussee wrote on 11 December that some men were 'likely to suffer therefore', and a week later confirmed that among those imprisoned were Sir William Essex and Sir George Throckmorton.[46]

The full story, or at least a plausible version of it, emerges from a lengthy confession which Sir George produced in January 1537.[47] On Saturday 18 November, Throckmorton came up to London, and on the following day attended a morning sermon at St Paul's, where he met his friend Sir John Clarke. The two men repaired to the Horse Head tavern in Cheapside, where the landlord placed them in a little parlour, and they began to discuss the rebellion in the north, Clarke asking what news Throckmorton had heard on his way up through the country. These were tense times in the capital. Only a few days earlier, one of Throckmorton's fellow MPs from the Reformation Parliament, the City burgess Robert Packington, had been shot dead in the street in Cheapside. The perpetrators were never caught, but were assumed to be conservative sympathisers with the rebels, for Packington was well known as an evangelical and an anticlerical.[48] Evidently, Throckmorton was interested in the rebels' demands. He had seen a copy of the Lincolnshire rebels' articles in print, but not those of their Yorkshire counterparts. Clarke promised him the details, and that evening sent his servant to Throckmorton's lodging with a bill containing the Pilgrims' Oath, the five York Articles of October 1536, and a proclamation issued by the rebel leader, Robert Aske. Not long after, Throckmorton was dining at the Queen's Head with another friend, Sir William Essex, and the talk turned once more to the demands of the rebels, about which Essex was as curious as Sir George. Throckmorton sent his servant to fetch the papers he had received from Clarke, and loaned them to Essex, who, before returning them to Throckmorton, had his servant copy them, warning him that he should 'not babble of it, for it was no alehouse matter'.

---

[46] *The Lisle Letters*, ed. Muriel St Clare Byrne (6 vols, Chicago, 1981), vol. 3, pp. 551, 571.
[47] *LP*, 11: 1405; TNA, SP 1/113, fols 60r–65r (*LP*, 11: 1406), from which all quotations in the following paragraphs are taken.
[48] Peter Marshall, 'The Shooting of Robert Packington', in *Religious Identities*, pp. 61–79. On tensions in the capital, see also Susan Brigden, *London and the Reformation* (Oxford, 1989), pp. 248–52.

Yet political news in Tudor England was not so easily suppressed or controlled, and within days the matter was out of hand. Travelling through Berkshire on a planned visit to Sir William Essex's house near Reading, Throckmorton met with an entourage headed by the Berkshire justices. They told him they were on their way to court, as divers priests and laymen of Reading had made copies of the rebels' demands, and the king and council were greatly displeased. Throckmorton affected surprise at this, 'for they be universall att London', but nonetheless straight after burned his own copy of the articles. When he arrived at Sir William's his host explained that the clerk who transcribed the articles had secretly made another copy and given it to a fellow servant, Geoffrey Gunter. From Gunter, the articles had passed to the host of the Cardinal's Inn in Reading, and within days copies were proliferating in the town. A local clergyman was perturbed when a copy came into his hands, and reported the matter to the bailiff. By 2 December an investigation had been carried out locally by the mayor and JPs, and its results despatched to Cromwell. Throckmorton and Essex knew at once that their part in the business must come out, but Sir George trusted all would be well, 'seyng the matter is so common'.

Yet by the time Throckmorton followed Essex into the Tower, it was apparent that he was going to have to do more in order to clear his name than profess an innocent thirst for news. Sir George was now charged with certain words 'that I shold speke att supper'. In response, he claimed that somewhere at table (he couldn't remember where, or who else was present) someone had asked what were the demands of the rebels, at which 'everi man lokid apon other, and no man wold make awnser'. The silence was broken by Throckmorton, saying that the matter was in everyone's mouth, and that since all present were true men, they might talk of it. Throckmorton then rehearsed the rebels' demands as well as he could remember them, remarking that 'the false knave Aske wolde rewle the King and all his realme'. He denied having spoken approvingly of the demand that Katherine of Aragon's daughter, the Princess Mary, should be made legitimate. There were also serious questions to answer about the loyalty of the troops Throckmorton had brought to the muster at Ampthill at the time of the Lincolnshire Rebellion. Sir George heard a report from a servant of his brother-in-law, Thomas Burdett, that one of his soldiers had been claiming that the earl of Shrewsbury, Lord Steward of the Household, was preparing to join the rebels, and that if he did so, Sir George would follow suit. Throckmorton was not able to find out which 'lighte person' among his following had so spoken, but Thomas Cromwell's subsequent investigation was more painstakingly thorough. The culprit was one Fischer, Sir George's standard-bearer no less, and he had spoken the words at an inn in Daventry. Cromwell had also received a report that two of Sir George's soldiers among the 100 sent north to

Lincoln had fled to join the rebels (36 had deserted and gone home after not being paid). Throckmorton protested that 'yt makithe mi harte blede withyn mi bodie' to imagine the king might suspect any of his followers went to the rebels by his assent, or that by any words or any outward signs 'yt mai be provid that my harte whas that wei'.

There is, in all of this, little suggestion of active treason or plotting of any sort. But underneath Sir George's professions of loyalty, and of disgust for the pretensions of Aske, we can discern a profound interest in the progress and aims of the Pilgrimage of Grace, and most likely a degree of sympathy for the pilgrims' cause, particularly as it touched on the position of the Lady Mary. For a known opponent of the break with Rome and the Boleyn match, this was playing with fire. Essex and Throckmorton were still in the Tower on 14 January 1537, when John Husee 'doubted of their lives'. But 11 days later he was able to report that they had been released.[49]

It was a close shave, but no permanent damage seemed to have been done, and Throckmorton was almost immediately restored to his position on the Warwickshire commission of the peace.[50] Yet Sir George's troubles were far from over. In October 1537, he found himself back in the Tower, where he produced another long and detailed confession – this one providing our source for his oppositional activities in and out of parliament in the early 1530s. The 'bruit' (rumour), according to Sir Thomas Palmer, was that Throckmorton had been denounced by Sir Thomas Dingley, the same Dingley to whom he had boasted in 1532 of his frankness to the king.[51] The accusation against Sir George was not a random or unsolicited one, for Dingley himself was in serious trouble: he had been committed to the Tower on 18 September 1537 on charges of treason, and closely interrogated there. Dingley was a glamorous and international figure, a Hospitaller knight of St John of Jerusalem (or knight of Malta), an order with whom the Throckmorton family had close associations. Dingley had received significant patronage from the prior of the order in England and was constantly on the road between England, southern France and Malta in the mid-1530s. But a furious row had erupted in 1537 among the English knights about a preceptory to which Dingley claimed right of possession, and it seems that some of his confreres denounced him to the English government for treasonous words spoken at the house of the English ambassador in Genoa. Dingley had allegedly accused the king of bloodthirstiness, and discussed the possibility of his deposition. In 1539, he

---

[49] *Lisle Letters*, vol. 4, pp. 242, 250.
[50] *LP*, 12 (i): 539 (3, 4).
[51] *Lisle Letters*, vol. 4, p. 426.

was beheaded on Tower Hill, one of many victims of the Act of Attainder of that year.[52]

Throckmorton's arrest was thus an accidental by-product of Dingley's misfortunes. Dingley confessed to hearing from Sir George an account of the interview between the latter and King Henry in 1532, and the government was naturally interested in discovering who else Throckmorton had been talking to about Henry's prolific interest in the female members of the Boleyn family. But there was another important context to this latest bout of official displeasure. Sir George was a marked man in late 1537, not just because of his history of political unreliability, but also because of the sudden prominence on the government's radar of Michael Throckmorton.

Michael was a younger half-brother of George, a child of Sir Robert's second marriage to Elizabeth Baynham, born sometime after the turn of the sixteenth century. He was a resident in Florence at the time of his father's death in 1518, and next appears as a student of law in Padua in 1533. In Italy, he was drawn to humanist scholarship, and to the religious reform movement of the *spirituali*. He was also drawn into the orbit of the *spirituali*'s leading light, Henry VIII's cousin, Reginald Pole, whose service he entered in 1536 and remained in for the rest of his life.[53] Henry had hoped that his cousin would support his break with Rome, but Pole delivered an excoriating judgement on it in his *Pro ecclesiasticae unitatis defensione*, composed over the winter of 1535–36, and thereafter became the leading and most feared English opponent of the king's proceedings. A copy of Pole's treatise was despatched to Henry in May 1536, and it seems likely that the bearer was Michael Throckmorton.[54] At the end of the year, Pole was created cardinal, and in early 1537 was made papal legate with a brief to liaise with princes for the summoning of a General Council, though his real objective was to solicit aid for the Pilgrimage of Grace. In these activities, Michael Throckmorton was constantly by his side. Cromwell, however, believed Michael was really working for him. Though the details are murky, it seems most likely that Throckmorton was stringing the minister along, feeding him a diet of low-grade information, while remaining the cardinal's man.[55] When he eventually realised he had been hoodwinked, Cromwell reacted with fury, and in September

---

[52] O'Malley, *Knights Hospitaller*, pp. 215–19.

[53] WRO, CR 1998/Box 73/2; Thomas F. Mayer, 'Throckmorton, Michael (d. 1558)', *ODNB*; M.A. Overell, 'An English Friendship and Italian Reform: Richard Morison and Michael Throckmorton, 1532–1538', *Journal of Ecclesiastical History*, 57 (2006): 478–93.

[54] *The Correspondence of Reginald Pole. Volume 1. A Calendar, 1518–1546*, ed. Thomas F. Mayer (Aldershot, 2002), p. 97.

[55] Marshall, *Religious Identities*, pp. 233, 242, 249.

1537 sent Michael a letter of bitter remonstrance, threatening him with a traitor's fate if he continued in his 'malice and perverse blyndnes'. He also hinted at possible consequences for the family at home, shamed by Michael's actions. 'I pray god they byde but the shame of it. This am I sure of, thoughe they by and by suffer no losse of goodes, yet the lest suspicion shalbe ynowghe to undo the greatest of them.'[56]

The greatest of Michael's kinsfolk was, of course, his eldest brother, George, whose copybook was already severely blotted in the government's eyes. Unsurprisingly, the regime was intensely interested in the nature and extent of Sir George's contacts with his Italianate, papalist brother, and was in little mood to be understanding or forgiving. It may be significant that on the same day Throckmorton was arrested, Cardinal Pole's brother, Sir Geoffrey, reportedly 'came to the court to have done service, but the king would not suffer him by no means to come in'.[57] Sir George admitted to hearing some news of Michael. About midsummer last he had been at a dinner at St John's Priory, Clerkenwell with Sir Thomas Dingley, where a young man had told him 'your brother Michael is in good health, for I saw him of late in Antwerp in a chapel at mass'. To this, Sir George claimed to have retorted that 'I would he had never been born', though (suspiciously?) he could not remember exactly who had given him the report. Beyond that, he knew only that since his departure 'my unthrifty and unnatural brother' had written a letter to Nicholas Wotton, and that he himself had written to him once at Cromwell's behest. But Sir George professed himself ready, should the king wish it, to pursue his brother and Reginald Pole to the gates of Rome, and 'die upon them both in that quarrel'. Thus, if the king had 'conceived any thing in your heart concerning me touching him', he begged him to put it away, 'for I had liefer end my life in perpetual prison than to live at large having your indignation'.

Sir George's confession of 1537 is an exercise in abjectness and professed self-loathing extreme even by Tudor standards. There were good reasons for this. He had been caught 'very lewdly and naughtily' discussing the king's most intimate affairs with a range of 'light' persons, even if these words were 'spoken so long ago and to no ill intent'. He thus threw himself on the king's mercy, humbly beseeching him to have 'pity of me, my wife and poor children for the service that I and all my blood hath done to you and your progenitors in time past'. He was also acutely aware of how fortunate he had been to escape punishment for previous recalcitrant behaviour, 'seeing how good and gracious lord ye were to me at Grafton to pardon and forgive me all things past concerning the Parliament, as all other speaking and lewd demeanour misused to your highness in time past'.

---

[56] *Life and Letters of Cromwell*, vol. 2, pp. 86–90, quotes at 89–90.
[57] *Lisle Letters*, vol. 4, p. 426.

But, by his own account, there was more underlying Sir George's confession than a sense of having done wrong, and a desire to avoid punishment. Blaming his past misdemeanours on the counsel of traditionalist clerics and his attachment to 'the long custom of old time', Sir George claimed that he had suffered from a 'great blindness', but had now come to see the world in a very different light. This change of heart he ascribed to his reflection on the 'oft and divers' warnings Cromwell had given him to beware of the papalists' counsels, and also to 'the books I have lately read'. These were the New Testament in English and *The Institution of a Christian Man*, otherwise known as *The Bishops' Book* – a semi-official statement of the Church's doctrine drawn up by a committee of bishops in 1537, which leaned in a noticeably evangelical direction on some key issues such as purgatory and the importance of images.[58]

Is it the case, then, that Sir George had undergone a profound religious conversion, coming to regard the traditions and allegiances of his forefathers as scales that had at last dropped from his eyes? If so, he would not have been the only middle-aged Henrician to have turned towards the message of 'the gospel', after initially regarding it with suspicion and hostility.[59] Perhaps Sir George did mean what he wrote. We should not underestimate the psychological impact of a close brush with the might and majesty of the Tudor state, embodied in the person, and the displeasure, of the king. Nonetheless, recent scholarship has taught us to read against the grain of Tudor recantations, and to pick out the discordant notes of resistance in refrains of loyalty and compliance.[60] There are reasons to doubt the sincerity of Sir George's 'conversion', and not only in subsequent attitudes and actions. Writing to his old friend Richard Morison from Rome in February 1537, Michael Throckmorton had asked to be commended to his brother and his wife, and to all his nephews, which does not suggest that contact between Sir George and his 'unnatural' brother had been quite as minimal as he was to claim later that year.[61]

Sincerely contrite or not, Sir George's life must have hung in the balance in the autumn of 1537. Writing to Lord Lisle in November, Sir John Wallop confessed that 'how Throckmorton shall do I know not'.[62] Throckmorton

---

[58] Guy, *Public Career of Thomas More*, pp. 209–10, 212.

[59] See Peter Marshall, 'Evangelical Conversion in the Reign of Henry VIII', in Peter Marshall and Alec Ryrie (eds), *The Beginnings of English Protestantism* (Cambridge, 2002), pp. 14–37.

[60] Susan Wabuda, 'Equivocation and Recantation during the English Reformation: the 'Subtle Shadows' of Dr Edward Crome', *Journal of Ecclesiastical History*, 44 (1993): 224–42; Alec Ryrie, *The Gospel and Henry VIII* (Cambridge, 2003), pp. 69–80.

[61] *LP*, 12 (i): 430.

[62] *Lisle Letters*, vol. 4, p. 179.

tradition portrayed Sir George's second incarceration as the great crisis of the family's fortunes. The *Legend of Sir Nicholas Throckmorton*, a first-person verse life of Sir George's fourth son, probably composed by one of Nicholas's nephews in the later part of the sixteenth century, dwelt with pathos over several stanzas on the time when 'my father's foes clapt him through cankered hart / In Tower fast, and gap'd to joint his neck.' According to this source, Sir George was only released after Katherine Parr became queen, and interceded with Henry on his behalf.[63] The chronology here is warped and telescoped, for Katherine did not marry Henry until July 1543, and Sir George was released from the Tower in or around April 1538.[64] But a Parr connection may nonetheless have been instrumental in securing Throckmorton's freedom. Lady Throckmorton was, by virtue of her mother's first marriage, a first cousin of Katherine's uncle, Sir William Parr. Thanks to William's good offices, young Nicholas Throckmorton had been placed some years earlier as a page in service of the king's illegitimate son, the Duke of Richmond, of whose household Sir William was chamberlain.[65] In her anxiety, Katherine Throckmorton wrote to Parr on 20 October 1537: 'Good brother, Mr. Throkmerton is in trouble, as I think you know. Come up here immediately on the coming of my son to you; as I think you have business here this term. Not that I desire you to speak to my lord Privy Seal for him, but merely to give me your best counsel what to do for the help of him and myself [and my children].' Conceivably, Parr may have talked Sir George into making the abject confession the authorities wanted to hear, or otherwise deployed influence on his kinsman's behalf.[66]

Remarkably, after his release Sir George was once again rehabilitated as a central figure of local government: he was on the sheriff roll for Worcestershire (though not pricked) in November 1539. Nor was he deprived of marks of royal favour – Sir George, along with his son Robert, was summoned to attend the reception of Henry's ill-fated new bride, Anne

---

[63] *The Legend of Sir Nicholas Throckmorton*, ed. J.G. Nichols (London, 1874), pp. 5–8. Family tradition, as well as the work's first editor, believed the author to be Sir George's grandson, Thomas Throckmorton: cf. 'The Legend of Sir Nicholas Throckmorton ... by (his nephew) Sir Thomas Throckmorton, kt', in *New Memoirs of the Life and Poetical works of Mr. John Milton*, ed. Francis Peck (London, 1740). The attribution is followed by A.L. Rowse, *Ralegh and the Throckmortons* (London, 1962), p. 9. But the poem's generally positive comment on the Reformation makes this authorship unlikely.

[64] *LP*, 13 (i): 878.

[65] See genealogical table in Alford, *Kingship and Politics*, p. 152. HOC, p. 459.

[66] *LP*, 12 (ii): 951. That the confession came about through Parr's persuasion is suggested by *HOC*, p. 454, where Parr is inaccurately referred to as Lady Katherine's 'half-brother'.

of Cleves, at the end of 1539.⁶⁷ Sir George's freedom also coincided with the culmination of the domestic centre-piece of Henry VIII's Reformation – the dissolution of the monasteries. There is no record of what Sir George thought of this wrench with tradition, though his actions before and during it suggest attitudes of considerable ambivalence.

Like many of his class, George Throckmorton was comfortably familiar with the world of monasticism, used to dealing with abbots and priors as fellow landowners and occasional litigants in court, as much as fathers in God. Sir Robert had been steward of the Augustinian house of Studley, Warwickshire, a position George inherited after 1518. He also became steward of Evesham Abbey in 1527.⁶⁸ Sir George benefited from Wolsey's dissolutions in the 1520s, leasing the lands of the former priory of Ravenstone, Buckinghamshire, in 1525.⁶⁹ In the mid-1530s, Sir George became more than ever involved in the affairs of religious houses in his locality. In December 1533, he was granted an annuity of 20 shillings by the Cistercian Abbey of Combe; in 1534 Studley Priory granted him a 40-year lease of all its lands and tenements in Coughton, and the farm of tithes of hay; in 1535 the Benedictine Prioress of Wroxall, Agnes Little, appointed him steward of all the lands of the priory in England; the same arrangement was made with the Augustinian canons of Maxstoke. Also in 1535, the Benedictine Abbot of Reading created Throckmorton steward of the estates of Rowington in Warwickshire and Wigston in Leicestershire. In 1539, Prior Weston made George and his son Robert stewards of the preceptory of Balsall.⁷⁰ This flurry of grants almost certainly did not indicate a sudden interest in monastic estate administration on Sir George's part. Rather, it was the local manifestation of a national phenomenon in these years, the tendency of monastic houses in the immediate pre-dissolution phase to alienate annuities and fee-paying nominal offices to influential local gentry whom they hoped might help shield them from the coming storm.⁷¹

There is little evidence that any of these institutions witnessed much return on their investment, and all were swept away in the great expropriation of the late 1530s. But there was one religious community

---

⁶⁷ *LP*, 14 (ii): 619 (38); 15: 14 (p. 6).

⁶⁸ *LP*, 4 (ii): 4543; 7: 1004; WRO, CR 1998/Box 61/folder 3/6; *VCH Warwickshire*, vol. 3, p. 81; *HOC*, p. 451.

⁶⁹ *LP*, 4: 1087.

⁷⁰ WRO, CR 1998/Box 45/GG7/2; Box 59/4, 9, 10, 11; *Abstract of the Bailiffs' Accounts of Monastic and Other Estates in the County of Warwick*, ed. W.B. Blickley, Dugdale Society, 2 (London, 1923), pp. 24, 136.

⁷¹ See Joyce Youings, *The Dissolution of the Monasteries* (London, 1971), pp. 57–61; Knowles, *Religious Orders*, p. 353; Peter Marshall, 'The Dispersal of Monastic Patronage in East Yorkshire, 1520–90', in Beat Kümin (ed.), *Reformations Old and New* (Aldershot, 1996), pp. 134–8.

Throckmorton did assist in a directly practical way, for it was one where the interests of his family were immediately involved. Sir George's aunt, Elizabeth Throckmorton, was a nun of the house of Poor Clares at Denny in Cambridgeshire, and since 1512 had been abbess there. Denny was no rural backwater, or dumping ground for the barely literate unmarriable daughters of the gentry. Erasmus may have visited the house during his Cambridge stay in 1513, and two of the sisters of one of his pupils, Thomas Grey, were later to be professed there. At Grey's urging the great humanist exchanged letters with the community in 1525, greeting the 'most religious lady' abbess, and asking for the prayers of the house. Elizabeth clearly had an interest in Erasmian spirituality, for around this time she requested a (probably manuscript) copy of an English translation of Erasmus's *Enchiridion Militis Christiani* from the London alderman Humphrey Monmouth, a generous benefactor of the house. But this was a sensitive transaction, for the author of the translation was William Tyndale, a disciple of Luther and now a wanted heretic. Monmouth was an evangelical, and financial backer of Tyndale's English New Testament, who in 1528 was hauled before the Bishop of London to account for himself.[72]

Was Elizabeth Throckmorton a sympathiser with the radical reformism of Tyndale and Luther? It seems unlikely. At around the time of receiving the *Enchiridion*, she was the recipient of a devotional text composed and sent by the thoroughly orthodox Bridgettine of Syon (and confrere of Richard Reynolds), William Bonde, and she is known to have owned other orthodox vernacular texts. But there was an indirect personal association with Tyndale, which may have alerted her to the existence of the Erasmus translation. Elizabeth's sister, Margaret Throckmorton, had married the Gloucestershire gentleman William Tracy. Tracy was an acquaintance, and partisan, of Tyndale, who suffered the ignominious fate of being posthumously burned as a heretic, after leaving an overtly solafidian will in 1530. His son, Richard Tracy, was a notable evangelical activist of the 1530s and 1540s. From almost the earliest date, therefore, the ideological fractures of the English Reformation were present inside the Throckmorton family.[73]

Not all was well at Denny in the years immediately preceding its closure. Cromwell's visitor, Thomas Legh, reported in October 1535 that some of the nuns wished to leave their vows, half a dozen of them 'instantly kneeling upon their knees desired to be delivered of such religion as they have ignorantly taken upon themselves'. Nonetheless, when the house fell under the terms of the first dissolution act of 1536, the abbess

---

[72] John Strype, *Ecclesiastical Memorials* (3 vols, Oxford, 1822), vol. 1/ii, pp. 364–7.
[73] Erler, *Women, Reading and Piety*, pp. 108–9; Alec Ryrie, 'Tracy, Richard (*b.* before 1501, *d.* 1569)', *ODNB*.

successfully petitioned for its continuation. It must have been surrendered to the Crown before October 1539, when the house and site of the abbey was granted to Edward Elrington.[74]

The 'plight of the nuns' is one of the great imponderables of the dissolution of the monasteries.[75] It is usually supposed that most went back to their families, and Elizabeth Throckmorton's is one of a few cases where this can be demonstrated to have happened. Elizabeth returned to Coughton and died there on 13 January 1547, just a fortnight before her dispossessor, Henry VIII. Her brass inscription, likely set up by Sir George, requested readers, in time-honoured but now contentious fashion, to 'Of your charite pray for the soule of Dame Elizabeth Throkmerton the last Abbas of Denye and aunte to Syr George Throkmerton Knyght … on whous soule and all chryssten soules Jhesu have m[er]cy.' But with Elizabeth were buried two of her nuns, whose remains were discovered when the present tomb occupying the site was built in 1862.[76] An explanation is supplied by the eighteenth-century antiquary William Cole, who recorded a family tradition passed on by his 'most worthy friend', George Throckmorton. This revealed that Elizabeth and two or three of her nuns lived quietly in an upper room at Coughton, where they continued to wear their habits and 'prescribed to themselves the Rules of the Order as far as it was possible in their present situation'. The identity of the nuns who accompanied Elizabeth cannot be known with certainty, but it is likely that they too were family members. Sir Robert's will of 1518 left bequests to his daughters Dame Margaret and Dame Joyce, apparently nuns of Denny. A third may have been Joanna Peto, also a Denny Franciscan, and a granddaughter of Elizabeth's sister Goditha, as well as a niece of the fiery Observant, and sometime spiritual counsellor to Sir George, William Peto. The former abbess also had a servant, Katheryn Tanner, who was remembered in a will of 1543.[77] Such attempts to maintain monastic and communal life after the dissolution were extremely rare, though we know of a few other instances.[78] The arrangement at Coughton may help account for one of the most interesting items still preserved at the house, the wooden dole-gate of Denny Abbey, with its inset wickets for conversation and for passing out doles to the indigent (Figure 2.1).

---

[74] *LP*, 9: 651, 694, 708; 10: 1238 (p. 516); 11: 385 (35); 14 (ii): 435 (49).

[75] G.W.O. Woodward, *The Dissolution of the Monasteries* (London, 1966), pp. 154–7; Kathleen Cooke, 'The English Nuns and the Dissolution', in John Blair and Brian Golding (eds), *The Cloister and the World: Essays in Honour of Barbara Harvey* (Oxford, 1996), pp. 287–301.

[76] *VCH Warwickshire*, vol. 3, p. 85.

[77] WRO, CR 1998/Box 73/2; Erler, *Women, Reading and Piety*, pp. 111–12.

[78] Woodward, *Dissolution of the Monasteries*, pp. 152–4; Knowles, *Religious Orders*, pp. 412–13.

Figure 2.1   The Denny Dole Gate, Coughton Court.

This item, bearing the name of Elizabeth Throckmorton, was discovered in 1836 at a cottage 20 miles away in Ombersley, Worcestershire. But it seems virtually certain that it was taken by Elizabeth to Coughton, and at least plausible that it may have performed some ritual function inside the house, demarcating the 'enclosed' space of the domestic convent.[79]

Sir George, then, was the patron of a semi-clandestine religious community, a discreet counter-enactment of a central policy of the Henrician Reformation, functioning at the heart of his family seat. It was an arrangement in a gentry manor house that has no known parallel, and one that could hardly have been contemplated if Sir George had really undergone the evangelical conversion he claimed to have done in 1537. Nonetheless, to call Sir George an 'opponent' of the dissolution of the monasteries is to go beyond what the evidence will sustain. In fact, like many in the landed classes he was a beneficiary of the process, and sought to reap what profit he could from the final harvest of English monasticism.

In this endeavour, he had the advantage of being on distinctly good terms with the official overseeing the transfer of property to the Crown, Chancellor of the Court of Augmentations, Richard Rich. Rich is known to posterity, as he was to contemporaries, as the betrayer of Thomas More, and he was a *bête noire* of the northern rebels with whom Throckmorton had felt some sympathy in 1536.[80] But once again, blood was thicker than spilt milk. Throckmorton and Rich were kinsmen, with a great-grandfather in common. They also shared a conservative outlook in religion, for despite his willingness to bend to whatever wind was blowing hardest, Rich was never a sympathiser with the evangelicals. By 1541, if not before, he had taken Sir George's son Kenelm into his service.[81]

Not long after Sir George's release from prison in 1538, Rich was already seeking to do him a favour. Following the suppression of Bordesley Abbey in Worcestershire, Rich wrote to John Scudamore, a receiver of the Court of Augmentations, commanding him to enquire into unauthorised sales of the abbey's possessions. At the same time, he asked him 'for my sake, to graunte unto Sir George Throgmerton, knight, the preferment of all suche stone, glasse, and iron as is at the said late monastery lefte to be solde'.[82] Other benefits Throckmorton acquired from the dissolution included a lease of the manor of Uckington, Gloucestershire, formerly a

---

[79] E.A.B. Barnard, 'A Sixteenth Century Dole-Gate from Denny Abbey', *Proceedings of the Cambridge Antiquarian Society*, 29 (1928), pp. 72–5.

[80] See P.R.N. Carter, 'Rich, Richard, first Baron Rich (1496/7–1567)', *ODNB*.

[81] *HOC*, p. 449. For the relationship of Throckmorton to Rich, see the genealogical information at www.tudorplace.com.ar.

[82] *Three Chapters of Letters relating to the Suppression of Monasteries*, ed. Thomas Wright, Camden Society, old ser. 26 (1843), pp. 279–80.

property of Tewkesbury Abbey, and a lease of the tithes of Oversley and of the manor of Beauchamp Court, lately held by Alcester Priory. By 1540, he was also leasing from Augmentations a number of the former properties of Evesham Abbey in Worcestershire: grain rents from Aldington and Wickhamford, tithes of Church Honeybourne and the manor of Middle Littleton. Closer to home, he acquired all the property in Coughton held by the Priory of Studley, along with the advowson of the parish church.[83]

The association of Sir George Throckmorton and Sir Richard Rich at the start of the 1540s had, however, one result infinitely more momentous than the disposal of surplus monastic glass. Together, they played an instrumental role in the fall, and execution at the block, of the second most powerful man in England, the Lord Privy Seal and newly created Earl of Essex, Thomas Cromwell. In one of those episodes which we might regard as an irony of history, and contemporaries might have seen as the turn of Fortuna's wheel, Sir George Throckmorton turned out to be the final nemesis of the man who, on more than one occasion, had so nearly been his.

Throckmorton and Rich were, it is true, bit-players in the fall of Cromwell, who at the start of 1540 had opened himself up to his conservative enemies in court and council by saddling the king with an unpleasing spouse, in the form of Anne of Cleves, and an embarrassing foreign policy, in the form of an alliance with the German Protestant princes. Nonetheless, the bit Throckmorton played in Cromwell's downfall was not an insignificant one. It is certified in the minister's own words, the letter the fallen minister wrote to Henry on June 12 1540, combining confession, attempted exculpation, and fulsome pleas for mercy and forgiveness – an eerie parallel to Throckmorton's own confession letter of October 1537. Cromwell invoked a fearful punishment on himself – 'all the devylles in Hell conffounde me and the vengeaunce of god light appon me' – should any faction be able to prove him a traitor to the king. Cromwell had evidently been accused of speaking incriminating words in the presence of Rich and Throckmorton, for he denied any memory of ever having spoken with them together at one time. Moreover, in true lawyerly fashion, he attempted to discredit the witnesses against him. What Richard Rich had been towards him, 'God and he best knoweth'. As for the other, Cromwell urged Henry to remember, with some good reason, 'what manner of man Throgmerton hathe ever bene ever towards your grace and your proceedings'. Nonetheless, the case against him went forward. We cannot say for certain what the alleged treasonous words were, but it seems plausible that they were those specified in a 10 June circular letter announcing Cromwell's arrest, sent by the council to English ambassadors.

---

[83] *LP*, 15: 564; SCLA, DR 5/938; *LP*, 15: 1032 (76); *VCH Warwickshire*, vol. 3, p. 86.

He was supposed to have said that if the king turned away from his opinions in religion 'he would fight him in the field in his own person, with his sword in his hand'. The act of attainder sealing Cromwell's fate alleged that these words had been spoken on 31 March 1539, in support of evangelical preachers.[84]

How much reliable substance there was to the charges of Rich and Throckmorton is now impossible to ascertain. As his involvement in the trial of Thomas More demonstrates, Rich was quite capable of judicial perjury in the cause of self-advancement, and Throckmorton had of course no reason to love the falling minister. Nonetheless, Rich was generally regarded as the Lord Privy Seals's protégé, and Cromwell may have believed in 1539 that Throckmorton was a genuinely changed man. In other words, it is conceivable that he allowed himself to become indiscreet in their company, and did say something of the sort that was alleged against him.

There can be little doubt that Cromwell's demise was a source of considerable satisfaction to Sir George. It was also a source of material enrichment. In 1541, Throckmorton petitioned for, and was allowed to purchase from the Crown, the extensive and valuable manor of Oversley, 'parcel of the possessions of Thomas Cromwell, late Earl of Essex, attainted.'[85] Lying only a couple of miles from Sir George's seat at Coughton, Oversley was an attractive acquisition. It may also have been a cause of long-standing tension. According to the *Gens Throckmortoniana*, a manuscript history of the family composed in the eighteenth century, Cromwell had looked out from Oversley 'with a rapacious eye' at Sir George's estate in the vale below, and for that reason had him clapped in the Tower. Some modern commentary, too, has asserted that the real issue between Sir George and Cromwell had always been land, rather than religion.[86] But it is impossible to explain the ruthless factional quarrels within the Henrician regime in terms of purely material motivation. Cromwell was, as everybody well knew, the lay patron of the evangelical cause. Throckmorton's part in his downfall may be viewed as a last sting

---

[84] *Life and Letters of Cromwell*, vol. 1, p. 296; vol. 2, p. 265; Glyn Redworth, *In Defence of the Church Catholic: The Life of Stephen Gardiner* (Oxford, 1990), pp. 121–5.

[85] *LP*, 16: 878 (80). In addition to the purchase price of £774 9s 2d, Throckmorton exchanged with the Crown the manor of Roxton, Bedfordshire.

[86] Vincent Hemingway and Jeffrey Haworth, *Coughton Court and the Throckmortons* (Norwich, 1993), p. 4; 'Gens Throckmortoniana, or A History of the Family of the Throckmortons' (WRO, CR 1998/EB/22), fols 9–10. The claim here that the ostensible reason for Sir George's arrest was 'refusing the oath of supremacy', and that he was 'preparing to lay downe his life for religion after the example of Bishop Fisher and Sir Thomas More', is an interesting illustration of the martyrological impulse at work among Hanoverian Catholic families.

of the 'Aragonese' connection of Queen Katherine's partisans, a grouping that Cromwell believed he had crushed the life out of five years earlier.

With Cromwell gone, Sir George's oppositional career seemed to be behind him, and in the generally more conservative climate of the 1540s he took up a more active role than ever in local administration. In addition to functioning as a JP, he served on successive commissions of Oyer and Terminer for the midlands circuit in 1542–44. He was active in raising a forced loan in Warwickshire to meet the king's military expenses in 1542–43, and a 'benevolence' in 1544–45. Sir George was listed prominently in the muster book drawn up for the royal invasion of France in 1544 (a campaign in which four of his sons served), and in 1546 he headed the muster commission for Warwickshire, with the promise of a contingent of 500 men. He continued to appear on the sheriff roll for Worcestershire, and was finally pricked sheriff in 1542, an office he also performed (after a 16-year gap) for Warwickshire and Leicestershire in 1543.[87]

The 1540s were also years of further consolidation of the Throckmorton estates. In 1544, Sir George bought the manor of Tanworth from the Crown for the imposing sum of £630 17s 2d. This purchase was likely linked to a longstanding connection with the Archer family, who were also major landholders in Tanworth. Richard Archer, a former ward of Sir George, was attainted for murder in the later 1540s, and Sir George was involved in the inquisition post mortem, and in much correspondence advising his widow Maude of her rights and prospects. The business may have impinged heavily on his other responsibilities, for in the course of a letter concerning it, Richard Catesby had to chivvy Throckmorton to 'send uppe your certificate of the musters, for all shires have certified save this'.[88]

Religious controversy did not disappear from England with the death of Cromwell. If anything, religious divisions in the country hardened and clarified over the course of the 1540s, even as the religious path taken by Henry VIII remained balanced precariously, schizophrenically even, between aversion to evangelical theology and unremitting hostility to Rome. As a brother of the right-hand man to Cardinal Pole, Henry's public enemy number one, Sir George was inevitably in an exposed position. Pole's own family was destroyed in the wake of the putative 'Exeter Conspiracy' of 1538, and Michael Throckmorton was one of

---

[87] *LP*, 16: 305 (80), 1391 (67); 17: 194, 312, 443 (25), 1154 (55), (75); 18 (i): 226 (9), 856; 18 (ii): 449 (79); 19: 273; 20 (i): 622, 623 (pp. 323, 326); 21 (i): 91.

[88] SCLA, DR 37/2/Box 88/19/1. See also DR 37/2/Box 72/13, 16; Box 87/5; Box 88/19/2; Box 88/21, 22, 24; *LP*, 3 (ii): 2074 (19); 21 (i): 504 (18); *Calendar of Patent Rolls, Edward VI*, ed. R.H. Brodie (6 vols, London, 1924–29), vol. 3, p. 67. *HOC*, p. 454, confuses Tanworth with Tamworth. It is not clear on what basis his *ODNB* entry asserts Throckmorton married for the second time in 1542.

those officially declared a traitor in the massive Act of Attainder which followed in 1539. Any contact with English exiles was dangerous – it led, for example, to the execution of Germaine Gardiner, nephew of the powerful Bishop of Winchester, Stephen Gardiner, in 1544 – and there is no evidence of Throckmorton remaining in communication with Michael in these years.[89] Nonetheless, Sir George remained capable of discreet acts of support for the conservative cause. In 1545, he presented the cleric John Feckenham to one of the rectories in his gift, that of Solihull. Conceivably, this was an expression of benign local patriarchy. Feckenham was an ex-Benedictine of Evesham in Worcestershire, where his confreres at the time of the dissolution included Richard Throgmerton, conceivably a kinsman of Sir George. Like all Benedictines, Feckenham took his name in religion from the place of his birth, and the village of Feckenham lies barely 4 miles from Coughton Court. But Feckenham was also a religious conservative with a growing reputation, who in 1543 had become a chaplain to Bishop Bonner of London, the most resolute opponent of heresy on the episcopal bench in the final years of Henry VIII.[90]

It was in the 1540s that the religious divisions of the country manifested themselves openly within Sir George's nuclear family, as all seven of his surviving sons reached adulthood. Like any responsible paterfamilias, Sir George had looked to the prospects of his younger sons, arranging suitable marriages, and settling small freehold estates on them. Clement was by 1541 in the service of Richard Rich; Kenelm had entered the household of Thomas Cromwell in the 1530s, transferring after his fall to that of William Parr, where, as we have seen, his brother Nicholas had already taken service. The marriage of Sir William Parr's sister Katherine to the king in 1543 was a major boost to Throckmorton family fortunes, as through their mother the boys could claim kinship with the new queen. Kenelm, Nicholas, Clement, George and John all found court positions through the good offices of Katherine Parr. A combination of Sir George's authority in the Midlands and the queen's wider influence ensured an extraordinary Throckmorton presence in parliament in the last years of Henry VIII, though Sir George did not again take up his Warwickshire seat. In the parliament of 1542, Clement sat for Warwick. In 1545 he represented the borough of Devizes (part of Katherine Parr's jointure), while Kenelm sat for Warwick, Nicholas for Maldon and John for Leicester.[91]

[89] Marshall, *Religious Identities*, pp. 238, 253.
[90] Charles S. Knighton, 'Feckenham, John (*c.*1510–1584)', *ODNB*; *The Letter Book of Robert Joseph*, ed. Hugh Aveling and William A. Pantin, Oxford Historical Society, new ser. 19 (1967), p. xv.
[91] *HOC*, pp. 449, 450, 454, 455, 457–8, 459; Susan E. James, *Kateryn Parr: The Making of a Queen* (Aldershot, 1999), pp. 44–5, 147.

Yet along the way, several of the young Throckmortons – Kenelm, Clement, Nicholas, George – had become estranged from the traditional religion of their father and grandfather, and began to espouse the new evangelical faith. It would be unwise to attribute this directly to the influence of Katherine Parr, though the circles around her were of a reformist character, and increasingly so as the decade progressed.[92] One figure on the edges of court evangelicalism was a runaway gentlewoman from Lincolnshire, Anne Askew. In 1546, Anne was arrested on charges of heresy, and her case rapidly became a political football as leading conservatives sought an opportunity to score a decisive goal against their enemies at court and, if possible, disqualify the queen herself. Anne freely admitted her sacramentarian beliefs, but refused to supply incriminating information about her contacts among the court ladies, even after she was wracked in the Tower at the hands of Sir Richard Rich and Lord Chancellor Wriothesley. A stream of priests and ex-evangelicals came to her (fruitlessly) in prison to try to persuade her to recant and thus avoid the stake. But not all of Anne's visitors were ideological enemies. One eyewitness of her execution on 16 July 1546 was John Louth, Elizabethan archdeacon of Nottingham, who later recalled that with him on the day were 'iii. of the Throkmorton's, Syr Nicholas being one, and Mr Kellum the other' (the third is unnamed). An unknown bystander had shouted to them 'ye are all marked that come to them; take heede to your lyffes', suggesting that the Throckmorton brothers had comforted Anne and her fellow evangelicals in prison.[93]

With the death of Henry and accession of Edward VI in January 1547 the evangelical faith of the young Throckmortons became the official ideology of the regime. The extent to which religious differences were now causing tensions within the family is impossible to ascertain. The *Legend of Sir Nicholas Throckmorton* suggests a strained relationship between Nicholas and his father in these years, with the latter privately berating his son on a visit to Coughton as a 'foolish boy', though 'thou think'st thyself a goodlie man!' But religion is not suggested as the cause; rather Sir George's perception that his son, now a successful courtier, thought himself too good for the homely comforts of Warwickshire, combined with resentment that Nicholas had been knighted by the king before his eldest son, Robert.[94] The

---

[92] Rowse, *Ralegh and the Throckmortons*, p. 11; Diarmaid MacCulloch, *Thomas Cranmer: A Life* (New Haven and London, 1996), p. 326, noting that Katherine's piety only became discernibly evangelical after her marriage to Henry.

[93] *Narratives of the Days of the Reformation*, ed. J.G. Nichols, Camden Society, old ser. 77 (1859), pp. 41–3. For the Askew case, see the introduction to *The Examinations of Anne Askew*, ed. Elaine V. Beilin (Oxford, 1996).

[94] *Legend of Sir Nicholas Throckmorton*, pp. 24–5.

one surviving letter we have from Sir George to Nicholas, dated 1548, is formal and restrained, a request for heraldic information.[95]

There is no evidence that Sir George cast himself in the role of an opponent of the Edwardian Reformation, or that he was perceived by the regime as such. On the contrary, he continued to function loyally as a local representative of the Tudor state. In July 1550, Sir George was commissioned by the Earl of Warwick, Lord Lieutenant of Warwickshire, as one of the new deputy lieutenants for the county, offices established in the wake of the popular rebellions of 1549. The commission specified 'thapprovyd fydelyties, circumspecon and promtnes that hath alwayes bene found in you to serve his majesty' – formulaic words, but not, in Sir George's case, totally inappropriate ones. In September 1550, the Privy Council asked the Chancellor of Augmentations to reduce Sir George's annual rent for the lease of the lordship of Alne by a hefty £20, 'as of his Majesties rewarde, during the lief of the saide George for his good service'. That service expressed itself in a wide variety of ways: serving on a commission to enforce a royal proclamation about grain prices, and on another for the collection of parliamentary taxation; pursuing a gang 'who have lately set up a coyning house in Worcestreshire'; inquiring and certifying to Chancery whether his kinsman John Peyto of Chesterton, 'lately being lunatic, is now of sound mind and memory'.[96]

More remarkably, he was also appointed in 1552 to commissions established to draw up inventories of church goods for Warwickshire, Worcestershire and the City of Coventry. These were to list 'plate, iuelles, vetyments, belles and other ornaments within every parisshe', and to check against previous inventories to make sure parishes were not realising their assets. This was the prelude to a campaign of wholesale expropriation of church plate, an act of fiscal desperation by Northumberland's government, dressed up as Protestant reform, and a final nail in the coffin of traditional parochial piety.[97] In the face of the Edwardian Reformation's dismantling of Catholicism, Sir George appears, then, as a conformist, if not a collaborator. Indeed, he gained materially in a small way: in October 1547, the priest serving the chantry at the Throckmorton ancestral home of Fladbury, Worcestershire, was granted permission by letters patent to

---

[95] WRO, CR 1998/Box 61/Folder 1/2.

[96] WRO, CR 1998/ Box 72/15; *APC*, vol. 3, pp. 119, 385, 409; *Patent Rolls, Edward VI*, vol. 3, p. 175; vol. 4, p. 142; vol. 5, p. 360–61.

[97] WRO, CR 1998/ Box 45/ GG 10/7; *APC*, vol. 4, p. 396–7. Cf. Eamon Duffy, 'The End of It All: The Material Culture of the Medieval English Parish and the 1552 Inventories of Church Goods', in Clive Burgess and Eamon Duffy (eds), *The Parish in Late Medieval England* (Donington, 2006), pp. 81–99.

surrender his chantry to the 'founder', George Throckmorton.[98] With a complete dissolution of the chantry system looming, this was a sensible recouping of family investments, though hardly an act of resistance. After the Chantries Bill passed through parliament in December 1547, the perpetual chantry Sir Robert Throckmorton had founded at Coughton was presumably wound up, and formal prayer for the souls of Throckmortons in purgatory came whimperingly to an end.

Sir George's own final reckoning arrived not long after the church goods commission was issued. His final sickness began in July 1552, and he died on 6 August. Looking back over his life, Sir George had reason to feel satisfied. The family estates had been expanded and consolidated, and a pre-eminent position in Warwickshire society had been maintained. His reputation among his neighbours was an enviable one. More than 20 years later, the Earl of Warwick's steward would remember, in the course of a bitter local dispute, 'that Sir George Throckmorton in his tyme, when he heard of controversy between his neighbors, woold call the matter before him; and what order he took in any matter, his word stood, and none of the parties woold or durst break any jote of it'.[99] Moreover, he had seen his daughters well married, and his sons proper. As the *Legend of Nicholas Throckmorton* noted, Sir George was only 'summon'd hence' when 'all of us at yeares: when two made knights: / when five of us had beene of Parliament: / All forwarde in the world: when all these sightes / Our father sawe'.[100]

But while all these family triumphs were taking place, Sir George had also lived to see the overthrow of the devotional world in which he had grown up, and in which we can imagine he had hoped to die. In fact, we can do more than imagine here, for there are clues in the last and most personal document he has left to us, the will written in his own hand on 20 July 1552.[101] Wills are notoriously tricky sources to interpret, but they nonetheless open an unparalleled window on the priorities of early modern people as they contemplate their imminent mortality. The main and most overt business of Sir George's will was, of course, to see to the disposition of his estates, and ensure that widow and children were properly provided for. Several manors were specified as a jointure for Lady Katherine (Figure 2.2), 'for the greate paynes that she hath and hereafter shall take with me'.

The bulk of the estate of course devolved upon Robert as eldest son and heir, but he was sternly admonished 'to permytt and suffer every of my younger sonnes quyetlye and without vexacion trouble or interruption' to

---

[98] *Patent Rolls, Edward VI*, vol. 1, p. 58.
[99] Cited in E.I. Fripp, *Shakespeare: Man and Artist* (Oxford, 1938), pp. 172–3.
[100] *Legend of Sir Nicholas Throckmorton*, p. 25.
[101] TNA, Prob/11/36.

Figure 2.2   Katherine, wife of Sir George Throckmorton, c.1489–1552, Coughton Court.

enjoy all the manors, tenements and rents 'as I have before tyme severally granted, assured and geven them'. Nowhere in the will is there any suggestion that sons were discriminated against on grounds of religious affiliation. There was a substantial cash bequest of £400 to Clement, a manor in Gloucestershire to John and Anthony, annuities to Kenelm and Nicholas, and a further cash payment of £20 each to Kenelm and Clement. Only £10 in cash was to go to John and to Nicholas 'for that he hath lesse need than any other of my younger sonnes' – a recognition perhaps of Nicholas's rising stature in the echelons of the Protestant regime.

The will also tells us much about Sir George's religious beliefs, though it requires a close reading, and a sensitivity to the meaning of formulae and silences. The contrast with his father Sir Robert's will of 1518 is marked. There is no lavish expenditure on refurbishment of the parish church, no panoply of bespoke masses, trentals and prayers, just as there were now no religious orders from which to request such services. The will is dated by the regnal year of Edward VI, not only defender of the faith, but 'of the Church of Englande and also of Irelande in earth Supreme Head'. Politically, and it seems spiritually, Sir George had learned to conform.

But in other important ways, Sir George's will is about as Catholic a document as it was possible to produce at the zenith of the Edwardian Reformation. He bequeathed his soul conventionally to 'almightie god my maker and redeemer', but hoped also to dwell 'amongest the holy company of heven' – an invocation of the saints anathema to Protestant sensibilities. He also stipulated that the residue of all his goods, after debts settled and legacies paid, should go to his wife 'to bestowe yearlie therof in dedes of charity for the wealth of my soule', thus declaring, albeit in a muted way, an unseasonal belief in the value of intercession for souls passing through purgatory. Sir George's will also aligned his charitable bequests firmly with those of his Catholic pilgrim father. His executors were to see to the continued good ordering of the alms house at Coughton 'according to my father's will'. They were also, intriguingly, to ensure that 'all other thynges specified in my fathers will not yet done shalbe well and truly performyd in every poynte according as I have declared to myne executors.' Among the four witnesses to the will was Throckmorton's protégé John Feckenham, sometime monk of Evesham Abbey, and later to become dean of St Paul's and abbot of Queen Mary's restored Benedictine foundation at Westminster – a crucial link figure between the establishment Catholicism of the late Middle Ages and the first stirrings of the English Counter-Reformation.

Sir George too was in some ways a transitional figure, though that tidy phrase does little justice to the complexity of lives as they were lived and negotiated on a day-by-day basis. Paradoxically, the key to understanding the career of this serial dissenter may be the concept of loyalty. In times of trouble (as Sir George seriously was in 1536 and 1537), dissidents had a vested interest in loud protestations of fidelity. Yet when Sir George fashioned himself as a loyal subject of Henry VIII, it is hard to avoid the conclusion that he meant, viscerally, what he said. What else should we make of his outpouring to Francis Bryan in 1535 that 'yt ys dethe to me' (figurative, not literal) to think that the king 'in whom should be my most worldly comeforte' should in anything 'be in displeasure with me', and his defying the world as 'God be my juge' to 'lay any untrowth unto me or yet dyssemulacion'?[102] When Sir George constructed his magnificent gatehouse at Coughton, he had both the Throckmorton arms and the royal arms set underneath its oriel windows, in what has been called 'a statement of flamboyant loyalty'.[103]

Loyalty to the king is often seen as the trump card of the Henrician Reformation, but too often we imagine contemporaries contemplating which way to travel at a well-signposted fork in the road. An influential recent study, for example, sees the Henrician Reformation as creating a clear 'bipartite division' among religious conservatives, splitting the nation's Catholic majority into 'conformist Catholics' who supported the regime and 'non-conformist Catholics' who opposed it.[104] But Sir George Throckmorton's career confounds the clarity of these classifications. Simultaneously a conformist but a dissenter, a plotter but not a traitor, a patriot with close family links to overseas enemies of the state, Sir George accommodated himself to a changing world while retaining core Catholic beliefs. He would doubtless have rejoiced, had he lived to see the accession of Queen Mary and the reconciliation with Rome. Yet he would not have passed muster with the high standards of a later Catholic generation: he did not (family tradition notwithstanding) refuse the oath of succession under Henry, and he honed to a fine point the skill of not becoming a martyr. In fact, the ability of a figure like Sir George to modulate between dissidence and loyalism underlines the complexity of 'Catholic' allegiance at a crucial moment of English religious identity-formation. Issues of how to believe and behave like a good Catholic were fluid and experimental throughout the 1530s and 1540s, and only finally began to resolve themselves in

---

[102] TNA, SP 1 /89, fol. 14r (*LP*, 8: 26).

[103] David Starkey, *Elizabeth: Apprenticeship* (London, 2000), p. 245. The dating of the gatehouse is frustratingly obscure: stylistic similarities to Thornbury Castle, Gloucestershire, might imply an early sixteenth-century construction, but John Leland's failure to mention it in his account of Coughton in his travels (1535–43) suggests it went up in the later part of Sir George's life. See Geoffrey Tyacke, *Warwickshire Country Houses* (Chichester, 1994), p. 77; Anthony Woodward, 'Coughton Court Warwickshire – I', *Country Life* (23 March 1995), 76.

[104] Ethan H. Shagan, *Popular Politics and the English Reformation* (Cambridge, 2003), pp. 29–60, quote at p. 59.

the course of the next generation. Sir George's children, like those of his gracious lord and occasional sparring partner, Henry Tudor, can be placed much more clearly in rival religious and political camps.

CHAPTER 3

Reputation, Credit and Patronage: Throckmorton Men and Women, c.1560–1620

Susan Cogan

In the early modern period, the Throckmortons were a very large kinship network whose various lines of descent populated the English Midlands, particularly Warwickshire, Worcestershire and Buckinghamshire. During the Reformation years some members of the family remained Catholic, while others embraced the new Protestant religion and still others became identified as Puritan. Most of the main branch of the family, seated at Coughton Court in Warwickshire, remained Catholic, and this chapter will focus primarily on these descendants of Sir George Throckmorton. An examination of the records of the family in the late sixteenth and early seventeenth centuries provides a wealth of insight into the dynamics of a family group and suggests some conclusions not only about how similar these Catholics were to other Catholics but, more importantly, how similar they were to other members of the gentry, regardless of religion.

Although the lives of the Throckmortons of Coughton were affected by their commitment to Catholicism, and although their experiences illustrate some patterns common to other recusant families, I will argue that their attitudes and practices were in many respects similar to religiously conforming families of their same social and economic status level. Members of the Throckmorton family performed specific tasks, such as managing estates and instructing their children on appropriate adult behaviour, and petitioning patrons and government officials in ways similar to those of their Protestant counterparts, though because they were Catholic the application of values and strategies was sometimes different. The surviving letters in the Throckmorton Papers at the Warwickshire Record Office illustrate the relationships that the Throckmortons formed with one another and with others outside of their family group. The letters also reveal important information about the roles and activities of individual members of this family, particularly with respect to women's roles, child-rearing practices and engagement with patronage networks. These particular topics are important for what they tell us about the accumulation and sustaining of non-economic forms of credit, and about how that credit could be utilised to construct and maintain relationships with patrons.

Recent work on early modern English Catholics has begun to explore the degree to which Catholics remained integrated into the social fabric rather than suffering severe marginalisation because of their religion. Norman Jones has argued that post-Reformation English people (Protestant and Catholic alike) agreed to disagree on matters of religion, preferring instead to maintain familial and community harmony despite differences in religious ideology.[1] Michael Questier's examination of the entourage that surrounded Anthony Browne, first Viscount Montague, a prominent Catholic in Sussex, demonstrates that Browne's position as a powerful south-coast aristocrat engaged him and his family with other leading peers in his region and with the national political structure.[2] In these analyses, Catholics held a healthy measure of agency even in the face of increasing recusancy fines.

The study of women has been a topic of interest among scholars of Catholic history since Marie Rowlands's pioneering essay on recusant women appeared in 1985.[3] Scholars have emphasised the significant role that women of both upper and middling status groups played in sustaining the Catholic faith in early modern England. But in the main, the agency of Catholic women, in constructing networks of protection and in working to build and maintain relationships with patrons for the benefit of husbands and sons, has been overlooked. Sara Mendelson and Patricia Crawford have argued that women were much more deeply engrained in English politics than either their contemporaries or modern historians have recognised, but their investigation did not include a focus on the activities of recusant women.[4]

Other than some incidental mentions of patronage being used as a protective device by Catholic recusants, no one has yet examined how Catholic men and women constructed and maintained patronage relationships, or how they might have acted as patrons themselves. Further, despite the importance of non-economic forms of capital (such as social and cultural capital) to individuals and families in this period, the connection between such forms of credit and a recusant's ability to

---

[1] Norman L. Jones, *The English Reformation: Religion and Cultural Adaptation* (Oxford, 2002).

[2] Michael Questier, *Catholicism and Community in Early Modern England: Politics, Aristocratic Patronage, and Religion, 1550–1640* (Cambridge, 2006).

[3] Marie Rowlands, 'Recusant Women, 1560–1640', in Mary Prior (ed.), *Women in English Society, 1500–1800* (London, 1985), pp. 149–80.

[4] Sara Mendelson and Patricia Crawford, *Women in Early Modern England, 1550–1720* (Oxford, 1998).

engage in the patron–client network has yet to be fully explored.[5] Careful maintenance of credit and reputation could help to create and cement patronage relationships (moving both up and down the social scale) and to affect one's social status. Catholics accrued and maintained the social and cultural capital necessary to secure and retain a patron, or a number of patrons, through various means. These included good behaviour, cultural conformity, assurances of loyalty to Crown and country and invoking their identity as ancient families or families with long records of service to Crown and government.

I hope to build on the valuable body of scholarship about early modern English Catholics by demonstrating the degree to which the Throckmorton men and women carried out activities that were typical for their status group, and to show that despite their practice of a prohibited religion, they were not very different from those who adhered to the Protestant faith prescribed by the state. This parallelism included but was not limited to their engagement with late-Elizabethan and early-Jacobean patronage practices. I will begin by placing the Coughton line in the context of Warwickshire's political and social structure, then explore how women's roles and conduct, the family's approach to child-rearing and its engagement with patronage helped to create the social capital necessary for the Throckmortons to remain integrated into the society in which they lived.

The Coughton Line

Sir George Throckmorton established the Coughton line as a political dynasty in Warwickshire early in the sixteenth century. Despite Thomas Cromwell's admonition to Sir George to 'stay at home and meddle little in politics', he and his sons quite certainly did involve themselves in politics.[6] The returns from Warwickshire for members of the House of Commons were heavily populated with Sir George's sons in the years between 1529 and 1558: in that period five of George's seven sons were returned as MPs

---

[5] Throughout this chapter, I draw upon Pierre Bourdieu's ideas of capital, particularly social and cultural capital. Social capital derives from one's social status in the community together with one's behaviour within that community; cultural capital denotes culturally valued preferences such as child-rearing and education as well as patterns of consumption and display. See Richard Harker, Cheleen Mahar and Chris Wilkes (eds), *An Introduction to the Work of Pierre Bourdieu: The Practice of Theory* (New York, 1990), pp. 8–15; Pierre Bourdieu, *Outline of a Theory of Practice*, trans. Richard Nice (Cambridge, 1977).

[6] 'History of Parliament Trust Documents' CD-ROM [hereafter HPTD] sub 1509–1558, section VII. See also Peter Marshall's chapter in this volume.

in seven different parliaments.⁷ In addition to his sons, Sir George appears to have helped along the careers of his friends William Newenham and Thomas Holte. In 1532 he recommended Newenham's appointment as sheriff of Northamptonshire, and he seems to have influenced the election to parliament of Newenham, Holte, John Butler, Robert Burdett, Ralph Broune and perhaps also Sir Marmaduke Constable II and Edward Ferrers.⁸ His influence was so great that his contemporaries regarded him as the 'chief patron' in Warwickshire through the mid-Tudor period.⁹

By mid-century, men of the Coughton line held a great deal of authority within Warwickshire governance. Sir George served as a Justice of the Peace (JP) for Warwickshire from 1510 until his death in 1552; he was elected to parliament as senior knight of the shire for Warwickshire in 1529; he was sheriff of Warwickshire and Leicestershire in 1526–27 and again in 1543–44, and sheriff of Worcestershire in 1542–43; he sat on a number of commissions in Warwickshire (for example, subsidy in 1512 and 1523, loan in 1542, musters in 1546) and was Custos Rotulorum in 1547.¹⁰

His son and heir, Robert, had a career similar to that of his father. He was bailiff for Warwick in 1544–45; JP for Warwickshire from 1547–70; was sheriff of Warwickshire and Leicestershire in 1553–54; sat as knight of the shire for Warwickshire in the parliaments of 1553 and 1555; and served as the constable of Warwick Castle during Mary's reign.¹¹ Early in Elizabeth's reign, Robert still held a measure of social and political authority in Warwickshire – or at least in the region around Coughton. Less than one year into Queen Elizabeth's reign, Robert Throckmorton and Edward Greville wrote to the corporation officials of Stratford-upon-Avon to complain about the corporation's treatment of the minister, Roger Dyos. The vicar's wages, due the previous Michaelmas, were in arrears. Throckmorton and Greville insisted that there was 'no reson that yow schulde kepe that from hym wyche he hath servyde for nor this lawe wyll not permyt yow so to do … We schall bothe desyre yow to se hym payde hys dewtie.' Throckmorton and Greville ended with what sounded like

---

⁷ HPTD sub Warwickshire; Coventry; Warwick (1509–58); Clement, George, John, Kenelm, and Robert served as MPs for Warwickshire during this period. Nicholas was returned for other counties; Anthony was not returned as an MP during this period.

⁸ HPTD sub Warwickshire (1509–58); HPTD sub Burdett, Robert; HPTD sub Constable, Sir Marmaduke II.

⁹ HPTD 1509–1558 sub Warwick.

¹⁰ Sir George held many more offices than are detailed here. For a full account, see HPTD sub Throckmorton, George. The names of the MPs for Warwick are unknown for the years 1510–23, 1536 and 1539.

¹¹ HPTD sub Throckmorton, Robert.

an ominous threat from two of the most powerful men in the county: that if the vicar was not paid, 'we schall not thynke so well of yow As we have donne'.[12] Such strong words probably inspired corporation officials to move quickly to settle the vicar's pay dispute rather than risk further damage to their own access to influential patrons.

By the 1570s, however, the openly Catholic Throckmortons of Coughton had less of a presence in county politics. The rapid descent of the parliamentary career of Robert's son Thomas was typical for many Catholics in Elizabeth's reign. Thomas went to parliament as knight of the shire for Warwickshire in the last meeting of Queen Mary's reign and was elected from the borough of Warwick for Elizabeth's first parliament in 1559. He served alongside his father as a JP for Warwickshire from 1564 until both were removed in 1570, perhaps for failure to swear to the Act of Supremacy.[13] Thomas does not seem to have held even a minor public office after this time. Neither his son John nor his grandson Robert appears to have held positions in county government. In practice, Catholicism did not necessarily prohibit one from involvement in town or county government, or even, occasionally, from a seat in parliament, but it was unusual for an openly recusant Catholic to remain in such a prominent office. More typical was the experience of the Throckmortons' kinsman Sir Thomas Tresham, who after 1580 served only in minor positions such as commissioner of the Rockingham Forest.[14] But a gentleman's absence from court did not necessarily signal marginalisation. As Felicity Heal and Clive Holmes have demonstrated, the way to build or preserve a family's fortune was to focus on extracting revenue from one's estates rather than on building and maintaining a career as a courtier.[15] In light of this consideration, perhaps Catholic families such as the Throckmortons of Coughton minded less about their forced retirement from Court and politics than modern scholars have assumed.

The impact of religion is made clear by the fact that the Protestant descendants of the Coughton line still held important public offices in Warwickshire in the 1570s and thereafter. Clement Throckmorton, the third son of Sir George, settled at Haseley, Warwickshire, in the late

---

[12] SCLA, ER 1/1/30; for a full examination of religion in early modern Stratford-upon-Avon and a more in-depth look at the Dyos dispute, see Robert Bearman, 'The Early Reformation Experience in a Warwickshire Market Town: Stratford-upon-Avon, 1530–1580', *Journal of Midland History*, 32 (2007): 68–109.

[13] John J. LaRocca, SJ, 'Time, Death, and the Next Generation: The Early Elizabethan Recusancy Policy, 1558–1574', *Albion*, 14/2 (1982), 104.

[14] HMC, *Report on Manuscripts in Various Collections*, vol. iii (London, 1904), p. 149.

[15] Felicity Heal and Clive Holmes, *The Gentry in England and Wales, 1500–1700* (Stanford, 1994).

1550s. He served as JP for Warwickshire from 1547 to 1572, went to parliament for Warwick in 1542, 1547 and 1553, and was elected MP as knight of the shire for Warwickshire in 1563 and 1572. He served as a member of the Ecclesiastical High Commission in 1572 and as constable of Kenilworth Castle from 1553 until his death in 1573.[16] His heir, Job, went to parliament for Warwick in 1586, but 'never achieved prominence in the affairs of his county', possibly because of his own Puritan leanings and suspicions over his involvement with the Martin Marprelate tracts.[17] Job's son, Clement, was a JP for Warwickshire in the early seventeenth century and heavily involved in the local political scene of the market town of Stratford-upon-Avon. Although Clement was influential within his town – certainly more politically influential than his Catholic relations in this period – neither he nor any other Throckmorton of the Coughton line achieved the level of authority in Warwickshire held by Sir George in the mid-sixteenth century.[18]

Despite the diminished political presence in Warwickshire of the Catholic Throckmortons of Coughton, the family remained influential members of their local community. They continued to maintain the parish church of St. Peter, which adjoined Coughton Court, even after it became a Protestant church with the implementation of the Elizabethan Religious Settlement. Arguably, this kind of conformity with state policy could have helped to build and maintain capital through continued demonstrations of loyalty to the state as expressed in support of the parish structure, though a status-driven desire to maintain the connection with the patronal church of their ancestors, and with what in effect was a family mausoleum, may have been more important considerations here.

The activities of the Throckmorton women reveal that they carried out duties very similar to those of other women of their status group. The family's values with respect to child-rearing demonstrate that the Throckmortons shared the same concerns about this responsibility as did other gentry and noble families, both Protestant and Catholic. The family did indeed feel and express anxieties about their legal status as ones who recused the state Church. But their behaviors and values served to reinforce their integration in their communities, helped to maintain relationships with patrons who could ease the level of prosecution or

---

[16] HPTD sub Throckmorton, Clement. Clement also served as MP for Devizes in 1545, for Sudbury in 1559 and for West Looe in 1571.

[17] HPTD sub Throckmorton, Job. Job Throckmorton appears to have conformed to the state Church, so it does not seem that his lack of political prominence in Warwickshire was related to any sort of Puritan recusancy.

[18] See HPTD sub Throckmorton, Clement; Throckmorton, Job.

punishment imposed by Elizabeth's and James's governments and allowed them to function as patrons themselves, not just as clients of others.

Women's Actions and Activities

The Throckmorton women were acutely aware of the gender expectations placed on them by early modern patriarchal society. They demonstrated that they were skilled at working within the confines of early modern gender expectations, while at the same time serving as effective estate managers, household managers or voices for their immediate and extended family. Their behaviour and roles allowed them to construct and maintain social capital, which they as individuals and the family as a group could use in their construction and maintenance of patronage relationships.

Mary Throckmorton, the unmarried daughter of Thomas (d. 1615), engaged in activities that were related to her role as a *de facto* deputy estate manager of her father's house at Weston Underwood in Buckinghamshire. Because she was single, her work life did not follow all of the same courses that a married woman's would have done – she had no children of her own to care for, although she may have at times been responsible for instructing children put into service in Thomas Throckmorton's household. Her primary responsibility within the household appears to have been as a household manager. Women commonly fulfilled roles as household managers; they were trained to do so as part of their contribution to the household economy and at least some of the advice literature advocated such roles for women.[19] In this capacity, Mary carried out activities similar to those of many prosperous married women. For example, she arranged to provision the house with rabbits from neighboring estates.[20] When provisions from her aunt, Lady Terringham, fell through in 1607, she was able to easily secure another supplier, which indicates that she was both aware of and a participant in the local network of provisioners.[21]

Her role as a deputy estate manager was more significant, and more unusual, than her role as a household manager. It appears that Mary's status as a single woman placed her in a position not only to work in her natal households, but also – especially after the death of her mother – to assist her father in the business matters of his estates. Mary kept track of and informed her father about the state of affairs at his estate at Weston

---

[19] William Gouge, *Of domesticall duties eight treatises. I. An exposition of that part of Scripture out of which domesticall duties are raised. ... VIII. Duties of masters* (London, 1622), pp. 288–93 *passim*.

[20] Mendelson and Crawford, *Women in Early Modern England*, p. 307.

[21] WRO, CR 1998/Box 60/Folder 3, fol. 11.

Underwood when he was away at other residences or in prison for his recusancy. In a letter of Christmas, probably 1607, she reported that the 'mault making' at Weston 'goeth forwarde very [well] the time is very good'.[22]

In her capacity as deputy estate manager, Mary sometimes had to defend her family's property in her father's absence. One of these situations provides a good example of the balance she had to strike between public and private roles. When she found herself in the midst of a dispute between her uncle's family, the Terringhams, and her father, she acted submissively in her public interactions with the Terringhams, but more forcefully when speaking privately to her father. Shortly before Christmas 1607, Mary's cousin, Thomas Terringham, and two of his men stole a horse from Thomas Throckmorton's servant while the servant was out hunting. Mary attempted to resolve the dispute in an exchange of letters with her uncle, Sir Thomas Terringham. She reported to her father that she had replied to Terringham's letter 'like a woman very submissively ... for I perceive that they can not indure to be tolde of theyr faults'.[23] She went on to say that she hoped her father would not suffer any 'preiudice' from the dispute, but that for her own part, she 'care not what they conceive' of her. Mary's acknowledgment of the behavioural expectations of women, and that she answered a man's letter 'like a woman very submissively', demonstrates that she could perform the public role of deferential woman. Yet in private, among members of her immediate family, she was less concerned with or confined by such norms. This dual role allowed her to serve as an effective estate manager – overseeing and reporting on matters such as malt-making – and also to protect family property by challenging male members of her extended family who attempted to take advantage of the absence of the male head of household.[24]

Agnes Wilford Throckmorton displayed an understanding of the delicate balance between authoritative and submissive in her conversations with her father-in-law, Thomas Throckmorton. In these exchanges, Agnes had to temper her often assertive tone with a degree of deference that acknowledged his position as family patriarch and her own subordinate

---

[22] Ibid. Although this document is undated, its arrangement in the larger collection and the relationship to the surrounding documents suggests it was probably written in 1607.

[23] Ibid.

[24] The family dispute with the Terringhams seems to have been a long-standing one, and it is probable that Mary grew up with an understanding of her natal family's broader dispute with the Terringham branch. In March 1584, a tenant of Terringham's son-in-law, Edmund Apreece, cut down a tree at Weston Underwood and was interrupted by Thomas Throckmorton's men. Rights to the woods in question belonged in 1583 to Throckmorton, but in 1584 that ownership was contested by Terringham, who claimed ownership of the land for himself. See WRO, CR 1998/TribCD/F. 48, fols 23, 24.

position. Still, she did not back down when Thomas tried to exclude her from roles that she felt she should rightfully fill. For instance, Agnes maintained that she should have a part in the marriage negotiations of her children, as women of her social and economic rank often did, and offered sharp criticism to Thomas when he attempted to circumvent her involvement. She reminded him that he had admitted to her that his attempts at previous marriage negotiations had failed, and that he had done her son 'wronge to send him so sonne a woinge, and therfor you wolde (requite) that wronge to brede him experiens by trauell'.[25] Agnes complained that her father-in-law's exclusion of her opinion and dismissal of her role in marriage negotiations 'did not a littell greave me ... that I shoulde be made a stranger in thes procedinges' and asked him to consider whether 'it wolde not greve a mother that hath broght a childe into the worlde with grefe, paine, and danger of my life, to have aney caus geven to thinke that I shoulde be made a stranger in his bestoinge, and by his best frinde, and one that I my self doe relithyon'.[26]

Although Agnes used language that acknowledged Thomas's position as family patriarch, at the same time she spoke to him not as someone fearful of losing favour or support, but as a woman intent on protecting her position and her authority over her own family group. Agnes was not willing completely to abrogate headship of her household and decisions over the lives of her children, even to Thomas. Still, she had to tread carefully. Thomas was the head of the family, and he could easily overrule her wishes. Her task was to develop strategies that balanced submissiveness and authoritativeness in order to protect her own position and that of her children without alienating the family patriarch. In so doing, Agnes maintained the family harmony that was vital to the preservation of her own individual social capital, both within and without her household, as well as the social capital of her household collectively.

Margaret Throckmorton Griffin made clear the importance of maintaining harmony among members of an extended family, and the damage to one's credit that could ensue from failure to attend to such relationships. When Margaret's father, Thomas Throckmorton, and her husband, Rice Griffin, became locked in a land dispute, Margaret wrote to her father in an attempt to persuade him to settle the disagreement. She told her father that her husband 'doth not knowe of the contents of this letter', and maintained that Mr Griffin would surely be seen as the more patient and virtuous if the matter went to trial (and became a more public matter), since 'he hath sought peace by so many meanes and hath

---

[25] WRO, CR 1998/Box 60/Folder 1, fol. 1. See also Jan Broadway's chapter in this volume.

[26] WRO, CR 1998/Box 60/Folder 1, fol. 1.

forborne the matter so long, in hope of agreement'.²⁷ She asked her father to 'give me leave to remember unto you' the ill effects his continuation of the dispute could cause to his own credit, reputation and spiritual condition. She urged Thomas to think of the 'good example you shold give towards men, by the charitable regard that ought to be of neighbourhood by the consideration of avoiding your owne troble and expense'.²⁸ In other words, his continued argument with his son-in-law disrupted the family unity and good neighbourhood that he was honour-bound to maintain, and could have a detrimental effect on his own social capital. Margaret ended with a different kind of manoeuvre. In case she had failed to achieve her objective by reason, perhaps she could appeal to Thomas's fatherly affection by invoking the hurt that the dispute caused her as Thomas's 'wofull child'.²⁹

Mary Throckmorton echoed her sister's concerns when she reminded her father of the possible detrimental effects of grief on a family economy and on those whom the patriarch was bound to protect. When Mary's mother died in April 1607, Mary wrote to her father to say that since his wife had made a good death that was 'was very comfortable to us all, she trusted that he would 'shewe your self wise as the worlde doth holde' and to consider how many depended on him.³⁰ His grief, Mary feared, would be a 'great hinderence to your health' and could result in hardship for those who relied upon him.³¹ Mary assured her father that his wife had had the support of family members on her deathbed, which Ralph Houlbrooke describes as a 'prerequisite of the "good" death'.³² Further, Mary's admonition to her father to grieve in moderation reflects the views offered in advice books, namely, that one should beware not to allow their grief to interfere with their earthy duties, including to those for whom the bereaved was responsible. It also interestingly inverts the contemporary stereotype, that it was women who were more given to 'immoderate' grief.³³

---

²⁷ WRO, CR 1998/CD F. 52, fol. 9.

²⁸ Ibid.

²⁹ Ibid.

³⁰ WRO, CR 1998/Box 60/Folder 3, fol. 10.

³¹ Ibid.

³² Ralph Houlbrooke, *Death, Religion, and the Family in England, 1480–1750* (Oxford, 1998), pp. 191–2.

³³ Barthélemy Batt, *The Christian mans closet. Wherein is conteined a large discourse of the godly training up of children*, trans. William Lowth (London, 1581), fols 58r, 58v; *The Office of Christian Parents: shewing how children are to be gouerned throughout all ages and times of their life* (Cambridge, 1616), pp. 117–18. Cf. Houlbrooke, *Death, Religion and the Family*, pp. 238–9.

Clearly, the Throckmorton women were well aware of the importance of credit, reputation, and protection of one's honour. The maintenance of such non-economic forms of capital took on greater significance when members of this family became embroiled in political intrigue. In 1583, Mary Throckmorton Arden, the daughter of Sir Robert Throckmorton and sister of Thomas, found herself and her family unwillingly thrust into the political sphere. John Sommerville, Mary Arden's son-in-law, plotted in 1583 to assassinate Queen Elizabeth in favour of Mary Stuart, but was apprehended en route to London. During questioning, Sommerville said that he, along with his wife and his in-laws, the Ardens, had been present at Park Hall to hear 'one Hawle a priest [deliver] certayne speaches ... that towched hir Majestie greatlie ... which wrought in him a hatred towards her Majestie whereuppon he grewe to this resolution' to kill the queen.[34] Officials charged with investigating the plot acknowledged with some relief that Sommerville's wife and her family attempted to dissuade him from his plans, but this incident clearly damaged the reputation of the Ardens in their local community.[35] Despite being known in the county as papists, the Ardens had until this time succeeded in keeping a low profile with respect to their Catholicism, despite their occasional harbouring of the priest and gardener, Hugh Hall – who also sometimes lodged with their kinsman John Throckmorton.[36] From this point on, however, local officials monitored the family more carefully. In September 1592, the recusancy commissioners for Warwickshire presented the widowed Mary Arden and her servant John Brown as recusants from the parish of Coughton.[37]

Political engagement was not restricted to Throckmorton women from the Coughton line. Recusant kinswomen of the Coughton Throckmortons intentionally involved themselves in political activities, and potentially quite dangerous ones. By 1583, Catholics were prohibited by law from sending their children abroad for education without permission from the state, legislation that had become necessary in light of the large numbers of young English Catholics entering continental seminaries and nunneries. Yet in October 1583, Lady Margery Throckmorton wrote to her son Francis to say that she had 'spoken with Owen, Mr Talbot's man, who recommends her son Thomas go to Lady Arundel at Arundel Castle, who will obtain a passage by ship for him'.[38] It seems that Margery tried to

---

[34] TNA, SP 12/163, fol. 67r.
[35] TNA, SP 12/163, fol. 140v.
[36] TNA, SP 12/164, fols 141r–v.
[37] TNA, SP 12/243, fol. 208r.
[38] TNA, SP 12/163, fol. 23. Francis Throckmorton was a cousin of Thomas Throckmorton of Coughton, their fathers both having been sons of Sir George Throckmorton. Francis's father, Sir John, held the manor of Feckenham in Worcestershire and was thus head

arrange passage out of the country for her son in the immediate aftermath of the Throckmorton plot, prior to his arrest. Margery's actions were politically subversive and could have resulted in severe financial penalties (or worse) for herself and her sons. Indeed, in December 1583 she was questioned for her role in this attempted transportation, but the results of that examination are unclear.[39] Still, her attempts to arrange unlicensed transportation out of the realm must have damaged her own credit in relationship to the Crown, credit that she would need to recapture through assurances of loyalty to the queen and government.

After Francis's arrest for his role in the plot, Lady Margery visited her son in prison and implored him to 'deale playnlye and loyally with her Majestie, and to discover such practyses as he knowe to be hurtfull to her Majestie and state.'[40] In June 1584, Sir Owen Hopton, Lieutenant of the Tower of London, asked Sir Francis Walsingham that Lady Throckmorton be allowed to continue to visit her son, as she gave him 'good & motherly Counsell'.[41] Walsingham and the queen agreed that Francis's mother and his wife 'shall have accesse to youe to parsuade you to dischardge your dewtie towards her highnes. And the speaches that shall passe betweene youe and them, shalbe in my [Walsingham's] hearinge.'[42] Francis's mother and his wife were interested in his well-being and in trying to elicit mercy from the queen, but Lady Margery must also have been concerned about rebuilding her own capital. The overtly treasonous actions of some Throckmortons made it even more important for loyal but recusant members of the family to cultivate every bit of social capital they could. Her demonstration of loyalty to the queen and state through her good counsel to her son presumably created some credit with his gaolers and any other witnesses; they at least helped her to maintain enough credit that she was allowed to continue to converse with her son, although she was not able to prevent his execution.

Through their successful fulfilment of their roles, the Throckmorton women built and maintained social capital. Although most of the Throckmorton women did not engage in the political arena, the maintenance of capital proved vital for those who did, in their attempts both to protect themselves and to protect men to whom they were related. Other roles they undertook were typical of English gentlewomen – Catholic or Protestant – seeking to accumulate and maintain non-economic forms of credit and capital.

---

of the Feckenham line of Throckmortons until his death in 1580. *VCH Worcestershire*, vol. 3, p. 114; HPTD sub John Throckmorton I.

[39] TNA, SP 12/164, fols 16r– v.
[40] TNA, SP 12/171, fol. 1r.
[41] Ibid.
[42] TNA 12/171, fol. 4r.

Child-rearing

The child-rearing practices of the Throckmortons of Coughton exhibited a conscious effort by both men and women to build up social capital. In matters such as preparing the heir to lead the family, protecting the honour and reputation of the house through effective guidance of children or composing a letter of instruction for a son, the actions of the Throckmortons reflect the advice offered in the prescriptive literature and also bear striking similarity to the actions of other families of upper status.

Aristocratic families in early modern England, whether Catholic or Protestant, understood that the overall credit of their house depended on the state in which the heir was left. Financial health was vital even to the non-economic capital of a house. This was particularly true for Catholics, as the continual assessment of financial penalties for recusancy in Elizabeth's and James's reigns made it incumbent on such families to ensure that they left a solid legacy for their heirs to inherit. The Throckmorton family's position as one of the leading Catholic recusant families in England demanded that the family – as individuals and as a corporate body – work together to accumulate and protect their economic and social capital. If the wealth of the house had diminished over the previous generation, if the heir was inadequately prepared to head the house or if his upbringing produced an individual deficient in the qualities that a gentleman or nobleman should possess, then not only could the credit of the house suffer, but also the credit of the individuals who had allowed these things to happen would be weakened.

Thomas Throckmorton and Thomas Wilford, Robert's paternal and maternal grandfathers, were concerned that Throckmorton's heir, Robert, protect both his economic and his social credit. After the death of his son John, Thomas Throckmorton wrote regularly to Robert to remind the young man that he had debts that needed payment and to urge him to 'to come hither to me whereby I may understand what course you have taken therein'.[43] Prescriptive literature on child-rearing in the late sixteenth and early seventeenth centuries cautioned parents that the family's social credit depended on their good parenting. Authors exhorted parents to nurture their children, to teach them restraint and respect for elders, to be God-fearing, to educate them well and at all costs to avoid producing 'degenerate' sons.[44] It was incumbent upon Thomas Throckmorton to

---

[43] WRO, CR1998/Box 60/Folder 3, fol. 16.
[44] Batt, *The Christian mans closet*, fol. 10r. See also *The Office of Christian Parents*.

assume the role his deceased son could not, and to take on the father's responsibilities in Robert's instruction.[45]

Thomas regularly wrote to Robert, both to inquire on health and business matters and to admonish his grandson for what he considered to be poor behaviour. On 1 October 1612 Thomas summoned Robert to his presence immediately, so that Thomas could discuss with Robert

> a greate erroure which you haue this daye committed and thoughe you dow nott presenttly consider of your oversighte you will taste of itt here after when you cannott tell howe to mende itt ... I hope you will nott neglectt my ffatherly admonition butt thatt you will presenttly come to me.[46]

A few weeks later Thomas again summoned Robert to 'come hither to me uppon Twesday morninge next for there is a matter which doth muche concerne me that I would conferr with you aboute'.[47] The surviving evidence does not indicate that Thomas Throckmorton offered similar admonitions or instructions to any of his other grandchildren. Guidance of this sort agrees in practice with the prescriptive literature, namely, that energies should be focused on the eldest male child, the heir. The unnamed author of *The Office of Christian Parents* (1616) argued that the eldest sons of 'great men' were those most in need of a proper education, 'for who hath more neede of learning, and wisedome by learning, then he that hath most, and the greatest estate to governe?'[48]

Robert's maternal grandfather, Thomas Wilford, offered his grandson further direction, and in some cases quite pointed criticism of the way Thomas Throckmorton had run his household – the implication being that Wilford could guide his grandson more wisely than Throckmorton.[49] Wilford cautioned his grandson about living beyond his income, a concern shared by Robert's mother, Agnes.[50] Thomas Throckmorton's household expenses for the previous year had outweighed his income by £500, and both Agnes and Thomas Wilford were intent that Robert should not follow his paternal grandfather's example. Wilford had little patience for Thomas Throckmorton's tendency to live beyond his means, and warned

---

[45] John Throckmorton, Thomas's only surviving son and heir, died in February 1604; *VCH Buckinghamshire*, vol. 4, p. 499.

[46] WRO, CR 1998/Box 60/ Folder 3, fol. 25.

[47] WRO, CR 1998/Box 60/ Folder 3, fol. 21.

[48] *The Office of Christian Parents*, p. 96.

[49] WRO, CR 1998/Box 60/ Folder 3, fols 24, 26.

[50] Agnes discussed with her father the state of fiscal affairs at Throckmorton's house, but does not appear to have voiced her concerns to her son. WRO, CR 1998/Box 60/Folder 3, fol. 26v.

Robert that such a habit would only result in deminishing your howshold a greate deale & with the sale of some landes for the discharge of all or greatest part of the debtes'.⁵¹ Less than a month later he wrote again and said that he would be 'glad to heare of the Lessening of your howshould otherwyse you will growe as fast in debt as your Grandfather was wount to doe'.⁵² Wilford had valid concerns about the effect that a house in economic distress could have on the credit formation and credit worthiness – both economic and non-economic – of the heir, and about the habits his grandson formed in following his paternal grandfather's example.

The honour and reputation of the house were predicated not only on financial solvency but also on settling one's personal and spiritual estate. A letter of advice that appears to be directed to Thomas Throckmorton underscored the importance of sound fiscal management in safeguarding an heir's economic and social capital. The writer urged his recipient to ensure that four main tasks were carried out in preparation for his death. First, to settle the estate of his eternal soul, to 'examine carefully the whole course of your life; to call to mynde all your humayne fraylties and lapses, to bewayle with true sorrow all your synnes and offenses, and to purge and cleanse your soule from them by a generall Confession'.⁵³ Although this personal introspection would be difficult or 'troublesome' at times, as it had been for the writer, he insisted that in the end it would bring Thomas 'great comforte and consolation ... and will settle your soule in a very secure estate'.⁵⁴ Next, Thomas was to settle his debts. If he neglected to do so he would endanger those who depended on him and those who had entered into bonds for him. The result would be scandal, loss of previous good reputation and peril of his soul. To further protect his reputation, Thomas was to be sure to provide well for his single adult daughter, Mary; for his servants and for the future health of his house. He needed to ensure that his own heir, and the heir's wife and mother, lived 'in perfect amitie and ffreindshipp that all dislikes and hart burnings being layd aside they maye live sociably and charitably, togeather and one helpe and Defende an other'.⁵⁵ To do so would protect the future of the house, the credit of the house, and would also be 'highly pleasing to god, who desireth nothing more then to have peace unitie and charitie among his people.'⁵⁶

---

⁵¹ WRO, CR1998/Box 60/Folder 3, fol. 26r.
⁵² WRO, CR 1998/Box 60/Folder 3, fol. 24.
⁵³ WRO, CR 1998/Box 60/Folder 4, fol. 20. The author and recipient of this letter are unclear, but the mention of the recipient's single adult daughter, Mary, suggests that the letter was directed to Thomas Throckmorton.
⁵⁴ Ibid.
⁵⁵ WRO, CR 1998/Box 60/Folder 4, fol. 20.
⁵⁶ Ibid.

Family honour also depended on the behaviour and conduct of the next generation. As Richard Cust has pointed out, 'an enduring family line was a divine acknowledgement of virtue'.[57] For Catholics, a parent's need to protect the reputation of the family from the youthful indiscretions of their children took on even more significance than it did for Protestant neighbours. Reckless or potentially offensive behaviour, such as gambling, jeopardised not only the reputation of the house, and of the parents as good parents, but also the standing of the broader Catholic community. In their adulthood, Robert Throckmorton and his younger brother Tom sometimes engaged in horse racing and gambling; when gossip about it reached their mother, Agnes, she was furious. She complained to Robert that 'all the Contrye tallketh of It that Papist hath so much monis that thaye run It a Waye'.[58] As Catholics, the family had to be particularly careful not to incur the disrespect or resentment of their neighbours. If there were a widespread perception that Catholics were wasteful and reckless with their money it might provide enemies of Catholics with a reason or incentive to push for an increase in financial penalties or for harsher prosecution of recusants. Thus, Agnes's admonition to her son had greater relevance than merely worrying about what the neighbours might think. She was concerned not only for the reputation of her sons and the house, but also for the fiscal situation of Catholics more generally.

Agnes might also have been concerned about the ramifications Robert's behaviour could have on her image or reputation as a good Renaissance parent and to her own good name. Part of Agnes's personal credit depended on the social and economic standing of her child, especially that of her heir. Thus, Robert's bad behaviour had the potential to erode some of the credit that Agnes had laboured to accumulate. Indeed, part of a woman's virtue was located in the nurturing and proper education of her children, even into their adult years. The anonymous author of *The Office of Christian Parents* told his readers that 'parents have a perpetual interest in their child, and their office to care, counsell, admonish, and helpe them, endureth always'.[59] Agnes regularly inquired after the health of Robert and his family and appeared particularly concerned when Robert and his wife had been ill while in London. She wrote that she hoped to hear that the couple would soon be restored to good health and ready to depart London, especially since the city's 'smoky are did neyer agree with nether of you I wish you both well out of It and at home with your littel one'.[60]

---

[57] Richard Cust, 'Catholicism, Antiquarianism, and Gentry Honour: The Writings of Sir Thomas Shirley', *Midland History*, 23 (1998), 51.

[58] WRO, CR 1998/Box 60/Folder 1, fol. 6.

[59] *The Office of Christian Parents*, p. 216.

[60] WRO, CR 1998/Box 60/Folder 1, fol. 5.

She provided a glimpse of her grandmotherly affection when at the close of one letter to Robert she referred to her grandchildren as her '2 littell swet lams'.[61] She offered counsel, although she avoided talking directly to her son about money matters and instead fretted to her father, who in turn instructed her son on proper management of his household. And when need arose, as in the case of the horse racing, she admonished. Parental missteps did not go unnoticed in a society deeply invested in appearance and reputation. Muriel Throckmorton Tresham's husband, Sir Thomas, described to her his concerns about the way their kinsman, Lord Vaux, had raised his children, saying that 'If they had been ruled by us, his lordship [the heir] should not have been so spoiled as he had been.'[62]

In their child-rearing values and practices, the Throckmortons of Coughton were strikingly similar to other gentry families. Anxieties about their religious position were present, as revealed in Agnes Throckmorton's worrying about what effect her sons' gambling might have on Catholics. Yet the Throckmortons were able to use social practices such as child-rearing to underscore their resemblance to other English gentry and also to reinforce their honour. In so doing, the family accumulated credit that they could utilise in forming relationships with patrons.

Patronage

Although patronage was an important part of the machinery of early modern English politics and society, the construction and maintenance of patronage relationships was particularly vital for English Catholics. Through relationships with influential Protestants, some Catholics – especially those of high social and economic status – were able to enjoy a measure of protection from prosecution or punishment for their religious practice. Accumulation of social capital was vital to Catholic recusants' survival because it allowed them to build relationships with patrons who could shield them from the full brunt of the recusancy statutes.

Patronage could assume multiple forms. In all cases, an individual (the client) sought office, protection or favour from another individual (the patron) who had access to more power or influence (or to other individuals with such connections) than did the client. In return for the patron's support, the client offered his or her loyalty and service. In their pursuit of patronage, clients turned not only to friends and relations, but also to unrelated individuals whose position could prove helpful – for example, someone who had the ear of the monarch. Although a patron is usually

---

[61] Ibid.
[62] *HMC Various iii*, p. 84.

considered to be someone of higher status than the client, patronage could also function laterally, between people of roughly comparable status. The Throckmortons of Coughton sought patronage from friends and kin such as Sir Walter Raleigh, from individuals with whom they developed and maintained long-term relationships of protection, such as the Earl and Countess of Warwick, and from more distant relationships they deliberately cultivated, such as that with the earl of Leicester and Robert Cecil, Earl of Salisbury. They dispensed patronage to kinsmen who had positions similar to their own, such as Sir Thomas Tresham.

The high political and social status of Thomas Throckmorton's patrons indicates that the Throckmortons of Coughton continued to enjoy social prominence in the West Midlands. In 1587 Thomas wrote to the earl of Leicester to ask his help in being released from the Bishop of London's prison to confinement at Throckmorton's own house at Holborne, and noted that 'ever sithens my first comittement into trobles I haue fownde you my good Lord and protecter'.[63] Leicester's brother, Ambrose Dudley, Earl of Warwick, also acted as patron to Thomas Throckmorton. Although Throckmorton faced frequent imprisonment for his recusancy throughout the late Elizabethan period, he was often 'spared of that restraine at the request of the … Earle of Warwicke while he lived … namely for that he hath bene thoughte a man not malitiouslie affected to the state, nor busie in corruptinge other with erronious doctrine and opinions but otherwise a quiett man'.[64] Simon Adams has underscored the degree to which the Dudley brothers, Leicester and Warwick, agreed on matters of policy and administration. Apparently they also sometimes agreed on the people to whom they would direct their patronage.[65]

The patronage of the Dudley brothers to the Throckmortons did not function as a blanket patronage of the family or of all the descendants of the Coughton line. Neither Leicester nor Warwick extended their patronage to the Protestant Throckmortons of the Coughton line, probably because these had cultivated relationships with other patrons. In the early 1570s, Job Throckmorton of Haseley, Thomas's first cousin, enjoyed the political patronage of the third Earl of Rutland. Job Throckmorton's bid for a parliamentary seat in 1586 had the support of Sir John Harrington, Fulke Greville and some prominent townsmen, while the Earl of Warwick's endorsement went to Thomas Dudley.[66]

---

[63] WRO, CR 1998/Box 60/Folder 3, fol. 3.

[64] Lambeth Palace Library, Fairhurst Papers 2004, fol. 41.

[65] Simon Adams, 'Dudley, Ambrose, earl of Warwick (c.1530–1590)', *ODNB*.

[66] HPTD sub Job Throckmorton; Job was the heir of Clement Throckmorton of Haseley, who was himself the third son of Sir George Throckmorton.

Although the Protestant branch of the family does not appear to have served openly as patrons to their Catholic relations when the latter ran afoul of the law, the family connections cannot have hurt. Job served as a JP and was entrusted with carrying out searches for priests in Warwickshire, but there is no indication that he, his son or his grandson, all of whom served in Warwickshire county government, ever searched the homes of their Catholic relations.[67] The lack of extant correspondence between the Catholic and Protestant branches of the family suggests that the association between the two branches was not particularly close, but it clearly was not a hostile relationship. On his travels, Nicholas Throckmorton's son, the diarist Arthur Throckmorton, periodically stayed with his Catholic relations at Coughton and elsewhere.[68] When the anti-Catholic legislation of 1593 required recusants to secure a licence from their county JPs to travel more than 5 miles from home, a Protestant Throckmorton was often one of the JPs from whom the Catholic Throckmortons received their licence, and they seem to have had no trouble in securing such licences.[69]

The Throckmorton's status as clients of powerful patrons placed them in a position to dispense patronage to those of status equivalent to their own. John Throckmorton, the son and heir of Thomas Throckmorton of Coughton, acted as patron to his uncle, Sir Thomas Tresham, when Tresham's son Francis became embroiled in the Essex rebellion.[70] In 1600, Francis Tresham, perhaps seduced into a lapse in judgement by his somewhat hot-headed nature, joined the Earl of Essex in his abortive uprising against Queen Elizabeth's advisers. In the aftermath of the abortive rebellion, Sir Thomas Tresham scrambled to secure his heir's release from prison and exoneration for his involvement in the revolt. Lady Mounteagle, Francis's sister, alerted John Throckmorton to the difficulty the Treshams were having in finding a patron to work for Francis's exoneration. Lady Katherine Howard, to whom Sir Thomas Tresham had appealed for help, 'hadd (at three severall tymes) desired them to fynd other means for the stay of his arraignmente and attainder' because she doubted that she could

---

[67] TNA, SP 12/167, fol. 54r–v.

[68] A.L. Rowse, *Ralegh and the Throckmortons* (London, 1962), pp. 96, 190.

[69] WRO, CR 1998/Box 62, fol. 40.

[70] Francis Tresham joined in insurrection against a monarch and government he felt had persecuted the recusant community and his family in particular. Francis's father, Sir Thomas Tresham, spent most of the 1580s and a healthy portion of the 1590s in prison for his Catholicism. He, like Thomas Throckmorton, was one of the Catholic recusants whom the government rounded up whenever the religious–political temperature grew too hot. John, the son of Thomas and one of the second generation of recusants that could have been involved himself in more militant recusancy and insurrection, opted instead for more passive, or conservative, recusancy than Francis Tresham supported, and may have been an occasional conformist. Sir Thomas Tresham's wife, Muriel, was John Throckmorton's aunt.

'p[ro]mise any securyty of his lyef by pardon butt utterlie disclaymed of any hope she had to helpe him'.⁷¹ John Throckmorton had been a 'meanes for ... Relief' for his nephew Robert Catesby (another Essex conspirator). When he sought assistance for Francis Tresham, he turned to the same 'three most honorable parsons and one especiall instrument' who had helped him with Catesby's release.⁷² The identities of the four individuals to whom Throckmorton alluded are unclear, but his appeals for his cousin's life were successful – and expensive. Sir Thomas Tresham was required to submit a bond that he would pay £2,100 to William Ayloffe over the following three months on Francis's behalf, to 'save his lyef attainder in bloode'.⁷³

The surviving evidence suggests that John Throckmorton's patronage was in the end more instrumental than that of Lady Katherine Howard, although Howard vehemently disputed that. Lady Howard, despite her initial doubts, continued to work towards Francis's release and hoped to secure a reprieve after judgement had been decided. When Tresham escaped prosecution, individuals close to the case maintained that 'this favour had come by a second means and not by her' and that the other party had been 'moved to undertake it when she so much doubted to effect it' – the other party being moved through the efforts of John Throckmorton.⁷⁴

In parallel with Katherine Howard's assistance to the Tresham family, the Throckmorton women were actively involved in the pursuit of political patronage. Muriel Throckmorton Tresham (Thomas Throckmorton's sister) regularly sought patronage and protection for her husband when he was imprisoned throughout the 1580s. In March 1589, when Sir Thomas Tresham was incarcerated in the bishop's prison at Ely for his recusancy, Muriel wrote to Lord Burghley to ask that her husband be moved to Banbury, 'alonely for his health's sake'.⁷⁵ On the same day, she also wrote to Burghley's son, Thomas Cecil, to ask that he 'use his interest with his father that Sir Thomas Tresham might be prisoner at Banbury instead of at Ely', perhaps because Banbury was more comfortable and closer to the Treshams' seat at Rushton, Northamptonshire.⁷⁶ When Tresham was

---

⁷¹ BL, Tresham Papers, Add. MS 39829, fol. 51.

⁷² Ibid. It is not clear who these individuals were, although John Throckmorton described them as 'most ho[norable] p[ar]sons under whom I must live', which suggests they were people with whom Throckmorton had cultivated and maintained relationships of patronage.

⁷³ BL, Tresham Papers, Add. MS 39829, fol. 51; *HMC Various iii*, p. 108.

⁷⁴ *HMC Various iii*, p. 109.

⁷⁵ Ibid. p, 50.

⁷⁶ BL, Tresham Papers, Add. MS 39828, fol. 137. Muriel Throckmorton Tresham was the daughter of Robert Throckmorton of Coughton, sister of Thomas Throckmorton of

imprisoned for a dispute over a debt in 1599, his wife once again called on her patrons for help. In January 1599 Muriel wrote to Lady Egerton to ask that she 'move her husband, Lord Egerton, on behalf of Sir Thomas Tresham'.[77]

In their pursuit of patronage, the women of the Throckmorton Coughton line were similar to other Catholic or Protestant women. Both Catholic and Protestant women utilised patronage relationships in their attempts to secure release from prison for their husbands, or for other women's husbands. In 1582 the Catholic Margaret Gage asked Sir Francis Walsingham to release her husband from the Marshalsea prison to the custody of the high sheriff of Sussex.[78] The Catholic Anne, Countess of Arundel, made similar appeals when her husband, Philip, was imprisoned in 1585.[79] Margaret Whorwood Throckmorton petitioned the Privy Council that her husband, Thomas, have liberty to attend to 'his weightie cawses in law' at Westminster in May 1590.[80] Their actions were similar to those of Protestant women such as the Countess of Warwick. After the Earl of Warwick's death in 1590, the countess took over her deceased husband's role as Thomas Throckmorton's patron. In 1592 she succeeded in securing from the queen a stay of imprisonment for Throckmorton, on the grounds that he was in such a weakened condition that 'emprisonmente were verie likely to shorten his dayes'.[81]

Muriel Throckmorton Tresham appears to have been one of the most active women in the Catholic recusant patronage network, although it may be only that we know more about her because her letters have survived in bulk. During the lifetime of her husband, Sir Thomas, Muriel frequently wrote to assorted women and men to appeal for relief for her husband; her two most frequent patrons were Lady Egerton and Robert Cecil, Earl of Salisbury. It is not always clear, however, whose voice is reflected in those letters. Many of Muriel's letters were drafted in her husband's hand, which suggests that one of the strategies of Sir Thomas or the family strategies for securing patronage was to have both Sir Thomas and Muriel working towards the same objective simultaneously while writing to a number of different patrons or potential patrons. Even after her husband's death in September 1605, Muriel maintained relationships with patrons, particularly with Robert Cecil.

Coughton, and aunt to John Throckmorton, Thomas's heir.

[77] BL, Tresham Papers, Add MS 39829, fols 35, 36.

[78] TNA, SP12/159 fol. 139r.

[79] *The Lives of Philip Howard, Earl of Arundel, and of Anne Dacres, His Wife*, ed. Duke of Norfolk (London, 1857), p. 73.

[80] *APC*, vol. 19, p. 102.

[81] Lambeth Palace Library, Fairhurst Papers 2004, fol. 41.

The preservation of patronage relationships became particularly necessary once a Catholic recusant woman was widowed. The change in a woman's legal status from wife to widow meant that she could be held legally responsible for her refusal to attend Protestant services. In March 1609 Muriel Tresham wrote to Robert Cecil to complain about her treatment at the hands of the proctor of Northampton, John Lambech. Despite her age and infirmity, Muriel explained, Lambech 'continually laboureth to have me presented [at the] Spirituall Court, & to be indighted at each sessions & assises'.[82] According to Muriel, Lambech's aggressive pursuit of an aged recusant widow was more an effort to seize her lands than to carry out a moral compulsion to prosecute local Catholic recusants.[83]

The experience of the Throckmortons of Coughton helps to illustrate how deeply ingrained patronage was in early modern English society. The Catholic Throckmortons cultivated and maintained patronage relationships as did other upper-status families, Catholic and Protestant. Philip and Anne Howard, Earl and Countess of Arundel, maintained patronage relationships with Lord Burghley and Christopher Hatton. Robert Brokesby, a Catholic, sustained a patron–client relationship with the Protestant (and sometimes Puritan) Hastings family, the third and fourth earls of Huntington.[84] The Hastings family, in turn, maintained relationships with Walsingham, Burghley and Essex.[85] Individuals or families of upper status had ready access to the patronage network, so long as their credit was sound. Few, if any, patrons wished to risk their own social or economic capital in support of an unworthy client. The efforts of the Throckmortons of Coughton to build and maintain their own individual forms of capital, as well as that of the family as a corporate body, allowed them to continue to engage with a network of patrons that helped them to navigate the increasing legal strictures against Catholic recusants.

Conclusion

The Throckmortons of Coughton were acutely aware of how important the maintenance of credit and reputation was to English society, perhaps especially to recusant Catholics. This chapter illustrates some of the ways

---

[82] TNA, SP 14/44, fol. 100r. Muriel (Throckmorton) Tresham was the daughter of Robert Throckmorton of Coughton and the sister of Thomas Throckmorton of Coughton.

[83] During the same period that Lambech presented Muriel Tresham for recusancy, he also pursued suits against her in Chancery and Exchequer for leases in Rothwell that Muriel held of King James. TNA, SP 14/44, fol. 100r.

[84] Huntington Library, Hastings Personal Correspondence, Box 7, HA5437.

[85] Huntington Library, Hastings Personal Correspondence, Box 4, HA5278, HA5279.

in which they devised and carried out strategies that allowed them to remain integrated into English society. By fulfilling roles typical of English gentlewomen, women of the Coughton line of Throckmortons emphasised their likeness to other women of their rank. They accrued and maintained both economic and non-economic forms of capital, as in the case of Mary Throckmorton's management of her father's estate in his absence. The Throckmortons, individually and as a family, shared concerns with their peers about child-rearing and judicious preparation of the heir, and they were very aware of the detrimental effects an unsound heir could have on the reputation and the longevity of the house. Such practices illuminate the degree to which some Catholics remained integrated into the larger corpus of English society. The Throckmortons of Coughton did not become ostracised, but rather remained integrated within their local communities in Buckinghamshire and Warwickshire, and also within the larger body of English gentry society. To be sure, members of this family paid fines, endured imprisonment, were probably frustrated or angered by the increasing pressure of anti-recusancy statutes and – in a few cases – participated in overtly treasonous actions against the Crown. But this family also devised strategies by which to deal with the challenges they faced, strategies that helped them to remain active members of early modern English society.

CHAPTER 4

Coughton and the Gunpowder Plot

Michael Hodgetts

The most dramatic event in the history of Coughton Court was also one of the most dramatic events in English history – the Gunpowder Plot. Two of the plotters, the ringleader Robert Catesby and Francis Tresham, were nephews of Thomas Throckmorton; several others were related to the family. In October 1605, Coughton was borrowed by another conspirator (who was not so related), Sir Everard Digby of Gayhurst in Buckinghamshire. But the Throckmortons themselves are a curious absence at the heart of the plot, and the family papers contain no material on it. Thomas himself was not privy to the Plot or present at Coughton during it,[1] and most books mention (briefly) only three events there: on 30 October 1605, the arrival from Gayhurst of Lady Digby and the Jesuit superior Henry Garnet; on 1 November, the Masses of All Saints in the Tower Room; and, on 6 November, the delivery to Garnet of a letter from Catesby and Sir Everard. After that, attention shifts to the conspirators' desperate ride to Huddington Court and Holbeach House, their last stand at Holbeach and the subsequent arrests, interrogations, trials and executions. Garnet himself reappears in January 1606, when he was arrested at Hindlip, near Worcester, together with his colleague Edward Oldcorne, his servant Nicholas Owen, the hide-builder, and Oldcorne's servant Ralph Ashley. But in the scramble to keep up with the Plotters on their flight, many other characters are mentioned by historians only in passing, and without much examination of their associations and connections. Moreover, clues are bound to have been missed since, after 400 years, there is still no comprehensive edition of the examinations and confessions.[2] As a contribution to both regional and national history, therefore, it may be worth taking a closer look at what happened in and around Coughton in the crucial months and weeks preceding and following 5 November 1605.

---

[1] A receipt for his recusancy fines for ten (lunar) months from 1 September 1604 to 7 June 1605 describes him as 'late of Weston Underwood', near Gayhurst (WRO, CR 1998/Box 62, no. 34). He was at Weston also on 18 December 1597 and on 16 August 1608 (Box 61/Folder 4/no. 9; Box 60/Folder 3/no. 11). But on 1 December 1594 he was 'at old Lady Sheffield's at Highgate' (Box 62/nos 6, 26); and in Warwickshire on 10 February 1615/16 (Box 62/no. 31).

[2] For this reason, to documents quoted from previous writers on the plot I have added the references to TNA, SP 14 (State Papers Domestic, James I) and *CSPD, 1603–10*.

There will be more questions and suggestions than firm answers, but by paying close attention to the movements of some key individuals in and around Warwickshire, as well as carefully unpicking some of the Plotters' Midlands connections, a picture will start to emerge that makes the whole conspiracy seem considerably more formidable and less of a hopelessly madcap scheme than convention usually dictates.

The Headquarters of the Rising

First, however, there is what did *not* happen at Coughton.[3] It is often implied that Sir Everard Digby had borrowed the house as a headquarters for the rising which would follow the explosion in London. But he was not recruited to the Plot until four weeks before the day. Unlike his distant cousin Sir Robert Digby of Coleshill, he was not a leading figure in Warwickshire; he never in fact reached Coughton, and if he had, with his household and Garnet's there would have been no room there for the court of the young Princess Elizabeth, who was to be kidnapped from Coombe Abbey, near Coventry, and proclaimed queen. In 1642, when her brother, Charles I, moved his capital to Oxford, even Christ Church, the largest of the colleges, was not spacious enough for both him and the queen, who had to take up residence at Merton instead. Coughton consisted of a single small quadrangle on a site so cramped that even the kitchen was outside the moat, and it was 27 miles west of Dunsmore Heath, where the insurgents were to muster under cover of a hunt. It seems an unlikely nerve-centre for a rebellion. But there is another possible scenario.

In 1601 three of the five original plotters (Catesby, Thomas Percy and John Wright) had been implicated in the attempted rebellion of the Earl of Essex, and their planning must have been shaped by that experience. As before, there must be a commander with a famous name, like Essex, who is at least a peer, preferably an earl. He must be sympathetic to Catholics, out of favour at court and, in view of Catesby's well-known instinct for keeping things within the family, related to one of the original five. Near Coombe Abbey there must also be somewhere to serve as the base for an army and as a dramatic and symbolic setting for the young queen. All of these conditions are met by Kenilworth Castle, and by Sir Robert Dudley (1574–1649), who was the surviving son of the Elizabethan Earl of Leicester, step-brother (some said half-brother) to Essex and husband of Alice Leigh, the sister of Catesby's wife Catherine Leigh. In 1594 he had been the first Englishman to explore the Orinoco (in search of El Dorado) and in 1596

---

[3] This section is adapted and developed from my 'The Plot in Warwickshire and Worcestershire', *Midland Catholic History*, 12 (2006): 16–32.

he had gone with Essex on the expedition to Cadiz. In 1604 he began a suit in Star Chamber, claiming Warwick Castle and the earldoms of Leicester (as heir to his father) and of Warwick (as heir to his uncle Ambrose). His claim was supported by the Howards (the Earl of Northampton and the Lord Admiral, who was Dudley's uncle), but opposed by Robert Cecil, Earl of Salisbury, between whose father, Lord Burghley, and Dudley's there had been a long rivalry. In May 1605 the claim was rejected because of the doubtful validity of Leicester's marriage to Dudley's mother Lady Douglas Sheffield (the Admiral's sister). James I remained grateful to Essex for promoting his claim to the English throne, and if Leicester's second marriage was valid, then his third, to Essex's mother, was bigamous and she would lose her jointure. Attorney General Coke had declared that Dudley's witnesses were 'not worth a frieze jerkin', and in 1604 the king had pre-empted the legal decision by granting Warwick Castle (though not the earldom) to Sir Fulke Greville (1561–1628) of Beauchamp Court, a mile south of Coughton.[4] In addition, Dudley arguably had a better claim than Lord Harington both to the 'governorship' of the young princess and to Coombe Abbey itself, which had belonged to his grandfather, John Dudley, Earl of Warwick and Duke of Northumberland.[5]

Dudley did, however, have possession of Kenilworth Castle under the will of his father, who had transformed it into a great Renaissance palace and four times entertained Elizabeth I there, most famously during the 17 days of 'princely pleasures' in 1575. The Jesuit Oswald Tesimond, who was at Coughton on 6 November, stated that Guy Fawkes and two or three others surveyed 'suitable sites for building fortifications' in case the rising turned into a civil war, and that they consulted experts in Flanders on this point.[6] This precaution was also a consequence of the Plotters' previous experience: in 1604–05 Thomas Percy was constable of Alnwick and Warkworth castles, and in 1601 Essex had been forced to surrender when Essex House in the Strand was bombarded by a force led by the Lord Admiral and including Sir Fulke Greville and Lord Compton of Compton Wynyates.[7] Coughton was no more defensible, as was to be shown in 1643, when the defenders vainly hung bedding out of the windows to deaden the impact of the Royalist cannonade. But Kenilworth, unlike many castles, was still a formidable fortress, protected by the great

---

[4] For Greville's previous support of Essex and his removal from the Treasurership of the Navy in 1604 see Ronald A. Rebholz, *The Life of Sir Fulke Greville, First Lord Brooke* (Oxford, 1971), pp. 99, 120, 123–4.

[5] *VCH Warwickshire*, vol. 6, p. 73.

[6] Oswald Tesimond, *Narrative of the Gunpowder Plot*, ed. Francis Edwards (London, 1973), p. 102.

[7] Rebholz, *Life of Sir Fulke Greville*, p. 124.

artificial mere which had defied the besiegers for nine months in 1266 and been the setting for much of the pageantry of 1575. Leicester had kept an artillery train there, as well as powder and a great stock of firearms and armour. For Catesby's purposes, nothing better could possibly have been devised, and there were precedents which would have been familiar to him and Dudley. In 1553 the coup by Dudley's grandfather had been foiled when Queen Mary set up her standard at Framlingham Castle in Suffolk (which had belonged to the Howards until 1546 and was restored to them in 1613). The Throckmorton Plot of 1583 had turned on an invading force to be quartered at Arundel Castle (which, of course, still belongs to the Howards).[8] And, strategy apart, the symbolism of another Earl of Leicester entertaining another Queen Elizabeth at Kenilworth would have created an immensely potent image in favour of the revolution.

On 2 July 1605, however, Dudley went abroad on a passport for three years,[9] taking with him, disguised as a page, Elizabeth Southwell (1585/6–1631), who was a maid of honour to the Queen and a grand-daughter of the Lord Admiral.[10] There he proclaimed himself a Catholic, got his marriage to Alice Leigh annulled, married Elizabeth, entered the service of Ferdinand I, Grand Duke of Tuscany, and was created Earl of Warwick and Duke of Northumberland in the peerage of the Holy Roman Empire. He also became involved in the tangled dispute between English priests, known as the 'Appellant Controversy'. On 21 May 1606 Robert Moore of Dummer in Hertfordshire, a suspected recusant, was examined about his contacts with Dudley and with the Jesuit Fr Robert Persons and Sir Francis Roper in Rome.[11] On 2 June 1606 Dudley's mother warned him against some 'unquiet priests abroad', who, to her knowledge, were reporting back on him and others to the English government; on 26 November 1606 Dudley himself reported a conversation with a Scottish priest named Fraser, who was a friend of the Appellant Christopher Bagshaw and had revealed the Appellants' plans to him.[12] It is odd that he should so quickly

---

[8] Cf. John Bossy, *Under the Molehill: An Elizabethan Spy Story* (New Haven and London, 2001), pp. 76–7, and my review in *Recusant History*, 28 (2006–07): 159–61.

[9] *CSPD, 1603–10*, p. 225.

[10] Bernard *Burke, A Genealogical History of the Dormant, Abeyant, Forfeited, and Extinct Peerages of the British Empire* (London, 1866), p. 287; James Balfour Paul, *The Scots Peerage* (9 vols, Edinburgh, 1904–14), vol. 2, pp. 441–2; *The Visitation of Norfolk in the year 1563*, ed. G.H. Dashwood et al. (Norwich, 1878), pp. 125–7.

[11] *CSPD, 1603–10*, p. 317 (SP 14/21/26).

[12] Both statements in *Letters of Thomas Fitzherbert, 1608–10*, ed. Leo Hicks, CRS, 41 (London, 1948), p. 12n, quoting Archivium Vaticanum, Borghese II, 448, ad. fols 354, 428. It was Bagshaw who in 1574 had got Persons sacked from his fellowship at Balliol and had the bells of St Mary Magdalen's rung in celebration: J.H. Pollen (ed.), 'Father Persons' Memoirs (concluded)', in *Miscellanea IV*, CRS, 4 (London, 1906), pp. 17–18, 21–2.

become embroiled in this quarrel, unless he had already been in touch with the Jesuits in England.

Meanwhile, when he did not return, another commander would have to be found, and that explains the late and unsuitable choice of Sir Everard, who, for his own household and Garnet's, would then want a house well away from London (so not Gayhurst) and well away from the action at Kenilworth. In his own words,

> Catesby advised [him] to seek out some convenient house in Warwickshire or Worcestershire where [he] might live this winter, the better thereby to be able to protect himself upon any occasion and do good to the cause, having most assistance in those parts. According to which direction [he] did borrow a house from Thomas Throckmorton for one month, purposing to take it longer or to enquire out some other (if that were not to be had), if [Lady Digby] should like to live there.[13]

Catesby could still hope to use the Castle and its armoury: it still belonged to Dudley and its officers were still Dudley's men. Even after the Plot, its confiscation was a slow procedure. On 2 July 1606, the stewardship of the manor of Kenilworth was granted to Sir Robert Sidney, who had already been created Viscount Lisle (a Warwick title) and was later created Earl of Leicester.[14] On 2 February 1607 Dudley's passport was revoked, on suspicion of disloyal conduct. But it was not until 10 September 1609 that a Crown survey was made of the castle and manor, and not until 11 August 1610 that Dudley's lands were leased to Sir Richard Verney, Edward Boughton and William Barnes.[15] Sir Richard (1564–1630), of Compton Verney in Warwickshire, was sheriff in 1605 and his wife Margaret (1561–1631) was a sister of Sir Fulke Greville, but in 1617 their son Greville (1586–1642) married Catherine Southwell of Woodrising in Norfolk, a sister of Elizabeth Southwell, Dudley's second wife.[16] Perhaps contact was maintained on the distaff side between Warwickshire and Tuscany. The final twist did not come until 1644, when Charles I created Alice Dudley a duchess in her own right. This unprecedented honour is

---

[13] Godfrey Anstruther, *Vaux of Harrowden* (Newport, 1953), p. 280 (SP 14/16/94). According to Tesimond, *Narrative*, arms had to be assembled at 'the place where they would set up headquarters' (p. 98), but John Grant also needed arms at Norbrook because he was to organise the force to capture the Princess (p. 100), though Digby would *lead* it (p. 105).

[14] *CSPD, 1603–10*, p. 323.

[15] Ibid., pp. 347, 543, 628 (SP 14/ 26/41; 48/26; 57/15).

[16] *Visitation of Norfolk 1563*, p. 128. In June 1606 Verney complained to the Earl of Salisbury that his 'extraordinary charge' at the time of the Gunpowder Plot had been ignored and 'favour ... denied me': *Calendar of the Manuscripts of the Most Honourable the Marquis of Salisbury* (24 vols, London, 1883–1976), vol. 18, p. 156.

sometimes said to have been compensation for the Crown's failure to pay her the purchase price of £14,500 for the castle.[17] But, legally, Alice was merely the abandoned wife of a knight, while the Earl of Worcester at Raglan Castle, who contributed nearly £1,000,000 to the Royalist cause, was only raised to marquis for it. There must therefore have been some other reason. Was it Alice who warned Harington to move the Princess from Coombe Abbey to within the walls of Coventry?[18]

Garnet at Coughton

How did the Jesuit Henry Garnet come to be at Coughton with Lady Digby? This was a question which he himself did not want to be asked. In a letter written from the Tower and in 'interlocutions' with Oldcorne there, he noted:

> The time of my coming to Coughton is a great presumption, but all Catholics know it was a necessity ... There is one special thing of which I doubted they would have taken an exact account of me: *id est*, of the causes of my coming to Coughton, which indeed would have bred a great suspicion of the matter... I was prest again with Coughton, which I most feared, questioning me of my times of coming thither, the place at such a time, and the companie.[19]

For an attempted explanation it is necessary to go back a couple of months. Until August 1605 Garnet had a small house in Thames Street, near the Tower, and two houses outside London: White Webbs in Enfield Chase and the manor house of Erith on the Kentish side of the Thames estuary. But both of these had come under suspicion.[20] Since White Webbs was only two miles from the Earl of Salisbury's great house at Theobalds Park, it is remarkable that Garnet had been able to use it for 5 years. So he decided to fill in the late summer, and take a holiday, by

---

[17] VCH *Warwickshire*, vol. 6, p. 138; Simon Adams, 'Dudley, Sir Robert (1574–1649)', *ODNB*.

[18] George Blacker Morgan, *The Great English Treason for Religion for Religion known as the Gunpowder Plot* (2 vols, London, 1931–32), vol. 2, pp. 199–200, prints a letter (SP 14/216/22) informing Harington that the Plotters had taken horses from the castle stables in Warwick at about three on the morning of 6 November. But by itself this did not constitute any threat to the princess.

[19] *Records of the English Province of the Society of Jesus*, ed. Henry Foley (7 vols, London, 1875–83), vol. 4, pp. 84, 150, 152 (SP 14/19/11; 18/117, 122). For Garnet's letters (to Anne Vaux) see Anstruther, *Vaux*, pp. 343–50.

[20] Anstruther, *Vaux*, pp. 275–6; Philip Caraman, *Henry Garnet and the Gunpowder Plot* (London, 1964), p. 324.

visiting St Winifred's Well in North Wales with a party of nearly thirty.[21] During the 16 days that this took they stayed, both going and coming, at Daventry (which probably means with Lady Catesby at Ashby St Ledgers, near Daventry); at Norbrook with the Grants; at Huddington with the Wintours; and at Kinlet, just into Shropshire, with the Lacons.[22] When he reached Gayhurst on the return journey, about 13 September, the Digbys invited him to stay there.[23] Six weeks later, when Sir Everard borrowed Coughton, Garnet still had nowhere else to go and so, apparently, had to move there with Lady Digby, though he 'perceaved also an intention in [Sir Everard] to draw us to that country for their owne projects'.[24] But if Thomas Throckmorton was willing to harbour Garnet at Coughton, why not at Weston Underwood, which is only three miles from Gayhurst? And if Garnet perceived an ulterior motive in the invitation (perhaps when he discovered how far from Coughton the hunting match would be), why could he not go to any of the other Midland houses where he had been welcome in September, especially Kinlet?

In June 1606 the informer William Udall, who had been a servant of Essex and of Sir Everard Digby, was sure that Tesimond was in hiding at Kinlet.[25] During the pilgrimage itself, 'Ambrose Rookwood and his wife [had been] at Mass [there] … and some three or four young men which were said to be priests, the one whereof was named Rookwood'.[26] This may have been Robert Rookwood, Ambrose's brother, who had just returned to England and was described in 1624 as 'a little black fellow, very compt and gallant, lodging about the midst of *Drury-lane*, acquainted with collapsed Ladies'.[27] But he may also have been Garnet's nephew St Thomas

---

[21] He left White Webbs on 29 August: John Gerard, *Narrative of the Gunpowder Plot*, in *The Condition of Catholics under James I*, ed. John Morris (London, 1872), p. 78; cf. Caraman, *Garnet*, p. 324; Anstruther, *Vaux*, p. 276.

[22] The itinerary can be reconstructed from the examinations of two servants, James Garvey and William Handy: SP 14/216/121, 153, both printed in M. Hodgetts, 'Shropshire Priests in 1605', *Worcestershire Recusant*, 47 (June 1986): 27–31.

[23] Lady Digby had been one of the pilgrims. On arriving at Rushton in Northamptonshire on the way back they found that Sir Thomas Tresham had just died, on 11 September: Anstruther, *Vaux*, p. 277.

[24] Garnet's 'Second Declaration', 10 March 1606, Hatfield House, Cecil Papers 110/30: printed by S.R. Gardiner in *English Historical Review*, 3 (1888), p. 518. Cf. Gerard, *Narrative*, p. 79; Caraman, *Garnet*, p. 325. 'Apparently' because this declaration may have been tampered with: Anstruther, *Vaux*, p. 351.

[25] *CSPD, 1603–10*, p. 252 (SP 14/216/47 = SP 14/216/75/15); Philip R. Harris, 'The Reports of William Udall', *Recusant History*, 8 (1965–66), 217, 220, 224.

[26] SP 14/216/151, in Hodgetts, 'Shropshire Priests', 27.

[27] Godfrey Anstruther, *The Seminary Priests* (4 vols, Ware and Great Wakering, 1968–77), vol. 2, p. 271; *John Gee's Foot out of the Snare (1624)*, ed. T.H.B.M. Harmsen (Nijmegen, 1992), p. 253.

Garnet, alias Rookwood, who was executed in 1608, having been arrested, according to one account, on his way to the Rookwoods' at Coldham in Suffolk.[28] Whichever he was, he had clearly come from Coldham with Ambrose and Elizabeth Rookwood to Huddington, where they stayed until Michaelmas before moving to Clopton House, near Stratford-upon-Avon.[29] Moreover, at White Webbs Henry Garnet passed as 'Mr Meysey' and Anne Vaux, who kept house for him, as 'Mrs Perkins'.[30] Three miles south of Kinlet is Shakenhurst Park, the home of Thomas Meysey and his wife Susan, daughter of Henry Perkins of East Ilsley in Berkshire.[31] Afterwards it was reported that early in November Anne Vaux had been at Hartley Court in Berkshire, which was close to Burghfield, another house of the Meyseys, and to Ufton Court, the main house of the Perkinses.[32] Ufton itself had been searched in 1586, when Francis Perkins was 'at Illesley, tenne miles of, a-hawking' but a Mr Measea, 'a man ill-affected', and his wife were lodging at Ufton; in 1599 it was searched again, on a warrant for the arrest of Garnet and his fellow Jesuit, John Gerard.[33] Had Garnet and Anne Vaux met the Meyseys at Kinlet and asked them to find a house in Berkshire? On 4 October, four days before Catesby inveigled Digby into the Plot, Garnet wrote to Persons from Gayhurst that 'we are to go within a few days nearer London; yet are we unprovided of a house'.[34] But, if he did have to leave Gayhurst, it is puzzling that he could not go to Kinlet, rather than to Coughton, which was not on the itinerary to Holywell.

However that may be, it is certain that on 29 October Lady Digby set out for Coughton. With her went Garnet, Nicholas Owen, the Digbys'

---

[28] Foley, *Society of Jesus*, vol. 5, p. 541; cf. vol. 2, pp. 475 ff.

[29] Hugh Ross Williamson, *The Gunpowder Plot* (London, 1951), pp. 129, 141.

[30] Anstruther, *Vaux*, pp. 255, 283, 285.

[31] Treadway Russell Nash, *Collections for the History of Worcestershire* (2 vols, London, 1781), vol. 1, pedigree between pp. 54 and 55; cf. John Hobson Matthews (ed.), 'Records Relating to Catholicism in the South Wales Marches', *Miscellanea II*, CRS, 2 (London, 1906), p. 295; *Recusant Documents from the Ellesmere Manuscripts*, ed. Anthony G. Petti, CRS, 60 (London, 1968), pp. 130, 144 n.7; Hugh Bowler (ed.), *Recusant Roll No. 3 (1594–1595) and Recusant Roll No. 4 (1595–1596): An Abstract in English*, CRS, 61 (London, 1970), pp. 131–2. In 1619 their son Matthias married Frances Middlemore of Edgbaston near Birmingham; cf. Michael Hodgetts, 'The Holtes of Aston Hall, Birmingham', *Midland Catholic History*, 9 (2002–03), 23.

[32] *Calendar of Salisbury Manuscripts*, vol. 17, p. 500; Anstruther, *Vaux*, p. 281. For Hartley Court and Hugh Speke, from whom Anne Vaux borrowed it, see N. Pevsner, *The Buildings of England: Berkshire* (1966), p. 216; *VCH Berkshire*, vol. 3, pp. 261, 265.

[33] Michael Hodgetts, 'Elizabethan Priest-Holes – II: Ufton, Mapledurham, Compton Wynyates', *Recusant History*, 12 (1973–74): 100–13.

[34] Printed in *Dodd's Church History of England*, ed. Mark Aloysius Tierney (5 vols, London, 1839–43), vol. 4, pp. cii–cvi; cf. Anstruther, *Vaux*, p. 279; Caraman, *Garnet*, p. 325.

Jesuit chaplain John Percy, Anne Vaux and her sister Eleanor Brooksby, the Digbys' children, most of their servants, Sir Everard's horses and greyhounds, and a cart containing 'great provision of armour and shot'.[35] This cavalcade could not have travelled the 50 miles to Coughton in a day: they probably stayed the night of 29 October at Ashby St Ledgers (did they leave the cart there?) and arrived at Coughton on Wednesday 30 October. Sir Everard himself and seven servants stayed behind to close up Gayhurst: it was not until Monday 4 November that they left and rode to the Red Lion at Dunchurch, where they stayed the night.

None of the examinations suggest that any of Thomas Throckmorton's household were at Coughton to receive the party. But it seems unlikely that the keys were left under the mat for them to let themselves in. Arrangements must have been made about fires, bedding, close-stools or garderobes, laundry, the dairy and the kitchen (and this was just before the Martinmas slaughter and salting of livestock). By the first evening the servants would need plate, wines, spices and other valuable items. To allot rooms to the company, the priests and the ladies would need to know the locations of the chapel and priest-holes, and where to find, or hide, vestments and church plate.[36] This information might have been supplied by a trusted servant. During the search at Hindlip, for example, Sir Henry Bromley wrote to Salisbury about two servants to be examined there: 'the on is the horskeper [William Glandish] that receaveth all strangers' horses; the other is on [Edward] Gerrard, Mrs Dorritie Abington's man, that ever attendeth on thes prests, bringeth them up thear vittayles and hideth them when thear is occasion'.[37] After their arrest, Oldcorne stated that on 19 January, on the way back from Evesham, he and Garnet met with an old man, sometime servant unto old Mr [John] Habington, on horseback also; and three or four miles before they came to Mr Habington's house, the old man took their horses, and they went there on foot. And when they came to the house, they were carried into a gallery by that old man; and because they were afraid to be troubled, they were showed to the place into which after they went.[38]

---

[35] Williamson, *Gunpowder Plot*, pp. 161–2.

[36] By the early 1590s John Gerard (1564–1637) found vestments ready in most houses that he went to: *John Gerard: The Autobiography of an Elizabethan*, ed. Philip Caraman (London, 1951, 1956; new impression with introduction by Michael Hodgetts, 2006), p. 40. Those at Coughton would include the cope now on display there and the chasuble now at Cleobury Mortimer: Paul Sidoli, 'The Catherine of Aragon Chasuble from Mawley Hall', *Cleobury Chronicles*, 4 (1996): 35–44.

[37] Foley, *Society of Jesus*, vol. 4, p. 76 (=SP 14/18/52); cf. pp. 76–7 (SP 14/18/64/i).

[38] Ibid., pp. 223–4 (SP 14/216/187).

This was confirmed by Ashley, who stated that 'a servant of Mr Habington's called Robert brought this examinant into the Gallery, where [Oldcorne] his master and Garnet the Jesuit were together'.[39] So, although Garnet may have known Coughton since 1586,[40] it is likely that someone like Gerrard was there to receive Lady Digby.

Who this might have been is suggested by Garnet's later request for 'some consideration of Mr Yates for his horse he gave me'.[41] One of Agnes Throckmorton's household at Moor Hall, two miles from Coughton, was a J[ames?] Yate. On 11 July 1608 he wrote to Elizabeth Russell at Little Malvern Court in Worcestershire about a hat left to her late husband and some books of Aristotle left to her sons by her old friend Mr Foxe and then in the custody of 'one Mr Browne out of Buckinghamshire'. 'If', he added, 'you send yor mind to Mrs Throckmorton's at Moorsall any time before St James tide, yor answeare shall bee sent unto him'.[42] Elizabeth was the eldest sister of Humphrey Pakington of Harvington Hall, near Kidderminster;[43] her husband Henry had been a colleague of the Jesuit martyr Edmund Campion at St John's College, Oxford, and principal of Gloucester Hall. When Campion was arrested at Lyford in 1581, a don named Yate was there, together with Henry Russell and Justinian Stubbs, who was later tutor to the sons of Henry and Elizabeth Russell.[44] Mr Yate of Moor Hall may not have been the same man, but he could have been at Coughton on 30 October and later supplied Garnet with the horse.[45]

On the other hand, there is a list of Thomas Throckmorton's servants with a note which begins: 'According to our charge we have demanded a note of the names of all Mr Throckmorton's servants and other recusants'.[46] This was probably made in 1593, when Coughton was searched and the

[39] Ibid., p. 269 (SP 14/216/194).

[40] Michael Hodgetts, *Secret Hiding-Places* (Dublin, 1989), p. 37.

[41] Foley, *Society of Jesus*, vol. 4, p. 104 (SP 14/20/11).

[42] Worcestershire Record Office, BA 1546, 899:169, C. 8. This letter is included in a volume of *Little Malvern Letters, 1482–1737*, which I am editing for publication by the CRS in 2010.

[43] Harvington was owned by the Throckmortons from 1696 to 1923; the portraits and the original great staircase from the Hall are now at Coughton.

[44] *APC*, vol. 13, p. 170.

[45] In a later letter to Anne Vaux, Garnet 'desyred to know … what money Richard [Blount] hath of ye Society and of ye grocer's money and the hundreth pound that was given me of curtesy' (Foley, *Society of Jesus*, vol. 4, p. 108 = SP 14/216/242). Was 'ye grocer' John Grove, who came from Alveley, near Bridgnorth (and Kinlet), a member of the Grocers' Company and acted as banker for Russell, Pakington and other recusants? Cf. John J. LaRocca (ed.), *Jacobean Recusant Rolls for Middlesex: An Abstract in English*, CRS, 76 (London, 1997), pp. 39–41, 111–12.

[46] Throckmorton MSS, Box 86, Folder 1, no. 11.

Privy Council ordered that Mary Arden, Thomas Throckmorton's sister, was to be imprisoned and examined, along with 'the rest of her servauntes whom you shall thincke fitt to be restrained'.⁴⁷ It names 23 men and three women; since none of them are in the Recusant Rolls for 1592–96 or in the list of 1592 to be considered below, it may refer to Weston Underwood. But the first of them was George Throckmorton, and in 1605–06 a George Throckmorton was returned as a recusant from Temple Grafton, which is four miles from Coughton.⁴⁸ It might have been fitting for Lady Digby and the Vaux sisters (as daughters of a peer) to be received by one of the family, rather than by a servant.

On Friday 1 November, All Saints' Day, Garnet said Mass in the Tower Room at Coughton, and preached on a couplet from the hymn of the day, *Gentem auferte perfidam Credentium de finibus*: 'Cast out the tribe of treachery From the believers' territory'. This was construed at his trial as inciting treason, and by the historian Hugh Ross Williamson as 'one last effort to prevent the "stir"'.⁴⁹ But it is hard to make sense of either reading, since the congregation consisted only of the three ladies, Nicholas Owen and three or four other servants.⁵⁰ Catesby and Digby, says Garnet, had 'promised to come to us at Allhalowtide, but they broake; and I assuredly (if they had come) had entred into the matter with Mr Catesby and perhapps might have hindered all'.⁵¹ Had he prepared a sermon aimed at them, which they were not there to hear? The only other priest recorded at Coughton that day was John Percy. So who usually served there, and where was he? Or did local Catholics go to Mass at Moor Hall, not at Coughton?

Soon after dawn on Wednesday 6 November, Catesby's servant Thomas Bates arrived with the letter from Catesby and Digby. He handed it over in the hall, which was probably on the east side of the quadrangle, where there is now a gap between the two wings.⁵² While he was reading it, Tesimond came in and asked what the news was. Bates heard the answer:

---

⁴⁷   *APC*, vol. 24, p. 148 (where 'Laughton' should read 'Coughton').

⁴⁸   The 'Second Certificate' (1592) mentions Mary Arden and four servants: Michael Hodgetts, 'A Certificate of Warwickshire Recusants, 1592: I', *Worcs. Recusant*, 5 (1965), 30. There is no entry for Coughton in the earlier list (also of 1592): John Tobias, 'New Light on Recusancy in Warwickshire, 1592', *Worcs. Recusant*, 36 (1980): 8–27.

⁴⁹   Williamson, *Gunpowder Plot*, p. 162.

⁵⁰   Examinations of Owen (Foley, *Society of Jesus*, vol. 4, pp. 259 = SP 14/216/194); Handy (Michael Hodgetts, 'Shropshire Priests in 1605', *Worcs. Recusant* 47, p. 27 = SP 14/216/121); and Michael Rapier (*CSPD, 1603–10*, p. 261 = SP 14/216/111).

⁵¹   Garnet's 'Second Declaration', in Samuel Rawson Gardiner (ed.), 'Two Declarations of Garnet Relating to the Gunpowder Plot', *English Historical Review*, 3 (1888), 516 (= Salisbury MSS 110/30).

⁵²   *CSPD, 1603–10*, p. 279 (SP 14/216/166).

'They would have blown up the Parliament House and were discovered, and we all utterly undone.' Then Bates asked Tesimond to ride with him to Robert Wintour's house at Huddington, eight miles away, where the conspirators intended to halt.[53] A few hours later Lady Digby sent four of Sir Everard's great horses to Huddington and

> willed [James Garvey] to put on his boots and to ride with the groom, called Anthony [Brightwell], and with one Mr Shelton, servant to Sir Francis Fortescue, whom he had seen often at his master's house; which Shelton came on Monday before to Coughton. Saith the said Shelton, after the traitors were come to Robert Wintour's house that Wednesday night, rode away with another gentleman unknown, taking their leave of the traitors openly. But saith that at their first coming to Wintour's house the house was presently guarded with shot, as he and others could not escape.[54]

The 'unknown gentleman' must have been Tesimond, who rode the four miles from Huddington to Hindlip, hoping to recruit Thomas Habington to the cause. But who was 'Mr Shelton'? Sir Francis Fortescue of Salden, ten miles south of Gayhurst, was a Church Papist, but his wife (Grace Manners) had been converted by John Gerard in 1600 and the couple harboured a Jesuit, Anthony Hoskins.[55] Their son Adrian (1601–53) also became a Jesuit and was chaplain to Sir George Wintour at Huddington, where he is commemorated by a fulsome brass in the church. Adrian's sister Dorothy married Thomas Throckmorton's grandson Sir Robert, who succeeded in 1615. Sir Francis was the son of Sir John Fortescue, Chancellor of the Exchequer, who may also have been a secret Catholic.[56] Sir John's steward, John Robinson, sent his sons to the Jesuit school at St Omer in France; one of them, another John, became the tenant of the Blackfriars Gatehouse in 1613, when Shakespeare bought it from John Fortescue of Lordington in Sussex, Sir John's nephew and former 'servant'. In 1599 a priest, Richard Dudley, was reported to be 'in Robinson's house...

---

[53] Foley, *Society of Jesus*, vol. 4, pp. 107 (SP 14/216/241), 145 (SP 14/18/86), 146 (SP 14/18/87), 155 (SP 14/19/40), 188 (British Library, MS Add. 21203, Plut. Ciii.F: Garnet's trial). John Grant's brother-in-law Henry Morgan saw Tesimond both at Norbrook and at Huddington, wearing 'coloured satin done with gold lace': *CSPD 1603–10*, p. 279 (SP 14/216/165 and 165/i).

[54] SP 14/216/153, in Hodgetts, 'Shropshire Priests', 30–31. For Anthony Brightwell see Blacker Morgan, *Great English Treason*, vol. 2, p. 216.

[55] Caraman, *John Gerard*, pp. 161–3, 252. But John Percy was still Lady Fortescue's spiritual director in 1609: ibid., p. 163.

[56] Tesimond describes a search at Fortescue's house in the Wardrobe in March 1598: *Troubles of our Catholic Forefathers*, ed. John Morris (3 vols, London, 1872), vol. 1, pp. 144–7, 174.

over against Sir John's door'.⁵⁷ On the night of 5–6 November 1605, Chief Justice Popham reported to Salisbury that 'Sundry letters lately sent over are yet Remayning at fortescue's house by the Wadrop [Wardrobe], but yt wylbe hard to fynd any thing in that house.'⁵⁸ So why did a servant of Sir Francis who had 'often' been at Gayhurst come to Coughton on 4 November and go on to Huddington and Hindlip?

Was he the Jesuit lay-brother Hugh Sheldon (c.1566–1612), who in 1599 had been arrested with Nicholas Owen at Kirby Hall in Northamptonshire? Though banished in 1603, Sheldon seems to have been back in England by 1606,⁵⁹ and he may have been a connection of the Throckmortons: he was born in Staffordshire, and Walter Fowler of St Thomas's Priory, Stafford, had married Mary Sheldon, daughter of Anne Throckmorton and of Ralph Sheldon of Beoley (1537–1613), who also owned Lower Skilts, four miles from Coughton.⁶⁰ Another Jesuit brother, Richard Fulwood, was 'bidden [by Garnet] to come down to Coughton' and 'went from him two or three days before he went into the hole at Hindlip'.⁶¹ In other words, he was with Garnet from, at latest, 4 December until 17 or 18 January. Fulwood was from 'Weston in Warwickshire' (probably Weston-by-Cherington in Long Compton, where the Sheldons had another mansion), and was employed by Garnet to arrange passages for young men going to the colleges abroad.⁶² If he was at Coughton and Hindlip, so may Hugh Sheldon have been.

Next day, Thursday 7 November, two priests, Thomas Strange and William Singleton, and five laymen were arrested at Kenilworth while,

---

⁵⁷ E.K. Chambers, *William Shakespeare* (2 vols, Oxford, 1930), vol. 1, pp. 166, 169; cf. Anstruther, *Seminary Priests*, vol. 1, pp. 106–7; Michael Hodgetts, 'A Topographical Index of Hiding-Places – III', *Recusant History*, 27 (2004–05), 494–5.

⁵⁸ SP 14/216/10, quoted in H.H. Spink, *The Gunpowder Plot and Lord Mounteagle's Letter* (London, 1902), p. 311; cf. *CSPD, 1603–10*, p. 240.

⁵⁹ Caraman, *John Gerard*, pp. 148–9, 158–60, 250; Foley, *Society of Jesus*, vol. 1, p. 63 (not by name) and vol. 7/2, p. 705; John Morris, *The Life of Father John Gerard* (London, 1881), pp. 331–3.

⁶⁰ Thomas M. McCoog, *English and Welsh Jesuits, 1555–1650: II – G–Z*, CRS, 75 (London, 1995), p. 292; Patrick Ryan et al. (eds), 'Diocesan Returns of Recusants for England and Wales, 1577', in *Miscellanea XII*, CRS, 22 (London, 1921), p. 92n; *VCH Warwickshire*, vol. 3, pp. 177–8 with a plan; cf. E.A.B. Barnard, *The Sheldons* (Cambridge, 1936), pp. 39, 16.

⁶¹ Foley, *Society of Jesus*, vol. 4, p. 193 (SP 14/20/44).

⁶² Ibid, vol. 1, p. 488 (SP 12/248/40); Brendan Minney, O.S.B., 'The Sheldons of Beoley', *Worcs. Recusant*, 5 (May 1965): 1–17; *VCH Warwickshire*, vol. 5, p. 55; Edgar E. Estcourt and John Orlebar Payne, *The English Catholic Nonjurors of 1715* (London, 1885), p. 279. Cf. Foley, *Society of Jesus*, vol. 1, p. 499; Caraman, *John Gerard*, p. 240 (SP 14/20/47); Anthony Kenny (ed.), *The Responsa Scholarum of the English College, Rome: I – 1598–1621*, CRS, 54 (London, 1962), pp. 76, 78.

according to John Gerard, trying to reach Garnet. They had come from Harrowden in Northamptonshire, where Elizabeth Vaux, Anne and Eleanor's sister-in-law, also harboured Gerard himself and another priest, Thomas Laithwaite.[63] On 5–6 November, Popham had already named four Jesuits as implicated: Gerard, Garnet, Tesimond and Strange.[64] But Strange, though tortured, was never brought to trial, either as a priest or for the Plot: in 1611 he was banished or allowed to escape and spent the rest of his life in the Spanish Netherlands.[65] Moreover, Gerard's account of the arrests omits as much as it records.

Near Harrowden, at Irthlingborough, the Vauxes had a dower-house, which Elizabeth had lent to Henry and Dorothy Huddleston of Sawston, near Cambridge. On Monday 4 November, Henry met the conspirators Catesby, Thomas Wintour and John Wright at 'Purney's house behind St Clement's', where he had gone to pick up his cloak and other items. That evening, he and his man, William Thornborough, left London and stayed the night at The Bull in St Albans, where they met Sir Francis Fortescue. Early on 5 November, they were overtaken by John Wright and Catesby and rode with them as far as Brickhill. There two of the other plotters, Thomas Percy and Christopher Wright, caught up with them, and Huddleston and Thornborough left the Watling Street and galloped to Harrowden to give the news to Mrs Vaux and the priests. That evening, Francis Swetnam, Mrs Vaux's baker, went to Wellingborough with Strange's servant Matthew Batty (who had also been a servant of Lord Monteagle) to buy 20 pounds of gunpowder. Next day, Wednesday 6 November, or so they claimed, Huddleston fetched Dorothy back to Harrowden from Irthlingborough, and Batty took the gunpowder to Kettering, where he left it with a carrier to send down into Lancashire. Early on Thursday, Huddleston, Strange and Singleton supposedly left Harrowden with Batty and three other servants.[66] Laithwaite had already left, apparently on the Wednesday morning.[67] Perhaps Strange and Singleton had done so too. From Harrowden to Kenilworth, as the crow flies, is 35 miles. On horseback, through Northampton, Daventry, Southam and Warwick, it was forty-five, on a day of heavy rain when it took the Plotters sixteen

---

[63] Caraman, *John Gerard*, p. 195; A. Fraser, *The Gunpowder Plot* (London, 1996), pp. 93–4; Gerard, *Narrative*, p. 55.

[64] *CSPD, 1603–10*, p. 240 (SP 14/216/10).

[65] Foley, *Society of Jesus*, vol. 4, pp. 3–16; Anstruther, *Vaux*, pp. 300–310; Nadine and John Fendley, 'Thomas Strange, S.J., of Cirencester', *Journal of the Gloucestershire and North Avon Catholic History Society*, 26 (1995): 3–9.

[66] Anstruther, *Vaux*, pp. 300, 303–8, 313–14; *CSPD, 1603–10*, p. 256 (= SP 14/216/93).

[67] Caraman, *John Gerard*, p. 198.

hours to ride the thirty miles from Huddington to Holbeach. Had Strange and Singleton really left Harrowden on the Wednesday and stayed the night at Ashby St Ledgers? And were their tall stories of what happened on the Wednesday attempts to cover up that fact?[68]

Huddleston and Strange claimed to be making for Grove Park, Sir Robert Dormer's house near Warwick, which was plausible, since Dorothy Huddleston was a Dormer. From Grove Park, Strange had 'determined to have gone to [his] cousin Mr Thomas Habington' at Hindlip,[69] while Huddleston and Singleton 'should have gone to Farington in Lancashire', which was the Huddlestons' house in Penwortham near Preston.[70] But, 'coming within two miles of Warwick, they heard of the troubles at Warwick and found the gates of the town were shut, and thereupon they altered their journey and rode to Kenilworth', where about five o'clock 'they were apprehended'.[71] They were interrogated by the sheriff, Sir Richard Verney, who suspected that they were all priests but gave a pass to some of Sir Robert Dormer's men to take a letter to Dorothy.[72] The year before, a nephew of Sir Richard, Sir George Simeon of Baldwin Brightwell in Oxfordshire, had married Elizabeth Vaux's daughter Mary; and on 12 November Elizabeth wrote to Sir Richard asking for the prisoners' release, and giving detailed descriptions of them.[73] Sir Richard received her letter at Warwick the following evening and sent it straight up to Salisbury.[74] By February, Strange was in the Tower, where he was severely tortured and repeatedly examined by the Council; on at least one occasion, the king himself was present behind a curtain.[75]

Although Gerard says that all four wanted to reach Garnet, and that he himself had suggested that Laithwaite should try to do so, Kenilworth is not on the way from Warwick to Grove Park or Coughton.[76] Did Strange and his companions think that Garnet might be at Kenilworth Castle? And

---

[68] Dorothy was apparently not at Harrowden six days later: Anstruther, *Vaux*, p. 312.

[69] Strange's declaration of 13 March 1606: Foley, *Society of Jesus*, vol. 4, p. 15; Anstruther, *Vaux*, pp. 309–10 (SP 14/19/43; *CSPD 1603–10*, p. 300).

[70] Huddleston's examination, 6 December 1605: Anstruther, *Vaux*, pp. 307–9; Foley, *Society of Jesus*, vol. 4, pp. 10–11 (SP 14/17/13; *CSPD 1603–10*, p. 268); M.M.C. Calthrop (ed.), *Recusant Roll No. 1, 1592–3*, CRS, 18, p. 175.

[71] Foley, *Society of Jesus*, vol. 4, pp. 10–11.

[72] Anstruther, *Vaux*, pp. 304–6, 301.

[73] Cf. Michael Hodgetts, 'The Chimney Hide at Mapledurham', *Midland Catholic History*, 11 (2005), 19; Anstruther, *Vaux*, pp. 301–2.

[74] Anstruther, *Vaux*, p. 303.

[75] Foley, *Society of Jesus*, vol. 4, pp. 1–7, 11–15; Anstruther, *Vaux*, pp. 304–5, 306–10, 340–42. In the end, the king was satisfied that Strange was innocent, but by then he had been crippled for life by the torture (Foley, *Society of Jesus*, vol. 4, pp. 5–8).

[76] Caraman, *John Gerard*, pp. 198–9.

why was Laithwaite, whose story is even more remarkable than theirs, not with them? Early in August he had been condemned to death at the Exeter assizes. The sentence had been commuted on payment of a bribe by his brother, but the ship which was taking him into exile had been wrecked off Hurst Castle. For another bribe the captain had let him go, and he had made his way to Garnet, asked to join the Jesuits and been sent to join Gerard at Harrowden.[77] After leaving Harrowden on Wednesday 6 November he was rearrested – where is not recorded. He and his captors stopped at an inn, where he offered to take his horse down to the river to water it, leaving his cloak and sword behind on a bench. He then mounted and made his way back to Harrowden, where a search for Gerard was in progress and he was arrested yet again. He claimed to have been in London and to have spent the night of 12 November at The George in Dunstable, which should have been easy enough to check.[78] So he had been away for at least a week – and Dunstable is nearly as far south of Harrowden as Kenilworth is west. Had he gone to White Webbs, or to Lady Gray's at Brentford (whose 'servant' he was later said to have been)?[79]

Elizabeth Vaux has been thought naïve for appealing to Verney. Gerard calls him 'faithless' and says that he acted 'more like a Puritan, which he was, than a kinsman, as he should be'. Anstruther implies that the only ground for her request was the marriage of her daughter and his nephew.[80] But about 1592 the musician John Bolt (c.1563–1640) had left his post at court on becoming a Catholic, even though the queen offered to overlook his lapse. For two years he taught music in Catholic households which included Braddocks in Essex, where Gerard was then living, and 'Mr Verney his house' in Warwickshire, where Bolt 'went ... to teach Mr Bassett's children to sing and play on the virginals'.[81] He was threatened with torture by the notorious priest-hunter Richard Topcliffe but released at the intercession of Lady Penelope Rich, who was Essex's sister and a friend of Gerard. He went abroad in 1594 and was ordained at Douai in

---

[77] Foley, *Society of Jesus*, vol. 4, pp. 630–40. Since we have no date for either the reprieve or the shipwreck, we do not know whether Laithwaite met Garnet at White Webbs, at Gayhurst or at Coughton, or, therefore, how long he had been at Harrowden.

[78] Anstruther, *Vaux*, p. 316 (SP 12/118/20: *sic*: the document is misdated to 1577).

[79] Morris, *Life of Gerard*, p. 404 and n.1. Cf. Anstruther, *Vaux*, p. 383; Michael Hodgetts, 'A Topographical Index of Hiding-Places – II', *Recusant History*, 24 (1998–99), p. 27, no. 235; Hodgetts, 'A Topographical Index of Hiding–Places – III', *Recusant History*, 27 (2004–05), 492–3, no. 330; McCoog, *English and Welsh Jesuits: II – G–Z*, CRS, 75, p. 226; Anstruther, *Seminary Priests*, vol. 1, p. 204; Caraman, *John Gerard*, p. 198. For Singleton, see also Anstruther, *Seminary Priests*, vol. 1, p. 318.

[80] Gerard, *Narrative*, p. 140; Anstruther, *Vaux*, p. 301.

[81] Caraman, *John Gerard*, pp. 49, 55n, 230. For Bolt's examinations of 20–21 March 1593/4, see Morris, *Life of Gerard*, pp. 155–8 (= SP 12/248/37).

1605; in 1613 he attended the profession of Sister (later Prioress) Margaret Magdalen Throckmorton at St Monica's in Louvain and stayed there as chaplain and organist for the remainder of his life.[82] It is not clear why Bassett and his children were at Compton Verney, but they were a recusant family.[83] This precedent might have led Elizabeth Vaux to think that Verney would stretch a point. But on this occasion Verney's first concern would be to cover his own back.

Tesimond, however, records that Verney 'wondered not a little' about the Plotters' motives,[84] a remark which could imply a source within the household at Compton Verney. Tesimond's informants included Nicholas Hart (who said Mass for the hunting party at Dunchurch on 5 November and for the remaining conspirators at Huddington on 7 November) and a Mr Taylor, whose house at Kidderminster was searched, like Hindlip, on 20 January. Nearly a dozen times he gives as his source 'someone who found himself with these gentlemen' or a similar phrase, who was in fact Tesimond himself.[85] So his statement about Verney is also likely to be well founded. Even if Verney was a Puritan, his wife's physician was Justinian Stubbs, whose patients also included several daughters of the Catholic Earl of Worcester, and Mrs Cassandra Cassey and her daughter at Deerhurst in Gloucestershire. On 21 April 1608, writing from Deerhurst, Stubbs told Elizabeth Russell that he would be with her in eight or ten days, but that first, 'uppon Monday next, I am to ride to my Lady Verney in Warwickshire: she hath sent unto me twice'.[86] Perhaps Elizabeth Vaux had other reasons for thinking that Sir Richard might release his prisoners.

Lady Digby left Coughton on Sunday 10 November or Monday 11. The date is fixed by a letter written to Salisbury on Wednesday 13 November by William Tate from Harrowden, where he was conducting the search for John Gerard: 'There is neither armour nor stranger in the house. Sir Everard Digby's lady would in her return out of Warwickshire on Monday last (as we hear) have entreated a lodging for one night, and could not prevail.'[87] She went to London, discovering on the way that Gayhurst had been ruthlessly pillaged; it is not clear whether John Percy went with

---

[82] Anstruther, *Seminary Priests*, vol. 2, p. 32; *The Chronicle of the English Augustinian Canonesses Regular of the Lateran, at St Monica's in Louvain 1548 to 1625*, ed. Dom Adam Hamilton OSB (Edinburgh and London, 1904), p. 94.

[83] See *CSPD, 1591–4*, pp. 379–91 (SP 12/245/138); Anstruther, *Seminary Priests*, vol. 1, pp. 135–6; Foley, *Society of Jesus*, vol. 4, p. 49; vol. 2, p. 228 (SP 14/19/59).

[84] Tesimond, *Narrative*, p. 131.

[85] Ibid., pp. 82, 102, 105, 107, 109 (twice), 117, 120, 131, 192 131, 135 (Hart); cf. pp. 81, 99, 103, 104, 132.

[86] Worcester Record Office, BA 81, 705:24, 616 (1).

[87] Anstruther, *Vaux*, p. 312.

her.[88] But Garnet stayed at Coughton until 4 December, when, being 'in some distress' there, he accepted Oldcorne's offer of shelter at Hindlip.[89] (Was he under pressure to leave from Thomas, or Agnes, Throckmorton?) Clearly, at both houses he was still dealing with the business of the Jesuit mission, which would explain why after his arrest he was so anxious not to be interrogated about Coughton. Such enquiries might lead to the uncovering of his arrangements for placing and escorting priests, and to the imprisonment or death of those who harboured them. But it is still not clear why he had to go to Coughton in the first place.

The Rising in Warwickshire

'Whatever the truth about the mine or the gunpowder', wrote Hugh Ross Williamson, the rising in the Midlands 'undoubtedly existed and is the most important part of [the Plot]'.[90] But neither he nor his successor historians of Gunpowder Plot have given it more than a page or two, and the sources for it are so scrappy that the late Fr Francis Edwards, SJ, held that no rising was ever intended at all: the muster on Dunsmore Heath, he claimed, was merely a get-together of men who intended to serve in the English regiment then being raised for the Archduke's forces in Flanders.[91] Yet the precedent of the Essex Rebellion is worth considering: among those arrested for the Rising with Edward Throckmorton and Francis Smith of Wootton Wawen had been the Earls of Southampton and Rutland, two of Rutland's brothers (Francis and George Manners), Lord Sandys of The Vyne in Hampshire, Sir Henry and Sir Edward Bromley (who were first cousins of Sir Francis Fortescue) and Sir Christopher Blount (1555/6–1601). This last, a brother of Sir Edward Blount of Kidderminster, was a pupil of the future Cardinal Allen at Louvain and a student at Douai before marrying Leicester's widow Lettice Knollys and so becoming, like Leicester before him, stepfather to Essex.[92] The ramifications of the Powder Plot may have been even more extensive, and it is worth asking who in Warwickshire (apart from Dudley) might have been involved.

Only one of the hunting party on Dunsmore Heath stayed with the Plotters throughout their flight to Holbeach: John Grant's brother-in-law,

---

[88] Lady Digby to Salisbury, 3 December 1605, in ibid., pp. 324–5.
[89] Foley, *Society of Jesus*, vol. 4, pp. 225, 260 (SP 14/216/197, 194).
[90] Williamson, *Gunpowder Plot*, p. 124.
[91] Francis Edwards, SJ, *Guy Fawkes: The Real Story of the Gunpowder Plot?* (London, 1969).
[92] *Calendar of Salisbury Manuscripts*, vol. 11, pp. 86–8, 98, 102; Paul E.J. Hammer, 'Blount, Sir Christopher (1555/6–1601)', *ODNB*.

Henry Morgan.[93] Sir Robert Digby of Coleshill (1575–1618) not only left them but helped in the subsequent arrests.[94] But two cautious remarks of Tesimond suggest that others would have backed a winning horse. The Plotters, he says, 'commissioned Mr Guy [Fawkes] with other particular negotiations, but I will say no more about them, either because they are uncertain, or else because they could touch the reputation of English gentlemen still living in those parts. They themselves deny the truth of what the plotters said about them.' But, he adds, 'if the insurgents had succeeded at any time in putting [Verney] to rout, it is believed certain that many others would have joined the conspirators'.[95] In fact, the surviving Plotters said next to nothing about the planned rising – hence the problem of reconstructing it – and by the time that Verney and his father-in-law, old Sir Fulke Greville (1536–1606), had raised their posse, the fugitives were out of Warwickshire, leaving only their servants and retainers to be rounded up.[96] All the same, Tesimond's other local information suggests that in this too he should be taken seriously. It is not possible here to examine all the hundred-odd peers and gentry of the county, from Sir Humphrey Ferrers at Tamworth Castle in the north to the second Lord Compton at Compton Wynyates in the south. But it may be instructive to consider, first, the other two Warwickshire houses which, like Coughton, were borrowed by conspirators (the Wrights at Bushwood Hall in Lapworth and Ambrose Rookwood at Clopton House) and, second, the alliances of Catesby's (and Dudley's) father-in-law, Sir Thomas Leigh of Stoneleigh Abbey. This much will at least illustrate the intricate web of friendship and kinship out of which a faction might be constructed, and perhaps was.

The examinations apart, some further clues about Bushwood and Clopton can be found in the returns of recusants and unlicensed alehouses in the hundreds of Barlichway and Kineton for 1605–06; in the remarkably vivid 'Second Certificate' of 25 September 1592; and in what seems to be Sir Fulke Greville's copy of a draft for the lost 'First Certificate' of

---

[93] For the itinerary see Blacker Morgan, *Great English Treason*, vol. 2, pp. 185–283. Those who left Huddington on the morning of the 7th are listed on p. 229.

[94] *CSPD, 1603–10*, p. 242 (SP 14/216/42); Williamson, *Gunpowder Plot*, p. 175; *ODNB*, under Digby, Lettice, Lady Digby. Sir Robert was a former adherent of Essex, MP for Warwickshire in 1601 and husband of Lettice Fitzgerald, heiress to the Earls of Kildare, so that the couple spent most of their time in Ireland, where he was later a Privy Councillor. His brother Sir John was later created Earl of Bristol. Their paternal grandmother was Anne Throckmorton (William Camden, *The Visitation of the County of Warwick in the year 1619*, ed. J. Fetherston, Harleian Society, 12 (1877), p. 17).

[95] Tesimond, *Narrative*, pp. 103, 132.

[96] *CSPD, 1603–10*, pp. 246, 271 (SP 14/16/34, 14/17/41); *CSPD, 1580–1625 (Addenda)*, pp. 468–9 (SP 15/37/87); *Calendar of Salisbury Manuscripts*, vol. 18, pp. 529, 532; and *CSPD, 1603–10*, p. 246 (= SP 14/16/34).

March or April that year, formerly at Warwick Castle and now in Warwick Record Office.[97] The return for Barlichway of 14 March 1606 includes 26 recusants at Coughton, 22 in Alcester, 17 at Sambourne and 29, headed by George and Agnes Throckmorton, at Temple Grafton.[98] But its compilers (Sir William Somerville, Thomas Spencer and Bartholomew Hales) kept to their brief and ignored the Plot, though surely they could have found evidence concerning it if they had wanted to.

Ambrose Rookwood, after staying with the Wintours at Huddington and with the Lacons at Kinlet early in September, moved at Michaelmas to Clopton House, which is a mile north of Stratford-upon-Avon. Its owner, Sir George Carew, had been president of Munster in Ireland since 1600, in succession to Sir Thomas Norreys, who had been killed there in 1599 and whose widow, Bridget (Kingsmill), a connection of Sir Richard Verney, had since married Humphrey Pakington of Harvington, Elizabeth Russell's brother.[99] On 4 May 1605 Sir George became Lord Carew of Clopton, and later Earl of Totnes. He had acquired Clopton by marrying Joyce Clopton, whose sister Anne confusingly married William Clopton of Sledwick in Co. Durham. In 1622 four daughters of Anne and William entered the convent of St Monica at Louvain on the same day, the chronicler recording that their parents had not been Catholics until after their marriage.[100] Nevertheless, Sir Fulke's list of 1592 included under Stratford both William Clopton and his wife (Joyce and Anne's parents), though six months later the 'Second Certificate' noted that William had

---

[97] Elizabeth Guise-Berrow and Aileen M. Hodgson (eds), 'Return of Recusants in Kineton and Barlichway Hundreds, County Warwick, 1605–6', *Worcs. Recusant*, 17 (June 1971): 2–18; and 18 (December 1971): 7–32 (= Warwick Borough Records W.19/3). Michael Hodgetts (ed.), 'A Certificate of Warwickshire Recusants, 1592', *Worcs. Recusant*, 5 (June 1965): 18–31, and 6 (December 1965): 7–20 (= SP 12/243/76, fols 235–48). John Tobias (ed.), 'New Light on Recusancy in Warwickshire, 1592', *Worcs. Recusant*, 36 (December 1980): 8–27 (= WRO, 1886/BL.2662).

[98] Guise-Berrow and Hodgson, 'Return of Recusants in Kineton and Barlichway', pp. 25, 28–9, 31–2.

[99] In 1602 Bridget negotiated a Crown lease of Pakington's sequestrated estates, including Harvington Hall, to Verney, to whom she was related through the Raleighs of Farnborough in Warwickshire: L. Anderton Webster and Veronica Webster, 'The Pakingtons of Harvington', *Recusant History*, 12 (1973–74), 208–9; Camden, *Warwickshire Visitation*, pp. 24–25. At least some of these Raleighs were also recusants: Hodgetts, 'Warwickshire Recusants, 1592', *Worcs. Recusant*, 5, p. 26; 6, p. 12; Guise-Berrow and Hodgson, 'Return of Recusants in Kineton and Barlichway', 9, 11; Tobias, 'New Light on Recusancy in Warwickshire', 10.

[100] Hamilton, *Chronicle of St Monica's*, p. 244. For a family tree, see Foley, *Society of Jesus*, vol. 6, p. 326.

died and that his wife 'was mistaken and goeth now to the church'.[101] It is not clear how or why Rookwood borrowed Clopton: on his own account he was not brought into the Plot until about 23 September.[102] But according to one of his servants, John Flower, he and his wife had been 'in Warwickshire and elsewhere for one year last past'.[103] Afterwards it was reported that at Clopton 'mye pepeoll hath seene Ser Edward bushel [and] mr robeart Catesbee with diuers others'. These included Rookwood himself, Thomas Rookwood, John Grant, one of the Wrights, one of the Wintours and Robert Keyes and his wife.[104] Thomas may have been the priest who was at Kinlet, though in his examination he stated merely that he was going to Worcester to pay for a hawk but returned because he heard that the town was disquieted.[105] Ambrose, however, was back at Coldham on Tuesday 29 October, from where he rode to London, leaving Flower and another servant, Stephen Kirke, to convey horses and £300 in money to Norbrook (not Clopton).[106] On Monday 4 November, Thomas Bates was at Clopton. Another of Rookwood's servants, Robert Warren, described how Bates came out into the courtyard, put a sack into Mrs Rookwood's coach and instructed Warren to drive it and him to Ashby St Ledgers.[107] On 8 November, Thomas Tempest, the Carews' steward, informed Lady Carew that old Sir Fulke Greville was raising the county against the traitors and that Clopton had been searched.[108] The finds included chalices, crucifixes, red and black vestments, Latin books and 'praying beads' made of bone.[109] These items may have been used in the attic chapel in the south range, which, as befits the varied views of the

---

[101] Tobias, 'New Light on Recusancy in Warwickshire', 21; Hodgetts, 'Warwickshire Recusants, 1592', *Worcs. Recusant*, 6, p. 20.

[102] Blacker Morgan, *Great English Treason*, vol. 1, pp. 170–71 (SP 14/17/9, 14/216/136; *CSPD, 1603–10*, p. 266).

[103] Blacker Morgan, *Great English Treason*, vol. 1, p. 172 (SP 14/216/142; *CSPD*, p. 266). In summer 1605 Rookwood had sent 'about twelve trunks' in two carts to Huddington: Blacker Morgan, *Great English Treason*, vol. 1, p. 172 (Cecil Papers 113/44).

[104] Spink, *Gunpowder Plot*, pp. 300–303. For Bushell, see Williamson, *Gunpowder Plot*, p. 151; Granville Squiers, *Secret Hiding-Places* (London 1933), p. 68; and Hodgetts, *Secret Hiding-Places*, p. 78.

[105] *CSPD, 1603–10*, p. 252 (= SP 14/216/75/ix).

[106] Williamson, *Gunpowder Plot*, p. 141; Blacker Morgan, *Great English Treason*, vol. 1, p. 275 (*CSPD, 1603–10*, pp. 253, 266; SP 14/216/78, 142, 144); Spink, *Gunpowder Plot*, p. 307 (*CSPD*, p. 240; SP 14/16/11). Rookwood left Coldham on Wednesday 30 October and Flower and Kirke on Saturday 2 November.

[107] Anstruther, *Vaux*, p. 274 (SP 14/216/77; *CSPD, 1603–10*, p. 252).

[108] *CSPD 1603–10*, p. 246 (SP 14/16/34).

[109] Fraser, *Gunpowder Plot*, pp. 145, 175. Cf. Hodgetts, 'A Topographical Index of Hiding-Places – I', *Recusant History*, 16 (1982–83), pp. 159, no. 31; 194, no. 137.

owners, is decorated with a mixture of religious paintings and Scriptural texts in black letter.[110]

By a quirk of ecclesiastical geography, Bushwood Hall was also in Stratford parish, though it is nine miles north of Clopton. In 1592 a Thomas Bates was there and accused of taking a 'man-child' to be christened at the house of Mrs 'Elizabeth' Brooksby alias Edwards in Tanworth-in-Arden, who was since thought to have gone into Leicestershire.[111] This was Eleanor Brooksby (Mrs *Edward* Brooksby of Shoby in Leicestershire), though she was probably living at Baddesley Clinton rather than at Tanworth.[112] In 1605 John Wright 'harboured this half-year' at 'Nicholas Sly's in Lapworth', was named as a recusant at Bushwood on 24 September, and was still there on 14 October.[113] It appears that he found time to remarry there,[114] and that the household also included Thomas Percy's wife (or one of them; he seems to have had two 'wives') and Mistress Stanley, a sister of the Wrights.[115] But on 15 September Christopher Wright and the Wintours were at Gouthwaite in Yorkshire,[116] and on 23 October he was at a party at the Irish Boy in London, where Catesby had lodgings.[117] As with Rookwood at Clopton, it is not clear what either Wright did at Bushwood, or how long they were there.

Bushwood had once belonged to Catesby (who is said to have been born there), but he had sold it to Sir Edward Greville of Milcote, near

---

[110] *VCH Warwickshire*, vol. 3, p. 234; Edgar I. Fripp, *Shakespeare's Haunts near Stratford* (Oxford, 1929), p. 133.

[111] Tobias, 'New Light on Recusancy in Warwickshire', 12, 13, and cf. 11, 22; Hodgetts, 'Warwickshire Recusants, 1592', *Worcs. Recusant* 6, pp. 7, 12, and cf. p. 20. The identification is not quite certain: in 1592 Thomas Bates of Lapworth was described as 'milner' and his wife's name was given as Anne, whereas the conspirator's wife (in 1605–06) was Martha. Calthrop, *Recusant Roll, No. 1*, p. 350.

[112] For a discussion of the evidence see Michael Hodgetts, 'Elizabethan Priest-Holes – III: East Anglia, Baddesley Clinton, Hindlip', *Recusant History*, 12 (1973–74): 174–84.

[113] Blacker Morgan, *Great English Treason*, vol. 1, p. 219 (SP 14/216/52); Guise-Berrow and Hodgson, 'Return of Recusants in Kineton and Barlichway', 8; Williamson, *Gunpowder Plot*, p. 153 (= SP 14/216/77; *CSPD, 1603–10*, p. 252).

[114] Spink, *Gunpowder Plot*, p. 311, Popham to Salisbury, 5 November 1605 (SP 124/216/10; *CSPD, 1603–10*, p. 240). John and Dorothy Wright had a daughter who was eight or nine in 1605: Mark Nicholls, 'Wright, John (*bap.* 1568, *d.* 1605)', *ODNB*.

[115] *CSPD, 1603–10*, p. 251 (SP 14/216/75); Blacker Morgan, *Great English Treason*, vol. 1, p. 86 (TNA, Transcripts of Montacute (Phillips) MSS, fol. 49). On Percy's 'wives': Williamson, *Gunpowder Plot*, pp. 70, 255–6.

[116] Ibid, p. 146. Lady Yorke of Gouthwaite was an aunt of the Wintours. See also Morris, *Condition of Catholics*, p. cclvii; Anstruther, *Vaux*, p. 391; J.D.H. Aveling, *Northern Catholics* (London, 1966), pp. 206, 289, 320.

[117] Blacker Morgan, *Great English Treason*, vol. 1, p. 213, from SP 14/216/132, a facsimile of which is opp. p. 214.

Stratford, who by 1598 had sold it on to Sir Thomas Holte.[118] Although such 'sales' might be merely mortgages, investments or devices for avoiding sequestration, Holte was living at Bushwood until he moved to Duddeston, near Birmingham, in April 1602, and two of his children were born there: Robert in 1597 and Margaret in 1599.[119] (It was not until 1618 that he began the great Jacobean mansion of Aston Hall, a mile and a half from Duddeston.) He is usually said to have been a Protestant. But in 1614–15 his wife Grace (Bradbourne) was a recusant, and he disinherited their eldest surviving son Edward (1600–43) for marrying a daughter of the bishop of London. Moreover, his brothers Francis and Robert were benefactors of religious houses on the continent; Francis had three daughters who were Franciscan nuns; and Sir Thomas's daughter Elizabeth died at Harvington in 1647 and is buried in the Pakington chapel at Chaddesley Corbett, a mile away.[120] Her will, of which Sir Thomas was joint executor, includes bequests to the priest at Harvington, Humphrey Lutley, and to others whose names are the same as those of priests. Furthermore, on 20 December 1605, William Askrigg of Birmingham alleged that Sir Thomas had split his cook's head in half with a cleaver. In the ensuing action the court found for Sir Thomas, but the verdict was reversed on appeal, on the grounds that Askrigg had not alleged that the cook was killed. This bizarre story would make excellent sense if one of the Holtes was concealing a head which had been not cloven but impaled and which did not belong to a cook but to a Cocks – that being one of the aliases of John Sugar, who had been executed at Warwick for his priesthood on 16 July 1604. And if such an explanation of the slander was suspected in London, then to deny Sir Thomas damages on this quibble would be a coded warning about his future behaviour.[121]

Sir Thomas Leigh of Stoneleigh Abbey had three sons (John, Thomas and Francis) and two daughters: Catherine, who married Catesby in 1593 and died in 1598, and Alice, who married Sir Robert Dudley at Ashow, near Kenilworth, on 11 September 1596.[122] Since he was one of the

---

[118] *VCH Warwickshire*, vol. 5, p. 111.

[119] Fripp, *Shakespeare's Haunts*, pp. 78, 79n. According to the pedigree in Alfred Davidson, *History of the Holtes of Aston* (Birmingham, 1854), Robert was Sir Thomas's first son.

[120] Humphrey Pakington's second wife Abigail, whom he married in 1607, was a daughter of Henry Sacheverell (of Morley and Hopwell in Derbyshire) and Jane Bradbourne.

[121] Michael Hodgetts, 'The Holtes of Aston', *Midland Catholic History*, 9 (2002–03): 13–26.

[122] Adams, 'Dudley'; Mark Nicholls, 'Catesby, Robert (*b*. in or after 1572, *d*. 1605)', *ODNB*; cf. Camden, *Visitation*, pp. 80–81. Sir Thomas Leigh noted that 'my daughter Catesby' had her first child on 18 March 1593/4: Blacker Morgan, *Great English Treason*, vol. 1, p. 93.

commissioners who signed the 'Second Certificate', Williamson describes him as 'an influential Warwickshire Protestant', and Lady Antonia Fraser speculates about the guilt which Catesby may have felt over marrying a Protestant.[123] But on 19 September 1593 Topcliffe reported to Burghley about a priest named Francis Ridcall, formerly Lord Montague's steward, who had fled northwards and met a number of papists at Buxton in Derbyshire. These included Sir Robert Dormer, his wife and their priest Harris; 'Sir Henry Constable of Holderness' (Burton Constable in Yorkshire), his wife and their priest Johnson; and 'Sir Thomas Lea of Stoneley and his wife'.[124] The mention of Sir Robert Dormer (1552–1616) suggests a Warwickshire connection; Lady Dormer was a daughter of Lord Montague; Lady Constable was Sir Robert's sister; and 'Lea of Stoneley' suggests Sir Thomas of Stoneleigh.[125] In 1593 Sir Thomas was in fact living at Fletchamstead, near Coventry, where he built a new house, while his widowed mother had the domestic quarters of the former abbey at Stoneleigh. But after her death in 1603 he moved to Stoneleigh, which by the 1660s was the largest house in Warwickshire, with seventy hearths.[126]

Sir Thomas's wife, Catesby's mother-in-law, was Katherine Spencer, one of the eight daughters of Sir John Spencer (d. 1586) of Wormleighton in Warwickshire and Althorp in Northamptonshire, and of Katherine Kitson of Hengrave in Suffolk, a notably recusant family. Sir John and Lady Spencer also had five sons; the eldest, another Sir John, had died in 1600 leaving a son, Sir Robert Spencer (1570–1627), who married Margaret Willoughby of Wollaton, near Nottingham, and was created Baron Spencer of Wormleighton in 1603.[127] The second of the five brothers, Thomas Spencer, was one of the justices who drew up the Barlichway and Kineton

---

[123] Williamson, *Gunpowder Plot*, p. 72; Fraser, *Gunpowder Plot*, p. 92; cf. Blacker Morgan, *Great English Treason*, vol. 1, pp. 90–98.

[124] Foley, *Society of Jesus*, vol. 2, pp. 273–4 (*CSPD, 1591–4*, p. 372; SP 12/245/98). 'Ridcall' may have been Simon Fennel; the other two priests were probably William Harris (*c.*1550–1602) and Cuthbert Johnson (*c.*1559–1624+). Anstruther, *Seminary Priests*, vol. 1, pp. 115, 150, 190.

[125] T.B. Trappes-Lomax, 'Some Homes of the Dormer Family', *Recusant History*, 8 (1965–66): 175–87, esp. 178–80.

[126] Geoffrey Tyack, *Warwickshire Country Houses* (Chichester, 1994), pp. 178–9. See also Richard K. Morris, 'From Monastery to Country House: An Architectural History of Stoneleigh Abbey, 1156–*c.*1660', in Robert Bearman ed., *Stoneleigh Abbey: The House, its Owners, its Lands* (Stratford, 2004), pp. 15–61.

[127] G.K. Cokayne, *Complete Peerage of England* (14 vols, London, 1910–65), vol. 12/1, p. 160; cf. Camden, *Visitation*, p. 285. The Willoughbys, who also owned Middleton Hall, near Kingsbury, were recusants until at least 1715: Hodgetts, 'Warwickshire Recusants, 1592', *Worcs. Recusant* 6, p. 11; Tobias, 'New Light on Recusancy in Warwickshire', 15, 20; Estcourt and Payne, *English Catholic Nonjurors*, pp. 33, 756, 190–91, 270.

recusant returns of 1605–06. Of Lady Leigh's seven sisters, something should be said about three: Anne, Elizabeth and Alice.

Anne Spencer (d. 1618), Edmund Spenser's 'Phyllis', married first William Stanley, third Lord Monteagle (grandfather through his first wife Anne Leybourne of the Powder Plot Monteagle). He died in 1581, after which she married Henry, first Lord Compton of Compton Wynyates, who died in 1589, and finally, in 1592, Robert Sackville, second Earl of Dorset (1561–1608/9).[128] Lord Compton had been a friend of William Weston, Garnet's predecessor as Jesuit superior, and on at least one occasion Campion had been at his house in London.[129]

Elizabeth Spencer (1552–1618), Spenser's 'Charyllis', married first, in 1574, George Carey, second Lord Hunsdon (1546/7–1603), who was Lord Chamberlain from 1597 and patron of Shakespeare's company, the Lord Chamberlain's Men, from 1596 until 1603, when they became the King's Men. He was also, from 1583 until his death, Captain of the Isle of Wight, where he employed the Italian engineer Giambelli to reconstruct the defences of Carisbrooke Castle in the most up-to-date fashion. In or after 1613, Elizabeth married a second husband, Ralph, third Lord Eure, who was president of the Council of the Welsh Marches and was buried at Ludlow in 1617.[130]

Alice (1559–1637), 'Amaryllis', married first Ferdinando, fifth Earl of Derby (previously the Lord Strange of Lord Strange's Men), who himself had a claim to the Crown and died mysteriously in 1594. By him she had three daughters: Anne (1580–1647), Frances (1583–1636) and Elizabeth (1587–1633). In 1600 she married Sir Thomas Egerton, who in 1603 became Lord Chancellor Ellesmere. He is usually thought of as a man who had conformed for the sake of his career and was now a reliable colleague of Salisbury and Coke.[131] But by 1604 he was employing and conducting

---

[128] Michael A.R. Graves, 'Sackville, Robert, second earl of Dorset (1560/61–1609)', *ODNB*.

[129] Morris, *Troubles*, vol. 2, pp. 157, 379, 397, 408, 426, 427, 479, 492; Anstruther, *Vaux*, p. 121; Foley, *Society of Jesus*, vol. 2, p. 587.

[130] Ute Lotz-Heumann, 'Carew, George, earl of Totnes (1555–1629)', *ODNB*; Elaine V. Beilin, 'Carey , Elizabeth, Lady Hunsdon [née Elizabeth Spencer; *other married name* Elizabeth Eure, Lady Eure] (1552–1618)', *ODNB*; *Complete Peerage*, vol. 6, pp. 627–30; Camden, *Visitation*, pp. 282–5. See also *Love's Labour's Lost*, ed. R.W. David (The Arden Shakespeare, 1951), pp. xxxvii–xliii; Andrew Gurr, *The Shakespearian Playing Companies* (Oxford, 1996), pp. 258, 165–6.

[131] For Egerton's early recusancy see Geoffrey de C. Parmiter, *Elizabethan Popish Recusancy in the Inns of Court, Bulletin of the Institute of Historical Research*, Special Supplement 11 (November 1976), 10–12, 14, 23. For his enforcement of the laws against recusancy see *Documents from the Ellesmere MSS*, ed. Anthony Petti CRS, 60 (London, 1968).

confidential business through Humphrey Pakington of Harvington.[132] It is clear that Pakington greatly admired Ellesmere, who in turn was described in 1607 as 'his most honorable frende, who respecteth him his pryvat affayres above all men's expectations'. There were limits, though: in April 1606, when Pakington, 'all his busynes here [in London] sett aparte', attended the trials in Worcester of Oldcorne, Ashley, Humphrey Lyttelton and Thomas Habington, 'my Lord Chauncellor must not knowe so muche yf yt may be concealed from his Lordshipp'.[133] Ellesmere and his wife lived mainly at Ashridge in Hertfordshire and Harefield in Middlesex, but they had interests in the Midlands as well. He bought Maxstoke Castle, halfway between Coventry and Birmingham, from the second Lord Compton in 1597 and sold it in 1599 to Sir Thomas Dilke, whose descendants still live there.[134] In 1607 John Marston's masque *The Entertainment of the Dowager Countess of Derby* was performed in Alice's presence at Ashby-de-la-Zouch Castle to mark the engagement of her eldest daughter Anne to Lord Chandos.[135] In 1610 there was a quarrel between Sir Thomas Leigh and Sir Fulke Greville over the Recordership of Warwick, in which Leigh later got his own back through Ellesmere's intervention.[136] In the same year, a marriage was arranged between Leigh's grandson, also Thomas, later the first Lord Leigh, and Ellesmere's granddaughter, Mary Egerton, who was to be brought up at Stoneleigh until the young couple married.[137]

These connections explain why in 1605 Catesby 'could not find it in his hart to go to see the Lady Darby [Alice, now Lady Ellesmere] or the Lady Straunge [her daughter Anne, later Lady Chandos] at their houses, though he loved them above all others, because it pitied him to think that they must also dye'.[138] But nearly twenty years before, in 1586, the spy Nicholas Berden had reported being at the French ambassador's, where

---

[132] Worcester Record Office, BA 1546, f.899:169 (6), John Grove to Henry Russell, 5 February 1603/4.

[133] Worcester Record Office, BA 1546, f.899:169 (12); BA 81, 705:24 (Berington MSS) 376(9): John Grove to Henry Russell, 6 June 1607, 21 March 1605/6, (*Little Malvern Letters, 1482–1737*, nos 80, 76).

[134] *VCH Warwickshire*, vol. 4, p. 139.

[135] Peter Levi, *The Life and Times of William Shakespeare* (London and Basingstoke, 1988), pp. 345–58; Michael Hodgetts, 'Mrs Packington and a Shakespearian Emblem', *Midland Catholic History*, 2 (1992): 42–5.

[136] *VCH Warwickshire*, vol. 8, pp. 495–6; Philip Styles, 'The Corporation of Warwick, 1660–1835', *Birmingham Arch. Soc. Trans.* 59 (1935), 23–24.

[137] Mairi Macdonald, '"Not Unmarked by Some Eccentricities": The Leigh Family of Stoneleigh Abbey' in Bearman ed., *Stoneleigh Abbey*, p. 137.

[138] Garnet's 'Second Declaration', in *English Historical Review*, 3 (1888), p. 518, on information from Tesimond. Strictly, 'Lady Strange' was a courtesy title, but she did have a remote claim to the throne: *Complete Peerage*, vol. 3, p. 127; vol. 4, pp. 212–13.

Lady Compton (Anne Spencer) and the then Lady Strange (Alice Spencer) had been attended by Thomas Gerard (the future Jesuit's brother) and Francis Tresham.[139] And these connections may also explain a well-known Shakespearian puzzle. Harold F. Brooks, following Peter Alexander, thought that *A Midsummer Night's Dream* was written for the marriage on 19 February 1596 of Elizabeth Carey, daughter of Lord Hunsdon and Elizabeth Spencer, to Thomas, the son of Henry, Lord Berkeley. But he could not explain Oberon's famous description of the mermaid and the shooting stars (II.1.148–64), which seems to be an allusion to the 'princely pleasures' of Kenilworth in 1575 but to have no relevance to the Careys.[140] Was the play repeated, and given some local colour, seven months later at Kenilworth for the marriage of Elizabeth Carey's cousin Alice Leigh to Sir Robert Dudley?

Aristocratic authority was needed to justify a rising, and the Venetian ambassador was sure that some great lord was behind the Plot.[141] In 1585 Thomas Bilson (later, through Essex's intervention, bishop of Worcester) had asserted that 'if a Prince shoulde goe about to ... change the forme of the commonwealth from imperie to tyrannie ... if the Nobles and commons ioyne togither to defend their auncient and accustomed libertie, regiment and lawes, they may not well be counted rebels' – as long as 'the lawes of the land appoint the nobles as next to the king to assist him in doing right, and withhold him from doing wrong'.[142] Historical precedent (and the siege of Kenilworth in 1266) might suggest that in England that was indeed the law. It is clear that Catesby rubbed shoulders with great persons, and, according to Tesimond, he had won over to Catholicism 'a number of gentlemen, and those among the most important, who moved in London and court circles'.[143]

Whether any of Leigh's brothers-in-law were among them remains uncertain. Just how ambiguous great men might have to be is vividly

---

[139] *CSPD, 1580–90*, p. 373 (SP 12/195/75). Whether Tresham and Catesby were so friendly with Egerton is another matter, since at the time of the Essex Rising Tresham had forcibly held him incommunicado at Essex House in the Strand: Blacker Morgan, *Great English Treason*, vol. 1, p. 99.

[140] *A Midsummer Night's Dream*, ed. Harold F. Brooks (The Arden Shakespeare, 1979), pp. lvi, lxvii–lxviii.

[141] *Calendar of State Papers Venetian*, ed. R. Brown et al. (*40 vols*, London, 1864–1940), vol. 10, p. 293, no. 444; cf. p. 291, no. 443. The government suspected that the Earl of Northumberland would have become Lord Protector. The previous (eighth) Earl had been implicated in the Throckmorton Plot of 1583 and found dead in the Tower.

[142] Thomas Bilson, *The True Difference between Christian Subjection and Unchristian Rebellion*, pp. 520–21, quoted by Philip Styles, 'The Commonwealth', in Allardyce Nicoll (ed.), *Shakespeare in his own Age: Shakespeare Survey 17* (Cambridge, 1964), pp. 112–13.

[143] Tesimond, *Narrative*, p. 61.

illustrated by a letter which the Earl of Worcester wrote to Salisbury on 5 July 1605. Four days earlier, he had summoned the Bishop of Hereford and all the justices of Monmouthshire to Raglan Castle and treated them to a lengthy and sententious speech on the increase of recusancy, after which arrangements had been made for searches the following night throughout Monmouthshire, and on the night of Monday 8 July throughout Herefordshire as well. One of his deputy lieutenants, Sir Roger Bodenham, had come to Raglan asking what service he might do and had been told 'to endevor the apprehending of thos accused to bee at the [recent riots], and cheefly of seminaryes and popishe preestes that frequented that part of [Hereford]shere'.[144] Yet Sir Roger's own wife Bridget was a recusant,[145] and at Rotherwas, near Hereford, the Bodenhams preserved the twelfth-century enamelled chasse depicting the martyrdom of St Thomas of Canterbury which is now back in Hereford Cathedral. The earl himself, a patron of William Byrd and the dedicatee of his *Cantiones Sacrae* (1589), was described by Queen Elizabeth as 'a stiff Papist and a good subject'; his daughters were reconciled to Rome by Robert Jones, later the Jesuit superior, and by 1615 Raglan itself was a Jesuit centre.[146] William Taylor (1576–1611), having been refused a fellowship at Magdalen College, Oxford, because of his papistry, taught two of the earl's daughters at Raglan before going abroad to become a priest in 1600.[147] Worcester must have known that among the gentry assembled in his great hall were Church Papists and men with recusant wives, and that little would be found to compensate the justices for the loss of two nights' sleep. Clearly he was powerful enough, and far enough from London, to exercise his own judgement about what was a threat to the state and what could be winked at in corners. Even in Warwickshire, lack of documentation should not be taken to mean convinced Protestantism and loyalty to James I.

This lack of documentation is a serious problem. Granville Squiers wrote that at Coughton, 'where we have proof of priest-hiding and political conspiracy, one may be allowed some latitude for conjecture'.[148] Such conjecture is in fact unavoidable, because the Throckmortons did

---

[144] Cecil Papers, Hatfield House, 111, fols 109–10; cf. Roland Mathias, *Whitsun Riot* (London, 1963).

[145] Matthews, 'Catholicism in the South Wales Marches', p. 293.

[146] Byrd's two books of *Gradualia* (1605, 1607) were dedicated to the Earl of Northampton and to Lord Petre, whose wife, Katherine, was Worcester's second daughter, and a patient of Justinian Stubbs: Worcester R.O., BA 81, 705:24 (Berington MSS), 576 (8); cf. 576 (4); Foley, *Society of Jesus*, vol. 4, pp. 333–6, 470–76.

[147] Kenny, *Responsa Scholarum*, pp. 80–84; cf. Anstruther, *Seminary Priests*, vol. 1, p. 347. Taylor had known two of Worcester's sons at Magdalen.

[148] Squiers, *Secret Hiding-Places*, p. 38.

not keep records of either illicit activity. A priest was hidden at Coughton in 1593, and an old Marian priest had been there by 1575. But, apart from Garnet, Tesimond and Percy in 1605, the first *name* that we have is that of Alban East, alias West, alias Jerningham, who died there in 1671.[149] And of these, we only know about the three Jesuits because of the Plot, and about the Marian priest through a passing remark in St Robert Southwell's panegyric on Edward Throckmorton, who died in Rome in 1582.[150] Similarly, the inadequate evidence for the rising in Warwickshire suggests not that no extensive rising was envisaged or possible, but that the local justices agreed to blame only those who were safely dead. The Throckmorton family may not have been at the heart of the Gunpowder Plot, but it was shot through with their relatives and connections, part of an extensive Catholic network that was remarkably, or (from the state's perspective) alarmingly integrated into Midlands landed society as a whole. Moreover, through Garnet and Lady Digby, the Plot is irrevocably associated with Coughton; and in the Tower Room, with its priest-hole, bare brickwork and Elizabethan painted cloth, the events of 1605 still seem disconcertingly present.

---

[149] *APC*, vol. 24, p. 148; Anstruther, *Seminary Priests*, vol. 2, p. 92. For priests at Coughton mentioned in Sir Francis Throckmorton's wills of 1670 and 1676 (WRO, CR 1998/ Box 73/ no. 6) see Michael Hodgetts, 'The Yates of Harvington', *Recusant History*, 22 (1994–95), p. 167 and p. 179 n. 97; Anstruther, *Seminary Priests*, vol. 3, pp. 224, 214.

[150] Foley, *Society of Jesus*, vol. 4, pp. 296–8; cf. Christopher Devlin, *The Life of Robert Southwell, Poet and Martyr* (London, 1956), pp. 18–21, 26, 67, 263, 340 n.18. Edward enjoyed fishing in the pool which still exists close to Coughton Court.

CHAPTER 5

Agnes Throckmorton: A Jacobean Recusant Widow

Jan Broadway

Recusant gentlewomen have long been recognised as having played a pivotal role in the preservation of the Catholic religion within early modern England. As women they were protected by their legal and political invisibility, while their gentility provided them with a privileged position within society. While Catholic gentlemen were increasingly coerced into at least outward conformity to the established Church, their wives were able to preserve the Catholic character of the household and to raise their children in the old faith. Recusant gentlewomen also played an important part in the networks that supported the priests in their mission to England. Yet, although they could exploit their overt powerlessness to advantage in some circumstances, recusant gentlewomen inevitably suffered disadvantages because of their sex.[1] Among the most disadvantaged of early modern gentlewomen, regardless of religion, was the widowed mother whose young son was the heir to a large estate. All families feared the damage caused by the succession of a minor and the interference in their affairs of the Court of Wards. Recusant mothers had particular fears, because their religion was liable to undermine what maternal rights contemporary society was prepared to recognise. When John Throckmorton died in February 1604, his young son Robert became the heir of his 70-year-old grandfather, Thomas Throckmorton of Coughton and Weston Underwood.[2] From that moment his mother, Agnes Throckmorton, became embroiled in a battle to maintain her relationship with her son, defending her rights against both her father-in-law and the state. She also needed to fight in support of the claims of her other children. At the same time the death of her husband removed her legal protection and exposed her to the punitive measures inflicted on recusants. Through studies of the Brownes, viscounts Montague, and of the descendants of Sir Thomas More, Michael Questier has posited the importance of kinship as

---

[1] For an overview of the situation of recusant women, see Marie B. Rowlands, 'Recusant Women 1560–1640', in Mary Prior (ed.), *Women in English Society 1500–1800* (London, 1985), pp. 149–80.

[2] *VCH Buckinghamshire*, vol. 4, p. 499.

a cohesive force within recusant society.³ The following study examines how competing loyalties and interests created tensions within and between kinship circles. It is largely based on the surviving correspondence between Agnes, her father-in-law, and her eldest son, which allows us to gain some insight into the power struggles within the family precipitated by the death of her husband.⁴ Through it I hope to throw light on the important role of recusant widows in maintaining family cohesion across generations in often difficult circumstances.

The accession of James I to the throne of England brought renewed hope of relief from persecution for their religious beliefs to his Catholic subjects. Although the king did not repeal the recusancy laws, he did relax their operation for a few short months. Hence, in the summer of 1604 Thomas Throckmorton was relieved of the need to pay the fines charged on him for not attending church from the time of Queen Elizabeth's death.⁵ The honeymoon period was all too brief, as any desire James had to display toleration was overcome by the recognition that the exactions on recusants were a significant part of his income, and that he could not expect his Protestant subjects willingly to make up the shortfall. The death of his eldest son during the period of high expectation in the first year of the new reign was not simply a personal blow to Thomas and his wife, his daughter-in-law Agnes and his fatherless grandchildren.⁶ For Thomas, who had entered his eighth decade and could not confidently expect to see his grandson reach the age of maturity, it raised the spectre of a feudal wardship that would undermine an estate already suffering from the heavy expenses of recusancy. For Agnes, who was in her early thirties, her status changed from a wife sheltered legally by her husband to a widow, liable to prosecution for her religion. She also assumed prime responsibility

---

³ Michael C. Questier, *Catholicism and Community in Early Modern England: Politics, Aristocratic Patronage and Religion, c. 1550–1640* (Cambridge, 2006); 'Catholicism, kinship and the public memory of Sir Thomas More', *Journal of Ecclesiastical History*, 53 (2002): 476–509. Agnes Throckmorton was related to both these kinship circles through her mother.

⁴ There are eight surviving letters written by Agnes in the Throckmorton archive; two are addressed to Thomas Throckmorton (one written by an amanuensis, one in her own hand), five to Robert (one written by an amanuensis, four in her own hand with the draft of Robert's reply on the reverse of one) and one to Sir Francis Fortescue (written by an amanuensis): WRO, CR 1998/Box 60/3, 4; CR 1998/Box 60/Folder 1/1–3, 5–6 and CR 1998/CD/Folder 52/6C.

⁵ WRO, CR 1998/Box 62/14.

⁶ Edward Kimber and Richard Johnson (eds), *The Baronetage of England* (3 vols, London, 1771) gives nine children of John and Agnes Throckmorton (four sons and five daughters). I have found evidence that all four sons and three of the daughters survived their father, which corresponds with the number of children given in the manuscript life of Thomas Throckmorton: WRO, CR 1998/LCB/21.

for defending her own rights and those of all her children. This included ensuring that protecting the inheritance of her eldest son did not adversely affect his younger siblings. At the same time, she was obliged to recognise that her son's position as heir meant that others would claim a right in deciding his fate, people who would not cede her authority as his mother. The example of Agnes Throckmorton provides a case study of the tensions experienced by widowed recusant mothers; tensions that could threaten the family cohesion that nurtured the survival of their faith within a hostile environment.

John Throckmorton and Agnes Wilford had married in 1589.[7] There is no direct evidence about the nature of their marriage. No letters between the couple or other personal documents survive. For Agnes, her marriage was dominated by the experience of pregnancy and childbirth. Their eldest daughter Margaret was born in 1591 and there were nine children of the marriage.[8] Even assuming that there were no miscarriages or still births, which were a common feature of women's experience, this would mean that Agnes spent about half of her married life either pregnant or recovering from the immediate effects of childbirth. As Agnes lived into the 1640s, her widowhood lasted far longer than her marriage.[9] This was not an unusual experience in the seventeenth century. Some women undoubtedly enjoyed the comparative freedom they enjoyed as widows. As we shall see, Agnes was not afraid to express her opinions forcefully and she may have been reluctant to enter into a second marriage where she would have been at least nominally subject to her husband. Since both her own father and John's outlived him by a decade, Agnes did not want for male advice and guidance as she raised her family. There may also have been practical reasons why she did not remarry. The most obvious is that she may not have had an opportunity. Although she received a comfortable income from her jointure, Agnes was not the mistress of the sort of wealth that would attract numerous suitors. If she did receive proposals, Agnes may have been discouraged from accepting them. Her jointure was for life, which meant that, unlike many contemporary widows, she would not forfeit it by remarriage. However, as the interests of the children of a first marriage were commonly felt to be subjugated to those of a second

---

[7] The exact date of the marriage is unknown, but the couple held their first view of frankpledge for the manor of Tanworth in September 1589: SCLA, DR 37/2/Box 109/60.

[8] *The Chronicle of the English Augustinian Canonesses Regular of the Lateran, at St Monica's in Louvain 1548 to 1625*, ed. Dom Adam Hamilton, OSB (Edinburgh and London, 1904), p. 150; Kimber and Johnson, *Baronetage of England*, vol. 1, pp. 484–5.

[9] I have not traced the exact date of her death, but she was party to a demise in 1644 and had died before the Throckmorton estate passed to her grandson in 1650: SCLA, DR 165/1253/1; Birmingham Reference Library, IIR 60/242277.

husband, a sense of duty perhaps combined with familial pressure may have discouraged her from remarrying while her children were young.[10]

As a widow, Agnes held the manors of Moor Hall, Spernall and Samborne in Warwickshire for life as her jointure. She settled in the manor house at Moor Hall, which was described as an 'Anciente dwellinge howse with houses of Office and well maynteyned in good repaire'.[11] She was to live there for the rest of her life. Agnes was not by birth a member of the Warwickshire gentry and she had no kinship circle within the county. While the Throckmortons belonged to the medieval Midlands gentry and had long-established connections across the counties of Warwickshire, Worcestershire and Gloucestershire, Agnes came from a rather different social setting in the south-east of England. She was born in 1570 at Ridley Hall in Terling, Essex, the home of her maternal grandparents. Her grandfather, Sir James Wilford, had distinguished himself as a soldier in the service of the Tudors.[12] Although the Wilfords claimed descent from the medieval gentry of Devon, their immediate fortunes were based on mercantile wealth. Sir James Wilford had been the son of a Merchant Tailor and alderman of London, who purchased an estate at Cranbrook in Kent during the reign of Henry VIII. Other branches of the Wilford family continued to play an active and significant role in the economic and administrative life of London. They were part of the mercantile elite of Tudor England, who moved into gentry circles in the counties around London and formed links with the bureaucracy of Church and government at the highest level. One of Agnes's great-aunts had married Edward Sandys, Archbishop of York, while a more distant cousin was the wife of Sir Thomas Smith, a prominent civil servant and author of *De Republica Anglorum*. Agnes's father, Thomas Wilford, was born into a newly Protestant world which reverted briefly to Catholicism in his childhood. His family and the wider circle of merchants, bureaucrats and newcomers to the gentry to which they belonged displayed an ability to adapt to circumstances, as each change of government brought with it alterations in the official religious stance. While the Wilford family had connections to some early and devoted adherents to Protestantism, the circle in which Thomas Wilford was raised was religiously conservative. His mother's family supported the reinstatement of Catholicism in Mary's reign, while her husband's patron Sir John Baker exhibited sufficient zeal

---

[10] Amy Erickson, *Women and Property in Early Modern England* (London, 1993), p. 120. For an overview of the experience of widowhood, see Sandra Cavallo and Lyndan Warner, *Widowhood in Medieval and Early Modern Europe* (Harlow, 1999).

[11] SCLA, DR 5/3390: no manor houses are mentioned in the account of her other manors.

[12] J.D. Alsop, 'Wilford, Sir James (*b*. in or before 1517, *d*. 1550)', *ODNB*.

for the persecution of heretics to acquire the abusive epithet of 'Butcher Baker' from John Foxe. On the accession of Elizabeth, however, most of Thomas Wilford's kin adapted themselves to outward conformity, while their status allowed them to retain more conservative practices in their household devotions. In the first decade of Elizabeth's reign Thomas Wilford married Mary Browne, whose father, Humphrey, was a judge of Common Pleas. Although he had twice been demoted and imprisoned for his legal views, Humphrey Browne had managed to conform outwardly in religion sufficiently to serve in turn Edward VI, Mary and Elizabeth. His nephew, Anthony Browne, as chief justice of the Common Pleas, had shown more zeal for the Marian persecutions than could be palatable for Elizabeth and was removed from his post. His ability to continue a legal career, however, is indicative of the spirit of compromise and adaptability that permeated the circle to which Thomas Wilford and Mary Browne belonged.

Compromise is rarely attractive to the young. Nor did adaptability and the preservation of traditional practices within the private sphere seem sufficient to ensure the survival of Catholicism in England, let alone its triumphant restoration as the state religion. Thomas Wilford named his daughter Agnes after her maternal grandmother, whose father John, Lord Hussey, had opposed Henry VIII's religious policies and had been executed in the reaction to the Pilgrimage of Grace. In his turn, Thomas Wilford was drawn into the community of young Catholic gentry, who were excited by and supported the mission of the Jesuit priests to recover England for the faith. In this way he came into contact with Thomas Throckmorton of Coughton, his cousin Francis Throckmorton and his brother-in-law Thomas Tresham. The Wilfords' London house was used as a venue for meetings and unlawful books were found when it was searched. Following the defeat of the Armada, Thomas Wilford was imprisoned in Ely Castle. Although he was released after a comparatively short period, he was subsequently rearrested in 1592 and held at Banbury. He was finally released in 1597.[13] He was to remain a recusant for the rest of his life and to suffer the considerable financial penalties inflicted by the state as a result. Given her father's status as one of the most determined recusants of Elizabethan England, the choice of marriage partners for Agnes Wilford was restricted. Few Protestant fathers would have contemplated matching their sons with the child of an obstinate recusant, who was likely to insist on raising her children in the old religion, and many Catholic families would look for evidence of some willingness to compromise which would allow the outward conformity of the head of the household. If Agnes

---

[13] John J.N. McGurk, 'Lieutenancy and Catholic Recusants in Elizabethan Kent', *Recusant History*, 12 (1973): 157–70.

had been a significant heiress, she would have been more attractive as a potential bride. However, she was one of a large family and a younger brother, James, would eventually inherit the bulk of their father's estate.[14] Consequently, it was almost inevitable that Agnes should marry within the close-knit circle of ardent recusants, for whom her Catholic upbringing and determination to adhere to her faith were an attraction rather than a disincentive. Consequently, as their fathers languished in custody after the Armada, the marriage was arranged between Agnes and John Throckmorton which took place in the summer of 1589.

Following John Throckmorton's death fifteen years later, the greatest concern was that his son Robert would inherit the Throckmorton estate as a minor. If that happened, his marriage and the management of his lands would come under the jurisdiction of the Court of Wards. The threat of a feudal wardship was feared by all gentry families, since with the guardianship of the heir went the right to arrange their marriage. Although the ward retained the power of refusal, a guardian whose choice was rejected could demand compensation.[15] The Throckmorton family had direct recent experience of the potential advantages to a family of securing the guardianship of feudal heirs to provide marriage partners for their children. In the mid-sixteenth century this was how Thomas Throckmorton's own marriage to Margaret Whorwood, the co-heir of Henry VIII's attorney general, and that of Sir Thomas Tresham to his sister Muriel had been procured.[16] Feudal wardship was a particular threat to Catholic families, both because their estates were already depleted by recusancy fines and because the Court of Wards would attempt to ensure the heir was raised as a Protestant. Thomas Throckmorton had suffered heavy financial penalties for his recusancy, and also had a reputation for extravagance. In the summer of 1604, following his son's death, an act of parliament was passed which allowed Thomas Throckmorton to sell manors in order to settle his estate on a firmer financial basis.[17] The manor of Tanworth, which John and Agnes had held from the time of their marriage, was sold. Given the likelihood that Robert Throckmorton

---

[14] When the Wilford house was searched in 1584, the pursuivants reported the presence of six children: Hamilton, *Chronicle of St Monica's*, p. 94; James Wilford married Anne, the daughter and heiress of Thomas Newman of Quendon, Essex. He too was openly recusant and suffered the confiscation of two-thirds of his lands under the Stuarts.

[15] The standard work on feudal wardship in this period remains Joel Hurstfield, *The Queen's Wards* (London, 1958).

[16] Julian Lock, 'Tresham, Sir Thomas (1543–1605)', *ODNB*. William Whorwood's widow Margaret married William Sheldon, whose son Ralph married Anne Throckmorton, Thomas's sister.

[17] TNA, C 89/10/35; *Journal of the House of Commons: Volume 1: 1547–1629* (London, 1802), pp. 225–6.

would inherit his grandfather's estate as a minor and become a ward of the Crown, other measures were probably taken at the same time to settle the estate so as to minimise the damage this would cause. Although it had declined from its height in the mid-sixteenth century, the Throckmorton inheritance remained a substantial one. Robert's estate was valued shortly after his grandfather's death as having a yearly value in excess of £2,000, of which £242 was held by his mother for life. The annuities and marriage settlements for the younger children were to be paid out of the main estate, so their future welfare was tied to that of their elder brother. Under Robert Cecil, wardships were sold by the Court of Wards for three or four times their annual value and there was no guarantee that a ward's mother or immediate family would secure the direct grant of wardship themselves. In the case of Robert Throckmorton, given the recusancy of his family and the value of his estate, should his grandfather die while he was still unmarried and underage, his wardship would almost certainly be fought over by a number of suitors. This would mean that his family would have to pay substantially more than the official price to acquire the right to choose Robert's wife, if they were able to persuade the initial purchaser to part with the wardship. All in all, it was eminently desirable that Robert should be married during the lifetime of his grandfather, thus reducing his attractiveness as a ward.

The position in which Agnes Throckmorton found herself in 1604 was by no means unique. Medieval and early modern gentry women frequently found themselves responsible for estate and household management when their husbands were absent on military, legal or other business. The added responsibilities that came with widowhood were also widely experienced.[18] In fact, Agnes's position closely resembled that which her paternal grandmother had faced in 1550, when Sir James Wilford had died in his early thirties, leaving his son Thomas a minor and heir to his grandfather. However, her husband's will, which made Joyce Wilford executrix of his estate with authority over the inheritance of her children until they came of age, placed her in a more influential position than her granddaughter. Moreover, Joyce's husband had named his patron Sir John Baker as one of the overseers of his will, with authority to negotiate a settlement between the widow and her father-in-law should any disagreement arise over the estate.[19] Crucially, the will did not place any limitations on Joyce's ability

---

[18] The proportion of widowed householders may have averaged around one-fifth, with widows generally outnumbering widowers: Ralph Houlbrooke, *The English Family 1450–1700* (London, 1984), pp. 208–9.

[19] TNA, PROB 11/33/220; J.D. Alsop, 'Baker, Sir John (*c*.1489–1558)', *ODNB*. Sir James Wilford's father had remarried after the death of his first wife and had a second family, which he might be expected to favour over the children of his eldest son.

to remarry. It was not unusual for a husband to reduce the influence of his widow over his children should she remarry, in order to ensure that the interests of a second husband would not supersede those of his heirs. Sir John Baker, who was Chancellor of the Exchequer, forwarded a match between Joyce and Thomas Stanley, one of the under-treasurers of the Mint.[20] By this marriage Joyce further strengthened her position in relation to her children's future and secured the support of her immediate circle against the claims of her father-in-law. When her father-in-law died three years later, their contacts within the government enabled her husband to obtain Thomas's wardship. Half a century later, John Throckmorton appears to have died without making a will. The financial position of his widow was assured by the settlements made at the time of her marriage, but in the absence of a will Agnes was in a less strong position than her grandmother. She was not the appointed executrix of her husband's estate and no counterbalance to her father-in-law's authority had been nominated by her husband. Although she benefited from the support of her own father, his ability to influence Thomas Throckmorton was limited.

While Agnes kept her younger children with her initially at Moor Hall, her eldest son seems to have been taken immediately into his grandfather's household. Since her manors were close to Coughton, this would not have represented a significant separation if Thomas Throckmorton had been based predominantly in Warwickshire. However, Thomas preferred the newer house at Weston, with its closer proximity to London. The settlement of Agnes at Moor Hall also meant that Thomas could consider letting Coughton, as part of the measures to reduce his debts. Consequently, Coughton was fatefully available to be leased by Sir Everard Digby in 1605.[21] Robert's exact age at the time of his father's death is uncertain. He appears to have begun the process of suing his livery in November 1618, although he did not receive his grant of special livery from the king until a year later. This suggests that he was born around 1597. This date would be consistent with the timing of his first marriage, which took place in or just before January 1612, as fourteen was the legal age of consent to marriage for males.[22] Hence, his father died when Robert was around seven, the age at which young gentry males began to wear adult

---

[20] Joyce's sister Anne married Sir Martin Bowes, a goldsmith and another official at the Mint.

[21] Antonia Fraser, *The Gunpowder Plot* (London, 2004), p. 176: Fraser assumes that Coughton was let because Thomas Throckmorton had gone abroad rather than as a retrenchment. See Michael Hodgetts's chapter in this volume.

[22] WRO, CR 1998/Box 60/Folder 3/15; CR 1998/Box 64/11 and CR 1998/Box 73/3; SCLA, DR 5/965; WRO, CR 1998/Box 60/Folder 3/14. Children could be married before the age of consent, but were able to repudiate the marriage when they came of age.

clothes and to move from their mother's sphere into the world of formal education. While this might have taken place with a tutor in his family home, it was equally likely that Robert Throckmorton would have been sent to another gentry household at this time even if his father had lived. Physical separation from their children at an early age was a common experience for Jacobean gentry mothers. This doubtless contributed to the formal distance that is typical of early modern family correspondence.[23] Such distance is demonstrated in all but one of the surviving letters written by Agnes to her eldest son. She commences the letters with the formal 'Sun with gods blessinge to your selfe and your wife' and concludes 'your most loving' or 'most assured loving mother'. The only exception demonstrates the strength of maternal feeling normally masked by formal distance. This was a letter written when Robert had been seriously ill and had required the services of a surgeon. In this instance, which is the latest in date of the letters to survive, he was 'My deare Robin'. Here the handwriting is more irregular and the layout less neat than usual, bearing testimony to the strength of her maternal concern for her son overcoming the customary formality of their correspondence.[24]

Catholic mothers are frequently credited with ensuring that their children were raised in the old faith, even when their fathers compromised with the Protestant authorities and attended the parish church. It appears that John Throckmorton was less militantly Catholic than his father and other members of his extended family. He does not appear in the recusant rolls of the Exchequer and when Thomas Throckmorton and Thomas Wilford were imprisoned in the last decade of Elizabeth's reign, he remained at liberty. Following the Essex rebellion, John Throckmorton was in London, where he helped to raise the large sums of money which relieved his cousins Robert Catesby and Francis Tresham from the full vengeance of the Elizabethan state. He does not appear to have joined in the plotting and conspiracies that consumed his kinsmen.[25] Although he was described as 'a virtuous and good Catholic' when his daughter entered the Augustinian convent at Louvain in 1611, more emphasis was placed on his father, 'a famous Catholic', and his wife's conduct as a recusant widow. Agnes is described as 'doing many good deeds in inducing of Protestants to be reconciled, receiving and relieving of priests, bringing up her children in

---

[23] For an examination of all aspects of early modern correspondence, see Alan Stewart and Heather Wolfe, *Letterwriting in Renaissance England* (Washington DC, 2004).

[24] WRO, CR 1998/Box 60/Folder 1/5: I assume the letter dates from the 1630s because of the reference to Robert and his wife having two children.

[25] BL, Add. MS 39829, fol. 51. There are a confusing number of John Throckmortons who survive in the records, including one (the son of Sir George Throckmorton) who died in the autumn of 1604.

the fear of God', as befitted her status as a comparatively wealthy widow of impeccable recusant stock.[26] Following her husband's death Agnes became liable to the financial penalties associated with recusancy for her refusal to attend church.[27] She was also subject to the restrictions limiting recusants from going more than five miles from their homes without obtaining a licence. Although recusant gentry generally found little difficulty in obtaining such licences, except in time of heightened political tension, it was an unwelcome inconvenience.[28] During the long years of her widowhood Moor Hall was part of the network of safe houses for priests maintained in the Midlands. In 1608 one Mr Blount and his two 'little scollers' spent some time there before moving on to be sheltered by the Morgan family at Heyford, Northamptonshire. Five years later her daughter's profession as a nun was attended by John Bolt, a priest who had 'known her in the world' and remained at the convent as organist thereafter.[29]

In her relationship with her father-in-law Agnes Throckmorton had to maintain a careful balance between the requirements of filial respect for the head of the family and her own maternal instincts and desire for some control over the fate of her son.[30] In 1608 an attempt by Thomas Throckmorton to negotiate a marriage for his grandson without the involvement of his daughter-in-law threatened their delicate relationship, as demonstrated by two of her surviving letters. The first was written on 25 January, in response to one from her father-in-law that had been delivered by her son.[31] The letter was written by a scribe, although it was signed by Agnes herself. It recognisably belongs to the genre of suitors' letters. The wording and the use of space in the layout of the letter form part of the formal expression of respect by Agnes towards Thomas, expected in correspondence from a supplicant to the head of the family.[32] It appears

---

[26] Hamilton, *Chronicle of St Monica's*, p. 120.

[27] In November 1607 the financial benefit of the recusancy of Agnes Throckmorton and other Warwickshire recusants was granted by James I to Sir Richard Coningsby: *CSPD, 1603–1610*, p. 383.

[28] *APC, 1615–16*, p. 614.

[29] WRO, CR 1998/Box 60/ folder 1/2; Hamilton, *Chronicle of St Monica's*, p. 150. When arrested in 1594, John Bolt was being harboured by the Wisemans of Braddocks, Essex; Jane Wiseman was the first prioress at Louvain: Gerard Kilroy, *Edmund Campion: Memory and Transcription* (Aldershot, 2005), pp. 63–6.

[30] On the duty of obedience owed to parents by adult children, see Houlbrooke, *English Family*, pp. 167–71.

[31] WRO, CR 1998/Box 60/ folder 1/2.

[32] Lynne Magnusson, 'A rhetoric of requests: genre and linguistic scripts in Elizabethan Women's Suitors' Letters', in James Daybell (ed.), *Women and Politics in Early Modern England, 1450–1700* (Aldershot, 2004), pp. 51–66; Jonathan Gibson, 'Significant space in manuscript letters', *The Seventeenth Century*, 12 (1997): 1–8.

that Thomas's letter, which does not survive, told her that negotiations for Robert's marriage had been unsuccessful and that Thomas had decided he should go abroad to continue his education. Thomas had sent Robert to stay with his mother at Moor Hall so that he might take his leave of her. From her response we cannot tell whether Agnes had been consulted about the intended marriage, or had even been informed that the negotiations were taking place. The letter begins with Agnes remembering her 'duty' to her father-in-law and 'humbly' desiring his daily blessing. While giving Thomas 'humble thankes' for sending Robert to see her, Agnes was clearly unhappy with the prospect of his going 'so farre' from home to a 'strange place'. Although Robert was living with his grandfather rather than his mother, there was a significant difference between having your ten-year old son living with family members within fifty miles and resigning him to the uncertain dangers of a voyage abroad. However, she expressed herself willing to 'brydle my motherlye affection', if it was for her son's benefit, and to accept her father-in-law's decision: 'for if it please you to lett him take this Jorney I hope it will breed him so good experience & knowledge, that it will be a great comfort to vs & all the rest of his freindes'. In exchange, she negotiated for a delay in any further attempt to find Robert a wife. She hoped that Thomas would be 'so good [a] grandfather' to her son, that he would allow him to 'haue more yeres & greater experience' before negotiating a match for him. At the same time, Agnes was sending one of her daughters to her grandfather. She hoped that the girl would be taken into her grandfather's household 'for that place I most desire', but if Thomas preferred to send her to another family, she was willing to 'resigne my whole interest of her vnto you'. Thus, Agnes was prepared to cede authority over her daughter in return for some say in the future of her son. Two months later a licence was obtained for Robert Throckmorton to travel abroad for three years.[33]

Despite the decision to send Robert abroad, there was no let up in the negotiations for his marriage. Shortly after she had dispatched the first letter with her son and daughter to Weston, Agnes learnt from her father that Thomas was 'very forwardes in spech for the bestowinge of him'. Agnes was clearly infuriated by this denial of her maternal rights and the duplicity she felt had been practised. She gave vent to her anger in a letter to her father, in which she expressed her 'dislickes' of Thomas's actions. Clearly, she hoped to exert indirect influence on Thomas through her father. At the same time, she apparently refused to correspond directly with Thomas on the subject.[34] The extent to which Agnes was prepared to act in an attempt to frustrate the marriage plans is uncertain, since

---

[33] *CSPD, 1603–1610*, p. 418.
[34] WRO, CR 1998/Box 60/Folder 3/12.

she subsequently needed to deny any such intentions in order to seek a reconciliation with her father-in-law. In the second letter from Agnes to Thomas, written on 9 September, she attempted to defend her conduct and her rights, while maintaining a formally deferential attitude.[35] In this instance Agnes wrote the letter herself and its appearance is far less deferential than the previous letter; there are more insertions and crossings out and the whole of the sheet is utilised. The letter opens with the same formula concerning her duty and desire for his daily blessing as the earlier letter. Then she enters immediately into his charges against her. To the accusation from Thomas that she was 'decemling' with him, she countered by quoting from his own letter to her: 'you wrot vnto me by thes wordes; that you had don him wronge to send him so soune a woinge'. She justified herself by referring to the grief she had felt on realising that she was to be 'made a stranger in thes procedinges'. She was careful to focus her complaint on the lack of consultation rather than challenging his authority in arranging his heir's marriage: 'I neuer harde of it from you, beinge so longe in hande'. Emphasising her own claims, she asked him to consider whether this failure to involve her would not naturally 'greue a mother that hath broght a childe into the worlde with grefe, paine, and danger of my life'. At the same time she acknowledged her father-in-law's dominant position within the family, both as her son's 'best frinde' and as one that 'I my self doe relivyon, and without desemlinge both loue, and honor mor then aney man in the worlde, but my one father'. Rather than lay the blame for their disagreement on her father-in-law or accept it herself, Agnes chose to suggest that others for their own motives had 'cast the fire brand' between them. The limitations of public action placed on women such as Agnes by their sex, and the problems of communicating over a distance, meant that they were forced to rely on servants. In some cases, a close relationship with a steward or legal adviser could strengthen a gentry woman's position.[36] Equally, a widow's position could be weakened if she was reliant on servants who did not give their first loyalty to her or who saw their own position as strengthened by causing dissent. This letter suggests that in her dealings with her father-in-law Agnes suffered from the lack of a reliable mediator.

In the absence of a messenger who could be implicitly trusted, the physical distance between Agnes and her father-in-law inevitably exacerbated any problems of personal communication. Consequently, Agnes expressed a

---

[35] WRO, CR 1998/Box 60/Folder 1/1 – the date does not include a year, but this can be deduced from its relationship to the earlier letter.

[36] An example would be the relationship between Lady Elizabeth Berkeley and John Smyth of Nibley: see Jan Broadway, 'John Smyth of Nibley: a Jacobean man-of-business and his service to the Berkeley family', *Midland History*, 24 (1999): 79–97.

belief that their differences could be resolved by a personal meeting, where they would be able to communicate directly and with more freedom than through intermediaries. A month before, one of the intermediaries who shuttled between Moor Hall and Weston had himself assured Thomas that, when he spoke in person to Agnes, 'you shall finde her yeld that satisfaction, that you will knowe her to bee very cleare'.[37] Despite her letter's combative tone, Agnes was admitting defeat and a wish for reconciliation. Perhaps as a concession to her pride, she hoped Thomas would visit her at Moor Hall. Otherwise she undertook to go to Weston and do her duty to him in person. She assured Thomas that when they met he would be persuaded that 'I neuer thought of malis, nor horte to you, nor aney of yours'. This underlines the problem many widows faced, of being suspected of placing their own and their birth family's interests above those of their marital kin. Such suspicions would also have limited the usefulness of her father as a mediator. In her conclusion, Agnes consciously aligned herself with the Throckmortons, as she humbly took her leave, 'prayinge god to send you the vppor hand of your eneymis' rather than the 'much happynes' she had hoped for in her previous letter. In both letters to Thomas Throckmorton Agnes dutifully signed herself 'your daughter euer to commande'. Despite obvious difficulties in their relationship, an irrevocable breakdown appears to have been avoided. By his will written in January 1612 at the time of her son's marriage, Thomas left Agnes a bequest of £150 to supplement her jointure.[38]

Physical separation was also a feature of Agnes's relationship with her eldest son. As we have seen, Robert had entered his grandfather's household when he became heir and had subsequently been sent abroad for his education. Although separation from their children at an early age was a not uncommon experience for early modern mothers, the lack of control over Robert's future must have been particularly difficult for Agnes. If she had been responsible for negotiating her son's marriage, it is likely that Agnes would have preferred a match with the daughter of a Catholic family from among her acquaintance who lived in reasonable proximity to her home. In the event, Robert was married to Dorothy, one of the daughters of Sir Francis Fortescue of Salden, Buckinghamshire. Since it was customary for young couples to live with the bride's parents after their marriage, this placed Robert close to his grandfather at Weston. Since Agnes held land only in Warwickshire, she was dependent on the hospitality of others and possibly occasional visits from the couple to Moor Hall in order to see her son. Considered in the light of the social and political standing

---

[37] WRO, CR 1998/Box 60/Folder 3/12.
[38] WRO, CR 1998/Box 73/3. Apart from Robert none of his Throckmorton grandchildren are mentioned in the will.

of the bride's family, the match was a good one. Sir Francis Fortescue's father Sir John had held a number of important posts under Elizabeth and had been a member of her Privy Council. He had built a grand house at Salden, where he entertained James I in 1603.[39] Even a younger daughter would have provided a good dowry. The Jesuit John Gerard described Sir Francis as 'a schismatic (that is, a Catholic by conviction)', but he was not prepared to be openly recusant. His wife Grace, however, was converted by Gerard and under her influence their children were raised as Catholics. Robert Throckmorton's marriage thus gave him a father-in-law who had the wealth, social standing and political contacts to secure his inheritance against the worst depredations of the feudal apparatus of the state. It also drew him closer into the Catholic gentry circle centred on northern Buckinghamshire. As well as Sir Francis Fortescue's own extensive family, the household at Salden included the daughters of Sir Edward Stanley of Tong Castle, one of whom was to marry the Fortescue heir, whilst the other sister, Venetia, was the celebrated beauty and wife of Sir Kenelm Digby. The Digbys were part of the same circle, living nearby at Gayhurst. Although its head was ostensibly Protestant, the household at Salden also harboured a priest, who presumably acted as tutor to Robert and his brothers-in-law.[40]

Despite having secured an act of parliament following his son's death, resettling his lands and allowing him to sell certain manors to pay off his debts, Thomas Throckmorton owed considerable amounts of money by the time of his grandson's marriage. In part, the debts were the inevitable consequence of his recusancy and the related fines. These had cost him £260 a year in Elizabeth's reign and remained burdensome under her successor, although the resettlement of his lands was designed in part to alleviate them.[41] Thomas also lived in a grand, and expensive, style, being described as 'keeping house like a nobleman'. In 1612 Agnes told her father that the annual household expenditure at Weston that year had been £500 more than the revenues. Advising his grandson to reduce the size of his household after his marriage, Thomas Wilford warned him that if he did not he would 'grow as fast in debt' as his grandfather. Once Robert was married, it was intended that some land should be sold to reduce his grandfather's debts, and that the estate should be transferred to Robert. This manoeuvre was designed to relieve the estate of the burden imposed by Thomas's recusancy. The arrangement formed part of the marriage negotiations, but almost a year later Thomas Throckmorton was complaining that Robert and his new father-in-law were 'very backward'

---

[39] J. Andreas Löwe, 'Fortescue, Sir John (1533–1607)', *ODNB*.
[40] Alice Hogge, *God's Secret Agents* (London, 2006), pp. 205–6.
[41] WRO, CR 1998/Box 60/Folder 4/14.

in concluding the arrangement. Once married, Robert came under the influence of Sir Francis Fortescue, whose view of his son-in-law's best interest did not necessarily correspond with that of Robert's other advisers. For Sir Francis the future of his own daughter and any children she might have with Robert was of primary importance. He was not concerned with the future of Robert's siblings, whose annuities and dowries were to come from their brother's estate. He shared Thomas Wilford's belief that expenses should be reduced, but his idea was that Agnes should move from Moor Hall to Weston in order to keep house for the young couple. Her father was only willing to urge this course of action on Agnes if her daughter-in-law Dorothy would have no objection and there was a reduction in the size of the household at the same time. Since the loss of her own household would have restricted her independence, it is likely that Agnes would have opposed any such suggestion.[42] Ensuring that nothing was done to damage her own jointure or to undermine her younger children was a priority for Agnes. Within six months of the marriage she was having to write to Sir Francis about the failure to pay her daughter her annuity, and towards the end of the year her father's letters to Robert were reminding him that his brother Thomas was also waiting for his money, and might have to return home 'to his great hurt'.[43] When Agnes learnt what arrangement was being proposed by George Kempson, a Throckmorton tenant, and Sir Francis for the Warwickshire manor of Haselor, she wrote to her son expressing her misgivings. If they proceeded as suggested, the financial benefit would be little and George Kempson 'will be a lorde ther as well as you'. In an indirect criticism of Sir Francis, she advised her son from her 'motherly affection' to 'looke vnto your one affayrs and take aduise of your one frindes'. This letter also reveals her wider concerns. She did not think it would be wise for Robert to let Ombersley or the tithe of Coughton. However, if he decided to do so, she desired 'to haue the refusinge of them' before the Kempsons. For Agnes, the settlement of the Throckmorton estate was not simply a question of the best financial arrangements, but also of maintaining the prestige of the family. The authority of the Throckmortons was reduced by their inability to take a full part in the life of the community because of their religion and by the reduction of the size of their holdings under Thomas Throckmorton. The status of the Throckmorton name in Warwickshire was obviously of far greater significance to Agnes Throckmorton than to Sir Francis Fortescue. In a subsequent letter she advised Robert that, if Sir Francis did come to

---

[42] Hamilton, *Chronicle of St Monica's*, p. 120; WRO, CR 1998/Box 60/Folder 3/24 and 26.

[43] WRO, CR 1998/CD/Folder 52/6C; CR 1998/Box 60/Folder 3/24 and 26.

an agreement with Kempson, he should himself refuse to confirm it.[44] How likely it was that Robert would have been able to oppose his father-in-law is uncertain, but Sir Francis Fortescue's involvement in the affairs of the Throckmortons was destined to be shortlived. The letters concerning the settlement of Haselor also contain Agnes's hopes that Robert's wife was grown 'stronge' again. Dorothy Fortescue was not, however, destined for a long life. She died in 1617 without producing an heir.

Once he reached the age of maturity, Robert was able to please himself in his second marriage and his choice of Mary, the daughter of Sir Francis Smith of Wootton Wawen, brought him closer to his mother and her social circle in Warwickshire.[45] Like the Fortescues, the male members of the Smith family had been in the habit of practising the limited conformity required to avoid recusancy fines, while their wives raised their children as Catholics. As her eldest son moved closer to her once more as he grew older, the reverse progression occurred in Agnes's relations with at least some of her other children. In one case the physical separation was absolute, as her eldest daughter Margaret became a nun at Louvain in the Spanish Netherlands. According to the history of the convent, her family was opposed to Margaret becoming a nun, although it is unclear whether this refers to her mother or her grandfather. It may be significant that Barbara, one of Agnes's younger sisters, was a nun at Louvain and that it was while visiting her aunt that Margaret apparently made the decision to take the veil. Agnes had been separated from her daughter some time before, when she had gone to live with Sir William Roper and his wife Margaret as a companion to their daughter Anne. Unlike her brother, Margaret was placed within the network of her mother's kin. Margaret Roper, a daughter of Sir Anthony Browne, was a second cousin of Agnes's mother and the Ropers' property was predominantly in Kent close to the Wilfords'. Although Sir William Roper had been prepared to practise occasional conformity, he went abroad rather than be obliged to take the Jacobean oath of allegiance, taking his wife, his daughter and her companion with him. According to the account in the history of the convent, Margaret decided to become a nun after being taken to visit her aunt by Lady Roper and deceived her companions about her intentions. She entered the convent against their wishes, 'leaving many great matches which attended only her consent'. This may exaggerate the

---

[44] WRO, CR 1998/Box 60/3 and 4.

[45] The date of the marriage is uncertain, but probably occurred between 1618 and the death of Sir Francis Smith in 1629 (in his will he referred to his married and unmarried daughters without naming them). Mary's parents were married in 1596 and she was mentioned in her grandfather's will in 1605, so she was probably a few years younger than Robert: William Cooper, *Wootton Wawen: Its History and Records* (Leeds, 1936), pp. 19–29.

sacrifice Margaret made in giving up the world, since her sisters did not achieve great matches, although her mother may certainly have regretted the permanent separation from her daughter. Whatever Margaret gave up in order to become a nun, she certainly made a success of her chosen life. In 1633, twenty years after her profession, she was chosen to be prioress of the convent.[46] Of her sisters, Eleanor married Edward Golding of Colston, Nottinghamshire, and Winifred married Edmund Powell of Sandford, Oxfordshire. These were respectable marriages within the Catholic community, but they were comparatively obscure and suggest a decline in the fortunes of the Throckmorton family.[47] The impression of declining fortunes is reinforced by the failure of any of Agnes's younger sons to marry. Ambrose and Thomas apparently remained in England, although they may have spent some time abroad during their education or fighting in the continental wars.[48] They both fought for the king in the civil war. The youngest son George followed his elder sister abroad to continue his education, entering the English college at Douai in 1619. Since Catholics were barred from English universities by their refusal to take the oath of allegiance, they were obliged to go abroad if they wished to pursue an academic career. Although George was tonsured a year after entering the college, his intention was not to take orders and return to England as a missionary. He pursued his studies for almost two decades and appears to have died in Italy.[49] A series of letters from George to his eldest brother, written when he had been on the continent for more than a decade, show how difficult life was for such Catholic exiles. For his income George was dependent on an annuity from the Throckmorton estate, paid to him in biannual instalments by his brother, and on occasional gifts from his mother. The mechanics of transferring these funds abroad clandestinely were complicated, particularly as the recipient moved around. George's letters show him pursuing his studies with the Jesuits at Angers, La Flèche and Bourges, moving to Rochelle because of the plague and to Montpelier because of the wars in France. The surviving archive shows that George would take advantage of different messengers to acknowledge the receipt of a sum of money, in the hope that at least one letter would reach his family. The warning from his brother that 'it would be better to write seldome

---

[46] Hamilton, *Chronicle of St Monica's*, pp. 120, 107.

[47] Edward Golding was awarded a baronetcy for his service to the Crown during the civil war, but it is unlikely that his wealth or social position would have supported one under other circumstances.

[48] Robert Throckmorton's brother-in-law, John Smith, went abroad to fight for the Catholic powers: E.I. Carlyle, 'Smith, Sir John (1616–1644)', rev. S.L. Sadler, *ODNB*.

[49] *The Douay College Diaries: Third, Fourth and Fifth, 1598–1654*, ed. E.H. Burton and T.L. Williams, CRS, 10–11 (2 vols, London, 1911), vol. 1, pp. 150, 178.

then often' is a reminder that exiled Catholics and those in direct contact with them were regarded with particular suspicion by the authorities.[50]

Although convention demanded that children were respectful towards their parents throughout their lives, as they grew up it inevitably became increasingly difficult to influence them. This does not mean that a conscientious mother like Agnes did not attempt to correct her adult children, when she believed they were in the wrong. In the mid-1620s, Agnes learnt that her sons were indulging in the sport of horseracing, 'but very Carfully kept from me till all the Contrye tallketh of It that Papist hath so much monis that thaye run It a waye'. The concern here is clearly twofold: firstly, the expense and, secondly, the danger that arousing the envy or disapproval of their neighbours would damage the status and reputation of the Throckmorton family within the largely Protestant community. Robert's defence was that the race was his brother's idea rather than his and that there had been no reason to tell his mother about it. Moreover, he maintained that his estate was in better shape than when his grandfather died: 'therefore I would humblie beseech yow to have a better opinion then that I will spende my estate although sometimes I goe abroad to matches for good companie sake'.[51] This exchange is suggestive of the greater social integration that was possible for gentry Catholics under the Stuarts, as the persecution of Elizabeth's reign was relaxed and became a predominantly financial arrangement.[52] Nevertheless, at times of increased tension innocent events could be misinterpreted. In 1625, as events in Europe raised Protestant fears in England, Robert Throckmorton wrote to Secretary Conway concerning reports that recusants were meeting at Weston under cover of darkness and that horses were being trained there. He explained that his uncle Sir Henry Jernegan and his daughter had fallen ill at Weston on their way from Norfolk to Gloucestershire. During their illness, they were visited daily by Robert's aunt Mary Throckmorton, who was sent home after supper in a coach, giving rise to the reports of movements at night. This explanation did not entirely satisfy the Privy Council, and both his aunt and a priest who had allegedly been staying

---

[50] WRO, CR 1998/Box 60/Folder 1/7–17.

[51] WRO, CR 1998/Box 60/Folder 1/6. The dating of this letter to the mid-1620s is based on the reference to Sir Robert Gorges. CR 1998/Box 61/Folder 3/7 shows that Robert Throckmorton came to a settlement with Gorges in 1625.

[52] Recusants forfeited one-third of their lands, but were often able to lease them back from the Crown. In 1637 Robert Throckmorton was granted a 41 lease of his lands for £160 per annum: *A Calendar of the Chancery Docquets of Lord Keeper Coventry 1625–1640*, ed. Jan Broadway, Richard Cust and Stephen Roberts, List and Index Society Special Series, vol. 37 (2004), part 2, p. 274. See also Jan Broadway, '"To equall their virtues": Thomas Habington, recusancy and the gentry of early Stuart Worcestershire', *Midland History*, 29 (2004): 1–24.

with her were examined. The muted response from Secretary Conway, however, with its advice to Robert Throckmorton on how to avoid any trouble in future, is indicative of how the atmosphere for recusants had changed. Yet for Agnes, brought up in a more repressive atmosphere than her sons, the desire not to draw adverse comment from their neighbours remained strong. This did not prevent her involving herself in the clandestine activities of the recusant community. In the following decade she wrote to her eldest son about 'Tom Throck', to whom she was to give £100, but 'he Is so sodenly gon over I mistrust he was In Sum danger for being taken agayne'.[53] However, it seems that Agnes and her family did succeed in maintaining their position as accepted members of the local gentry society. Despite Robert's receipt of a baronetcy for his financial support of Charles I, and the military service of two of his younger brothers, when he died in 1651 he was described to the authorities in London as a recusant but not a delinquent. This meant that his son was able to inherit the estate. It is possible that the local community felt that the damage sustained by the manor house at Coughton was sufficient punishment for the Throckmortons' support of the king.

Like his father before him, Sir Robert Throckmorton died when his son was still a child. In his will he made his wife executrix of his estate, which was sequestrated on account of his recusancy. The abolition of the Court of Wards by the Long Parliament meant that the threat of feudal wardship had been removed, but the authorities did require that the child should have a Protestant guardian. Mary Throckmorton and her brother-in-law Thomas handed over her nine-year-old son Sir Francis to Thomas Salwey of Throckmorton, Worcestershire in March 1651. This enabled the sequestration of the Throckmorton estate to be lifted. Although this appears to be a separation not unlike that endured by Agnes Throckmorton half a century before, it was actually less severe. The boy was placed in the home of Mr East of Weston Underwood, a local gentleman.[54] This was not the separation that had been experienced by previous generations, but a pragmatic arrangement that allowed his mother a full part in the life of her young son. It is indicative of how the situation of gentry widows with young sons had improved over the course of the first half of the seventeenth century. Despite the intentions of the Protestant authorities, Mary Throckmorton was able to ensure that her son was raised in the Catholic faith.

[53] WRO, CR 1998/Box 60/Folder 1/5: Tom Throck may be Robert's younger brother, although it seems more likely that he was a more distant member of the family.

[54] TNA, PROB 11/229; Birmingham Reference Library IIR 60/242277, fols 3–15. See Malcolm Wanklyn's chapter in this volume.

CHAPTER 6

Stratagems for Survival: Sir Robert and Sir Francis Throckmorton, 1640–1660

Malcolm Wanklyn

The Catholic landed community as a whole was in a quandary in the middle years of the seventeenth century. On the one hand, the crisis of the Stuart monarchy, which began in 1640 with a war with Scotland and ended ten years later with the execution of the king and the establishment of a republic was, after all, a conflict between various groups of Protestants. In such circumstances keeping a low profile might seem the best course of action. Catholics, on the other hand, with their commitment to a hierarchy in the Church at the head of which sat an elected monarch, seem like natural royalists, especially as Charles's wife Henrietta Maria had done something to restore the respectability of Catholicism at court, if not in the country. Yet it could be equally well argued that Catholics at the start of the crisis had grounds for being cautious in supporting a king who had assiduously collected recusancy fines, which in the case of the Throckmorton family deprived them of about 15 per cent of their income from land between 1638 and 1642.[1] Moreover, there seems no reason why Catholics should not have been as alienated from the king as other landowners by the various financial exactions of dubious legality introduced in the 1630s. Robert Throckmorton, like several of his Protestant neighbours, had delayed paying Ship Money in 1637.[2] In his case this was not through penury or neglect, but because he had reservations about paying a tax that had not been approved by parliament. In the end he did pay, probably after listening to the advice of Richard Betham, one of his correspondents, to the effect that the tax had been collected in 1625 whilst parliament was sitting without the members taking umbrage, or indeed showing any interest.[3]

---

[1] Martin Havran, *The Catholics in Caroline England* (Stanford, 1962), p. 156; WRO, CR 1998/Box 62/ Folder 11. See note 48 for calculations of the Throckmorton family's income from rents in the mid-seventeenth century.

[2] Anne Hughes, *Politics, Society and Civil War in Warwickshire 1620–1660* (Cambridge, 1990), p. 109.

[3] WRO, CR 1990/Box 60/Folder 2, item 10.

However, simply letting the Protestants get on with what might seem a private quarrel was not an option for Catholics. They and their religion were already in the thick of the quarrel between king and parliament whether they liked it or not. Charles's opponents used the anti-Catholic card again and again during the late 1630s and the 1640s to discredit the king by playing on ingrained fears that international Catholicism was as significant a threat to England's religion and liberties as it had been in Queen Elizabeth's reign; not least because two generations later the threat was insidious rather than blatant.[4]

The association between the king and Catholicism was there for all to see, provided they did not keep their eyes shut. In the first place, Charles I's government prior to 1640 had been lax towards the old enemy at a number of levels. Its foreign policy during the 1630s had been antagonistic towards the Protestant Netherlands and at times very friendly towards Catholic Spain; Catholics, both native and foreign, had been shown favour at court; and Charles had encouraged a High Church group in the Church of England led by Archbishop Laud. Laud was in fact hostile towards Roman Catholicism, but because of their love of ritual and their Arminian doctrine of salvation, he and his associates could be seen as Catholic fellow travellers.[5] Finally, Catholics had raised money in 1639 to support a military campaign, the so-called First Bishops War, against the Scots, who were determined to defend their Presbyterian form of Protestantism against the king's attempt to force them to accept English styles of worship with a Laudian/Catholic flavour.[6] When fighting in earnest began in the following year in the Second Bishops War the king had employed over sixty Catholic officers in the army raised to impose his will on his Scottish subjects.[7] Charles I's failure to defeat a Scottish invasion, and the Scots' army's occupation of Northumberland and Durham, was followed by the election of a new English parliament with a majority determined to alter royal policies for good and for all by increasing parliament's control over government and decreasing that of the king. What had happened in 1639–40 laid the Catholics as a body open to attack. To make matters worse, the leading strategist amongst the king's opponents in the House of Commons was John Pym, who for the past twenty years had consistently sought to chill the blood of those who were prepared to listen with tales

---

[4] Robin Clifton, 'Fear of Popery', in Conrad Russell (ed.), *The Origins of the English Civil War* (London, 1973), pp. 144–67; Peter Lake, 'Anti-Popery, the structure of a prejudice', in Richard Cust and Anne Hughes (eds), *The English Civil War* (London, 1997), pp. 198–201.

[5] Richard Cust, *Charles I* (Harlow, 2005), pp. 122–30, 145–7.

[6] Havran, *Catholics in Caroline England*, pp. 134–55.

[7] TNA, SP 16/473, fols 104–12.

of an international Roman Catholic conspiracy to subvert the strongest Protestant power in Europe.[8]

The new parliament removed the Catholic officers from the English army in November 1640, including Thomas Throckmorton, Robert's brother. He had hoped that family influence would procure for him the captaincy of a troop of horse, but the best command he could get was lieutenant in Captain Minne's company in Colonel George Goring's regiment of foot.[9] A bill was prepared to allow the houses of the Catholic gentry to be searched for arms; an oath of loyalty to Protestantism was administered to all adult males to ascertain who was or was not a papist; and the king was presented with demands to remove Catholic peers from the House of Lords and to require their children to be educated as Protestants. Moreover, the king's indulgence towards Catholics was seen as a form of lunacy, and a prime justification of the political programme of Pym and his colleagues to reduce the powers of the Crown to a cipher. This was essential for the defence of England's Protestantism and its laws and liberties, as the king could not be trusted to stand by his coronation oath.[10]

Anxieties associated with the first few months of the new parliament can be seen in a series of letters from Robert Throckmorton's agents in London to their master written between November 1640 and March 1641. There were brief notices of the more significant political developments, such as the trial of the king's leading adviser Lord Strafford and the impeachment of Archbishop Laud, and matters of a Catholic interest, such as the threat that the estates of families which had not compounded for their recusancy fines might be seized, and that Catholics would be forbidden to reside within 10 miles of London or the court. Robert had also asked to be sent the text of certain acts of parliament. His interest in the taxation bills was financial, in that Catholics would have to pay double subsidies. This was customary and perhaps a relief. Robert's interest in the Triennial Bill, by which there was no longer to be a gap of more than three years between parliaments, may reflect a continued interest in the liberty of the subject suggested by his response to the Ship Money levy. But there were other concerns of a personal nature, and these take up much of the contents of the letters. They also probably explain why the letters stopped when they

---

[8] Conrad Russell, *The Causes of the English Civil War* (Oxford, 1990), pp. 105–6; Conrad Russell, *The Fall of the British Monarchies* (Oxford, 1991), pp. 267, 418–20; Anthony Fletcher, *The Outbreak of the English Civil War* (London, 1981), pp. 77–8, 138.

[9] Peter Young, *Edgehill: the Campaign and the Battle* (Kineton, 1967), pp. 168–9; WRO, CR 1998/Box 60/Folder 4, items 6, 8; TNA, SP 18/473, fol. 106.

[10] Religious anxieties run through the narrative of the 1641 sessions of parliament in Russell, *Fall of the British Monarchies*, chaps 5–11, whilst the constitutional threat is stressed in John Adamson, *The Noble Revolt* (London, 2007).

did. A legal dispute with the Sandys family over the tithes on meadowland at Throckmorton appears to have been settled; and a silver watch repaired or replaced and sent to Weston.[11] More serious was the threat that the recent conversion of common land into pasture at Weston might bring Robert into conflict with the state for breach of anti-enclosure legislation. He and his estate managers drew up a persuasive argument to the effect that all the freeholders and tenants had received compensation for the loss of their rights on the commons, that nobody had been forced to leave their houses for lack of livelihood, and the manure from the additional animals kept on the estate was sufficient to bring an extra 160 acres of arable into cultivation. However, in the spring of 1641 parliament was too busy to bother with enforcing anti-enclosure legislation.[12]

In the autumn of 1641 Pym's predictions about the Catholic menace appeared to take on flesh when a revolt broke out in Ireland in which thousands of Protestants were to be killed or die of exposure and maltreatment. Rumours then spread that English Catholics were plotting something similar, stoked up by such stage-managed events as Cornelius Burges's sermon, preached in the Temple Church in London on 5 November in celebration of England's delivery from the Gunpowder Plot, emphasising again and again that Catholicism was synonymous with treachery.[13] Ten days later, Thomas Beale, a London tailor, confirmed parliament's fears. Treachery was indeed afoot. There was to be general uprising of Catholics in England on 18 November preceded by the murder of 108 members of both Houses of Parliament in execution reminiscent of (and probably derivative from tales about) the St Bartholomew's day massacre in France 70 years earlier.[14] Alarm spread like wildfire. It led to the citizens of Warwick being woken at 4.00 am on that day by the sheriff's emissary with the news that the papists of the county were about to rise led by Robert Throckmorton, Thomas Morgan, Sir Charles Smith and several members of the Sheldon family, all of whom were promptly arrested.[15] Further west a letter from Sir Robert Harley, the radical MP for Herefordshire, to his wife to put their castle at Brampton Brian into a state of defence, caused fear of an imminent uprising to spread quickly to Ludlow and Bewdley, and then to Bridgnorth, where the inhabitants lit a huge fire in the High Street and sat round it drinking sack until dawn broke on 18 November.[16] Shrewsbury

[11] WRO, CR 1998/Box 60/Folder 2, items 20–37, 39, 48.
[12] WRO, CR 1998/Box 60/Folder 2, 51 and Folder 4, items 4, 5, 8.
[13] Adamson, *Noble Revolt*, pp. 424–5.
[14] *Journals of the House of Lords*, vol. 4, pp. 439–41.
[15] Hughes, *Politics, Society and Civil War*, pp. 133–5.
[16] Brian Manning, 'The Outbreak of the English Civil War', in R.H. Parry (ed.), *The English Civil Wars and After* (London, 1970), pp. 5–6; C.D. Gilbert, 'The Popish Plot of

and Gloucester set about repairing their walls and acquiring cannon and ammunition. Month by month the watch on the gates intensified as the country drifted towards civil war, whilst in the countryside village constables were ordered to keep a strict watch on all crossroads and to apprehend suspicious persons who might be carrying letters.[17]

With the outbreak of civil war in England in the summer of the following year, pressure on the Catholic landed community increased. As parliament's newly raised regiments left London to establish control over the south and the Midlands, so they plundered the houses of Catholics, egged on at first by their officers who did not have the means to feed or to pay them. Those who had scruples, like the London journeyman Nehemiah Wharton – a volunteer in Denzil Holles's regiment of foot – could see themselves as doing God's work. But this was no more than a fig leaf, as he wrote with approval of what can only be regarded as protection money, with soldiers demanding copious quantities of food and the households providing it in the hope that the soldiers would go away.[18] One brigade left London during the second week in August heading for Coventry, threatened by a siege. On 21 August it passed quite close to Weston. At about the same time other regiments were beginning to converge on Northampton, which was the rendezvous for the Parliamentary army commanded by the Earl of Essex.[19] One or other of these caused Robert Throckmorton to flee for his life to his West Midlands estates,[20] but it proved an unnecessary precaution as the house escaped the attention of the Roundhead soldiery, probably on account of the speed of their advance and Weston's sequestered position on the edge of Yardley Chase and away from major roads. However, Coughton would not provide a safe refuge. A month later the full Parliamentary field army passed close by on its march from Northampton via Warwick and Alcester to Worcester, shadowing the king's forces as they moved across country from Nottingham to Shrewsbury.[21] Essex's rearguard saw Coughton as a good billet for the night and pandemonium followed. In the words of a letter sent to the editor of one of the London weekly journals:

1641', *Worcestershire Recusant*, 44 (1984): 31–5.

[17] Ettwell Barnard, 'Some original documents concerning Worcestershire and the Great Rebellion', *Transactions of the Worcestershire Archaeological Society*, 6 (1929): 72–4; Hughes, *Politics, Society and Civil War*, p. 135; Andrew Warmington, *Civil War, Interregnum and Restoration in Gloucestershire* (Woodbridge, 1997), p. 32; Shropshire Record Office, Shrewsbury, Shrewsbury Borough Library MS, 270.

[18] TNA, SP 16/491/119.

[19] TNA, SP 16/492/2, 5.

[20] WRO, CR 1998/Box 86, item 26.

[21] Malcolm Wanklyn and Frank Jones, *A Military History of the English Civil Wars* (Harlow, 2004), p. 44; TNA, SP 18/492/21.

We lay at a place called Colfon in Warwickshire, and there lived a great papist, one Frogmorton, who hearing of our coming, fled away from his house, and his whole family, which the soldiers did plunder, and found abundance of images and pictures, which they brake and committed to the fire. They likewise burnt many popish books, some of them being almost as big as we could lift with one hand, printed in parchment, and others were thrown into a great moat. In the house we found 3 or 4 murthering pieces, brass pots and a great sheet of lead about 500 weight, which was hidden under the ground. The soldiers drank up his perry, cider and beer almost all. They did lie on his feather beds all night, and in the morning cut them, emptied out the feathers, and carried the ticks away with them and also silk hangings for beds. And abundance such like things they did there.[22]

Such outrages were random, and also visited on Protestant Royalists such as Lord Leigh of Stoneleigh, whose herd of deer found its way into the stomachs of Essex's soldiers on 27 August.[23] Indiscipline was causing concern, as soldiers were plundering Parliamentarian supporters or putting them under pressure, and Essex issued a book of martial law to curb such behaviour, which was read at the head of every regiment. However, Catholics were seen as fair game, the sack of Coughton taking place some weeks after its dreadful penalties were read to the soldiery. Matters did quieten down, but this was probably as much a result of the solidification of the front as of the introduction of martial law. Essex's army plundered Castle Morton twice, in late September 1642 and in early September 1643.[24] However, the settling down was followed by the systematic financial milking of Catholic landowners via sequestration in areas controlled by parliament. Whether they were active supporters of Charles I or not, their estates were seized and then let. Only a small fraction of the rent was allowed to them for the upkeep of the family, the rest being taken by the state as a form of taxation.[25]

Even in such circumstances keeping their heads down and offering no resistance were still possibly the best options for the Catholic peerage and gentry in areas of the country firmly under Parliamentary control, but this was not the case across the whole of north and central England

---

[22] BL, Thomason Tracts, E240 23. The 'murthering pieces' were probably the equivalent of duck guns designed to fire a shower of shot against a flock of birds, the brass pots possibly convertible into mortars by being melted down and recast. Of more immediate significance was the lead, presumably roofing material, which could be easily converted into musket balls.

[23] TNA, SP 18/491/138.

[24] *Mercurius Rusticus*, reproduced in facsimile in Robin Jeffs (ed.), *The English Revolution, III: Newsbooks 1: Oxford Royalist* (4 vols, London, 1971), vol. 4, pp. 132–4.

[25] Sir Charles Firth and Sir Robert Rait (eds), *Acts and Ordinances of the Interregnum 1642–1660* (3 vols, London, 1911), vol. 1, p. 107.

or in south-west and south-central England, which were occupied for much of the time by the king's forces or were in a disputed area. However, there were powerful incentives for siding with the king as the lesser of the two evils, which were something more than a reaction to their personal circumstances as victims of persecution for their faith's sake. In the first place, Catholic landowners must have shared some of the concerns that drove into the king's camp in 1642 many Protestant landowners; men who had had serious reservations about the policies he had pursued in the 1630s. The drift into lawlessness, the involvement of ordinary people in the political process, the threat to property as the country appeared to be drifting into anarchy: these were powerful incentives to join the Royalists, as Pym's supporters in parliament appeared to be recklessly dismantling the coercive powers of the Crown.[26] Second, loyalty to the anointed king was as potent a force for Catholic landowners as to Protestants. Unlike in previous reigns, there was no serious Catholic claimant to the throne; the king was married to a Catholic wife, whose patronage had helped to raise the hopes of the Catholic community for a measure of religious toleration; and the king himself appeared to have no hostility towards Catholics as individuals. When a Parliamentarian informed Edward, Lord Herbert, the future Marquis of Worcester, that the Civil War was between Protestants and papists, he replied that he did not recognise it as such but as one between those who were loyal to their anointed monarch and those who were not.[27] Edward Walsingham went one stage further: Charles was God's vice-regent on earth.[28] Finally, there was the self-interest factor. If Catholics were enthusiastic in their support for the Royalist cause, the lifting of the ban on celebrating Mass might be the king's reward for their loyalty. It is almost certainly with an eye to the latter that Walsingham wrote his three remarkable biographies of contemporary Catholic heroes, one of whom was Robert Throckmorton's brother-in-law, John, fifth son of Sir Charles Smith of Wootton Wawen, who had rescued the royal standard after it had been captured at the Battle of Edgehill, rose from the rank of lieutenant to that of major general and died of wounds sustained at the battle of Cheriton in Hampshire in March 1644.[29]

---

[26] Peter Newman, *The Old Service* (Manchester, 1993), pp. 197–8, 204. Fletcher, *Outbreak of the English Civil War*, p. 406, provides a neat summing-up of the factors that would have inclined landowners to support the king in the summer and autumn of 1642.

[27] John and Thomas Webb, *Memorials of the Civil War in Herefordshire* (London, 1879), pp. 30, 193.

[28] Edmund Walsingham, 'Hector Britannicus', Camden Society, 3rd series, 18 (1910), p. 119.

[29] These paragons were Sir John Smith, Sir Henry Gage and Sir John Digby. Edmund Walsingham, *Britannicus Virtutis Imago* (Oxford, 1644); *Alter Britannicus Heros* (Oxford, 1645); and 'Hector Britannicus'.

Nevertheless the commitment of Catholic members of landed families to the Royalist cause in the Civil War has been a matter of controversy over the years. After the Restoration it was alleged that 198 of the 500 officers who had died fighting for Charles I were Catholics, a claim strenuously denied by Low Church Anglicans such as William Lloyd.[30] More recently, Peter Newman has claimed that of the 603 men who attained the rank of colonel or above in the king's armies 117 were Catholics.[31] That is not far short of one-fifth of the total, at a time when the percentage of Catholics in the population of country as a whole is unlikely to have exceeded 2 per cent. He has also shown that an overwhelming percentage came from the landed classes. Admittedly the percentage of Catholics was considerably higher amongst the peerage and the gentry than amongst those below them in the status hierarchy, but not to such an extent.[32]

On the other hand, Keith Lindley has claimed that Catholic landowners responded to the outbreak of the Civil Wars, not by becoming enthusiastic Royalists, but by sitting on their hands. In his study of London and eight counties chosen for their social, economic and geographical diversity, he showed that many Catholic families had their estates sequestrated merely for recusancy; that is, refusing to attend Protestant forms of worship, not for delinquency, which was defined as giving support to the Royalist cause. In this he saw a similar pattern to that which Havran had discerned in the 1630s.[33] However, Lindley's hypothesis has been attacked very effectively on the grounds that very many of the Catholic families who were apparently neutrals came from the bottom end of the gentry hierarchy, where commitment to one side the other was equally low or even lower amongst non-Catholic families.[34]

Moving down from national to local level, very different findings have emerged from studies of the five contiguous counties of Lancashire, Cheshire, Staffordshire, Shropshire and Warwickshire. Blackwood's meticulous analysis of allegiance in Lancashire, where the percentage of Catholics at all levels of society was almost certainly higher than in any other part of England, showed a high level of support for the Royalist cause amongst

---

[30] Joyce L. Malcolm, *Caesar's Due: Loyalty and King Charles I* (London, 1983), p. 51, quoting nineteenth-century sources, which apparently used an eighteenth-century updating of the list compiled by Roger Palmer, Earl of Castlemaine, and printed in his *The Catholique Apologie* (London, 1673).

[31] Newman, *The Old Service*, p. 218.

[32] Ibid., pp. 227–8.

[33] Keith Lindley, 'The Part Played by Catholics', in B. Manning (ed.), *Politics, Religion and the English Civil War* (London, 1973), pp. 136–7; Havran, *Catholics in Caroline England*, p. 156.

[34] Peter Newman, 'Catholic Activists in the North', *Recusant History*, 14/1 (1977): 26–38.

the landed gentry apparently at all levels.[35] In the case of Cheshire, where the number of Catholic landed families was far fewer, John Morrill has commented on the lack of activity showed by the three major families in the Wirrall: the Masseys of Puddington, the Stanleys of Hooton and the Pooles of Poole.[36] However, the lack of activity displayed by the three Catholic families living in the Wirrall may not have been as pronounced as Morrill suggested. Sir William Massey sent his sons into the Royalist army, whilst James Poole, head of the family in 1642, almost certainly died of wounds suffered during the war, probably in an engagement at Christleton in January 1645.[37] Only the Stanleys seem to have kept their hands totally clean.

In my own work on Shropshire, where Catholic landed families were even thinner on the ground, both in numbers and in the acreage they owned, there was little evidence of support for the king even amongst those which had or had had close connections with the court, like the Brookes of Madeley and the Lacons of Kinlet.[38] In Staffordshire, where Catholic allegiance was much higher, Pickles found a marked lack of commitment to the Royalist cause.[39] Mosler's findings for Warwickshire were not dissimilar, but the range of evidence he used was limited and his tables are swamped with evidence pertaining to those families at the bottom of the gentry hierarchy.[40] The more intensive exploration of primary sources in Hughes's masterly account of county government in the 1640s and 1650s shows that the leading Catholic families of Warwickshire displayed considerably more support for the king at the outbreak of the war than Mosler had claimed.[41] Gilbert reaches a middle-of-the-road conclusion with regard to Worcestershire, but although his paper is thoroughly researched, I cannot agree with all the connections he makes between Royalist officers

---

[35] B.G. Blackwood, *The Lancashire Gentry and the Great Rebellion* (Manchester, 1978), pp. 63–6.

[36] John Morrill, *County Government and Society in the English Revolution* (London, 1974), pp. 17–18, 71.

[37] *Calendar of the Proceedings of the Committee of Compounding* [hereafter, CCC], ed. Mary Green (5 vols, London, 1889), vol. 3, p. 1802; George Ormerod, *The History of Cheshire* (3 vols, London, 1882), vol. 2, p. 424; Rupert Morris, *The Siege of Chester* (Chester, 1924), p. 222n.

[38] Malcolm Wanklyn, 'Landownership and Allegiance in Cheshire and Shropshire in the First Civil War', unpublished PhD thesis, University of Manchester (1976), p. 503.

[39] The findings of his MA Thesis, 'Studies in Royalism', are cited in Malcolm, *Caesar's Due*, pp. 51–2.

[40] David F. Mosler, 'Warwickshire Catholics in the Civil War', *Recusant History*, 15/4 (1980), pp. 259–62.

[41] Hughes, *Politics, Society and Civil War*, p. 167. Eleven out of 18 attended the commission of array put into execution by the Earl of Northampton in August 1642.

and recusancy.[42] In all of this the problem is one of quantification, both sides of the argument relying on the painstaking analysis of data that is not only incomplete and therefore possibly unrepresentative of Catholic landed society as a whole, but also bedevilled by the notion of who was or was not a Catholic and who was or was not a member of the landed gentry.[43]

In the last thirty years or so disenchantment with the possibility of constructing definitive narratives of the past grounded on quantification has placed the spotlight firmly on qualitative research, which in recusant history means intensive studies of individual families. The Throckmortons of Coughton and Weston are perhaps not an ideal case study, as documentation is patchy and problematic, and the process by, and even the extent to which they kept loyal to the Catholic faith under the nose of the Commonwealth regime is still to some degree veiled in mystery. Nevertheless, attention to their history during the 1650s offers fascinating insights into how a Catholic family managed to secure its position in landed society as the national crisis unfolded.

The head of the Throckmorton family was Robert, who was about fifty years of age in 1642 and married to Mary, daughter of Sir Charles Smith of Wootton Wawen.[44] She was his second wife. By his first wife he had had no children that survived, and his second marriage had not been that successful in demographic terms either. Several children died in infancy, the only survivors in 1642 being a daughter, Anne, probably born in about 1635, and a son, Francis, who was less than a year old.[45] The Warwickshire estate, though considerably smaller than it had been in 1560, still included a scattering of manors between Studeley and Alcester.[46] The family also owned the manor of Throckmorton in Worcestershire between Pershore and the county town, and the manor of Weston Underwood on the Buckinghamshire/Northamptonshire border. In 1642 the income from the entire landholding was probably in the region of £1,300 per annum, which would have placed the family amongst the upper/middling gentry

---

[42] C.D. Gilbert, 'Worcestershire Catholics and the English Civil Wars', *Recusant History*, 20/5 (1991): 336–57.

[43] *Inventories of Worcestershire Landed Gentry*, ed. Malcolm Wanklyn, Worcestershire Historical Society, new ser., 16 (1998), p. xviii; Malcolm Wanklyn, 'Paying for the Sins of our Forefathers: Catholic Loyalism in the Midlands in the Great Civil War', *Midland Catholic History*, 12 (2006), 40–41.

[44] See Jan Broadway's chapter in this volume.

[45] Ettwell Barnard, *A Seventeenth-Century Country Gentleman: Sir Francis Throckmorton 1640–1680* (Cambridge, 1944), p. 4; WRO, CR 1998/Exhibition Box 22, p. 27.

[46] The manors of Tanworth in Arden and Sheldon in Warwickshire, and also considerable quantities of land adjacent to the manor of Throckmorton, had been sold since 1560: Birmingham Reference Library, MS 3888/A1012; SCLA, DR 37/2/Box 109, item 60; WRO, CR 1998/Box 65/Folder 1, item 9.

in the part of the country where the estates were situated.[47] However, out of this had to come the composition for recusancy of £160 agreed with the Exchequer in 1638 for a period of four years, and annuities payable to Robert's younger brothers, at least three of whom were alive in the late 1630s, which probably amounted to £60 per annum.[48] The fact that Robert's mother had not taken a second husband, however, probably meant that the lands that had been settled on her as a jointure at the time of her marriage in about 1589 were managed as part of the estate.

The National Trust guidebook to Coughton describes the family as instinctively Royalist. This may have been the case. There is some evidence in the case of Robert Throckmorton, but it is not that convincing when put to the test. In the first place, it is a matter of record that he was awarded a baronetcy on 1 September 1642, three weeks after the king had raised the royal standard at Nottingham Castle, an action that is generally regarded as the start of the Civil War.[49] However, this was not a reward for services performed in the present or promised in the future. The title of baronet had been created in James I's reign as a means of raising money, and Sir Robert duly paid the sum of £1,095. Moreover, there are examples in other counties of newly created baronets who remained neutral, like the Salopians Sir Edward Corbet of Longnor and Sir Francis Lawley of Spoonhill.[50] The timing may have been no more than a coincidence, probably of little significance in terms of allegiance, and possibly no more than a blatantly financial transaction between an impecunious monarch and an ambitious member of the landed gentry.[51]

Second, Sir Robert appears in a list of Warwickshire gentry who were present when the earl of Northampton attempted to raise south Warwickshire for the king's cause at the end of August 1642.[52] Anne Hughes regards the list as an accurate one, as it was compiled within a few months of the meeting taking place, but goes too far in assuming

---

[47] A comprehensive rent roll for the Throckmorton estates does not exist for the second quarter of the seventeenth century, but evidence presented to parliament's sequestration committees valued the Warwickshire estates at £865 pa and the Buckinghamshire estate at £241 pa. There is no evidence relating to Throckmorton in the papers of the Committee for Compounding, but it is unlikely that the total gross annual income provided by the estate for the family exceeded £1,200: WRO, CR 1998/Box 65/Folder 1, item 9; CCC, vol. 1, p. 68.

[48] Thomas was entitled to £20 a year out of the estate, and Ambrose and George probably received the same amount: WRO, CR 1998/Box 60/Folder 1, items 7–12: Folder 2, items 2–4; and Box 62, item 11.

[49] WRO, CR 1998/Box 61/Folder 3, item 8.

[50] Wanklyn, 'Landownership and Allegiance in Cheshire and Shropshire', p. 102.

[51] The flush of baronetcy conferred in the early 1640s was spread over a period of 15 months beginning in mid-1641.

[52] Northamptonshire Record Office, Northampton [NRO], Finch-Hatton ms, 4284.

that turning up was a sign of anything other than exceedingly lukewarm royalism.[53] Several of those who attended seem to have taken no further action in support of the king, and Robert may well have been one of them. There is also no evidence that attending the commission of array and the award of the baronetcy had anything to do with the sack of Coughton several weeks later. The letter from the London journal reproduced above says nothing about 'Frogmorton' supporting the king. Robert and his family were Catholics, and that was enough.

A third piece of evidence that may indicate firm commitment to the royalist cause concerns not Sir Robert but his younger brother Thomas, who was in command of a company in Colonel Richard Bolle's regiment in the royalist field army at the start of the war. Most regiments were territorial in origin. Bolle's, which joined the king between Nottingham and Derby on 13 September 1642, fell into that category, having been raised by Lord Paget in Staffordshire.[54] It is just possible that Thomas's company was raised in south Warwickshire and east Worcestershire during the Earl of Northampton's recruiting operations, which had followed the proclamation of the commission of array at the end of August. But if this had been the case, one would have expected to find Thomas's company in the earl's own regiment, especially as Sir Robert's manor of Weston bordered the earl's immense Castle Ashby estate, and Sir Robert was one of Northampton's political supporters in 1640.[55] Regrettably, the fact that Thomas was an Edgehill captain is therefore merely evidence of his own allegiance, nothing more. It cannot be taken as evidence that Sir Robert's level of commitment to the king's cause extended as far as supporting or conniving at raising men to fight parliament. Moreover, if he had done, this would have been known in the area and counted against him when the Parliamentary authorities decided who was a Catholic Royalist and who a Catholic neutral. As it was, Sir Robert was treated as a recusant, not as a recusant delinquent when his lands came under the control of parliament.[56] And this is not surprising given the family circumstances. In Cheshire and Shropshire, landowners who showed little or no commitment to either side tended to be men who were 50 years of age or over, who had an heir who

---

[53] Hughes, *Politics, Society and Civil War*, pp. 158–9, 161.

[54] Young, *Edgehill*, pp. 16, 169, 221–2. Thomas himself may also have been a professional. Prior to the outbreak of the First Bishops War in 1639 he is described in one document as Captain Throckmorton: WRO, CR 1998/Folder 52, item 8, John Tyringham to Robert Townshend, 26 April 1639.

[55] WRO, CR 1998/Box 60/Folder 4, item 17; Hughes, *Politics, Society and Civil War*, pp. 144–9.

[56] WRO, CR 1998/Box 86, item 30.

was a minor, and whose family had sold land during the previous eighty years.[57] Sir Robert fitted all three criteria.

What little can be pieced together of the behaviour of Sir Robert and his wife during the war points to a conscious decision not only to avoid any outright commitment to the king's cause, but also to try to appease the king's enemies in whose quarters their estates were situated. Sir Robert did not take up arms himself or serve as a civilian administrator, and the claim that he was a Justice of the Peace in Worcestershire in 1644 is based on faulty editing of the document from which the evidence is supposed to derive.[58] In addition, Sir Robert's name does not appear on any of the quite extensive, if scattered, administrative documents produced by the royalists of Worcestershire and, unlike fellow Catholics Thomas Hornilow and William Sheldon, he was not taken prisoner at Worcester when it surrendered in August 1646.[59] The only direct evidence of involvement in royalist affairs is his signature on a petition sent to the king by the Worcestershire gentry in December 1644, which is to be found in the papers of Henry Townshend of Elmley Lovatt.[60] This petition formed part of a propaganda campaign waged through the south and west of England in areas under the control of the king's forces. Charles had made several efforts to bring parliament to the conference table in the late summer and autumn of 1644 but these had got nowhere. Impressed by the hankering after peace he found in Somerset during his march eastwards from his victory over the Earl of Essex in Cornwall in September, he encouraged the formation of provincial associations with a wider membership than before to petition parliament for peace, whilst threatening to raise new forces for the king if their efforts were spurned.[61] Signatories of the Worcestershire petition included a number of Catholic landowners who had yet to play a part in the war, including Sir Robert. There seems to have been a deliberate policy to draw Catholics into the fold at the time, which may be evidence

---

[57] Wanklyn, 'Landownership and Allegiance in Cheshire and Shropshire', p. 517.

[58] *The Diary of Henry Townshend*, ed. John Willis Bund, *Worcestershire Historical Society*, (2 vols, 1915, 1920), vol. 2, pp. 183–4.

[59] CSPD, 1645–47, p. 456. A family chronicle compiled 150 years after the Civil War claimed that Sir Robert went to Worcester after the first sack of Coughton, but this seems unlikely as the city was in Parliamentary hands until early December 1642. WRO, CR 1998/EB/ 22, p. 27; Wanklyn and Jones, *Military History of the English Civil War*, pp. 62–3.

[60] *Diary of Henry Townshend*, vol. 2, p. 185.

[61] Ronald Hutton, *The Royalist War Effort 1642–1646* (London, 1982), pp. 157–9, 162–3 provides an effective narrative of the progress of the associations, but sees it as a concession forced on the king by the weakness of his military position in the winter of 1644–45. For the argument that the associations of 1644–45 were a deliberate political stratagem dreamt up by the king and his more moderate advisers to drum up more support for the Royalist cause, see Wanklyn and Jones, *Military History of the Civil War*, pp. 198, 230.

of their previous neutrality, but it backfired, as one of the grievances of the Clubmen of the border counties was the involvement of Catholics such as the Earl of Shrewsbury.[62]

The evidence for the family's movements after the sack of Coughton is slight, but it suggests that Sir Robert spent all or part of the war at Moor Hall in Warwickshire, where his elderly mother had lived,[63] whilst Lady Throckmorton returned to Weston. It was to Moor Hall that she secured a pass in the autumn of 1644 to visit her husband who was seriously ill. She did not return until past the expiry date, when she made a full and contrite apology to the officer who had issued the pass, Sir Samuel Luke, the governor of Newport Pagnell, which dominated the upper Ouse valley where the Weston estate was situated. There is further evidence that she was keen to remain on good terms with Luke. When the Newport Pagnell garrison experienced a shortage of musket balls in June 1645, he instituted a search for lead in the vicinity focusing on recusant and Royalist houses. Lady Throckmorton and her fellow recusant chatelaine Lady Tyringham were very cooperative, in contrast to Lady Digby at Gayhurst. The latter not only abused Luke's soldiers but was also discovered to be hiding a sheet of lead in a dung heap. Lady Throckmorton also played host to Oliver Cromwell on the night of 12/13 June as he made his way from Cambridge with reinforcements to join the New Model Army at Northampton just prior to the Battle of Naseby.[64] Luke describes this as if it were a matter of course, not another chance to squeeze resources out of a recusant family. Finally, when the war was over and Sir Robert was anxious to leave Moor Hall for Weston, he obeyed all the legal niceties. Before the war he was not permitted to move about the country without the approval of the Privy Council. In October 1646 that body no longer functioned. Instead he made his appeal to the House of Lords, and it was granted without any question.[65]

[62] Hutton, *Royalist War Effort*, pp. 159, 162–3.

[63] She was still alive in September 1644: SCLA, DR 165/1253/1.

[64] WRO, CR 1998/EB/22, p. 27; Sir Samuel Luke, *Letter Books*, ed. H.G. Tibbutt, HMC, Joint Publications, 4 (London, 1963), items 724, 725, 739, 823, 965. A family tradition claims that Lady Throckmorton was treating a young cornet of horse in the Parliamentary army for a swelling of the face at Weston when a party of 'enemy horse' (that is Royalist) arrived at the house. She hid him in a 'wood hole', presumably a hole in a tree, until the danger had passed. Subsequently she was thanked by a general officer, who promised that 'he would stand like a wall of brass between her and danger'. The general concerned was likely to have been Major-General Phillip Skippon, who commanded a corps based at Newport Pagnell between October 1643 and January 1644, the only period when royalist horse were operating in the lower Ouse valley in force. This type of evidence is, of course, highly suspect, but if true it would explain why Skippon's son and young Sir Francis went on a fishing trip when Sir Francis was at Cambridge in 1655. WRO, CR 1998/EB/22, p. 27; ibid., Large Carved Box, item 39, fol. 43.

[65] *Lords Journals*, vol. 8, p. 514.

There he seems to have remained quietly until his death four years later. It is highly unlikely that the Robert Throckmorton captured in arms for the king in Hertfordshire in 1648 during the second Civil War was Sir Robert.[66]

The behaviour during the war of Robert's brothers, Thomas and Ambrose Throckmorton, was not such as to hazard the quietist line taken by Sir Robert and Lady Mary. After the Restoration, Thomas's name appears in a list of former Royalist colonels of foot and his brother Ambrose on a list of lieutenant colonels, but this in itself does not indicate that either had played a conspicuous role in the fighting.[67] Thomas had given up his command in Bolle's regiment before May 1643, by which time his lieutenant, Robert Skerrow, had succeeded him as company commander.[68] This does not necessarily mean that he had left the service. He could well have obtained a promotion elsewhere, like his brother-in-law, John Smith, who served for a time in Lord Herbert's regiment of horse before getting his own regiment and a major generalcy in the king's western army.[69] However, Thomas's name does not appear in the most fertile source of information, the Indigent Officer list of 1663, in which junior officers very frequently mentioned their company commanders.[70] The only other evidence of Thomas's military career in the king's army is a commission issued on 4 October 1643 appointing him colonel of a new regiment of infantry, 1,200 strong, which he was to raise from volunteers.[71] The timing is probably significant. Prince Rupert was about to launch a military initiative in the upper Ouse valley, in association with troops from the king's northern army, which were to advance through the Fenlands. The final objective was to make an incursion into East Anglia, parliament's main reservoir of recruits after London. The first stage was to be the occupation of Newport Pagnell, only 6 miles or so from Weston, as an army base. Possibly Thomas promised to raise his men from the estates of his brother and local recusant families, and it is not unlikely that Thomas chose his younger brother Ambrose to serve as lieutenant colonel.

Ambrose's portrait in armour duly appears on the grand staircase at Coughton today (Figure 6.1), but there is no evidence that the regiment was actually raised, largely because the Ouse valley campaign scarcely got off the ground.[72] None of Thomas's regimental officers made claims on

---

[66] *CSPD, 1648–49*, p. 184.
[67] TNA, SP 29/159/45.
[68] Young, *Edgehill*, pp. 221–2.
[69] BL, Thomason Tracts, E 53 10.
[70] TNA, SP 29/68.
[71] NRO, Finch-Hatton MS, 133. The volume is not paginated, but the commissions, which are reproduced in date order, make up the final section.
[72] Wanklyn and Jones, *Military History of the English Civil War*, pp. 127–32.

Figure 6.1   Ambrose Throckmorton, Coughton Court.

the Indigent Officer fund, and I have not come across mention of it in any Royalist sources for this campaign, which, though obscure, is well documented in terms of the military formations of troops involved.[73] If Thomas had managed to raise any men, they are likely to have served in the short-lived garrisons Rupert planted at Grafton Regis or Towcester, but there is no mention of them in the contemporary biography of the commander of Grafton Regis, Sir John Digby of Gayhurst, or in the letters and administrative papers associated with the short life and successful evacuation of the Towcester garrison between November 1643 and early January 1644.[74] Nevertheless, Thomas continued to be described as the colonel in subsequent documents in the family archive.

The Throckmorton estates appear to have been sequestrated as soon as the general ordinance to that effect passed through its parliamentary procedures.[75] By that date both Coughton and Weston fell within areas of the country under Parliamentary control, though both were close to disputed territory with royalist garrisons not too far away. This explains the fate of Coughton, which became an out-garrison of Warwick in the autumn of 1643, defending the approach to the town from the direction of the Cotswolds through an area that was pretty firmly under Royalist control from October 1643 onwards, as regiments returned from the First Battle of Newbury settled into new quarters. However, Coughton was abandoned before Christmas, not through Royalist pressure, but seemingly because it was no longer needed.[76] Nevertheless the house suffered appallingly, either in the process of making it defensible or whilst it was being abandoned so that the king's forces could not refortify it. A document written in 1648 describes major damage to the fabric – 'the gatehouse dismantled and the house quite ruined'.[77] This was almost certainly not a case of special

---

[73] Bodleian Library, Oxford, Firth MS, C6, fols 268–9, 278, 291 and Firth MS C7, fol. 51; BL, Add. MS 18980, fols 136, 159, 168; BL, Add. MS 18981, fols 1, 19.

[74] Walsingham, *Hector Britannicus*, pp. 91–4.

[75] Firth and Rait, *Acts and Ordinances of the Interregnum*, vol. 1, p. 107.

[76] *The Life, Diary, and Correspondence etc. of Sir William Dugdale*, ed. William Hamper (London, 1827), pp. 55–7. One of the military objectives of Colonel Bridges, the governor of Warwick, was to dislodge Lord Molineux's regiment of horse from its quarters at Chipping Camden. This was some distance away, but Bridges' horse, although they were able to carry out a successful attack on the town, were unable to dislodge the enemy permanently. In mid-November, however, Molineux's regiment marched into Cheshire under Lord Byron's command. Its departure was quickly followed by the abandonment of Coughton. (Bodleian, Firth MS, C6, fol. 252; HMC, Duke of Portland MS, vol. 1, p. 161; John Willis Bund, *The Civil War in Worcestershire 1642–1646 and the Scottish Invasion of 1651* (London, 1905), pp. 105–6.

[77] WRO, CR 1998/Box 86, item 26.

pleading. It can be inferred from the principal source on the 1650s that it could not be lived in.

The minute book of the sequestration committee for Warwickshire for the period 1646–50 contains copious information about the leasing of recusant estates in the county, but very little about the lands of the Throckmortons, other than the fact that they were leased in 1648 to Richard Kempson of Ombersley gent and Francis Waters of Sambourne gent, Kempson having been the sole tenant in the previous year.[78] The latter had been Sir Robert's correspondent in London in 1640–41,[79] whilst the former acted as a land agent and rent collector for the Throckmorton family throughout the 1650s.[80] This was not a fix by which the Throckmortons hoodwinked the Parliamentary authorities. A powerful resolution had been taken by the Warwickshire county committee only three weeks before the conclusion of the first arrangement to the effect that no agreement should be made with a tenant without the committee seeing 'exact particulars' of the rent roll. Any composition made without this evidence would be null and void.[81]

In 1648 Catholics were allowed to pay a compounding fine to regain control over their estates. The Throckmorton family, however, ignored the opportunity, probably on account of the size of the penalty, which in their case would have been between £4,000 and £6,000. On the other hand, there may have been an obstacle to compounding, as most of the revenue extracted from the estate via sequestration was reserved for a special purpose. It is an outstanding irony (or else the mark of a macabre sense of humour on the part of parliament) that it was paid to Charles I's eldest nephew, the fugitive Karl Ludwig, Elector Palatine, whose father had been evicted from his lands in Germany by Catholic troops during the early years of the Thirty Years War. One of the last entries in the minute book is to the effect that the estate was returning to the committee's hands, Karl Ludwig having been dispossessed in March 1649, six weeks after his uncle's execution, in what may be seen as the final act in the eradication of all traces of the Stuart monarchy.[82] However, Karl Ludwig would probably have lost his income from England whatever his uncle's fate. At that stage in the 1640s he was not in the frame as a possible replacement king. Moreover, he was no longer in need of poor relief, having recovered the Rhenish part of his ancestral lands by the treaty of Westphalia concluded in 1648, which brought the Thirty Years War to an end.

---

[78] The surnames appear in a list of Warwickshire and Worcestershire recusants compiled in 1655–56, but not these Christian names: TNA, C 203/4.

[79] WRO, CR 1998/Box 60/Folder 2, items 19–32.

[80] WRO, CR1998/ Box 86, items 46, 46a.

[81] BL, Add. MS 35098, fols 37, 41, 100.

[82] BL, Add. MS 35098, fol. 127.

On 16 January 1651 Sir Robert died at his house at Weston, having made his will three days earlier. He appointed Mary, his wife, as sole executor and left her the manors of Throckmorton in Worcestershire, Oversley, Coughton and Sambourne in Warwickshire, and the houses at Coughton and Moor Hall for the duration of Francis's minority. The revenues from them were to pay his debts and the costs of his funeral, and to provide a dowry of £1,000 for his daughter Anne. The remainder was to provide for Francis's maintenance and education until he came of age. In addition Sir Robert named three of his friends, William Sheldon senior of Beoley, John Caryll of Hartinge, Sussex, and Henry Farmer of Dunsmore, Oxfordshire, as overseers of the will.[83] This was a well-tried way of ensuring that the heir to a recusant estate was shepherded along the right path during his formative years, as all three were Catholics.[84]

However, on 21 January, with Sir Robert probably not yet in his grave, the Committee of Compounding in London was approached by one Richard Salwey, styling himself guardian of Francis, and informing them that Sir Robert was dead, that his son was a minor and that he would be brought up as a Protestant.[85] As the Throckmorton estates had been sequestrated for the recusancy of Sir Robert, not for supporting the king's cause in the Civil War, he asked for the sequestration order to be removed. But how had Richard become Sir Francis's guardian? Francis's twentieth-century biographer Etwell Barnard argued in one place that Salwey was named in Sir Robert's will, but this was not so. In another he asserted that Richard and his family, squires of Stanford-upon-Teme in Worcestershire, were friendly with the Throckmortons,[86] but this is seems inherently unlikely: their religious views were poles apart, devoutly Catholic on the one hand and committed Puritan on the other.[87] Another possibility is that Richard's guardianship was an act of central government. From the reign of Elizabeth I onwards, it had been intermittently government policy to seek to weaken the Catholic element in the landed classes by appointing Protestant guardians for the heirs of recusant families who inherited their estates whilst under age. There are certainly examples of

---

[83] TNA, PROB 11/229 (probate granted 14/06/1653); WRO, CR 1998/Box 86, item 29.

[84] *CCC*, vol. 3, p. 1953; Anthony Fletcher, *A County Community in Peace and War: Sussex 1600–1660* (London, 1975), pp. 309–10; *Calendar of the Committee for the Advance of Money*, ed. Mary Green (3 vols, London, 1889), vol. 2, p. 977.

[85] WRO, CR 1998/Box 86, item 28; TNA, SP 23/115, fols 207–10.

[86] Barnard, *Seventeenth-Century Country Gentleman*, pp. 13, 18.

[87] For evidence that the Salweys' allegiance to parliament was firmly founded on their religious beliefs, see C.H. Firth, 'Salwey, Richard (*bap.* 1615, *d.* 1685x8)', rev. Sean Kelsey, *ODNB*, and B. Worden, *The Rump Parliament* (Cambridge, 1974), pp. 128, 131, 135.

this practice during the Commonwealth period under the auspices of the Commissioners of the Great Seal,[88] but the process would have taken some time and there was less than a week between the death of Sir Robert and Richard describing himself as guardian. Another possibility, though there is no direct evidence of it, is that a pact with the devil in the form of Richard Salwey was a desperate measure devised by Lady Mary and her advisers to deal with the acute financial crisis caused by Sir Robert's death.[89] Year on year, sequestration had taken away two-thirds of the revenue of the estate, and taxation remained at a high level throughout the 1640s. Nothing is therefore likely to have been set aside to meet the additional burdens on the estate imposed by Sir Robert's will.[90]

Richard Salwey was the fourth son of Humphrey Salwey, MP for Worcestershire in the Long Parliament from 1640 until his death in 1654. Before the war, Richard had been in business in the City of London. During the war he attained the rank of major in parliament's armies and afterwards was elected as a recruiter MP for Appleby in Westmoreland, his fellow member being Oliver Cromwell's son-in-law Henry Ireton.[91] Richard was very close to Cromwell in matters of religion, but he and his father managed to avoid becoming involved in the trial and execution of the king. Nevertheless Richard was sufficiently in favour to be asked to serve as a commissioner in the army in Ireland very soon afterwards, probably on account of his financial expertise. He declined the offer for personal reasons but on grounds that were acceptable to parliament.[92]

One possible link between Richard and the Throckmortons, and a very tenuous one at that, is that he appears to have been in the Newport Pagnell area in 1644, where his civil behaviour towards Lady Conquest was a matter of comment in a letter she wrote to Sir Samuel Luke.[93] Another link, which pre-dates the Civil Wars, is more certain but even more circuitous. In a letter written in January 1641 to Robert Throckmorton at Weston, Anthony Salwey, who held land of the Throckmortons in Throckmorton

---

[88] CCC, vol. 4, p. 2408; vol. 5, p. 3232.

[89] Sequestration allowed the family to keep only about one-third of its landed income. This would have amounted to about £400 out of £1,200, but for the five years immediately following Sir Robert's death the estate was required by his will to pay £200 towards Anne Throckmorton's dowry, and also to discharge all Sir Robert's debts. This was in addition to the increasing costs of feeding and educating Sir Francis as he moved from childhood into adolescence.

[90] TNA, PROB 11/229.

[91] Members of the House of Commons who had supported the king in the First Civil War were expelled from parliament. Elections were then held in 1645 and 1646 to fill the vacant seats. The men elected at that time are often described as recruiter MPs.

[92] Firth and Kelsey, 'Richard Salwey'; Worden, *The Rump Parliament*, p. 31.

[93] Luke, *Letter Books*, item 648.

and may have acted as their land agent in Worcestershire, mentioned his cousin Thomas's hopes that Sir Robert would be pleased to exchange his lease upon the same covenants.[94] The connection between the cousins, however, was not a bond based on close friendship. Anthony, who had no male heirs at his death in 1643, did not mention Thomas in his will. Instead he left his estate to friends, servants and godchildren.[95] A possible reason for this was that Anthony was a Catholic and Thomas not.[96] There had been a split in the Salwey family. In the early years of the century Anthony was disinherited by his father Arthur, Richard's grandfather, and a good reason for doing so, given the firmly Protestant reputation of the rest of the family, would have been if Anthony had converted.[97] Thomas's exact relationship to Anthony and Richard is not known, but it is likely that he was descended from a junior branch that diverged from the main line of the family in Anthony's father's generation.[98]

Thomas Salwey of Throckmorton was to play a most important part in the affairs of the Throckmorton family for the next eight years, as it was he, not Richard, who actually became Sir Francis's guardian. This is evidenced by correspondence between the sequestration committees of Buckinghamshire, Warwickshire and Worcestershire and the Committee of Compounding in February and March 1651.[99] Richard probably declined the responsibility because of his growing involvement in central government. Later in the year, he was sent to Scotland as a commissioner to negotiate the union of the two countries after Cromwell's victories at Dunbar and Worcester. He then sat in the Council of State, the executive arm of government, in 1652 and 1653. Although he seems to have refused to play a part in the Protectorate government, he kept in with the regime and served as Cromwell's ambassador to Constantinople. After the downfall of the Protectorate he rose to prominence again, being appointed once more to the Council of State, but fell from power in early 1660 when he was

---

[94] WRO, CR 1998/Box 48, item 2; Box 60/Folder 2, item 26.

[95] Worcestershire County Record Office, Records of Probate, 1643, 121.

[96] *Worcestershire Quarter Sessions Papers*, ed. John Willis Bund, Worcestershire Historical Society (2 vols, 1900), vol. 2, p. 699.

[97] Shropshire Records Office, Shrewsbury [SRO], Joseph Morris's Volumes of Pedigrees, 6, pp. 3060–62.

[98] He cannot have been the Thomas Salwey, son of an unnamed younger brother of Anthony, who is described as dying without issue in a book of Shropshire pedigrees: SRO, R.C. Purton's Volumes of Pedigrees, 3, p. 460. If this had been the case, Anthony would have called him nephew. When Thomas Salwey, Sir Francis's guardian, died without issue in 1667, he left most of his estate to Major Richard Salwey, who by that date was a landowner in the Ludlow area. However, Thomas described Major Richard and his family merely as kin: TNA, PROB 11/ 330 (probate granted 12/07/1669); Firth and Kelsey, 'Richard Salwey'.

[99] WRO, CR 1998/Box 86, items 29, 30, 40.

imprisoned, albeit briefly, in the Tower of London for keeping too many options open. This was not a man to be trifled with. Although absent from England for long periods and not always in the political limelight, he stood behind Thomas and continued to take an interest in Francis's affairs until 1659.[100]

Apart from the letter mentioned above, Thomas's life prior to assuming the guardianship is veiled in mystery. It is unlikely that he had served in a Parliamentary regiment in the rank of captain or above, as he is never given a military rank, though his younger brother may have done. Thomas's will left a small bequest to his brother's executor, a Major Hill.[101] He may have been a land agent, possibly replacing his cousin Anthony on the Throckmorton manorial estate. The phraseology used in a document of 1658 setting out the financial problems of paying debts charged on the estate points in this direction.[102] However, it is most unlikely that he would have been a Royalist given the task he was set and the responsibility his kinsman Richard was placing on him.

The sequestration of the Throckmorton estates was removed on 25 March 1651, but the record of the first three years of the guardianship in the family archives is completely blank. Lady Mary married a second time to Lewis Mordaunt, a member of the family of the earls of Peterborough, whilst her daughter Anne married into a Kentish family of recusants, the Guldefords.[103] The only clear sign of the young baronet is an entry in the casebook of a Northampton physician, John Metfoote, to the effect that he had treated Francis for an eye condition soon after setting up practice in Northampton in 1652.[104] This suggests that he spent part of the time at Weston, only 10 miles from Northampton as the crow flies. However, in March 1654 an intense but narrow beam of light pierces the darkness of unknowing, the remarkably detailed expenditure account of Sir Francis's passage to manhood, kept for a period of six years by James Smith for Thomas Salwey and Sir Francis's mother, who had financial control of the estate.[105] However, it illuminates only the objects on which it is focused.

---

[100] Firth and Kelsey, 'Richard Salwey'. The major is mentioned on several occasions in the book of accounts. The last recorded meeting between him and Sir Francis was in January 1659: WRO, CR 1998/Large Carved Box, 39, fol. 96.

[101] TNA, PROB 11/330.

[102] WRO, CR 1998/Box 86, item 33.

[103] Barnard, *Seventeenth-Century Country Gentleman*, p. 74; SCLA, DR 5/1001.

[104] BL, Sloane MS 2812, fol. 9.

[105] WRO, CR 1998/Large Carved Box, item 39. Thomas Sheldon of Temple Grafton, a recusant, also played a prominent part in the running of the estate and the perusal of its accounts. He was probably Lady Throckmorton's financial adviser, not joint guardian as Barnard supposed: *Seventeenth-Century Country Gentleman*, p. 13.

Beyond that is a penumbra of uncertainty, where certain things can be inferred; but further than that the utter darkness remains, for Smith is merely recounting the ways in which he spent the money allotted to him for Francis's education. The account book therefore gives a reasonably full account of where Francis went, what he did and whom he met, but rarely explains why. It also contains almost nothing about his spiritual as opposed to his cultural life. It is possible to read the book at one extreme as evidence of an earnest, but ultimately failed, attempt by Thomas Salwey to bring the young man up as a Protestant, or at the other, as a record of an elaborate charade managed by Sir Francis's Catholic relatives, at which Thomas either connived or was the unwitting dupe.

The most immediate impression of the account book is the decidedly non-Puritan culture that pervades it from the very start. Practices that were supposed to be banned are shown as taking place, and the fact that they were noted down suggests that they were not seen as possible grounds for later prosecutions. There were mummers at Throckmorton on May Day in 1654; Christmas gifts were given; Sir Francis attended a stage play at Cambridge, where there was music on Shrove Tuesday prior to the beginning of Lent. He also attended bull and bear baiting. In 1658 and 1659 he twice attended an opera with several companions, paying for the 'play book' on the second occasion. Modern scholarship has removed some of the traditional picture of the bleakness of Puritan England in respect of Cromwell's court, where a high premium was placed on music and poetry, and where dancing was allowed on special occasions, but the evidence presented in the account book is in a different league.[106] Moreover, there is no evidence of any curtailment in such activities during the rule of the major generals when repression was supposed to have been at its most extreme, Christmas gifts being given in both 1655 and 1656.[107]

The accounts begin with Francis living with his guardian at Throckmorton and paying a visit to the senior line of the Salweys at Stanford-on-Teme. He then spent almost three years at Cambridge, followed by brief spells at London and Oxford, interspersed with visits to Weston and his West Midlands estates, and to the houses of various family friends. In 1659 he spent part of the year in London, where he married Anne, the only daughter of John Monson of Kinnersley, Surrey.[108] The young couple then resided at Weston and at Moor Hall until March 1660, when the account book comes to an end. It is tempting to describe the contents in great detail because of their great social interest, but the job has already been

---

[106] Roy Sherwood, *The Court of Oliver Cromwell* (London, 1977), pp. 135–43.
[107] WRO, CR 1998/Large Carved Box, item 39, fols 36, 53.
[108] SCLA, DR 5/789.

done by Barnard in the form of a youth's journey towards manhood.[109] Accomplished local historian that he was, he managed to tease out the significance of many of the individual entries, but his failure to gain access to the rest of the Throckmorton family papers and his inability, it seems, to consult the state papers and the probate registers in the Public Record Office, due probably to wartime restrictions, means that a rereading of the original text is absolutely essential for appraising the family strategy for survival as it developed during the 1650s.

A prime question must be whether the Protestant conversion mentioned in Richard Salwey's petition was any more than a sham. To Barnard, who did not have a sight of the documents that set up the Salwey guardianship, Sir Francis was clearly a practising Roman Catholic throughout the 1650s. Yet it is extremely difficult to see how this could have been the case whilst Sir Francis was living at Throckmorton under the direct supervision of Thomas Salwey, or during his visit to Stanford-on-Teme. Moreover, it seems out of the question that Major Richard, with his close association with the Commonwealth regime would have connived at any kind of cover-up.

At first sight the account book seems to provide plentiful evidence for the deception hypothesis. Between 1654 and 1659, whilst not at Cambridge, Sir Francis spent a high proportion of his time in the company of Roman Catholics.[110] He also married a bride who, if not herself a practising Catholic, had close family members who were.[111] However, the account book is almost devoid of references to the practice of religion. On many occasions small gifts of money are made to the poor, but this was not a specifically Catholic practice at the time and the words used to describe such acts of charity are not Catholic in tone. Moreover, his journeys to St Winifred's well at Holywell in Flintshire are not necessarily evidence of a visit to a Catholic shrine. Protestants and Catholics alike regarded the waters as having curative properties,[112] and Sir Francis seemed to have been

---

[109] Barnard, *Seventeenth-Century Country Gentleman*, pp. 6–74.

[110] Hughes's brief comment on this is misleading. She claims Sir Francis visited Lord Brooke at Warwick Castle, but all he did was visit the castle and donate some money to the soldiers there. There is no evidence that he met Lord Brooke. Hughes, *Politics, Society and Civil War*, p. 64.

[111] The estates of Anne Monson's aunt, Anne Saville, were sequestrated for recusancy in Yorkshire: *CCC*, vol. 4, pp. 2511–12. Her grandfather, Sir William Monson, Vice Admiral of England who died *c.*1643, was also reputedly a Catholic: Andrew Thrush, 'Monson, Sir William (1568?–1643)', *ODNB*.

[112] Havran, *Catholics in Caroline England*, p. 183. The visits took place in August 1657 and in August 1658: WRO, CR 1998/Large Carved Box, item 39, fols 63, 83. Cf. Alexandra Walsham, 'Holywell: Contesting Sacred Space in Post-Reformation England', in Will Coster and Andrew Spicer (eds), *Sacred Space in Early Modern Europe* (Cambridge, 2005).

both unhealthy and lucky, Smith's accounts recording numerous bouts of ill health and also the occasional injury. It is also probably significant that Smith went on an exploratory visit to Malvern in 1654, whose waters at that time were thought of as being efficacious in the treatment of complaints associated with the eyes.[113] Thus there is no unimpeachable evidence from the account book that Sir Francis was participating in religious practices that were unequivocally Catholic during the mid and late 1650s.

The entries in the account book that relate to Sir Francis's residence in Cambridge, however, are somewhat problematic. Although the purchases of writing materials, a lecture book and academic texts point to formal studying taking place during his first year, there seems to have been a falling off thereafter. Less time was spent at Cambridge, and whilst he was there more attention was paid to gentlemanly pursuits like fencing and playing the viol and the violin than to learning.[114] Expenses connected with the university occur quite frequently, but they are mainly concerned with showing visitors around the colleges.[115] In addition, although there were costs for being entertained in college, primarily meals consumed by himself and guests, expenditure is not focused on a single college.[116] Moreover, Sir Francis lodged not in the university but in the town itself during term time, first with Mr Lee and then with Mr Lilly.[117] Finally, although quite substantial payments were made to a tutor, William Bayly (whom Barnard identifies as having connections with King's College), the final occasion on which his name appears in the account book allows for a number of different readings, one of which is that his education had indeed all been a sham: 'Given to Mr Bayly who past as my master's tutor at Cambridge £2-00-00.'[118]

Barnard saw Sir Francis as being a kind of extramural student, unable to register with the university because he could not take the requisite oaths without prejudicing his faith. This may not have been the case. In the first place, it is just possible that he was formally attached to one of the colleges. Although the records for admittance are quite good by the 1650s, there are nevertheless some gaps and a single reference in the account book to 'the

---

[113] Bryan Smith, *A History of Malvern* (Leicester, 1964), pp. 171–2; WRO, CR 1998/Large Carved Box, item 39, fol. 6. A later example of Sir Francis experiencing trouble with his eyes occurred in early 1657: WRO, CR 1998/Large Carved Box, item 39, fol. 55.

[114] WRO, CR 1998/Large Carved Box, item 39, fols 35, 52.

[115] Ibid., fols 35 (Mr John Smith) and 42–3 (young Mr Neville and Dr John Throckmorton).

[116] Ibid., fols 23, 35, 44 (visits to Trinity, King's, Clare Hall, Peterhouse and Christ Church).

[117] Ibid., fols 24, 35–53, 54–7.

[118] Ibid., fol. 41 (14 May 1656).

college' rather than to a named one may be significant in this respect.[119] Moreover, even if he was tutored externally, this is not necessarily proof of recusancy. Convinced royalist Anglicans would also have had scruples about swearing the requisite oaths. However, it does seem odd that the Salweys did not check on Sir Francis's status, if their aim in sending him to Cambridge was for him to receive a Protestant higher education in a university staffed with Puritan academics that would reinforce the good work done during the first years of the guardianship. The purchases of books on his behalf are at first sight unexceptional. Most were stock texts such as works by Ovid and Petrarch, but James Howell's *Epistles* is of interest as it contained arguments by an ex-royalist in favour of supporting the Cromwellian Protectorate as a form of mixed monarchy.[120] Acquiring a Latin/English dictionary, however, may not have been as vocationally motivated as it might be supposed. Prior to the 1650s, it was important to be able to understand texts written in Latin, as Latin was the language in which legal disputes were conducted, but this was not the case between 1651 and 1660, when they were conducted in English. Such dictionaries were, of course, important for reading the classics mentioned above, but they also had other more sinister uses in the eyes of the Salweys.[121]

The key to understanding what was going on lies elsewhere in the Coughton archives. In the catalogue there is a brief reference, which can easily be missed, to two catechisms belonging to Sir Francis dated *c*.1656.[122] These turn out to be two substantial manuscript volumes that employ the stock question and answer format to explain and justify Roman Catholicism. The immediate reaction is that they were in some way related to Blessed John Wall, who first arrived in Warwickshire at this date, but that it not the case.[123] The preambles to the catechisms tell an interesting story, but not the whole story, of Sir Francis's spiritual odyssey. The implication is that Lady Throckmorton had given her son a copy of the manuscript, which had belonged to his father and was in the library at Weston. He had transcribed it into English, presumably using the dictionary he had acquired at Cambridge, and been totally convinced of the truth of Catholic

---

[119] *Alumnii Cantabrigiensis*, ed. John Venn and J.A. Venn (10 vols, Cambridge, 1922–54), vol. 1, pp. vi, viii–ix. Barnard believed Sir Francis had a particular affinity with Christs College, Cambridge, as he visited the college in 1671, but its records for the 1650s appear to be complete: *Seventeenth-Century Country Gentleman*, p. 35.

[120] D.R. Woolf, 'Howell, James (1594?–1666)', *ODNB*; Barnard, *Seventeenth-Century Country Gentleman*, p. 32.

[121] WRO, CR 1998/Large Carved Box, item 39, fol. 23.

[122] Ibid., fols. 69, 70.

[123] Bede Camm, *Life of Blessed John Wall*, cited by Michael Hodgetts, 'Recusants in the Midlands', *Worcestershire Recusant*, 48 (1988), 15.

doctrine as a result. In addition, the dedication to his mother, which is filial devotion writ large as she has set him to the right path for salvation, contains the potent phrase '*ingratissimus filiorum*'. He had been a bad boy, the implication being that he broken with the faith to some extent in the early 1650s, and possibly broken a promise made at the time of his father's death. However, the language is obscure, and it is possible that I am reading more into the dedication than Sir Francis actually intended.

Whether or not Sir Francis was a Protestant in the first half of the 1650s remains therefore a matter of conjecture. However, from 1656 onwards he had to keep his Catholicism concealed, and the anodyne entries in James Smith's account book provided some evidence that he remained a Protestant. Thomas Salwey would have examined it from time to time, and it was therefore important that it should contain nothing that caused concern. Indeed one post-conversion entry does suggest an ongoing interest in Protestantism, as James Smith purchased a prayer book on his master's behalf in September 1658. This could have been a Protestant or a Catholic volume, but to a Protestant reader it would suggest the Anglican Book of Common Prayer. The visits to Holywell could also be explained away, especially as Sir Francis and his colleagues stayed at inns on the way, not at the houses of Catholic landowners, as had been the case with the visit of family members and kin to Holywell uncovered during the official investigation into the Gunpowder Plot in 1606.[124] Finally, given the attendance of two of the Salweys, Thomas and Humphrey, at the wedding of Sir Francis and Anne, there can be no doubt that it was conducted in accordance with rites acceptable to the Commonwealth regime.

Surprisingly, the book continued to be kept after the marriage which brought the guardianship to an end.[125] Although Thomas Salwey's name disappears from James Smith's accounts, it was still essential not to get on the wrong side of Major Salwey who, after the collapse of the Protectorate in May 1659, was more important than ever in national politics. Moreover, sequestration raised its ugly head again after the suppression of Sir George Booth's uprising in August.[126] However, the account book does come to an end on Lady Day 1660. This was eight weeks after Richard Salwey's downfall. It could have not been known on 25 March that the republic itself had fallen and that the Stuart monarchy would replace it. It is, however, highly likely that the monarchy had been restored by the time the fair copy was made for Sir Francis's signature, and with it any real chance of a revival in the fortunes of Major Salwey.

---

[124] Marie Rowlands (ed.), *Catholics of Parish and Town 1558–1778*, CRS, monograph series, 5 (1999), p. 41. See Michael Hodgetts's chapter in this volume.

[125] From then onwards Sir Francis signs the entries as correct.

[126] CCC, vol. 5, pp. 3246–55.

The Throckmorton archives for the late 1650s and early 1660s show that the course of action adopted in 1651 had been a remarkably successful one, despite Thomas Salweys' worries about excessive expenditure in 1658. Minorities usually did provide landed families with the chance for putting their financial affairs in order, as expenditure on the household was much reduced; but the lifting of sequestration, which meant that the estate was better off in terms of income by at least £600 a year,[127] ensured that the various Commonwealth regimes placed no more financial burdens on the Throckmortons than would have been experienced by a landed family which had supported parliament during the Civil Wars. As Sir Francis was not formally a Catholic, the estate was not liable to pay taxes at double the normal rate; and as he had not supported the king, he did not fall within the provisions of the so-called decimation tax levied on Royalists to pay for the expenses of the regional government of the major generals established by Oliver Cromwell as a public order measure in the mid-1650s. In addition, as he had only one sister, there had only been a single dowry to pay, and this was probably offset by the dowry that Anne Monson had brought with her.[128] Finally, the costs of maintaining one less house, and the largest at that, would have represented a very substantial saving on the 1630s.[129] Indeed such was the turnaround in the family financial fortunes that Sir Francis was able to undertake extensive building work at Coughton between 1663 and 1665 at a cost that exceeded £2,000, thus making the house habitable once more.[130]

Thus the Throckmortons of Coughton were able to turn to their advantage the severe, if not potentially fatal, financial crisis caused by sequestration and the terms of Sir Robert's will, even if it was at the expense of Sir Francis at least outwardly laying aside his Catholic faith. Possibly this brought him close to apostasy, as he conformed to what was expected of him by the Salweys, but the catechisms show that he turned the corner in his mid teens and was reconciled with the Catholic faith that had guided his ancestors.

---

[127] Two-thirds of the income had gone straight to the Parliamentary authorities under sequestration, and in the case of the Warwickshire lands this amounted to £500: WRO, CR 1998/Box 65/Folder 1, item 9; BL, Add. MS 35098, fol. 41.

[128] Mrs Monson, Anne's mother, paid £500 prior to the marriage and £100 in the following year, but there is no record of the remainder, as Smith's entries in the account book came to an end in March 1660, and the settlement agreed between the two families does not still survive: WRO, CR 1998/Large Carved Box, item 39, fols 101, 127.

[129] Francis visited Coughton in May 1657 to shoot duck on the pools and to visit his tenants. A peal of bells was rung in the church, but there is no sign in the account book of the kinds of expenditure necessary for opening up the house. Instead Sir Francis seems to have lodged with his estate managers: WRO, CR 1998/Large Carved Box, item 39, fols 60–61.

[130] WRO, CR 1998/Large Carved Box, item 40.

CHAPTER 7

The Throckmortons at Home and Abroad, 1680–1800

Geoffrey Scott

The Throckmortons during these years remind us that there is no such thing as a typical recusant family. While Catholic kinship networks still remained important, and provided members of the family with a facility for investing in a degree of social intercourse and economic prosperity, the Throckmortons were never a hermetically sealed Catholic family; Protestant Throckmorton branches continued to flourish. If the Throckmortons in the long eighteenth century were no longer prominent in national political affairs as they had been in the past, they nevertheless maintained an equivalent position offering patronage and influence in other spheres. But what is particularly striking about the family in these years is how it broke free of its recusant constraints and produced a line of liberal grandees whose standing in the English establishment caused them to exploit all that was on offer, but whose Catholicism drove them to demand further civil and religious liberties. This striking commingling of recusancy and reform among members of this family has led them to be viewed as 'the lay heirs of Erasmus'.[1] How they achieved such distinctive celebrity status in this respect is the story of much of what follows.

Having endured a century of persecution and penal restrictions, members of the Catholic and main branch of the Throckmorton family were now too habituated to their circumstances to wish to change them radically. There is no escaping the evidence for enduring recusant attitudes and ways in the family even in the eighteenth century. The continual passage of legislation against recusants throughout the late seventeenth and eighteenth centuries had produced a predictable knee-jerk response among the Throckmortons, so inured had they become to such repression. The sequestration of the family's Warwickshire estates for recusancy had been discharged in 1651 when the second baronet, Sir Francis, succeeded his father, but recusant disadvantages remained. Thus, Sir Francis, as a Catholic recusant, was unable to be admitted formally to Cambridge University, though he studied there under dons between 1654 and 1657, and passes for recusant

---

[1] Patrick J. Doyle, 'The Origins of Recusancy: The Throckmortons of Coughton', *Worcestershire Recusant*, 13 (June 1969), 2, 8.

Throckmortons to travel more than five miles from Coughton and their other houses, as well as 'beyond the seas for their health', were obtained frequently throughout this century. Passes to go abroad were issued in July 1677 and in January 1679 for Sir Francis, his son Robert, who would succeed as third baronet in 1680, and for their servants, horses and goods, suggesting that being well known as notorious papists, they felt it best to be out of the country while the Popish Plot gathered momentum. This did not, however, prevent the absentee Sir Francis being charged at Warwick between 1679 and 1680 for recusancy and failing to attend the Anglican Church, but fortunately the process got no further. Sir Francis died in 1680, the last Throckmorton to face the full impact of the laws against recusants.[2]

The Survival of Recusant Culture

The family was lucky not to have suffered more during the Popish Plot scare, given its kinship network. Sir William Throckmorton, a kinsman, had acted as a go-between for Louis XIV and James, Duke of York, in the critical early 1670s, and the Yate family at Harvington, into whom Sir Robert would marry in 1686, had also secured passports in 1679 and 1680 to go abroad. Another relation, George Throckmorton of Chisfield, Hertfordshire, was involved in the Plot's aftermath. Recusants' fortunes markedly changed for the better, however, during the Catholic King James II's reign (1685–88) when the young Sir Robert gained a licence to attend the Stuart court in London, and was appointed a Justice of the Peace for Buckinghamshire, in which lay his principal residence, Weston Underwood, as well as a justice for Warwickshire, where the ancestral seat of Coughton Court was to be found. Sir Robert also received a commission to raise a troop of horse at his own expense. Meanwhile, in 1685 the family contributed to the new Catholic chapel in Birmingham. Such upward mobility ended with the Revolution of 1688 which ushered in another period of repression of leading English Catholics. A mob from Alcester destroyed the chapel at Coughton on 'Running Thursday', 18 December 1688, and at the same time an armed attack on Harvington Hall forced some members of the family into continental exile. At Weston, Sir Robert resented the attempt of the nearby parson of Ravenstone to search his property. In order to maintain his fortunes, Sir Robert found himself desperately torn between a traditional loyalty to Catholicism and the Stuarts, and the practical necessity of conformity to the post-

---

[2] Etwell Barnard, *A Seventeenth Century Country Gentleman (Sir Francis Throckmorton, 1640–80)* (Cambridge, 1944), pp. 5, 9, 11, 84; *CSPD, 1677–78*, p. 258; *CSPD, 1679–80*, p. 330; SCLA, DR 5/1919.

revolutionary *status quo*. With his marriage to the heiress Mary Yate in 1686, which brought into the family the lucrative estates at Buckland and Harvington, he had far more to lose than his father. He decided he was wealthy enough to remain true to his faith while displaying a rather lily-livered conformity to government policy regarding Catholics. The periodic attacks by the government on papists between 1696 and 1708 following various scares required the surrender of their horses and arms and their swearing the oath of allegiance. This made Sir Robert squeal. He gave up his dozen or so horses, surrendered himself to house custody in London and declared his loyalty to the government:

> I had never meddled in any public affairs, for I resolved at the beginning of William III's reign to behave myself always peaceably under it ... I have been encouraged to continue in this way, with an additional tie of gratitude to the king for his great clemency since he came to the throne in not executing the penal laws relating to religion against those who belong to my faith. For this favour I hope all Catholics are as ready as I am to declare their public thanks and acknowledgements with a detestation and abhorrence of the late intended villainy (i.e. the 1696 Assassination Plot). Practices opposed to fundamental Christian principles and to the laws of nature and nations, which might bring about the dissolution of human society, should be abhorred by all men of religion, honour, or understanding ... I have always lived peaceably under the king's government, realising his great clemency to all Catholics. I wish to show my intentions to continue in this manner by taking the Oath of Allegiance to him.

He does not, however, seem to have taken the oath.[3] After the deaths of Sir Robert in 1721, and his wife the following year, their joint estates, registered for the 1722 levy of the 'Great Tax' on papists, were valued at over £1,400, thus putting the family among the wealthiest of the country's Catholics.[4] Although the family's understanding of its place within English society was to change as the eighteenth century progressed, older loyalties survived and were exemplified in enduring attachments to the Old Faith fostered within a traditional household Catholicism. In the eighteenth century, the family generally resided at Weston Underwood in Buckinghamshire and later at Buckland House in Berkshire (Figure 7.1).

---

[3] John Kenyon, *The Popish Plot* (London 1972), pp. 34–6; Michael Hodgetts, 'The Yates of Harvington, 1631–1696', *Recusant History*, 22 (1994), 173; WRO, CR 1998/LCB/17; CR 1998/Folder 55/5; *CSPD, Jan. 1686–May 1687*, nos 268, 1669; C.A. Lowe, 'Politics and Religion in Warwickshire during the Reign of James II, 1685–1688', MA dissertation, University of Warwick (1992), vol. 2, pp. 166, 172, 173; *Recusant Documents from the Ellesmere Manuscripts*, ed. Anthony G. Petti, CRS, 60 (London, 1968), pp. 285, 289.

[4] *Anno Regni Georgii Regis Magnae Britanniae, Franciae, & Hiberniae Nono. At the Parliament Begun and Holden at Westminster, the Ninth Day of October, Anno Dom. 1721* (London, 1723), Appendix 2.

Figure 7.1 Buckland House, engraving of c.1827.

Private chapels used by the family, its servants and tenantry were to be found in these two, and also at Coughton and Harvington where estate agents and chaplains lived throughout prolonged absences of the family. All of these houses except Buckland, which was rebuilt in 1757, had priest-holes. After the death of Lady Mary Yate in 1696, Harvington was neglected by the Throckmortons, and this house thus preserved its recusant chapels' furnishings and ingenious priest-holes. Tradition has it that the Franciscan martyr, Saint John Wall, had celebrated Mass there for the devout Yate family around 1677. Coughton's house chapel had been finished in May 1687 by Sir Robert Throckmorton, a symbol of newly won Catholic emancipation under James II, but was destroyed by the mob in less than a year. It was soon succeeded by another which served the chaplain and the family's retainers until the nineteenth century, when it became the saloon. All these Throckmorton houses encouraged the formation of Catholic enclaves which relied heavily on the presence of the family for their survival. In the 1676 papist returns, for instance, Coughton, empty of family members at the time, had Catholics numbering a fifth of the total population, while at Weston, where the family was usually in residence, Catholics outnumbered the rest of the population. In 1691, 11 papists were recorded at Coughton, all male, who included the Throckmorton agent and servants, and Robert Waters, a long-standing tenant and family friend. In 1685 Waters had presented Sir Robert on his birthday with the sword with which Sir Robert's great uncle, Sir John Smith, had redeemed the king's standard after it had been lost at the battle of Edgehill. On that occasion, Waters invited Lord Carrington of Wootton Wawen and neighbouring Protestant gentry, as well as Throckmorton tenants, to the presentation dinner. This suggests that the family's royalist affiliations in the late seventeenth century were as strong as its Catholicism. Sir Robert's father, Sir Francis, had, for instance, commissioned the monument to commemorate Sir John Smith in Christ Church cathedral, Oxford, after he had fallen fighting for the king in 1644.[5]

It seems to have been the Pakington family especially, and its descendants the Yate family of Harvington and Buckland, into which Sir Robert, the third baronet, married in 1686, that kept old recusant ways alive among the Throckmortons. Many recusant families, for instance, treasured small

---

[5] Michael Hodgetts, *Secret Hiding-Places* (Dublin 1989), pp. 36–40, 51, 53; Hodgetts, 'The Recusant History of a County', *Worcestershire Recusant*, 1 (1963), 13; Hodgetts, 'John Wall at Harvington?', *Recusant History*, 8 (1965): 123–32; *The Compton Census of 1676*, ed. Anne Whiteman (London 1986), pp. 185, 369; Marie Rowlands (ed.), *Catholics of Parish and Town, 1558–1778*, CRS monograph series, 5 (1999), p. 85; Monica Ory and Kevin Down, 'List of Warwickshire Papists 1691 Part 3', *Worcestershire Recusant*, 35 (1980), 29; WRO, CR 1998/CD/Drawer 3/8, p. 5. Barnard, *Seventeenth-Century Country Gentleman*, p. 44.

collections of medieval manuscripts preserved by them after the dissolution of the monasteries. They were emblems of happier days of a single medieval Christendom. Thus, the fifteenth-century Norwich Missal from Harvington and the fourteenth-century Buckland Missal which originally belonged to a friary of the obscure English religious order of Grandmontines or Bonhommes, were almost certainly the property of the Yates. These, with other surviving medieval manuscripts, were carefully preserved by Sir Robert. The 'church stuff' of old Lady Mary Yate's chapel was inventoried on her death in 1696, and her granddaughter, Sir Robert's wife, inherited from her a jewelled locket, probably a reliquary, with the stipulation that it be given to Chaddesley Corbett church when it was returned into Catholic hands again. The surviving *Tabula Eliensis*, a painted canvas of 1596, unites the medieval, monastic and recusant worlds. Endorsed by Sir Robert, it depicts Norman knights quartered by the monks of Ely in 1076, but also shows the arms of recusants imprisoned in the reign of Elizabeth. Not surprisingly, Sir Robert's interest in recusancy encouraged his antiquarian and bibliographical interests. He was responsible for the establishment of the family's library, now widely dispersed, and in 1685 he was busy listing inscriptions on early Throckmorton tombs. How far into the eighteenth century such recusant medieval nostalgia survived is hard to gauge, but there is a hint of it as late as 1791 when Sir Robert's son, the fourth baronet and his namesake, was buried in the empty table tomb in the centre of Coughton parish church built for an earlier Sir Robert who died on his way to the Holy Land in 1518.[6]

That the culture of recusancy survived in the family at least into the early eighteenth century was due in large measure to the Throckmortons' close links with European centres of English Catholicism, a bond which was to point the family in a particular direction during this century. At about the same time that old Lady Mary Yate was endowing divinity professors at the English College, Douai (1677), her daughter's father-in-law, Sir Francis Throckmorton, donated an organ to the chapel of the Conceptionists (Blue Nuns) in Paris, where his two daughters, Anne and Mary, were being educated, as well as altar plate to the English Benedictine priory in Paris (1678). Furthermore, the surviving late seventeenth-century Mass cabinet at Coughton Court has Anglo-Dutch features (Figure 7.2).

It was Paris, however, which was to remain the Throckmortons' European home, and that city's intellectual and religious milieux were

---

[6] WRO, CR 1998/LCB/62 (Buckland and Coughton library catalogue) lists various liturgical 'manuscripts' and Sarum Use manuals, without further details. G.F. Pullen, 'The Harvington Library at Oscott', *Worcestershire Recusant*, 1 (1963), 19; Oxford, Bodleian Library, MS.Don.b.5 (Buckland Missal); Birmingham Diocesan Archives, C0204; WRO, CR 1998/CD/Drawer 3/8, pp. 14, 15.

Figure 7.2   Late seventeenth-century Flemish Mass cabinet, Coughton Court.

to have a crucial effect on the family in the following decades. In 1685 Sir Robert, the third baronet, described the collection of portraits in the gallery at Weston of Paris nuns from his Smythe, Fortescue and Markham relations, and he and his wife Mary erected a funerary monument in Saint-Sulpice, Paris, to Mary's brother, Sir John Yate, after his death in 1690. European Catholic devotional works such as the Spanish Jesuit Luis de la Puente's *Meditations* and the Portuguese Dominican Louis of Granada's sermons in Latin (Antwerp 1686) nourished the prayer life of the household, but were eclipsed by native recusant literature promoted especially by the Throckmorton women. Thus, the Benedictine Edward Byfleet alias Worsley's *Briefe explication of the office of the blessed virgin Marie* (Douai, 1652), carried a dedication to Lady Throckmorton in which the author noted his debt to her mother. In these years, Yate female relations were also attracted to the mystical teachings of the English monk Dom Augustine Baker and his disciples. In 1681, Sir Robert's mother promised to leave him on her death a prayer book of Queen Mary 'with a golden enamelled cover' which had been in her family for generations. Similarly, the cope and chasuble of Queen Katherine of Aragon, with their pomegranates of Granada, were precious heirlooms which went to the Catholic Blounts of Mawsley on the marriage of Sir Robert's daughter, Apollonia, to Edward Blount in 1722. Sir Francis, the second baronet, had been more demonstrative about his piety, visiting, as a teenager in 1657 and 1658, the well of St Winifrid at Holywell which was maintained by the Jesuits. Although the well seems to have been damaged during the Civil War, Sir Francis brought away with him moss and stones as relics.[7]

The Throckmorton genealogy in the eighteenth century is so complicated that it is best to refer to a family tree (see Appendix). Sir Robert, the fourth baronet, bestrides the century like a colossus (1721–91), and was married three times. Four other male Throckmortons shared his name. At no point from 1680 did the eldest male heir of the family inherit the title, thanks to infant mortalities and premature deaths. Where there is a uniformity, however, is in Throckmorton marriages to generations of established Catholic gentry families. Not only did these continue recusant affiliations, they were perhaps the most important factor in expanding the wealth and property of the family in the eighteenth century – although that wealth was also conserved by the unusually large number of female

---

[7] WDA, Old Brotherhood Archives, IV, 27–29; *Diary of the Blue Nuns*, ed. Joseph Gillow and Richard Trappes-Lomax, CRS, 8 (London, 1910), p.26; Douai Abbey, Benet Weldon, 'Memorials' II, p. 492; WRO, CR 1998/CD/Drawer 3/8, pp. 14, 22; CR 1998/CD/Folder 47/48. Barnard, *Seventeenth-Century Country Gentleman*, pp. 48, 55; Granada's *Conciones* at Coughton Court; Hodgetts, 'Yates of Harvington', 16; Paul Sidoli, 'The Catherine of Aragon Chasuble from Mawley Hall', *Cleobury Chronicles*, 4, Cleobury Mortimer History Society (1996), pp. 35–44.

members becoming nuns whose fathers did not have to find them large dowries. Catholic brides of Throckmorton husbands, many of whom were to be blessed with lengthy widowhoods – from the families of Yate of Buckland and Harvington, Herbert of Powis, Collingwood of Eslington, Heywood, Paston of Molland and Horton, Giffard, Stapleton, Plowden and Clifford – all brought with them ample dowries. Two brides, from the Yate and Paston families, endowed the family with a substantial landed inheritance. In turn, Throckmorton brides found Catholic gentry husbands from the Wollascott of Woolhampton, Blount of Mawsley, Hunloke of Wingerworth, Giffard of Chillington, Petre of Ingatestone and Fitzherbert of Swynnerton families. A Throckmorton family network thus became established, especially in the Midlands, composed of gentry rather than aristocratic members. And even if the eighteenth-century Throckmortons were to end up heading the liberal Catholic interest, they always seemed to fight shy of proposing to Protestant brides. The anxiety to find Catholic partners is a striking feature in much of the correspondence throughout the century. The marriage of Sir Francis, the second baronet, was to be the most notorious of Throckmorton matches. He had spent much of his youth trudging around his Catholic kin, and in 1659 had married the Catholic Anne Monson of Kinnersley, Surrey, from whom he separated in 1677, allowing her and her youngest daughter, Elizabeth, annuities of £300 and £50 respectively. Anne lived at Coughton, her estranged husband at Weston Underwood, and on his death in 1680, she immediately took up residence with the English Blue Nuns in Paris where she seems to have remained until her death in 1728. It is difficult to be certain of Sir Francis's relationship with Bridget Tyldesley, who became a major beneficiary of his will, from which his wife was cut out. But his dependence on her can be gauged by the help she gave in trying to reconcile him, albeit briefly, with his wife in 1670, and from her role in 1675 as governess to his children. Sir Francis's successor, Sir Robert, third baronet, blessed with a happier marriage to the wealthy heiress Mary Yate, had eight daughters to cope with and since a number became marriageable around 1720, he tried desperately to reduce the £6,000 dowry which each daughter was expected to take with her. The worry of this burden, together with those related to various encumbrances on the estate, the necessity of selling off part of his mother's estate to pay debts and the fear of renewed taxation on papists' estates, must all have contributed to the unexpected death in 1721 of this man of a 'good charitable and compassionate temper'.[8]

---

[8] Barnard, *Seventeenth-Century Country Gentleman*, ch. 7; Gillow and Trappes-Lomax, *Diary*, pp. 25, 29; Edgar E. Estcourt and John Orlebar Payne, *The English Catholic Nonjurors of 1715* (London 1885), p. 14.

English Society and European Education

We have traced so far the story of the family up until the beginning of the eighteenth century. In this new era of growing religious toleration and political freedom, the Throckmortons were to become socially and economically secure, and achieve a reputation as one of the best-known English Catholic gentry families. They never, however, loosened their ties with Europe. To initially predominant French influences were added those of Italy. This broadening world prevented them from retreating quietly like some other recusant families into bucolic provincial backwoods, and their Catholicism allowed them to mix far more easily in continental circles than might comparable Protestant families. The Throckmortons were able to derive benefits from participating in the Grand Tour as the phenomenon exploded in popularity during this period. Above all, Europe exposed the family to particular intellectual and theological stimuli which shaped it into becoming the leading English Catholic liberal family by the end of the century, with Sir John Courtenay Throckmorton at its head. What is remarkable is that whilst other equally grand Catholic gentry families with similar European interests, such as the Swinburnes of Northumberland and the Gascoignes of the West Riding, conformed to Anglicanism in the late eighteenth century as a prerequisite of entry into the establishment, the Throckmortons held out. It was almost as if Sir John Courtenay believed he had a divine vocation to make Catholicism, with its cultural and intellectual inheritance, acceptable to enlightened Protestant England.

The family's breadth of interests and experience would have been severely curtailed had it closeted itself in leafy middle England. Throckmortons were, as we shall see, frequent visitors to London and Bath, but it was their continuing exposure to France and adjoining countries which made them exceptional. Their European lifelines were their chaplains and the English Catholic schools and religious houses with which they were associated. The distinctive religious attitudes of the family's chaplains consolidated what young Throckmortons had already picked up in exiled academies, and these chaplains prepared their charges for their later Grand Tour. It is essential to note that the Throckmorton character, at least in its religious aspect, was formed almost totally by English Benedictine and secular clergy guides; Jesuit influence, by design or accident, was completely absent in this century, a blessing which must presumably have endeared the family to its Protestant neighbours. Behind this Benedictine and secular formation lay the intellectual and ecclesiastical world of Paris, which in this period enjoyed some notoriety as the centre of Gallican and Jansenist sentiment.[9]

---

[9] Thomas H. Clancy, *English Catholic Books 1641–1700. A Bibliography* (revised edn, Aldershot, 1996), no. 890, suggests the philosopher priest and apologist John Sergeant, who

Unlike other families where the family's priest combined his role as chaplain with that of tutor to the children, the Throckmortons seem generally to have separated these roles. Chaplain and tutor were treated and maintained quite separately. Furthermore, because of the peculiar circumstances of the family, the Throckmorton chaplains enjoyed a greater degree of independence from their host family than did other chaplains in English Catholic families, something that might explain why names and details of seventeenth-century chaplains are so sparse. Evidence indicates that the head of the family, as well as the branches, were mobile. Time abroad was balanced by stints in London, or in progresses around the four major landed estates that had fallen into the family's possession by the early eighteenth century. Meanwhile, the chaplains were left to their own devices at home, which is partly why they were able spread themselves in local society and to develop close friendships with personages of national repute such as the traveller William Cole and the poet William Cowper. This independence had a further curious effect, which was that Coughton and Harvington, from which the family were generally absent, became early rural missions whose priests functioned less as chaplains and more as parish priests to communities independent of the Throckmorton household. Harvington was effectively handed over to the secular clergy as an independent base for local pastoral work and became an English centre for intellectual research by Sorbonne graduates. Down the road, at Coughton, the resident monks developed a circuit and extended their pastoral ministry, taking in congregations from as far afield as Foxcote and Abbots Salford.

In a clergy directory of 1701, four chaplains, two monks and two secular priests, were supported by the Throckmortons, more than any other family on the list, and eight years earlier, at the Benedictine General Chapter of 1693 in Douai, Dom Augustine Constable proposed sending a letter acknowledging Sir Robert, third baronet, as a great benefactor to the Benedictine Order and English Benedictine Congregation. Of these four chaplains in 1701, the two seculars presumably resided at Harvington and the two monks at Coughton and Weston. They would have helped to mature the education, particularly in theological matters, which returning members of the family had received on the continent. A significant number of the secular priests at Harvington had studied in Paris in the early eighteenth century when the Jansenist controversy was raging. Pre-eminent among them was Hugh Tootell, alias Charles Dodd, who was at Harvington from 1722 until his death in 1743. The draft of his

---

generally lived abroad, dedicated his *Method to arrive at satisfaction in religion* (London 1671) to Lady Throckmorton ('T.E.'), arguing that women were more intellectual than men. Like him, Lady Throckmorton was not satisfied until her 'piercing wit' had established rigorous 'bottom-Principles' in any argument.

monumental *Church History of England* (Brussels [i.e. London], 1737–42) was already complete before he reached Harvington, which explains why he mentions no recourse to Throckmorton family libraries or archives. But Sir Robert, who became the fourth baronet in 1721, helped fund the work's publication. It is crammed with documentary evidence which Dodd had collected throughout Europe, and betrays that sympathy to Jansenism and violent hostility to the Jesuits found in his earlier works. What little we know of the third baronet's theological leanings suggests some affinity with Dodd's theological position.[10]

It was the Benedictine chaplains of the family, however, who particularly helped cement the Throckmortons to European culture and thought, and who, by their training on the continent in various secular disciplines, were able to find acceptance in English non-Catholic circles. Through the Benedictine procurator in London, annuities were paid by the Throckmortons to their ex-chaplains who had retired to the English monasteries in Europe, and family members, notably Anna Maria, wife of Mr George Throckmorton, kept up a lively correspondence with those chaplains close to the family who sent news of the progress of young Throckmortons in continental schools. Bernard Wythie, chaplain at Weston 1726–30, went on to become Benedictine procurator in Rome in 1737, where he was recommended for the service of the Pretender. Wythie's book, *The Creed Expounded* (London, 1735), seems to have been written whilst at Weston, where he must have made use of resources available in the baronet's library. Its interesting slant on Catholic attitudes to Protestant neighbours will be discussed later; here it is noteworthy for its use of classic expositions of Gallicanism like that of Louis Ellies Dupin (1657–1719) on the ancient creeds, and for its demonstration of Wythie's awareness of the current patristic revival then taking place in France. Wythie was succeeded as chaplain by the monk, Gregory Greenwood, a member of a gentry family from Brize Norton and a relation of the Throckmortons. He was at Coughton for an astonishing forty years (*c*.1704–44), during

---

[10] J. Anthony Williams, 'The Distribution of Catholic Chaplaincies in the Early Eighteenth Century', *Recusant History*, 12 (1973), 43; Douai Abbey, Weldon, 'Memorials', IV, p. 87; Michael Hodgetts, 'The Throckmortons of Harvington, 1696–1923', *Recusant History*, 26 (2002), 146; WRO, CR 1998/LCB/62 (Buckland and Coughton library catalogue) reveals a distinct Jansenist bias, with substantial numbers of works by Antoine Arnauld, Charles-Joachim Colbert, Pierre Nicole and Denis Raimond. Ushaw College, Durham, has five volumes from Sir Robert's library, three of which lean towards Jansenism: an edition of Augustin, *Les deux livres de la predestination des saints* (Paris 1676); Michel Bourdaille, *Theologie Morale de Saint Augustin* (Paris, 1681); and Pierre Nicole, *Instruction theologique et morale sur le symbole* (Paris, 1716). Coughton Court has Edward Hawarden's *The True Church of Christ* (London, 1714), with Sir Robert's armorial plate, originally from Weston. Hawarden was a popular and orthodox theologian who had been hounded out of the English College, Douai, for alleged Jansenism.

which time he compiled his manuscript devotional and catechetical works, including a translation of the notorious Jansenist Montpellier catechism which he finished in 1734. What his bizarre purpose was in drafting three discourses on late sixteenth- and early seventeenth-century French witches and witchcraft, which described in minute detail erotic villainies of the devil for the gentlefolk and peasantry of south Warwickshire, whom he addressed as 'Christian hearers', cannot be fathomed.[11]

Two Benedictine chaplains whose experience of Europe endeared them to English figures of national repute were Benedict Simpson and Gregory Gregson. Both were chaplains at Weston to Mr George and Sir John Courtenay Throckmorton, respectively the son and grandson of Sir Robert Throckmorton, fourth baronet. Simpson was at Weston in 1747–69, where he became friendly with the antiquary William Cole (1714–82), a neighbour and rector of Bletchley, who was himself drawn, he said, to a vocation 'after the monkish manner'. In 1765, Simpson provided Cole with Benedictine contacts in France which allowed him to visit Saint-Omer, Douai and Paris. In Paris, in the midst of listing antiquities, he met up with Horace Walpole, as well as English Benedictine monks and Miss Throckmorton, a *pensionnaire* in the school at Port-Royal. In Gregory Gregson, Simpson's successor as chaplain at Weston, who lived there from 1769 to 1800, European influence made more of an impact on the family and its neighbours, and especially on the poet William Cowper. Gregson seems to have become a physician while vestiarian in the English Benedictine monastery in Paris in 1753. At Weston, from where he made frequent return visits to Paris, 'the Doctor', as he was known to Cowper, was in great demand because of his medical expertise, attending members of the family and their friends, and freely giving his services to the local poor. Gregson seems to have been principally responsible for introducing Charles Throckmorton (1757–1840), son of Mr George, the squire of Weston, to the medical profession. As a young man, Charles helped to supply medicines to the Doctor's patients and went on to have a distinguished medical career after studies in Europe and in Scotland. His Edinburgh dissertation on the circulation of the blood was published in 1785. Gregson, Sir Charles's apparent mentor, was primarily a physician, with an extensive knowledge of *materia medica* which allowed him to prescribe with authority an impressive range of potions and to recommend, for instance, the type of embrocation to be applied to a flannel waistcoat covering the skin. Despite his early training in Paris, Gregson disagreed with some French physicians who attributed hiccup to rheumatism. Cowper the

---

[11] WRO, CR 1998/CD/Folder 44/1–3, 5–39, 40; Nancy, Dept. de la Meurthe, H 77 (Anna Maria Throckmorton). Gregory Greenwood's manuscripts are at Downside Abbey, Bath, including MS 566, 'Three Discourses on Witches and Witchcraft'.

poet, who lived close to Weston, frequently visited his friendly neighbours, the Throckmortons, and dined and walked with 'the skilfull Apothecary' Gregson, remarking once how physicians were inclined to affect an air of mystery in their profession by persisting in prescribing in Latin. He must have had Gregson's pedantic and complex remedies in mind, although he was eternally grateful to 'Griggy' for successfully treating his friend Mrs Unwin's tumour. Gregson's memorial tablet in Weston parish church speaks of him being 'a doctor and friend of the poor'.[12]

Such chaplains guided the heads of the family on their choice of education for the Throckmorton children. Tutors and schools were to play a formative part in influencing the character of the family. Tutors who accompanied their charges on their travels, popular with the family in the seventeenth century, seem to have been dropped by the early eighteenth century in favour of schools established in Europe, only to return in popularity at the century's end. Sir Francis, the second baronet, was guided by a number of tutors, and he also preferred his sons to have individual tutors. Francis, his eldest, died prematurely aged sixteen in 1676 in Bruges, suggesting he was being educated in that region. His embalmed heart was given to his brother Robert at Weston eight years later. This Robert, the second baronet's younger son and heir, was put under the Benedictine Francis Fenwick, a Sorbonne doctor who went on in the 1690s to become the agent of the monks at the Stuart court in Rome, and who excelled in preaching and had 'a most sweet affable temper'. On his inheriting the baronetcy in 1680, Sir Robert had rewarded Fenwick with a large annuity from the manor of Oversley, near Coughton. Two of Sir Robert's sisters, Anne and Mary, came to Paris with their governess in 1675 to be educated by the English Blue Nuns in the Rue de Charenton, a community traditionally favoured by the family, but they seemed to have finished their education with the English canonesses of St Augustine in the Fossés-Saint-Victor.[13]

Sir Robert, who became the third baronet at the tender age of 18 in 1680, had to supervise finishing school for his younger siblings as well as the formal education of his eleven surviving children. He was very generous in helping to fund the education of members of his extended family and of other English Catholics. George (1690–1714), his oldest

---

[12] William Cole, *A Journal of my Journey to Paris in the Year 1765*, ed. F.G. Stokes (London 1931), pp. xxiv, 4–5, 9, 141; BL, Add. MS 6401 fol.169; Charles Throckmorton, *Tentamen inaugurale, quaedam de sanguinis motu et quantitate complectens* (Edinburgh, 1785); Nancy, Meurthe, H 77, 3 Jan. 1771 (Gregson to Simpson, and undated letters of Anna Maria Throckmorton to Simpson); *The letters and prose writings of William Cowper*, ed. James King and Charles Ryskamp (5 vols, Oxford, 1979–86), vol. 2, p. 56; vol. 3, pp. 393, 396.

[13] Barnard, *Seventeenth-Century Country Gentleman*, pp. 4, 22, 80; WRO, CR 1998/CD/Drawer 3/8, pp. 2, 6; SCLA, DR 5/936; Douai Abbey, Weldon, 'Memorials', I, 480; Gillow and Trappes-Lomax, *Diary*, pp. xi, 25, 26, 29, 34.

surviving son, who was unfortunately to predecease his father, was the first to spend long periods having a European education. In 1699 his father was offered by the Benedictine president a choice of three young monks to accompany George as tutor. Their youth, intelligence and teaching skills clearly illustrate to what lengths the monks would go to continue to maintain the family's favour. In the end, George was on the continent from 1705 until 1712, probably attending the small school attached to the English Benedictines at Dieulouard in Lorraine and finishing off his education in Paris and the Low Countries with a monk as chaperone. His extended stay required the permission of the English government to travel in France, England's enemy at the time. George was accompanied by his cousin, Thomas Gage, for part of these travels:

> Mr Throckmorton here is very well, spends all his time with his cousin, Sir Thomas Gage, they are together from morning till night. Sir Thomas is gay & airy, my spark for the most part grave and serious.

They lodged in a 'public house', which 'the two young sparks' liked 'mightily well'. In Paris, George attended the opera, visited his aunt Anne, the nun, took his sisters out on jaunts from their convent school and 'treated' the religious communities which received him. He spent a huge amount enjoying himself, learning to fence, ride, sing and dance and play the bugle, whilst studying mathematics and history. But he had no staying power; he was sickly, had a speech impediment and was overconcerned about his health. He succumbed to smallpox and had eye distemper, so apothecaries, purgings and leechings were frequent. His tutor ruefully commented that in Brussels he was too backward to please the ladies and was apt to make faces at them from his coach. There was, therefore, no need for his father to worry about his 'falling into Intriques and Amours'. His early death aged 24 in 1714 came therefore as no surprise. As his tutor had commented earlier, ' I am apt to think that exercise discomposes him and puts him out of order, which makes him not love it, for he takes great care of his health and I think too much.'[14] Even though details of the curriculum which George followed are sparse, the correspondence of his monk tutor with Sir Robert, his father, is crucial because it reveals the latter's substantial financial support for a projected English translation of the New Testament originating in certain English secular clergy circles in Paris reckoned to be tainted with Gallican and Jansenist tendencies. With the publication of the papal bull *Unigenitus* in 1713, which encouraged further witch-hunts of

---

[14] WRO, CR 1998/CD/Folder 55/12; CR 1998/Box 65/Folder 2/2; WDA, vol. A, xxxvi, no. 19, p. 5; WRO, CR 1998/CD/Folder 44/41; WRO, Coughton Folder, 44/4, 6, 8, 17–19, 21, 23, 24, 34, 35.

Figure 7.3 'Child Robin', later Sir Robert Throckmorton, fourth baronet, Coughton Court.

Jansenist suspects, this support from the well-known leader of an English Catholic household could not have come at a more critical time and reveals, yet again, the particular theological and political colouring of the family.[15] It is unfortunate that there are few surviving details regarding the education of Sir Robert's son and heir, another Robert (1702–91), who became fourth baronet in 1721 (Figure 7.3), but part of it appears to have been conducted in small clandestine Catholic schools in England.[16]

Meanwhile, Sir Robert, despite the burdens of taxation at home and war abroad, favoured the English canonesses' school in Paris for his many daughters and Wollascott nieces (his sister Mary having married Martin Wollascott of Woolhampton, Berkshire), to which school they came with their governess, a Mrs Burrell. A number of these girls were themselves to become nuns. At school they were looked after by his sister, Anne (Sister Anne Frances), professed in 1687 and abbess 1720–28. The school careers of 'Nancy', 'Betty', 'Fanny', Charlotte, Apollonia, Frances and Catherine are charted in Anne's letters and accounts to her brother, which include bills for stays, 'mantos' and petticoats, 'harpsicalls' and paints, and describe the ravages of smallpox to which a number of them succumbed. They also visited their grandmother, the widow of the second baronet, still living in Paris, and went to Versailles accompanied by a secular priest 'that they might see what all strive to do before they leave these parts'. In this 'Convent of Our Lady of Syon', well known for its Jacobite sympathies, the girls lived for three years within the enclosure and were taught by two of the nuns and by the chaplain, a secular priest academic living in Paris. During this time, they had spells in French convents to improve their language skills. The school's rules survive from this period: rising at 6.00 am, daily Mass and many devotional exercises, home economics and 'casting account', with lots of craft and design, and learning by rote from

---

[15] Ibid, 44/17,19, accounts for 6 and 24 Oct. 1711; Folder 44/34, William Phillips's accounts for June–Sept. 1710; Godfrey Anstruther, *The Seminary Priests* (4 vols, Ware and Great Wakering, 1968–77), vol. 3., pp. 172, 211–13, 224–5. George's tutor, William Phillips, OSB, knew Francis Thwaites, the secular priest, who helped translate the Jansenist Pasquier Quesnel's *Reflections* on the New Testament. Phillips entered in his accounts contributions by Sir Robert to the translation of the New Testament by Thomas Plumerden, then in Paris, who was collaborating with Bishop John Talbot Stonor, an Anglo-Gallican, in the translation. It never seems to have been published, probably because all contemporary attempts to publish unofficial scriptural translations were treated suspiciously by the Roman authorities paranoid at any perceived Jansenist or Gallican influence: see H. Cotton, *Rhemes and Doway* (Oxford, 1855), pp. 34–46 and Patrick Fagan, *Dublin's Turbulent Priest, Cornelius Nary 1658–1738* (Dublin, 1991), ch. 6.

[16] WRO, CR 1998/Box 65/Folder 2/6, *c*.1712, Bushy House School, London; CR 1998/CD/Folder 44/43–46, *c*.1718, ?Twyford School, Hampshire.

the Douai catechism and Fleury's Gallican historical catechism.[17] From all these came accomplishments and habits of mind which the Throckmorton girls took with them back to England.

The next generation comprised the fourth baronet's son, another George, and his two surviving daughters, Mary Teresa and Barbara, all by his first marriage. They must have been educated in the 1730s and 1740s, but details are few. However, as we hear of the Throckmorton children travelling from Calais to Paris in 1731, we can assume they continued the tradition of an education in Europe, where the English schools had become more established and were attracting funding for bursaries; whilst in England, the very few Catholic schools were struggling. George (1721–1762), an inauspicious name in the family, was outlived by his father, the fourth baronet, but of his five sons, John Courtenay, George and Charles succeeded each other in turn as the fifth, sixth, and seventh baronets. The education of these three, together with that of their youngest brother William, was prolonged and firmly European. None of them had any hopes of immediately succeeding the strapping fourth baronet, who survived until the age of 89, so they moved seamlessly from school onto the Grand Tour, a new experience for members of the family at this date, which was encouraged by their grandfather and paid for from his commodious purse.[18]

The grandsons' education demonstrated the family's continuing preference for secular clergy and Benedictine tutelage. By 1763, two of the boys were attending the secular clergy's small school at Standon Lordship, Hertfordshire; John Courtenay could only have been 10 years old at this time. Later the young Throckmortons were educated by the monks at Douai. In October 1765, Mrs Anna Maria Throckmorton, then widowed, asked the antiquary William Cole to visit Douai and call on her three sons

> who were all sent to me by the Prior's Order to his Apartment: I found them all very well, & much grown... My Freind the late Mr Throckmorton's 3 sons were all dressed in close black Cassocks, being the common Habit of Students: being a very modest, decent & becoming Dress.

---

[17] WRO, CR 1998/CD/Folder 46/5–8, 18–22; CR 1998/CD/Folder 55/18; A.F. Allison, 'The English Augustinian Convent of Our Lady of Syon at Paris: Its Foundation and Struggle for Survival During the First Eighty Years, 1634–1713', *Recusant History*, 21 (1993), 486–7.

[18] Birmingham Diocesan Archives, C0418, Z5/3/84/1/1, 21 June 1731; Douai Abbey, Scott Box 54e; Lille, Nord, 18 H 27 (7 July 1778). In this period, some sons of Throckmorton tenants and members of the Coughton congregation were sent to the Benedictine schools at Douai and Lambspring in Germany: see Downside Abbey, Bath, MS 531, Greenwood's accounts. For a 1753 Benedictine educational fund for future monks established by a close friend of the Throckmortons (John Rawlins of Redditch), see Douai Abbey, Scott Box, 2. For struggling schools in England: WRO, CR 1998/Box 86/17, 4 March 1754.

Their mother showed constant concern for the welfare of her sons exiled in Douai. Robert, John Courtenay and George's time there in the 1760s spanned a momentous decade which saw this school in Douai expand, thanks partly to the suppression of the Jesuits and their schools in France, to fill a new set of fine buildings, still extant. Charles, Francis and William, her remaining sons, later followed their elder brothers to Douai. That they enjoyed close relations with the monks is seen in their attendance at various monastic professions, and evidence of their solid schooling can be judged by Charles's public defence in July 1776 of his philosophy thesis on metaphysics in the University of Douai. Douai was an essential grounding for Rome which soon followed.[19]

In the early eighteenth century, the Throckmorton girls and boys coped with their schooling so far removed from home and in a different culture by having family and friends living with them, whether it be aunts, cousins, brothers or sisters. Poor Mary (1749–63) and Anne ['Nanny'] (1751–83), George Throckmorton's daughters, had none of this companionship when they were sent to Paris in the early 1760s. At the convent of the English canonesses of Our Lady of Syon, their great aunt, who had become abbess, had unfortunately died in 1760, and when Mary also died there in 1763 Nanny was all alone, though at least the culture was English. William Cole was sent by her mother to visit Nanny in 1765, and while there, he noted the Throckmorton and Yate memorials in the nuns' chapel. A nun peeped at him from behind the grille curtain, then directed him to a parlour to meet Nanny, who was living and studying within the enclosure.

> She was much altered for the worse, according to my opinion, since I had seen her: seemed delighted to see a person she had known in England, & expressed herself very happy in her present situation with these English ladies; but seemed to dread very much her approaching leave of them for the French nunnery of Port Royal, where her grandfather, Sir Robert Throckmorton was desirous she should go for a time in order to perfect herself in the French language, as none but the ladies of the best families in France were educated in that monastery.

Nanny did indeed detest Port Royal, as Cole noted when he visited her there:

> As soon as the nun was retired, & she was alone with me, she began to let tears fall in abundance: she said, that she hoped her Mama would not let her remain

---

[19] Cole, *Journal*, pp. 18–20; Nancy, Meurthe, H. 77; Douai Abbey, Reading, Scott Box 2, 2; St Edmund's, Paris, Profession Book, entries for 1768, 1776, 1779; MS 44 (Charles's thesis); Geoffrey Scott, *Gothic Rage Undone: English Monks in the Age of the Enlightenment* (Bath, 1992), p. 179.

in that convent for a long time, where she had not one mortal to speak to in her own language (there being about 30 pensioners of all sorts). I told her I would have her make herself as easy as the awkward situation of being a stranger in the midst of foreigners would admit: that it was upon this very account of being bred up with persons of the first distinction, who consequently spoke their language in its purity, that she was placed there, where I told her, I apprehended she was not to stay long. She regretted leaving the English Canonesses of St. Austin on the Fossez St Victor, & seemed to think it long that she had been at Port Royal, tho' she had not been there a week.[20]

One senses behind Nanny's unhappiness the anxiety of a mother which rubbed off on her daughter, having to wrestle with and abide by the demands of an influential and stubborn grandfather. Nanny eventually returned home and never, it seems, married.

The Throckmortons had plenty of daughters during the eighteenth century (albeit a number of these daughters were sickly, suffering recurrent bouts of smallpox and measles), but far fewer sons. Unsurprisingly the paucity of sons meant that the family produced no priests, but many of the daughters (at least seven) became nuns on the continent. At home in England an abundance of daughters was reckoned a disability because of the generous dowries which had to be paid on their marriages, and the burden of high dowries is a constant theme running through the family's correspondence in these years. Much cheaper, then, to encourage daughters, sickly though they might be, to be professed as nuns and to provide them with small annuities. In addition, they would help to maintain the family's European links. Sir Francis, the second baronet, was friendly with the English nuns of the Third Order of St Francis at Princenhoff, near Bruges, where his heir and namesake had been buried in 1676, and with the English Conceptionists in Paris, for whose chapel he donated an organ that same year. His daughters Anne and Elizabeth, who had had to cope with the early separation of their parents, had settled with their widowed mother in Paris and been educated at the Austin canonesses' school, whose secular chaplains were friends of the family. Anne (1644–1734) was professed a canoness in 1687 (Sister Anne Frances) and was abbess from 1720 to 1728. Her sister chose a more enclosed community and became an English Poor Clare of Rouen. Three of their nieces also became Austin canonesses in Paris: Mary (born 1696) and Frances (1708–51) – daughters of their sister Mary and her husband Martin Wollascott – and Elizabeth, daughter of Sir Robert, third baronet and his wife Mary (née Yate). This Elizabeth (1694–1760), known in religion as Sister Elisabeth-Theresa-Pulcheria, was abbess twice (1736–44, 1756–60), despite her extreme poor health. She had been touched for the King's Evil at Saint-Germain-en-Laye in 1704

---

[20] Cole, *Journal*, pp. xxv, 145, 201, 286–7.

by the Pretender in an effort to restore her health, and at her profession in 1714, her father insisted she was granted various dispensations because of her infirmities. Sister Anne Frances, who also suffered from recurring bouts of smallpox – which seems to have been endemic in the convent – kept a close eye on the education and health of her Throckmorton nieces in the convent school. These Throckmorton nuns had literary pretensions: Sister Anne Frances composed 33 pieces of devotional poetry, Sister Elisabeth-Theresa-Pulcheria devised antiphonal mnemonics in her psalter; and being an enclosed Poor Clare at Rouen did not prevent Sir Robert's sister Elizabeth from offering to procure for her brother the scriptural commentaries of the contemporary French Benedictine Augustin Calmet (1672–1757). The fourth baronet continued to treat the nuns to regular feasts of 'pigge', pigeon pie, strawberries and wine even when he had returned to England.[21]

Of the three Throckmorton canonesses in Paris, two assumed high office in the convent. Anne Frances was novice mistress (1706) and her niece, the physically handicapped Elisabeth, bursar, before both became abbess. Abbess Anne Frances, solicitous for the well-being of her community, petitioned the Grand Almoner of France in 1726 for the continuation of a pension to one of her old nuns whose sister had died and left a bursary for that purpose. These Throckmorton nuns and their niece and cousin, Sister Frances Wollascott (1708–51), are familiar to us through their sensitive and subtly textured portraits, painted in 1729 by Nicolas de Largillière (1646–1756) on the instructions of Sir Robert, fourth baronet, when he was in Paris. Other English Catholic families had to make do with dolls or miniatures sent home to remind the family of their loved ones abroad in the religious life, but the Throckmortons were sufficiently wealthy and cultured to commission from one of the greatest portrait painters of the French and Jacobite courts these fine portraits of the three nuns, with their transparent black veils and pleated white Augustinian rochets. The tired old abbess, Anne Frances, holds the seal of her office; her niece, Abbess Elisabeth, looks pale and badly scarred from the ravages of smallpox as she holds her prayer

---

[21] WRO, CR 1998/CD/Drawer 3/8, p. 6; Gillow and Trappes-Lomax, *Diary*, p.25; WDA, Chronicles of the Convent of Our Lady of Sion in Paris, vol. 1, 1695–1738, especially 5 Dec. 1702, 2 Sept., 29 Oct., 5 Dec. 1704, 3 Aug. 1705, 18 Dec. 1708, 9 Sept. 1711, 26 May 1712, 12 Jan. 1713, 7 Feb. 1716, 11 Nov. 1719, 11 July 1734, 8 Sept. 1737. Thomas Witham, *A short discourse upon the life and death of Mr. Geo. Throckmorton* (1706), p. 116, and longer MS version now at Coughton Court, pp. 235, 296, for Sister Anne's verses. Sister Elisabeth's annotated *Liber Psalmorum* (Paris, 1679), now at Coughton Court. WRO, CR 1998/CD/Folder 47/2 (Calmet). Other Throckmorton nuns include Catherine (c.1693–1792), a Benedictine, and Frances Fitzherbert, d. of Mary Teresa Throckmorton and her husband, Thomas Fitzherbert, who was clothed as a Franciscan at Princenhoff, Bruges, in 1767.

book, while young Sister Frances, aged 21, energetically sews a brocaded coat and peers straight at the viewer (Figures 7.4 a, b, d).[22]

In Paris, Sister Anne Frances was heavily reliant for knowledge of family business on her brother George Throckmorton (1670–1705), her 'chief helper in all things'. It was recounted that when his mother, who was to become the estranged wife of Sir Francis, second baronet, was carrying him, her body sparkled on going to bed each night. George's earliest education was with the Oratorians at their royal academy at Juilly outside Paris, where he was known as 'le petit Chevalier de St. George', but he was only given there 'a Tincture of Belles Lettres'. His vain course was continued in a Grand Tour of Italy during which he was accompanied by Sir Francis Andrews from Norfolk and the monk, Francis Fenwick. In 1696, he returned to the Throckmorton household but was soon bored by rural domesticity and returned to France, with horses and hounds, to cut a fine figure at Fontainebleau. Two riding accidents by which he narrowly escaped death brought this prodigal son to his senses, and at last he heeded the advice of his sister, the nun. He made a serious confession and became converted to a life of three years of penance and mortification in Paris. After falling seriously ill, he died on 6 April 1705. The crowds of Parisian poor who attended his funeral proclaimed him as a saint and father of the poor. His embalmed heart was given to the convent where his sister and two nieces were nuns, while his sister composed devotional verses to commemorate his passing. In 1712, the Throckmortons paid for a neatly inscribed wall monument to cover the cavity in which his heart lay. George Throckmorton was the nearest the family came in this period to producing a saint, even though he never had a vocation to the religious life as such. His early death at the age of 35 in the odour of sanctity was commemorated in a published biography by his close friend Thomas Witham, a secular priest and doctor of the Sorbonne, then superior at St Gregory's College, Paris. Witham was well known for his Jansenist sympathies, 'complaints had been carried to Rome against him concerning the respect due to the Popes Decrees (against the Jansenists)'. This 'Life' of George was published in 1706, almost certainly at the behest of the Throckmorton family, and survives also in another, longer manuscript version, full of eye-witness accounts, which claims to be a copy of a second edition of 1710, although this was not in fact published.[23]

---

[22] F.-M.-Th. Cédoz, *Un Couvent de Religieuses Anglaises á Paris de 1634 á 1884* (Paris, 1891), ch. 13, and pp. 228–35; G. Daumet, *Notice sur les Etablissements religieux anglais, écossais, et irlandais fondés è Paris avant la Révolution* (Paris, 1912), pp. 3, 10, 112–13; BL, MSEg.1,671 (petition).

[23] Thomas Witham, *A short discourse upon the life and death of Mr. Geo. Throckmorton, decesas'd the 5th of April, N.S., 1705 in the 34th year of his age* (1706); Coughton Court MS,

George Throckmorton's biography, and nothing else in English resembles it, is of particular importance not only because it shows how deeply the Throckmortons had inserted themselves into the mainstream of French religious life, but because it also belongs to that genre of contemporary fashionable Jansenist hagiographies of virtuous youth and penitents; Jansenist, that is, in the sense of describing a life of austere piety rather than in the promotion of theological heterodoxy. The most famous of these Jansenist accounts was that of the miracles and convulsions at the tomb in Paris of the young deacon François de Pâris, who died in 1727 and who had been a bitter opponent of the papal bull *Unigenitus* of 1713 which had condemned Jansenism. Significantly, George Throckmorton's death in 1705 coincided with an earlier papal attack on Jansenists in the bull *Vineam Domini*. His *Life* is, therefore, as much a Jansenist tract as a panegyric, and in a more nuanced way, given the peculiar nature of English Catholicism, was published partly to lend support to a party among English exiles in France sympathetic to Jansenism who felt persecuted and under threat. Throughout the biography, Jansenist influences predominate: on the eve of his conversion, George was reading the works of Pierre Nicole, the most distinguished Jansenist spiritual author, to whom he believed he owed his conversion. Nicole's works had been given him by Dr Richard Short, a leading English Jansenist sympathiser who was to be George's executor. Besides Nicole's tracts, George absorbed the works of the Jesuit Paolo Segneri and Louise de La Vallière, the mistress of King Louis XIV who became a Carmelite nun, on how to lead a penitential life. George's deeply serious approach to confession and the lengthy emphasis given to this in the biography, where it is contrasted with Jesuit laxism, also reveals Jansenist sympathies. Since such an extreme penitential life was impossible with his family in England, he had been persuaded by Thomas Witham and Thomas Plumerden, themselves attracted to Jansenism, to stay in Paris where he would be near his sister, the nun, and where he could practise private retirement and attend public liturgies as a *dévot*. There followed three and a half years of prayer, fasting and alms-deeds, chronicled in great detail in the manuscript 'Life', in which he waited upon God's grace 'like a poor beggar standing waiting for alms'. He lived first with the Fathers of Christian Doctrine and then in his own house some doors down from his sister and nieces in the convent, while he continued

'A short discourse upon the life and death of Mr. George Throckmorton who dyed at Paris the fifth day of April new stile 1705. In the 35th year of his age by Thomas Witham Doctor of Divinity of the Faculty of Paris. The 2d. Edition with the addition of some few particulars by another hand. Printed Anno 1710', with postscript by Eugenius Martin, 1712. For Martin, see *The Register Book of St. Gregory's College at Paris, 1667–1786*, ed. Edwin Hubert Burton, CRS, 19 (London, 1917), pp. 238, 250; John Kirk, *Biographies of English Catholics in the Eighteenth Century* (London, 1909), pp. 232–3; Cole, *Journal*, p. 289.

to read classic Jansenist authors such as Nicolas Le Tourneux. Thomas Witham preached at the immuring of George's heart in the convent chapel in 1712, and later sent letters to the Throckmorton nun nieces – one of whom, Mary, was George's goddaughter – urging them to meditate before the heart in its monument and despise worldly things. Witham, we are told, had had 'a very particular connexion' with George and, through him, with all the family, an indication of how Witham's own theological and spiritual interests must have been absorbed in some measure into the Throckmortons generally.[24]

During the rest of the eighteenth century, Europe continued to be attractive to the Throckmortons, not so much for the schools of devotional austerity which had influenced George Throckmorton, but more particularly for its art and culture. It continued to widen their experience and their vision, set, as they were, within the narrow confines of English insular society and the even narrower English Catholic circle. George's nephew Robert became fourth baronet in 1721, aged 19, and spanned the century, being married three times and dying in 1791. It was he who was principally responsible for seeing that his grandsons, John Courtenay, George, Charles and William, derived maximum advantage from their time on the Grand Tour. Sir Robert's reputation as a continental connoisseur survives in his art commissions and in the splendid Palladian villa at Buckland, west of Oxford. He was imbued with that same spirit of English Catholic liberalism found in his ancestors which he imparted to his descendants, notably Sir John Courtenay, the fifth baronet. Thus, while other Catholic families rigidly adhered to the cause of the exiled Stuarts up to the death of Bonnie Prince Charlie in 1788, there is a noticeable absence of any abiding interest in Jacobitism by Sir Robert after his return from the Grand Tour in 1729. The garter ribbon of Prince Charles Edward, the drawing of the young prince by Giles Hussey and a glove of his father, James Edward, together with Stuart locks of hair, all forlornly preserved at Coughton today, do not essentially detract from this view. By the time of the '45, the Throckmortons had slipped into a platonic Jacobitism; witness the wager that the Catholic John Chichester of Arlington made with George

---

[24] WRO, CR 1998/LCB/62, Buckland and Coughton library catalogue, for printed and manuscript 'Life'. For contemporary Jansenist tensions in Paris, see B. Robert Kreiser, *Miracles, Convulsions, and Ecclesiastical Politics in Early Eighteenth-Century Paris* (Princeton, 1978). For Jansenism and the English secular clergy, Eamon Duffy, 'A Rubb-Up for Old Soares; Jesuits, Jansenists and the English Secular Clergy, 1705–1715', *Journal of Ecclesiastical History*, 28 (1977): 291–317. For Witham, WDA, Old Brotherhood Archives, Calendar, MSS 1700–1750, Burton, *Register Book*, pp. 121–2, and Ruth Clark, *Strangers and Sojourners at Port Royal* (Cambridge, 1932), p. 174, note 4.

Throckmorton in 1747 that if Bonnie Prince Charlie ever appeared in the United Kingdom he would repay Throckmorton ten guineas.[25]

Sir Robert had married the Catholic Lady Theresa Herbert, daughter of the wealthy Marquis of Powis in 1720, and was introduced to French portraitists of Jacobite subjects by his wife, she bringing with her the portrait of her aunt, Lady Mary Herbert, as the goddess Diana, painted by François du Troy (1645–1730) about 1692. Du Troy frequented the exiled Stuart court at Saint-Germain-en-Laye. Within three years of the marriage, Sir Robert had become a widow. On 30 August 1728, the monk Thomas Southcott in Paris informed the Old Pretender that Sir Robert was departing imminently for a tour of France, then progressing to Italy where he was to visit Rome, and seek entry to Jacobite circles, and Naples. He was accompanied by his neighbour, Mr Carrington of Wootton Wawen, a relative of his wife, and by the monk Joseph Howard. In Paris, Sir Robert commissioned from Nicolas de Largillière the famous set of four family portraits of himself and his three nun relatives mentioned earlier (Figures 7.4a–d). Largillière had completed many Jacobite and English portraits in the past, but these four represent a late flowering of his skill.

Sir Robert's is a 'rhetorical portrait' in the French style, and if the group was commissioned by him to mark the retirement of his aunt as abbess in 1728, the clue to the group's unity appears to be the richly brocaded waistcoat which his niece, Sister Frances Wollascott, is depicted as embroidering and which is deliberately set alongside the similar waistcoat the baronet is himself wearing. Orders for fancy French waistcoats are often items in Throckmorton correspondence of the eighteenth century. Sir Robert's art collection, including these portraits, was eventually exhibited at Buckland House, Berkshire, designed and built by the Bath architects Sir John Wood, father and son, between 1753 and 1759. The Throckmortons often visited Bath, but one wonders if the original inspiration for neo-Palladian Buckland came from houses Sir Robert had seen on his European travels; it is supposed to have a bedroom modelled on one at Versailles. Buckland is 'an extraordinary Anglicization of a pyramid-capped Palladian cupoid, its spare fenestration wonderfully at odds with the dark northern climate'.[26]

Such was the fourth baronet's attraction to Europe that he was determined his grandsons should derive maximum advantage from the continent after they had left school at Douai. By 1769, Robert, his eldest

---

[25] WRO, CR 1998/Box 61/Folder 2/1.

[26] Windsor, Royal Archives, Stuart Papers 119/134; John Ingamells, *A Dictionary of British and Irish Travellers in Italy 1701–1800* (New Haven, 1997), pp. 186, 942–3; A. Meyer, 'Re-dressing classical statuary, the eighteenth-century "hand-in-waistcoat" portrait', *The Art Bulletin*, 77 (1995): 59–60; Andor Gomme, 'Wood, John', *ODNB*.

Figure 7.4a Abbess Frances Anne Throckmorton, by Largillière.

Figure 7.4b Abbess Elizabeth Throckmorton, by Largillière.

Figure 7.4c Sir Robert Throckmorton, fourth baronet, by Largillière.

Figure 7.4d Sister Frances Wollascott, by Largillière.

grandson (1750–79), had arrived in Rome where he lived for two years in 'a wretched situation in Trastevere' with Augustine Walker, the English Benedictine procurator at the papal court. In 1772 Robert had his Grand Tour portrait painted by the leading portraitist, Pompeo Batoni, where he is shown holding a drawing of the Pantheon (Figure 7.5).

Figure 7.5   Robert Throckmorton (1750–79), by Pompeo Batoni, Coughton Court.

This was eventually to be hung at Weston. Mr Robert's face demonstrates the anatomical precision and texture which made the artist famous, and the dark background and gold-braided black coat reflect the sobriety of Batoni's later works. In gratitude to Walker, Sir Robert paid him an annuity of £20 for the rest of his life. In 1773, Mr Robert was succeeded in Rome by his brothers John Courtenay and George, who were guided around the city by Walker and their cousin, James Paston. John Thorpe, an English Jesuit in Rome, commented:

> They frequent low English company, because there (in Trastevere) is the favourite card table of their tutor (Walker), unless he chooses to exhibit with Cups & Balls, or declaim against the Jesuits in the vile hole of an English Coffee House … The two young gentlemen appear to be very capable of improvement, & the elder of them (Mr. Courtenay) to be of a most agreeable character.

Charles, their younger brother, was due to go to Rome in 1777 for two years to learn civil law, 'Italian well, belles lettres and Italian, poetry, fencing & dancing', but, in the end, he never came and ended up in Paris, where Walker had been installed in 1777 as English Benedictine president-general.[27] John Courtenay immersed himself fully into Italian culture in this, the first of his two sojourns in Italy. His surviving notebooks, with accompanying sketches, record his visits to churches, palaces and villas in and around Rome, Naples and Florence. Italy was for him the source of his abiding interest in art and architecture, and the home of his distinguished artist friends who were members of the circle around James Byres, the Roman *cicerone*.[28]

---

[27] Nancy, Meurthe, H 77, 4 April 1770, 6 Oct. 1772, Walker to Naylor, 25 Feb. 1772, Bennet to Naylor; Lille, Nord, 18 H 27, 27 Dec. 1774 , 25 Aug. 1775, Bennet to Welch; 18 H 28, 27 Aug. 1777, Bennet to Walker, 18 H 62, 18 Jan. 1778, 13 May 1780, J.C. Throckmorton to Walker, 18 H 63, 25 Feb.1775, Walker to Welsh; Douai Abbey, Scott Box, 54e; London, Farm Street, Jesuit Archives, Thorpe Letters, 9 March 1774, 25 Feb. 1775; Windsor, Royal Archives, Stuart Papers 400/67; Edgar Peters Bowron and Peter Björn Kerber (eds), *Pompeo Batoni* (New Haven and London, 2008), pp. 74–5; Ingamells, *British and Irish Travellers in Italy*, p. 942.

[28] Lille, Nord, 18 H 62, 7, 10 July 1788, J.C. Throckmorton at Weston to Walker, thanking him for Walker's present of the architectural draughtsman Charles-Louis Clérisseau's *Antiquities of Nimes*, and Throckmorton's criticisms of the new classical portico at St Gregory's Priory, Douai. Lille, Nord, 18 H 62, 18 January 1778, J.C. Throckmorton to Walker, asking to be remembered in Rome to James Byres (antiquarian guide and collector), Christopher Norton (engraver), Christopher Hewetson (sculptor), Solomon Delane (landscape painter) and Colin Morison (painter and antiquary). W.J. Blyton, 'A Puritan's Catholic Friends. Cowper and the Throckmortons', *The Month*, 49 (March, 1937), 222; WRO, CR 1998/LCB/62, Buckland and Coughton library catalogue, many entries of Italian works on art, architecture & topography, & 1792 Buckland inventory with 'drawing in crayons … by Mr. Throckmorton'.

The Maturing of Liberality

While their degree of European involvement made the Throckmortons distinctive, the liberal attitudes demonstrated by this Catholic family at home were equally remarkable, especially in the eighteenth century when xenophobic Englishmen prided themselves on their democratic sense, their reformed Christianity and their humanity and respect for justice, in comparison with the tyrannies of Catholic Europe and with French absolutism. Had it not been for the family's dogged adherence to Catholicism, some of whose more obscurantist tenets were not above criticism by certain of its members, the Throckmortons would have slipped early into mainstream English society. As it was, their successful blend of continental culture and sense of English justice enriched the Protestant nation. From Europe they brought to England an interest in the early Enlightenment, coupled with an Augustinian, even Jansenist, sense of a fallen world. Recent work on the emergence of a 'Country Party' in England during the first half of the eighteenth century has shown how attractive 'country' interests were to certain English Catholics like the Throckmortons, forced to remain outside the political establishment but nevertheless eager to demonstrate their patriotism and their adherence to classical virtue. It was to be a short step from their involvement in this 'Country Party' to the full-blown later Cisalpinism of John Courtenay Throckmorton, for the family was exemplary of a wider Catholic patriot body seeking toleration throughout the century.

It is curious that John Courtenay's immersion in the Cisalpine debates at the end of the century replicated the policies of his ancestor at its beginning. We have already noted Sir Robert, the third baronet's, determination to prove his loyalty to the government when under pressure. The background to his stance is reflected in his correspondence with his lawyer, the Catholic Nathaniel Pigott, between 1705 and 1706, when Catholics, already subject to punitive legislation and debarred from offices, parliament and the professions, were obliged to notify the government of their religious status in the returns of 1706. Sir Robert and Pigott feared this would unleash a further campaign against Catholics, and in the previous year had been alarmed by the arrest of the Jesuit Robert Beeston at the house of the Sheldon family, neighbours to the Throckmortons. Sir Robert had already financed Pigott in his campaign against the bill of 1700, which would have prevented Catholics inheriting estates if they refused the oaths. Both agreed that it was not sufficient for Catholics simply to live quietly in order to merit government protection; they must be prepared to take an oath of allegiance. This, Sir Robert insisted, was 'founded on the principles of the gospel and the practice of the primitive Christians'. He believed it was best to proceed cautiously, not by way of 'public petition', but by bringing foreign ambassadors onto the side of the English Catholics and arranging meetings of the Catholic nobility and gentry in London which Sir Robert would join.

> As owr enemies accuse us of favoring arbitrary power, I think wee ought to … declare owrselves for the English constitution which undoubtedly is the best in the world, to express owr sence of having lived without persecution under her present M[ajest]y, to promis to behave owrselves as becomes good subjects.

Unfortunately, the friends of the Catholics at court, who included the Duke of Devonshire, recommended no further action because of the 'critical juncture' of the times and that 'it was thought best to sitt still'.[29]

Catholics of considerable estates like the Throckmortons had been penalised by the government's enforcement of a double land tax, first imposed in 1692 and repeated until 1831, but only sporadically enforced. On top of this was the obligation, in the wake of the 1715 Jacobite rebellion, for papists to register their estates, which led in some cases to forfeiture and to a levy of £100,000 on papists in 1723. The Throckmortons seem generally to have weathered these encumbrances, thanks partly to their wealth and social acceptability. In 1718, Robert Eyston, Sir Robert's Catholic Berkshire neighbour, could report to the Oxford antiquary Thomas Hearne that Sir Robert was worth at least £5,000. Just before the 1723 levy, the third baronet had died (1721), having through marriage incorporated into the family estates those of Harvington and Buckland, and his successor increased the family's wealth by means of the generous portion which his first wife, Lady Theresa Herbert, daughter of the fifth Marquis of Powis, brought with her.

The Throckmortons complied with government orders to send in the requisite returns regarding their property, but the tensions typical of a landed Catholic family of the time can be seen in a valuable document written between 1718–23, at the time of a renewed attempt by Bishop John Stonor and the Abbé Thomas Strickland to negotiate Catholic oaths of allegiance and abjuration with the Protestant Hanoverian government. This overture coincided with the threat of the imposition of the papist levy. The document begins with a copy of the preface to a book by the English secular clergy agent in Rome, Lawrence Mayes, which insisted on English Catholic loyalty to the Old Pretender, but this is followed by an anonymous response suggesting how Catholics might best face the threat of the levy. The answer was simple: through a new oath of allegiance which

---

[29] M.W. Farr, 'Correspondence between Sir Robert Throckmorton and Nathaniel Pigott, 1706-7', *University of Birmingham Historical Journal*, 8 (1961): 82–92; WRO, CR 1998/Box 65/Folder 2/11. G. Glickman, *The English Catholic Community 1688–1745. Politics, Culture and Ideology* (Woodbridge, 2009), for Throckmortons and the 'Country Party'.

'the more considerable RC Ecclesiasticks as well as Laicks, have already declared their readiness to take'. This would separate loyal Catholics from the disaffected. This rebuttal, with its clear understanding of Protestant and Catholic divisions in contemporary European states, and with its reference to the supremely conciliarist Council of Constance (1414–17) in relation to the necessity of concordats, might in a later decade easily have come from the pen of the knowledgeable John Courtenay Throckmorton himself. Indeed, a late eighteenth-century note inserted in the last page of the document seems to be in his hand, and urges the meeting of a group of Catholics to discuss the oath of allegiance. Once again, there is evidence not merely of passive conformity, but of a continuing thread of liberal attitudes within the family over several generations.[30]

If the family had difficulty maintaining a succession of male heirs, it was blessed with marriages into other comparable Catholic families, many of whose later members shared the liberal views of John Courtenay and also joined the Cisalpine Club in the 1780s. Thus Barbara, daughter of the third baronet, married Peter Giffard of Chillington in 1722, and her sister Anne married John Petre of Ingatestone, while their nieces Mary Teresa and Barbara married respectively Thomas Fitzherbert of Swynnerton and Thomas Giffard of Chillington. The three grandsons of the fourth baronet who were to inherit the title in turn, and their youngest brother, William, married into the Catholic dynasties of Giffard, Stapleton, Plowden and Clifford. Land remained the basis of eighteenth-century power and the Throckmortons' wealth was assured by generations of marriages of male Throckmortons to daughters of landed gentry families who brought with them comfortable dowries, while keen haggling ensured that Throckmorton daughters departing for marriage took with them moderate portions. Daughters were thus a key factor in Catholic family connections and marriages were carefully arranged partly with materialist motives in mind and often through the agency of go-betweens such as family chaplains. The correspondence of the family and its circle is full of this essential preoccupation. But ultimately, Throckmorton matches were conservative, made with landed gentry rather than with upwardly mobile commercial and business families, a growing trend in this period. Through such marriages, Throckmorton baronets were drawn into becoming executors for members of other Catholic families. Although the fourth baronet had three wives in descending order of grandeur, only the second, Catherine Collingwood (c.1705–61) has left anything of interest. She was

---

[30] *The Remains of Thomas Hearne*, ed. John Buchanan-Brown (London 1966), p. 212. Estcourt and Payne, *English Catholic Nonjurors*, pp. 3, 14, 216, 279, 291, for the extent of the family's propertied wealth in 1723. WRO, Coughton, Box 86/12, for the paper on an oath of allegiance.

the third daughter of George Collingwood, a Northumbrian Catholic and Jacobite rebel executed in 1716, and his wife, Catherine, daughter of Henry Browne, fifth Viscount Montague. Before and after her marriage to Sir Robert, Catherine mixed in high London society, being a member of the Duchess of Portland's circle and a correspondent of the artist and socialite, Mary Delany Pendarves (1700–88), who was relieved to hear in 1737 that Catherine had decided against burying herself alive in a convent and agreed instead to become Sir Robert's wife.[31] The wives of Sir John Courtenay and his brother, Sir George, Maria Catherine Giffard (c.1760–1821) and Catherine Stapleton, are well known for their friendship with the poet William Cowper. Perhaps the most influential Throckmorton wife, however, was Anna Maria Paston (c.1732–99), the Catholic wife of George Throckmorton, son of the fourth baronet, who brought the Molland estate in Devon into the family (Figure 7.6). She was widowed in her thirties, at which point she moved to Bath, and from that spa kept up an active correspondence with her numerous family and friends whilst managing her estates in Devon until her death.

The Throckmortons were at the hub of local Catholic networks around their houses and elsewhere. A monk, for instance, supplied the neighbouring house chapels of Coughton and those of the Cannings of Foxcote and Stanfords of Abbots Salford. Anselm Mannock, a chaplain at Foxcote, dedicated in 1726 his book *The Christian Sacrifice* to Sir Robert Throckmorton, William Stanford and Francis Canning and other Catholic gentry in the locality whom he had hoped would pay for the engravings. Weston's baptismal register was begun as early as 1702. Amongst its earliest entries were baptisms performed at Coughton but entered here. Coughton's register was begun in 1744, with some baptisms being performed at Abbots Salford and in private houses. Twenty converts are recorded at Weston between 1710 and 1719, mostly members of estate families, but including 'a married woman of Northampton' who 'seemed to have the thought of her conversion by a particular inspiration'.[32] Confirmation was administered to groups of local Catholics from 1687 at Weston, where 90 were confirmed, and was similarly administered at Coughton every few years during the rest of the century. Such lists provide details of the congregations attached to the family's chapels, which were

---

[31] WRO, CR 1998/ Box 72/ Folder 49; *The autobiography and correspondence of Mary Granville, Mrs. Delany*, ed. Lady Llanover (London, 1861); *Elizabeth Montagu The Queen of the Blue-Stockings; Her Correspondence from 1720 to 1761*, ed. Emily J. Climenson (London, 1906), p. 16.

[32] *The Catholic Registers of Weston Underwood, in the County of Buckingham*, ed. Frederick Arthur Crisp (privately printed, 1887); Birmingham Diocesan Archives, Coughton register.

Figure 7.6   Anna Maria Throckmorton (née Paston) (c.1732–99), Coughton Court.

attended by local Catholics as well as staff and tenantry, When Bishop Richard Challoner visited Buckland in 1741, he found a congregation of only 30. Buckland never seems to have had a continuous line of resident chaplains. At Weston, which Challoner visited the following year, he found 200 Catholics, who worshipped in an attic chapel on the west side of the house. The 1767 papist returns sent to the House of Lords indicated that Weston had 173 Catholics, Coughton 75 and Buckland 42, the fourth baronet being resident in the last since 1751, aged 67, with a young wife of 31 years. By the early 1780s, the congregation at Coughton was said to have been large and extensive. Around 1700, there had been a squabble at Coughton between the Throckmortons and a Catholic tenant, Mrs Frances Grey, a generous benefactress to the Benedictines. The argument centred on whether she, a Catholic tenant, had a duty to pay land tax levied on papist estates as well as the owner himself, an interesting local example of how anti-popish legislation might cause divisions within local Catholic society.[33] Bath, which the Throckmortons frequented throughout the eighteenth century, was a Benedictine mission staffed by some monks who had earlier been at Coughton. In this fashionable spa George Throckmorton's widow, Anna Maria, lived for over 30 years with her young son, another George, and a household of ten servants, gossiping with some authority about its Catholics and their fripperies.[34]

Despite their systematic endogamy, during the eighteenth century the Throckmortons lived less and less within the constraints of a Catholic bubble. They benefited from the fitful enforcement of the penal legislation and from the toleration granted to Catholics by the Catholic Relief Acts of 1778 and 1791. They consciously took their place among the landed wealthy gentry of the country in this time of social and political stability, having their pedigree compiled by Browne Willis (1682–1760), the high Tory antiquarian of Buckinghamshire, at the beginning of the century, and witnessed by Ralph Bigland (1712–84), garter king of arms, at the end. In 1789, Sir Robert, nearing his ninetieth year and quite blind, was commended for preserving and restoring Buckland's Anglican parish church, 'An excellent example to Roman Catholick gentry!' In 1794, a leading Benedictine noted of Sir Robert's grandson that 'the baronet (Sir

---

[33] Lille, Nord, 18 H 66, 28 Sept.1782, 8 March 1783, Warmoll to Walker; Edwin H. Burton, *The Life and Times of Bishop Challoner (1691–1781)* (2 vols, London, 1909), vol. 1, pp. 181, 202; *Returns of Papists, 1767*, ed. E.S. Worrall, CRS, Occasional Publications (2 vols, 1980–89), vol. 2, pp. 74, 108, 163–4; WRO, CR 1998/Box 65/Folder 1/11.

[34] J. Anthony Williams (ed.), *Catholicism in Bath*, CRS, 65, 66 (2 vols, 1975–76), vol. 1, pp. 77, 106, vol. 2, pp. 18, 22, 28, 48, 50, 53, 72, 153, 162.

John Courtenay) and Lady have lately lived in high and pompous style at Coughton, and shown great popularity to his surrounding neighbours'.[35]

This entry into the local English establishment was mostly due to the aggrandisement of their landed wealth, and the documents relating to their land tenure are the largest single item among the surviving eighteenth-century family records, although legend has it that the fourth baronet, embarrassed at his extravagant outlay on Buckland in the 1750s, burned all the papers relating to its development. Significantly, the erection of Buckland coincided with a marked increase in the signing of leases. The landed interest was at the height of its power in this contented century, but the family's Catholicism prevented its members supplementing its wealth through the usual channels of government offices and patronage. The Throckmorton property was rural and devoted to agriculture; the family never benefited, therefore, from urban land sales nor early industrial expansion. There was some willingness to lease property to city gents, but the only interest in industrialisation seems to have been an agreement in 1700 to give mining rights on Sambourne Heath, near Coughton, and to grant leases to needle makers near Coughton which lay close to a centre of that industry. The baronets were, however, unable to withstand the march of progress in agriculture, as witness their involvement in the enclosing of common fields on Sambourne Heath and outside Throckmorton village. The family was, furthermore, generally reluctant to sell its land, being anxious at all costs to preserve the estates accumulated mostly through marriage, and it did well out of rising land rents from mid-century. Thorough surveys were sometimes compiled when a young member of the family succeeded to the management of the estate, which shows a degree of continuing interest by the baronets. The outlying estates around Chaddesley Corbett, Worcestershire, were leased frequently, and at Molland in Devon, Mrs Anna Maria Throckmorton tended to prefer long leases, both suggesting perhaps a degree of disinterestedness in these more remote fiefdoms.[36] Even at Coughton, Weston and Buckland – the last the most desirable residence because of its proximity to Oxford and London – the family's absenteeism and increasing mobility as its members flitted between London and Bath necessitated leaving business in the hands of agents. Inevitably the management of all the Throckmorton estates brought the baronets and their agents into direct contact with their non-Catholic tenants and neighbours, and this was true also of involvement

---

[35] John Nichols, *Literary Anecdotes of the Eighteenth Century* (9 vols, London, 1812–16), vol. 3, p. 700; WRO, CR 1998/LCB/21, L3/791; Clifton Diocesan Archives, 1794, vol, no. 104, 22.

[36] Hodgetts, 'Throckmortons', 143; SCLA, DR 5/1047–50, 1056, 1105, 1155, 1185, 1196, 1202, 1207,1212, 1217, 1764, 1777; Berkshire Record Office, D/Ewe, E 3, e 14.

with the Church of England. We thus find Sir Robert, the third baronet, presenting to the parsonage of Spernal and helping to purchase the vicar of Coughton's robe in 1684, while his successor leased the advowson of Coughton church in 1775 to a neighbour. As we have seen, the third baronet had an angry exchange in the heat of the 1688–89 Revolution with the vicar of Ravenstone, near Weston, whom he accused of searching his house without authority. But the measure of the baronet's acceptance within local society is perhaps best indicated in the generous subsidies he gave to the repair and recasting of the peal of bells in Coughton and Weston parish churches. Local communities were often obsessed by their bells, symbols of self-esteem which created territorial identity. As Alain Corbin has perceptively written, 'Bells shaped the habitus of a community or, if you will, its culture of the senses. They served to anchor localism, imparting depth to the desire for rootedness and offering the peace of near, well-defined horizons.'[37]

An interest in literature, architecture and the arts helped the Throckmortons to identify with the English culture of the period, for the majority of them were well educated. The rebuilding of Coughton and Weston witnesses to the family's growth in self-confidence, but it is Buckland above all else which stands as the strongest symbol of the Throckmortons' coming of age. The family had owned Coughton since 1409, but had tended to forsake it for much of the eighteenth century. Only in 1780, when Sir John Courtenay, who had architectural pretensions, took up residence for part of the time, were the ruins of the east range cleared. The moat disappeared and a drive was built to the gatehouse, which was gothicised and extended on each side. At the east end of the south wing, a chapel was created which later became the saloon. During the 1790s these new interiors were furnished partly with materials from other Throckmorton houses. The symmetry achieved between old and new at Coughton is remarkable. At Weston, also inherited in the fifteenth century, where only outbuildings now survive, the third baronet, who made Weston his home, began in 1686 to make extensive changes, which culminated in the completion around 1710 of the north and principal front facing the park. Around it were the fish-ponds which he meticulously stocked.[38] Sir Robert, the fourth baronet, had possibly known at Bath the two John Woods, father and son, the architects he chose to rebuild Buckland House,

---

[37] WRO, CR 1998/CD/Folder 55/5; CR 1998/CD/Drawer 3/8, 9, 20, 21. Alain Corbin, *Village Bells. Sound and Meaning in the Nineteenth-century French Countryside*, trans. Martin Thom (Basingstoke, 1999), p. 97.

[38] WRO, CR 1998/CD/Drawer 3/8; Geoffrey Tyack, *Warwickshire Country Houses* (Chichester, 1994), p. 79.

Berkshire, between 1755 and 1759 in the Palladian style. This he made his home, and created around it

> an Arcadian landscape, complete with grotto and rotunda, winning the admiration of that much-derided Poet-Laureate Henry Pye who sings of his having 'Clothed the declining slopes with pendant wood, And o'er the sedge-grown meadows poured the flood'.

Pevsner called Buckland, 'the most splendid of smaller Georgian houses in the county'. A portrait of Sir Robert, now at Coughton, shows him with the plans of a temple he had built in the park, which is the earliest known to be designed by Richard Woods, a Catholic contemporary of Capability Brown. The house, with its two curious octagonal pavilions at the extremities, earned a place in *Vitruvius Britannicus*, 1767.[39] Buckland housed the collections of the fourth baronet, including portraits of the family, no longer now by Italian artists but by English portrait painters such as George Knapton (1698–1778) and William Hoare (*c*.1707–92), and a library which on his death comprised over 1500 books. This collection, strong in the classics and Church Fathers, was to be an invaluable resource for the researches of Sir John Courtenay, the most distinguished scholar in the family, although an anecdote by the Oxford antiquary, Thomas Hearne, about the third baronet suggests that earlier heads of the family were not without parts:

> He hath more than once sent for me to come over to him at Bucklands. The Person told him that I could not ride. I will send, says he, a Coach and six for him. But he can ride no way, says the Person. He always walks. Why, the Duce is in it, says Sir Robert, so all Antiquaries use to do. I have known several, and they have all walked, Anthony Wood not excepted. They are Men that love to make remarks, and they prefer walking to riding on that account.[40]

In 1791, Sir Robert, the old fourth baronet, died, leaving the baronetcy to his grandson, John Courtenay (1753–1819). Sir John represents the maturing of what we might grandiloquently call the Throckmorton spirit of the eighteenth century. He inherited his passion for field sports and horse racing from this grandfather, but he was more than a typical Jorrocks, for Sir John was a serious scholar whose European education in France and Italy,

---

[39] Berkshire Record Office, D/EWe.A.3; Mark Bence-Jones, *The Catholic Families* (London, 1992), p. 41; Nikolaus Pevsner, *The Buildings of England: Berkshire* (Harmondsworth, 1975), p.105.

[40] WRO, CR 1998/LCB/62, Buckland and Coughton library catalogue, 1792 Buckland inventory, including Knapton and Hoare works; Hearne, *Remains*, p. 212.

extending over a quarter of a century, made him a passionate champion of liberty. In contrast to many of his English Catholic contemporaries who sought advancement by conforming to the English political and religious establishment, he remained resolute in his inherited Catholic faith. His Grand Tour of the early 1770s was revisited in further trips to the continent in the 1790s as baronet, accompanied by his wife, when he took in Geneva, Venice, Florence, Rome and Naples.[41] This was followed by a fact-finding trip around England, during which his natural curiosity led him to investigate best practice in estate management and planning. Sir John was to know absolute monarchy in Europe, papal theocracy in Italy, democracy in America and revolution in France, all of which influenced from the late 1770s his leadership of the advanced Catholics in England who, as members of the Catholic Committee and later the Cisalpine Club, urged the government to provide toleration for Catholics. In return, Sir John and his fellow Cisalpines supported Catholics taking the oath of allegiance as well demanding properly constituted English Catholic bishops and the provision of wider educational opportunities for their co-religionists.

Sir John's brothers – George, an invalid; Charles, a medical doctor; and William, a lawyer – all shared his wide experience and liberal opinions. His rock, however, was his wife and cousin, Maria Catherine, from another Catholic liberal family, the Giffards of Chillington. They married in 1782 and lived at Weston before they established themselves at Buckland in 1791 on the old baronet's death. There were no children by the marriage. At Weston, Sir John and Maria Catherine's charming friendship with their tenant and neighbour, the poet William Cowper, is endearingly detailed by him. For Mrs Throckmorton, Cowper wrote epitaphs on her dogs Fop and Neptune and verses on the death of her bullfinch. She, in turn, copied his translation of Homer. Cowper and John Courtenay were keen horticulturalists: Cowper, 'Toot', was given the key to the garden of 'Mr and Mrs Frog'. In 1784 they invited him to watch a hot-air balloon take off from Weston. Lots of invitations to meals with the couple and their chaplain, Gregory Gregson, followed. At one of these, in 1786, Cowper famously acknowledged their generous tolerance:

> I happened to say that in all professions and trades mankind affected an air of mystery. Physicians ... persist in prescribing Latin, many times no doubt to the hazard of a patient's life, through the ignorance of an apothecary. Mr Throckmorton ... turning to his chaplain to my infinite surprise observed to

---

[41] See Michael Mullett's chapter in this volume.

him, 'That is just as absurd as our praying in Latin'. I could have hugged him for his liberality and freedom from bigotry.[42]

Sir John, whose reputation must have preceded him, was one of the first to be invited to join the liberal Catholic party which was campaigning for Catholic emancipation from 1778. In 1782, he was elected a member of the revived Catholic Committee and he soon showed himself a Whig in politics, attached to Charles James Fox, as well as an Anglo-Gallican in ecclesiastical affairs. His pamphlets, *A letter addressed to the Catholic clergy of England on the appointment of bishops. By a layman* (1790) and *A second letter* (1791), were two of the few works published by a Throckmorton and distributed free of charge. They argued from primitive and Gallican precedents for the election of bishops by the laity, opposed delegated episcopal commissions and supported reduced papal interference. Both demonstrated a breadth of reading and a clear line of argument. 'I have no other object in view in this Address to you, than the desire of seeing our religion practised in its primitive purity'. At the second meeting of the Catholic Committee in April 1785 Sir John had thundered, 'We don't want Bishops [present]'. He believed that his support for refractory clergy – like the monks Gregory Gregson, who insisted on a vernacular liturgy; Joseph Wilks, a member of the Catholic committee; and the secular priest Joseph Berington, a scourge of the bishops – furthered his campaign, as did his appointment to the board of Oscott College in 1794. In 1792, after the passing of the Catholic Relief Act of 1791 for which he had laboured, Sir John and other committee members formed the Cisalpine Club and, until his death in 1819, he remained a champion of liberty, either as a member of the Society of the Friends of the People or as a supporter of Irish Catholics' struggle for emancipation. He did not live to see the passing of Catholic Emancipation in 1829, but two surviving relics, the Throckmorton coat and his portrait by Thomas Phillips (1760–1851), best embody his energy and define him as a man of the enlightenment looking through the gates into the Romantic industrialising nineteenth century. At Buckland in 1811 Sir John laid a bet for 1,000 guineas that a team of his workers could make a coat by sunset from the wool shorn at sunrise from two of his sheep. The wager was won and the coat, 'illustrative of manufacturing celerity', according to the contemporary poster, is displayed today at Coughton Court. Thomas Phillips must have painted Sir John's iconic portrait at the peak of the latter's career, around 1800 (Figure 7.7).

---

[42] WRO, CR 1998/SS/1-22; *Letters and prose writings of Cowper*, vol. 2, p. 561, vol. 4, pp. xxxii, 11, 20–22, 60–62, 76–7, 125–6, 128–9, 190, 370, 375, 379, 382–3, 386–7, 398–400, 422–4.

Figure 7.7　Sir John Courtenay Throckmorton (1753–1819), fifth baronet, by Thomas Phillips, Coughton Court.

It now hangs in Sir John's saloon at Coughton and bears all the hallmarks of this great portraitist of the Romantic age who, through his bold use of *chiaroscuro*, sought to capture an individual's intellectual powers and creative imagination. Sir John, with those very characteristic bushy Throckmorton eyebrows and powerful visage, sits exhausted after a day's hunting, holding his hat and his crop, with his mind apparently on other, more important, things as light filters through the dark mysterious forest behind him.[43]

---

[43] [John Courtenay Throckmorton], *A letter addressed to the Catholic clergy of England on the appointment of bishops. By a layman* (London, 1790), p. 21. Burton, *Life and times of Challoner*, vol. 2, pp. 190, 195; Scott, *Gothic Rage*, pp. 141–2; Geoffrey Scott, 'Dom Joseph Cuthbert Wilks (1748–1829) and English Benedictine Involvement in the Cisalpine Stirs', *Recusant History*, 23 (1997): 318–40.

CHAPTER 8

An English Catholic Traveller: Sir John Courtenay Throckmorton and the Continent, 1792–1793

Michael Mullett

One of the most noteworthy of his family and its only published author of any significance, Sir John Courtenay Throckmorton, the fifth baronet, was born in 1753, son of Sir George Throckmorton and his wife Anna Maria. John Courtenay Throckmorton went to school in the 1760s with the English Benedictines at St Gregory's in Douai, beginning a familiarity with the continent which he further developed in a grand tour centred on Rome in the 1770s, where, described as 'of a most agreeable character', he acquired the training in artistic taste which was to serve him so well in his second continental tour – the subject in large part of this chapter – in 1792–93. Early in 1778 Throckmorton, back in England, took up residence at one of his family's estates, Weston Underwood in Buckinghamshire, and in 1782 married Maria Catherine (1762–1821), the daughter of Thomas Giffard (d. 1775) of Chillington and of the old Staffordshire recusant family of Giffard. Maria Catherine's mother was a daughter of the eighth Baron Petre, of the great Essex recusant dynasty, whose father featured in Pope's *Rape of the Lock*, so that the marriage confirmed the Throckmortons' position at the very centre of the intertwined and intermarried English Catholic elite. John succeeded to the baronetcy and estate on the death of his grandfather Sir Robert, the fourth baronet (b. 1702), in 1791 and set up home at Buckland House in Berkshire, upon which the younger brother, George, moved into Weston Underwood.[1]

The period following Throckmorton's return to England saw a sudden raising of the public profile of English Catholicism after some decades in which it was a largely invisible factor in national life. First of all, the Catholic Relief Act of 1778 made modest advances in establishing the civil

---

[1] Geoffrey Scott, 'Throckmorton, Sir John Courtenay, *ODNB*; Joseph Gillow, *A Literary and Biographical History, Or Bibliographical Dictionary of the English Catholics. From the Breach with Rome, in 1534, to the Present Time* (5 vols, London, 1885–1902), vol. 4, p. 542; *The Letters and Prose Writings of William Cowper Volume IV Letters 1792–1799*, ed. James King and Charles Ryskamp (Oxford, 1984), p. xxxii.

rights of English Catholics, perhaps most significantly allowing them to inherit property in a fully legal way. However, within that limited scope, the Relief Act was in fact to act as an overture to a series of gradualistic parliamentary enactments which, culminating in the Emancipation Act of 1829, would abolish the penal system built up, also by parliamentary legislation, ever since the reign of Elizabeth, and would allow the British Catholics to take a more or less full part in national life. The question that then arose concerned what kind of community – how governed and with what degree of balance of lay and clerical control, how linked to Rome, in what ways tied to the British state and British institutions, of what doctrinal and devotional temper – would come to occupy those broad and sunny uplands of the future.

For whatever reasons of background – a wealthy squire of a class used to having much of its own way in the running of the post-Reformation English Catholic Church – and of education, by the Benedictines, the heirs of the more Anglocentric traditions of the English Church rooted in the pre-Counter-Reformation middle ages, Throckmorton gravitated to the lay-led, patriotic, somewhat anti-clerical and even anti-Roman wing of English Catholicism known as Cisalpine, and was in 1782 voted onto its mouthpiece body, the Catholic Committee, which had been resuscitated in order to press for further Catholic freedoms beyond the quite narrow limits set in 1778.

Cisalpinism had as much to do with style and taste as it did with hard-and-fast ideology. As we shall see, from the viewpoint of the *bien-croyant* orthodox Sir John may have been wayward, but he was in fact far from irreligious: he built, for example, new chapels at Buckland in Berkshire as well as at Coughton, in the latter case to mark the Catholic Relief Act, 1791, which legalised such edifices. And whereas like-minded aristocrats such as Sir Thomas Gascoigne of Partington, in 1780, or Sir John Swinburne of Swinburne Castle, in 1786, or even his brother-in-law Thomas Giffard of Chillington, 'apostasised', Sir John kept the faith, even though it was of an idiosyncratic and undemonstrative stripe. He insisted on remaining a liberal Catholic inside the tent than an Anglican outside it. One indicator of his Catholic liberality was a kind of sociable ecumenism, for, while the Throckmortons were in every way insiders within the recusant upper class, they did not share its oft-alleged exclusivity, and their friendship with their tenant at Weston Underwood from 1786 to 1795, the emphatically Protestant poet William Cowper (1731–1800), testified to their breadth of spirit. Maria Catherine made copies of Cowper's translations of Homer and was the inspiration for three of his poems. Cowper, her regular correspondent, took up Maria Catherine's pet name of 'Frog' ('my dear Mrs Frog'), wrote verse 'On the Death of Mrs Throckmorton's Bullfinch' and acclaimed the couple as 'Papists, but much more aimable than many

Protestants': for sheer good sense, he did not know the 'equal' of Sir John, and when the couple moved from Weston to Buckland he felt 'the loss of them ... since kinder or more friendly treatment I never can receive at any hands than I have always found at theirs'. That eirenic friendship should also be seen as part of the mindset that the Throckmortons took with them to Catholic Europe in 1792, one certainly lacking in fanaticism or credulity, though not necessarily in conviction, and perhaps best summed up in David Mathew's characteristically evocative phrase about 'the polite unenthusiastic Catholicism of the Thames Valley'.[2]

At the same time, the broad Cisalpine outlook also aimed for what we might call a party-political and ecclesiological expression, the Cisalpine grouping of Catholic patriots of which Sir John had unmistakably become a leading member sought by all means at their disposal to emphasise the Englishness of their Catholicity: there was a programme to be implemented. For example, in seeking to adopt for the English Catholic community the highly contentious label 'Protesting Catholic Dissenters', the Cisalpines were clearly aiming to model themselves on the uniquely English and Welsh Protestant Nonconformist groupings known as 'their Majestyes Protestant Subjects dissenting from the Church of England'. These were the beneficiaries of the Toleration Act of 1689 – the measure whose concessions were broadly the kind sought in programmes for Catholic 'relief' and emancipation between the later eighteenth and early nineteenth centuries. And if that measure of the 1680s operated as a model of legislation in favour of a religious minority, agitation for Catholic rights in the late eighteenth century in exchange for professions of loyalty to a British constitution seemed validated by another late seventeenth-century text which the Cisalpines took to their hearts as a formula for creating a Catholic faith and life at ease in its English social and political environment. This was the Benedictine James Maurus Corker's work, originally of 1680 and bearing the title *Roman Catholick Principles, in reference to God and the King*, a classic summary of what has been termed 'Anglo-Gallicanism', proclaiming a faith Catholic in its doctrines but essentially Anglocentric in its political allegiances and opinions. The work was reissued in 1785 (with the 'King' in the original title updated to the more Whiggish-sounding 'The Country') as an attachment to a modernist work, *Reflections Addressed to the Rev. John Hawkins*, by the priest and leading Cisalpine writer Joseph Berington (1743–1827), who, in 1793, took up the post of chaplain to

---

[2] Mark Bence-Jones, *The Catholic Families* (London, 1992), pp. 129, 66–7; Scott, 'Throckmorton, Sir John Courtenay'; Geoffrey Scott, *Gothic Rage Undone: English Monks in the Age of the Enlightenment* (Bath, 1992), pp. 91, 100; *Letters and Prose Writings of Cowper*, pp. xxxii, 22; Tony Hadland, *Thames Valley Papists from Reformation to Emancipation* (n.p., 1992), p. 146.

the Throckmortons at Buckland in Berkshire, remaining in that ministry for 34 years. For the remainder of the decade of the 1780s and beyond, Throckmorton was committed to the political colours of his friend, the liberal Whig Charles James Fox (1749–1806), and was also inextricably and indeed volubly associated with the Cisalpine wing of the English Catholic community.[3]

From that ideological vantage point, having in 1786 tried to get the clerical leaders of the English Catholic Church to accept the message of *Roman Catholic Principles*, Throckmorton called for a virtual institutional severance of Catholic England from papal Rome in a trilogy of works of the early 1790s, written under the pen-name of 'a layman'. In particular, his scheme for laicising, if not democratising, the process of appointing regular 'bishops-in-ordinary' could be seen as a proposed declaration of ecclesiastical independence from Rome, inasmuch as the system then prevailing, and dating back to the 1680s, of episcopal vicars apostolic appointed directly by the Holy See – in Throckmorton's words 'the arbitrary uncanonical government of apostolic vicars' instead of 'a regular church-government and pastors properly appointed' – also provided a direct route for constant papal intervention in English Catholic affairs. Throckmorton published a *Second Letter* on episcopal appointments in 1791 and, when his first work was reissued the same year, it was denounced in a joint pastoral letter by the four vicars apostolic having jurisdiction over Catholics in the four 'districts' into which England and Wales were divided. The vicars' letter was in fact composed by the most uncompromising upholder of Roman authority amidst the ranks of the English Catholic clergy, John Milner (1752–1826), at that point priest in charge in Winchester and soon (1803) to be himself a vicar apostolic, for the Midland District. Subsequently, Milner's *Ecclesiastical Democracy Detected* (1793) unleashed its *ad hominem* fury against the 'absurdity' and

---

[3] Eamon Duffy, 'Ecclesiastical Democracy Detected: II (1787–1796), *Recusant History*, 10/6 (1970), 309; as Duffy shows (ibid., 309–10), the Cisalpines' protestation of maintaining a Catholicism doctrinally universal but institutionally Anglocentric was also subject to some erosion, Throckmorton certainly taking up Corker's initiative of seeking doctrinal common ground with English Protestantism; *English Catholic Books 1701–1800*, ed. F. Blom, J. Blom, F. Korsten and G. Scott (Aldershot, 1996), p. 85. For the conflict between the Cisalpines and their Romanist or 'Ultramontane' opponents, see also Bernard Ward, *The Dawn Of The Catholic Revival in England, 1781–1803* (2 vols, London, 1909); W.J. Amherst, SJ, *The History of Catholic Emancipation and the Progress of the Catholic Church in the British Isles* (2 vols, London, 1886); Michael Mullett, *English Catholicism 1680–1830* (6 vols, London, 2006), vol.1, pp. xxii–xxvii; vol. 3, pp. 257–60, 229–55. *Roman Catholic Principles* was a text beloved by the Cisalpines and was reproduced, with a full authorial history recalling its 35 editions, by one of their leading ideologues, the lawyer Charles Butler (1750–1832) in his *Historical Memoirs of the English, Irish, and Scottish Catholics, Since the Reformation* (4 vols, London, 1819–21).

the 'pernicious tendency of the errors in question' in the baronet's writings, his proposals on the election of bishops threatening, Milner wrote, even 'to degrade our religion from a divine to a merely human system of spiritual government, to deprive the pastors of their only authority in teaching and governing, and the faithful of their only comfort in hearing and obeying'. A polemicist of considerable ruthlessness as well as vituperation, Milner did not fail to add warnings on how Throckmorton's allegedly democratic proposals would send the English Catholic Church down the same road to destruction as that then being opened out to its once great sister, that of France, 'plunged into schism'.[4]

'Schism' apart, there was indeed no doubt that the Cisalpine movement of which Throckmorton was such an outspoken representative sought to broaden its own base of consensus with England's predominant Protestant culture, traditions and institutions, while at the same time narrowing its platform of accord with mainstream continental, Roman and global Catholicism. Hence, for example: the attack by one party spokesman on 'Mass and Service in an unknown tongue' (Throckmorton thought 'our praying in Latin' 'absurd'); the desire of the group to elevate the claims and rights of the British government over those of the Holy See; the party's extreme distaste for such terms as 'Roman Catholics or Papists'; their leanings toward the rationalism of the Enlightenment and their diffidence over the more ostentatious devotional features of European Catholicism that were likely to set English Protestant teeth on edge. It was, surely, the Cisalpines' attempt to square colliding allegiances – their Catholic opponents were likely to accuse them of seeking to 'form in England a Christian church in itself' – that justifies Eamon Duffy in terming their ideological vessel a 'crazy barque'.[5]

Even so, any portrayal of the Cisalpines as merely Catholic little Englanders betrays the complexity of their positioning. In many respects, in fact, far from being narrowly Anglocentric, their principles aligned them with the modernising momentum within the eighteenth-century Catholicism of the European Enlightenment. Thus, for example, Berington's reissue of

---

[4] John Courtenay Throckmorton, *A Letter Addressed to the Catholic Clergy of England, on the Appointment of Bishops. By a Layman* (London, 1790); *A Second Letter Addressed to the Catholic Clergy of England on the Appointment of Bishops. In which the Objections to the First Letter are Answered* (London, 1791); *A Letter Addressed to the Catholic Clergy of England, on the Appointment of Bishops ... To which are added Further Considerations on the Same Subject, and on the conduct of the English Catholics from the Reign of Elizabeth to the Present Time* (London, 1792); Blom et al., *English Catholic Books*, pp. 293–4; Mullett (ed.), *English Catholicism 1680–1830*, vol. 3, p. 230; vol. 5, pp. 403, 27; Duffy, 'Ecclesiastical Democracy Detected', 318.

[5] Scott, *Gothic Rage Undone*, p. 159; Duffy, 'Ecclesiastical Democracy Detected', 312.

Corker's tract came as a supplement to a wide-ranging survey of religious conditions in the Europe of the 1780s, its highest praise being reserved for the principal royal legislator of the progressive principles of the *Aufklärung*, the Emperor Joseph II of Austria (1741–90), the suppressor of monasteries, road-maker of religious toleration in his domains and architect of a post-medieval, or even post-Tridentine, Catholicism. 'What his Imperial Majesty has done in favour of his Protestant, and even Jewish subjects,' Berington wrote, 'is well known to all Europe; what was oppressive he has relaxed; and with the free practice of religion he gives to dissenters all the common rights of citizens. This fair example has been followed by other Catholic princes of the empire.'[6] Catholic Austria and Catholic Germany had already, according to this close associate of Throckmorton, realised the dream of toleration cherished by the 'Protesting Catholic Dissenters'.

So Catholic continental Europe offered conflicting visions to British Cisalpines. What, for example, did the prospect of Italy mean to them? Did it signify credulity and superstition? Berington derided the insistence of traditionalists that miracles reported in Ancona in the Papal States upheld the claims for the Church's continuing supernatural powers – arguments put forward by orthodox writers such as the vicar apostolic William Walton (1715–80) in *The Miraculous Powers of the Church of Christ Asserted* (London, 1756). Did the image of Italy signify perhaps the uncritical faith invested in the 'holy house' of Loreto, reputedly flown into the March of Ancona from Galilee by angels in the thirteenth century and which Throckmorton was to visit in 1793, commenting only on its artistic embellishments? Or did 'Italy' mean rather the welling up in the 1770s and 1780s of a liberal Catholicism under the rule in Tuscany of Joseph II's younger brother Grand Duke Leopold (1747–92), whose ecclesiastical reforms included the prohibition of penitential processions, a drastic reduction in the number of devotional confraternities and a campaign against superstition, as well as the simplification of ritual and the suppression of the Inquisition, all culminating in the near-revolutionary decrees of the Tuscan Synod of Pistoia (1786) which made the Grand Duchy the 'centre of a European movement' of Catholic modernisation? Again, did the image of Italy– and crucially of the Papal States – conjure up mental pictures of a black clericalist regime as politically and economically incompetent and regressive as it was repressive and illiberal? Or, rather, was Italy –including papal Italy – in fact a beacon of progress to embarrass even that land where Britons never, never, never would be slaves? Berington, in his European *tour d'horizon*, supplied his own answer to that kind of question: 'Even the court of inquisition in the papal states, has nothing

---

[6] Joseph Berington, 'Reflections Addressed to the Rev. John Hawkins ...', in Mullett (ed.), *English Catholicism*, vol. 3, p. 236.

terrible in it; and our Protestants know how kindly they are every where received. If you talk to me of religious freedom; I would rather be a Jew in Rome than a Roman catholic in the capital of an empire, where liberty is vainly said to have fixed her throne.' (As we shall see, Throckmorton was to witness to the fact that to 'be a Jew in Rome', at least when the city's bigoted mob was rampaging, was rather less enviable than Berington might have supposed.)[7]

Perhaps it was with some of those ambivalences in mind that Sir John, with Maria Catherine and a 'Mr. Dormer' (presumably the baronet's Coughton neighbour, Charles Dormer, of the renowned Catholic family of Grove Park near Warwick) set off for the continent in the summer of 1792, the little party to be joined in Geneva by Throckmorton's ideological sympathiser, the tempestuous Benedictine Joseph Cuthbert Wilkes (or Wilks, 1748–1829), the son of John, the Throckmortons' Coughton steward, who had been voted onto the Catholic Committee in 1787. A holiday out of England was no doubt in order, for even before the appearance of Milner's savage *Ecclesiastical Democracy Detected* Throckmorton had been trading blows, giving as much as he got, in an often intemperate and doubtless wearying combat. Then, too, in 1791 had come a major breakthrough for the English Catholic community that was also a serious blow for its Cisalpine elements. The Second Relief Act permitted open Catholic worship subject to legal restrictions, but omitted the cherished descriptive label for English Catholics that the committee had tried to intrude into the Act: 'Protesting Catholics Dissenters'. So Throckmorton's second continental odyssey came amidst a period of concentrated interest, controversy, excitement and also, no doubt, of some disappointment in his life and career. Perhaps, indeed, by 1792 Sir John needed some time for platonic reflection, but whether or not he did, he kept on his tour a manuscript journal (now in the Warwickshire Record Office), a rare text, hit upon almost by chance, that both opens up the extensive cultural hinterland of a well-educated, engaging, likeable man who was so much more than the stormy petrel of Cisalpine pamphleteering, while at the same time it reveals the tastes, presuppositions, prejudices, habits, experience and opinions – on agriculture, landscape, religion, politics, scenery, society, economics and the fine arts – of a cultivated Catholic Hanoverian landed gentleman. The Throckmorton Journal records, in short, the broadening effect of travel, at a time of extraordinary turbulence in Europe, on the development of an already well-stocked mind, as the evolving attitudes and outlook, especially on the natural world, political and religious life

---

[7] Mullett (ed.), *English Catholicism*, vol. 3, pp. 231, 127–49; Stuart Woolf, *A History of Italy 1700–1860: The Social Constraints of Political Change* (London and New York, 1991), pp. 134–5; Berington, 'Reflections Addressed to the Rev. John Hawkins', pp. 242–3.

and the arts, of this influential aristocrat were shaped by a quite lengthy and extensive European excursion. We shall uncover, then, what this observer observed, what he understood as well perhaps as misunderstood, of a large tract of Western Europe, how his views of it typified those of at least some of his contemporaries and how his own thought processes may have been shaped by his observations.[8]

Sir John Courtenay Throckmorton's second Grand Tour may also itself have reflected some traceable long-term change in the pattern of that particular form of travel and tourism, and in particular its evolution into a vacation – as John Brewer writes, 'an edifying family holiday'. Traditionally, the grand tour had combined a gap period for young *milords* as pupils in an itinerant finishing school, acquiring the gloss of European high culture – French language and literature, Italian art, sculpture, architecture and general connoisseurship – along with youthful release from Anglo-Saxon moral and sexual restraint, or at the very least a period of adolescent slumming. Throckmorton had earlier enjoyed or endured this in Rome, when, with his brother George, tutored by their uncle James Paston and the Benedictine Augustine Walker, they were reported as residing 'with the Monk Walker in a wretched situation in Trastevere. They frequent low English company, because there is the favourite card table of their tutor [Walker], unless when he chooses to exhibit with Cups & Balls, or declaim against the Jesuits in the vile hole of an English Coffee House.' Now, though, treading a route well traversed by any number of other upper-class English travellers, Sir John, a near 40-year-old prosperous south Midland country gentleman and a figure of some literary and political fame, or notoriety, had a wife to escort, so that the days of 'vile holes' and 'wretched situations' had given way to a discerning review of inns and hotels. The 'Lion d'Or' in Amiens was 'a bad Inn'; in Fontainebleau, where they slept at the palace, they were 'troubled by bugs'; and they 'slept at Auxerre (*très mediocre*) ... We lodged at the Chapeau Rouge [near Dijon] (- good)'.[9]

Throckmorton, however, was to offer rather more than a stand-up *Guide Michelin* to the *auberges* of provincial France. Amongst his varied interests was a commitment to agricultural improvement typical of the landowning generation that came into their estates in the reign of

---

[8] Bence-Jones, *The Catholic Families*, pp. 59, 121, 129; Scott, 'Throckmorton, Sir John Courtenay', Geoffrey Scott, 'Dom Joseph Cuthbert Wilks (1748–1829) and English Benedictine Involvement in the Cisalpine Stirs', *Recusant History*, 23/3 (1997): 318–40.

[9] John Brewer, *The Pleasures of the Imagination English Culture in the Eighteenth Century* (London, 1997), pp. 206–7: for the long tradition of the English trip to France, see Constantia Maxwell, *The English Traveller in France 1698–1815* (London, 1932); Scott, 'Throckmorton, Sir John'; WRO, CR 1998/Drawer 3 [3]: Sir John Throckmorton, 5th Baronet, Journal, containing brief entries ... [hereafter *Throckmorton Journal*], p. 1: 24 July 1792, p. 3: 8, 10, 11 August 1792.

'Farmer George' and evident, for example, in Sir John's celebrated and successful wager in 1811 of 1,000 guineas that his farm workers possessed the 'manufacturing celerity' to produce a coat on one day from wool off the backs of his Buckland, Berkshire, estate's sheep. Inevitably, then, Sir John would offer observations on the agricultural situation of what was traditionally renowned as 'the best garden of the world … our fertile France', favoured by nature as one vast and rich farm. So, virtually from his landfall in France, Throckmorton was either eulogising or rapturising *la belle France*:

> We left Calais & went to St Omer, through a very fine rich corn country, very populous. The barley already in many places out. … The road lies through a very fine corn country; the part which lies near St Omer & Air is particularly well cultivated, the crop as fine as possible: They grow in this country a great deal of Rape seed, with which they make oil; this crop is gathered about the beginning of July, after which the ground is prepared for wheat. They also grow for the same purpose a species of poppy with a light purple flower. Tobacco also is planted in great quantity. The villages are almost entirely hid by trees, above which the steeples rising have a good effect. … Soon after we had passed Clermont, the wheat harvest was begun … Throughout all Franche Comtè [*sic*] they cultivate a great deal of Turkey wheat.[10]

Sir John's Georgian georgic might suggest to us a sheaf of *idées reçues* about *la France profonde*, or even clichés concerning rural France that are often perpetuated, for example in French political rhetoric, down to the present day. Courtenay in short was subscribing to visions of Gallic bounty and of a simple cornucopia of plentiful subsistence supplied by generous indigenous harvests that were both early and successional – timeless, native grain crops, barley and corn, springing out of the earth's everlasting largesse, an essentially pre-modern, indeed ancient, autarchic arable, all observed through an English gentleman farmer's eye. To take only one parallel example, a near contemporaneous English visitor to France, in 1789, the Norfolk medical doctor and improving farmer Edward Rigby, was simply astonished by what appeared to be the country's enviable, unchanging, natural, spontaneous and everlasting fertility:

> We went through an extent of 70 miles, and I will venture to say there was not a single acre but what was in a state of the highest cultivation. The crops are great beyond any conception I could have had of them; thousands and ten thousands of acres of wheat superior to any that can be produced in England.

---

[10] Scott, 'Courtenay, Sir John', p. 693; *Throckmorton Journal*, pp. 1–2: 23–25 July 1792; p. 7: 14 (?) August 1792.

Fair France was indeed a lucky country: as Wordsworth wrote in 'October 1807',

> ... a chosen soil, where sun and breeze
> Shed gentle favours; rural works are there,
> And ordinary business without care.

Two further observations, though, might be made about what we might term the rhapsodic Anglo-Saxon appreciation, which Courtenay fully shared, of a seemingly self-sufficient French agriculture and its fabled riches. The first of these concerns what were in fact the economically advanced complexities and adaptations underlying what visitors such as Rigby and Courtenay saw as France's almost naturally abundant agriculture. French farming in fact involved sophisticated and extensive integration in a nationally organised, diligently assembled supply chain, fully caught up with rapidly changing industry and commerce. The rape seed harvest, for instance, mentioned *en passant* by our traveller, led indeed to oil refining, but it did so as part of a cluster of industrial processes that made the northern city of Lille an industrial heartland, involving there all kinds of tense political struggles over protectionism and industrial relations. Tobacco was, of course, the most obvious example of an industrial crop, once imported into France, along with other colonial exotica, through the great harbour of Bordeaux, but in Throckmorton's time colonising the fields of Normandy and supplying not a region's food needs, but, as Braudel's English translator put it, a nation's 'craving'. The poppies Sir John saw growing, however, were not intended for any narcotic or addictive product – those strains are better grown in warmer climes – but rather supplied the market with a range of culinary uses; while the 'Turkey wheat' Sir John witnessed flourishing in the Franche-Comté was not some time-honoured indigenous grain but a quite recent import, maize, otherwise 'Guinea corn' or 'Indian corn' – a transatlantic immigrant earlier let into the country via the south-west of France, literally putting down roots increasingly from around the 1640s and coming to play a complex role in a sophisticated and capitalising economy. In the Toulousain, for instance, it acted as a cheap, if not exactly always cheerful, grain which freed up wheat for sale in the commercial markets; but also, Braudel speculated, it helped bring to a close the famines of the 'age of the baroque', which had made rural France a constant zone of peasant insurgency in the years before 1680. Throckmorton was in fact seeing a

French agricultural sector itself subject to its own successive 'agricultural revolutions'.[11]

Our second caveat around the species of English euphoria that Throckmorton displayed over France as a garden has to do with the vastness and diversity of the kingdom itself, an accumulation of dramatically variegated *pays*, painstakingly put together over centuries by successive kings, statesmen and warriors. A closer, more professional, observer than Sir John, the Secretary to the Board of Agriculture, Arthur Young (1741–1820), whose visits in the late 1780s preceded those of the Throckmortons by only a few years, was fully aware of the complicated heterogeneity of the French landscape. In the 'miserable province' of Brittany in particular, 'the country has a savage aspect; husbandry not much further advanced, at least in skill, than among the Hurons ... the people almost as wild as their country ... such filth and poverty ... this hideous heap of poverty'. In the starkest contrast though, Young, like Throckmorton and Rigby, also idealised the agricultural richness of France's great northern prairies: 'This noble territory includes the deep, level, and fertile plain of Flanders, and part of Artois, than which a richer soil can hardly be desired to repay the industry of mankind.' And it was exactly that France – the *pays de grande culture*, that broad arc of fertility between Calais and Lille, the fields of Normandy and French Flanders, today including the long flanks of the Eurostar track – in which generations of English visitors, including Rigby and Throckmorton, caught their initial impressions of their host country as an allotment of abundance.[12]

If maize culture helped still insurgency in Bourbon France, it was only temporary. Throckmorton, an intensely political Foxite Whig, was on hand to watch the unfolding of revolution in the early 1790s. However, he was also a middle-aged and wealthy aristocrat, and his first-hand perceptions of the inexorable demolition of France's *Ancien régime* perhaps need to be understood partly in that light, as well as in the context of his positioning within the British party system. As a Whig, Throckmorton was bound to welcome the dawning of English-style constitutional rights in a country whose royal government even the doyen of conservative Whiggery, Edmund Burke, had to admit was characterised by the 'inconstancy and fluctuation natural to courts'. The problem was that by the time of the first centenary of the Glorious Revolution of 1688–89 the Whigs had taken

---

[11] Maxwell, *English Traveller in France*, p. 153; Fernand Braudel, *The Identity of France Volume II People and Production*, trans. Siân Reynolds (London, 1991), pp. 452–5, 576, 583, 392; Emmanuel Le Roy Ladurie, *The French Peasantry 1450–1660*, trans. Alan Sheridan (Aldershot, 1987), p. 315.

[12] Braudel, *Identity of France*, p. 265; *Travels in France during the Years 1787, 1788 & 1789 by Arthur Young*, ed. Constantia Maxwell (Cambridge, 1950), pp. 107, 270.

over possession of its ideological legacy. The radical Whig Charles, third Earl Stanhope (1753–1816), with whom Throckmorton was probably associated politically in 1788, was chair of the 'Revolution Society' (of which Burke disapproved) formed in 1788; but crucial to a traditional English understanding of that exemplary revolution was its 'bloodlessness', as well as its conservation of the established Church, with limited toleration, a parliamentary monarchy and care for property, law and order. Insofar as those normative Whig values, which were according to Burke the true legacy of the Glorious Revolution, were observed in France, the changes the country was putting in place were to be welcomed, and insofar as they were not, they were to be abhorred. And it is clear from the record of his French itinerary that such consideration shaped Throckmorton's view of rapidly and dramatically succeeding events. Though commitment to Fox's principles is still recorded, perhaps a little jocularly, in an addendum from Maria Catherine to a letter from Italy in February 1793 – 'Charles Fox for ever' – there is strong evidence that Throckmorton's own 'reflections on the Revolution in France' may have been influenced by a Burkean stance, fortified by first-hand experience. Certainly, the library at Coughton Court contains political writings strongly indicative of that ideologically positioning, including *A Letter from Mr. Burke, To A Member of the National Assembly; In Answer To Some Objections To His Book On French Affairs* (Paris and London, 1791) – Burke's own defence of his *Reflections on the Revolution in France* – along with the essayist Richard Hey's warning, in *Happiness And Rights A Dissertation Upon Several Subjects Relative To The Rights Of Man And His Happiness* (York, 1792), of 'a dreadful picture of actual Consequences in France'. Over the course of that momentous summer the Throckmortons were to be eye-witnesses to some of the 'actual Consequences' in Paris and in France at large of revolutionary change, recording the mounting violence as reporters. At the end of July, for example,

> 50 armed men from Marseilles entered Paris; in the afternoon a commander of a battalion of the National Guard was killed in a quarrel with a party of them. [3rd August] Petion the Mayor presented a petition in the name of his section of Paris, to the N. Assembly, requesting that the King may be dethroned.

In the following month, the Throckmortons themselves only narrowly escaped some of the Revolution's perils, for Cowper was to report a 'very kind letter' from 'Mrs Throckmorton' in which 'Sir John and Lady Frog she tells me were so fortunate as to leave Paris just two days before the terrible 10th of August': the date when the Tuileries was ransacked, the Swiss Guard slaughtered and the king and queen imprisoned. Such experiences must have strengthened Throckmorton's inclination away from Fox's adulation for French events, summed up in the latter's description of the Declaration of the Rights of Man and the Citizen as 'the most stupendous edifice of liberty' in the history of the world, and increasingly in the direction of Burke's sceptical and hostile response. In other words, while Throckmorton insisted on retaining the Foxite outlook of a 'democrat', his reception of events on the French ground may have drawn him ever closer to Burke's conservatism. To some extent, Sir John witnessed the flow of opinion on the provincial level, in the Auvergne country around Clermont-Ferrand (through which Louis XVI attempted to flee France) for instance, where 'the people, as far as I could judge in passing through the country, appear very much attached to the new constitution & to the king, in opposition to the Jacobins. The only thing with which they appeared dissatisfied, was the change in their curates.'[13]

Our traveller had plenty more to say about the tumultuous events in France in that extraordinary summer of his arrival on the continent – the pressure, for example, from Jacobin Paris to dethrone the king and create 'what they call a perfect equality'; the disorder and unrestrained partisanship in the debate in the National Assembly; the intrusive mob 'applauding every violent measure proposed'. However perhaps the clearest indicator of Throckmorton's view of the Revolution in France comes not so much in his travelogue, as in his letters home. There the distinctions we have seen in his travel journal are drawn with refreshing simplicity. First, as Burke admitted, Louis XVI had made some progress in the direction of reform, including, in 1786, projects for the overhaul of the country's woefully inequitable fiscal system, modernisation of the administration of the provinces and free trade measures. However, the Bourbon princes brought back to Paris in June 1791 after a failed attempt by the royal family to escape to the north-east were, in Throckmorton's eyes, for the most part congenitally stupid, blundering on in oblivion, vanity and ostentation, remembering nothing and forgetting nothing:

> The Princes do not stir without 50 Aid de camps, & their amusement has been to establish a household in the name of the king, in which all the reforms formerly made by this king are broken through & a greater retinue is created than he had at Versailles before the Revolution. They treat the gentlemen who have followed them with as much hauteur as if they were still at Versailles.

---

[13] Edmund Burke, *Reflections on the French Revolution and other Essays*, ed. Ernest Rhys (London and New York, 1935., p. 128; *Throckmorton Journal*, p. 2: 30 July, 3 August 1792; *Letters and Prose Writings of William Cowper*, pp. 191–2; *Throckmorton Journal*, p. 2: 25 July 1792; Maxwell (ed.), *English Travellers in France*, p. 153; WRO, CR 1998/TCD/fol. 2/16a: John and Maria Catherine Courtenay Throckmorton, Naples, to William Throckmorton, 8 February 1793; Fox, in Simon Schama, *A History of Britain 3 1777–2000 The Fate of Empire* (London, 2004), p. 48.

Nevertheless, nothing, not even this myopic arrogance, could, as far as Sir John was concerned, excuse Jacobin excesses: 'I am convinced the Jacobins have gone too far & are not to be defended ... I am as great a democrat as ever but I am convinced those <u>confounded</u> Jacobins have ruined the good cause.' Meanwhile, though, the old Whig suspicion of kings lay not far beneath the surface: 'the King of Poland has done the same – Nevertheless cela ira, cela ira.'[14]

Inevitably, given the intimacy of the ties that bound throne and altar in the France of the *Ancien régime*, the political and social revolution that followed 1789 was paralleled by a far-reaching *bouleversement* in the sphere of religion. Throckmorton's interest as a Catholic Cisalpine of the Enlightenment – one capable of distinguishing between true 'religion' and mere credulity – was, predictably, strongly engaged in the changes under way. To his disappointment, though, any attempt on the part the Revolutionaries to apply the rationalising principles of the *éclaircissements* to the sphere of religion was encountering apparently insurmountable barriers of popular 'superstition', even in the power-house of change, Paris: 'Although the people shew very little sense of religion, the old superstitions are not laid aside, the shrine of St. Genevieve is more frequented than for some years past, and I am informed that the convulsionaries have again appeared in considerable numbers.'[15]

The Throckmorton party was by this time about to leave France, amidst an atmosphere almost suggestive of *The Scarlet Pimpernel* or *A Tale of Two Cities*:

> We ... stopped at Ponarlier [Pontarlier, where the old route into Switzerland crossed the river Doubs], where our trunks &c were very strictly examined ...
>
> During the last three days we met a great quantity of men going to join the army, they frequently on this day stopped us to examine our passports; as we were English they were civil, but they shew a great apprehension at any

---

[14] *Throckmorton Journal*, p. 6: August 1792; WRO, CR 1998/TCD/fol. 21: Sir John Courtenay Throckmorton to William Throckmorton, 3 September 1792; at the time of the Revolution the Bourbon royal family included the seven 'princes of the blood' (*les princes du sang*) still, in 1792, either in exile or in Paris. Poland's last king, Stanislaw-August Poniatowski (1764–95), was unable to prevent the final partition of his country by Austria, Prussia and Russia in the latter year; the original anthem of the Revolution, dating from 1790, 'ça (or cela) ira' (approximately 'anything goes'), acquired vituperative anti-noble verses from 1793.

[15] *Throckmorton Journal*, p. 6: August 1792; Sainte Geneviève (c. 420–c. 500), patron of Paris, is said to have been a shepherdess and was reputed to have saved the city from the Huns in 451. Her deliverance of Paris from plague in 1129 was marked annually in the city's churches and her relics were conserved in the church of Saint-Etienne-du-Mont.

person quitting France & are particularly strict in preventing any money being exported.

Sir John added a footnote as if to emphasise his own direct involvement in this atmosphere of *grande peur*, 'apprehension' and general revolutionary *melée*: 'They stopped a pair of pistols which I had.'[16]

As Throckmorton entered Switzerland, his travelogue, always varied, took on another hue – that of observer of rugged nature. Indeed, even before leaving France, in the beautiful scenery of the Jura region shared by eastern France and western Switzerland, he seems to have been gearing himself up for an appreciation of wild landscape: near Besançon, for example, 'there is a very fine romantic view, & then a rapid descent almost the whole way to Ornans'. Then on arrival in Switzerland itself, Sir John's response to its scenery rose in the intensity of its appreciation, partly, perhaps, because he was conditioned by existing literary convention to see what he saw in exactly the way that he recorded it:

> … a considerable torrent … a beautiful vale, through which the river runs … Near Moutiers [Mouthiers, in the French *département* of the Doubs] is a pretty cascade which falls down the side of the hill & forms a brook which immediately joins the river [Loue]. After a few miles the valley is much contracted, & the river which before glided gently through the vale, encreased by several other streams, rushed rapidly along it's [*sic*] bed. … Nothing can be more beautiful than the scenery in this place …

The writing is, of course, carefully studied; and whereas in the France of *grande culture* Throckmorton had been observing 'very fine rich corn country', his 'Alpine' vocabulary instead has the requisite 'torrent', 'cascade', 'barren, perpendicular rock' and 'stupendous mountain', as Throckmorton responded to the standard requirements of reaction to the picturesque. And the landscape performed splendidly in response to his careful writer's brush: at Lake Lucerne

> the hills here rise to a great height, the shores are rocky & bold, in many places the borders consist of perpendicular rocks of a stupendous height, projecting into the lake, & of an extraordinary countenance [?] in some places the layers of them [?] appear like an ancient building, in others they are folded & twisted in a very extraordinary manner. Down the rocks in many places, fell cascades & torrents of water, which were considerably encreased by the late rains.

As it happened, Wordsworth was in Alpine Europe just a few months before the Throckmorton party, and we can see the differences between his

---

[16] *Throckmorton Journal*, p. 7: 15 August 1792.

reactions and Sir John's, for to the 'egotistical sublime' the Swiss scenery provided opportunities primarily for *self*-observation:

> Yet still in me, mingling with these delights
> Was something of a stern mood, an under-thirst
> Of vigour, never utterly asleep.

In other words, the differences between these two near contemporaneous tourists is that the poet was concerned to 'give his reader', through the recall of 'sublime features', an 'idea of those emotions which they have the irresistible power of communicating to the most impassive imaginations'. Throckmorton, in comparison, following something of what Wordsworth dismissed as 'the cold rules of painting', was a watercolourist – but not a self-portraitist – in prose, responding to, but also distancing himself from, the scenes which his fellow-Catholic, that Boileau of the picturesque, the Jesuit Thomas West (1720–79), insisted in his *Guide to the Lakes in Cumberland, Westmorland, and Lancashire* of 1779 should be tagged and recorded, *capturing* pieces of carefully observed landscape from formal 'stations'. As Sir John noted of one Swiss scene, 'The whole offers one of the finest objects which can be viewed.' It is also worth mentioning, though, that Throckmorton's anxiety to paint the sublime, when combined with his conscientious endeavour to record, like a latter-day Defoe, the productivity of environments, could easily lead him into bathos, as in describing 'A beautiful valley down which runs an impetuous torrent, which rolls violently on forming beautiful picturesque falls … I have often had occasion to observe the quantity of mills in Switzerland …' Evidently something of a gourmet, and taking a dislike to 'bad cooking in Swiss de la muscade [nutmeg] par tout', Throckmorton was also self-aware, and self-mocking, enough to put his ecstasies over landscape into their proper place in the queue of his priorities: 'I long for some roast mutton, all stewed and broiled, & fried. Frog says I am a great John Bull for when I am very hungry I say, Frog I had rather have a good dinner than see all the mountains in the world.'[17]

Increasingly important as the grand tour morphed into the tourist industry, Switzerland, like Venice, also had important pulling power for the English political, as well as visual, imagination. Probably the best-known literary tribute to the key feature of that country's constitution,

---

[17] Ibid., p. 7–8: August 1792 (includes 15 and 16 August); p. 21: 6 September 1792; Wordsworth, *The Prelude*, Book VI, ll. 488–90; Mary Moorman, *William Wordsworth A Biography The Early Years 1770–1803* (Oxford, 1969), pp. 144–5; *Throckmorton Journal*, p. 21: 6 September 1792; p.22: 7 September 1792; WRO, CR 1998/TCD/fol. 2/2b: Sir John Courtenay Throckmorton, Lucerne, to William Throckmorton, 20 September 1792.

freedom, is Wordsworth's *Thoughts of a Briton on the Subjugation of Switzerland* (1807), linking the Venetian and Swiss republics as outposts of liberty in Europe:

> Two Voices are there, one is of the sea,
> One of the mountains; ...
> They were thy chosen music, Liberty!

Other commentators too enthused greatly on Swiss freedom, and indeed Lord Stanhope's thirst for reform has been attributed his being educated in Geneva. However, amongst other English observers of Swiss politics, the landscape painter Joseph Farington (1747–1821) noted in addition the complex socio-political ballet performed in those major cantons that were 'perfect Aristocracies', where hereditary elites, monopolising public office, treated the peasantry, who were 'true to the old system', paternalistically, to the disadvantage of townspeople, 'encouragers of the reform proposed by France'. Throckmorton too was aware of those kinds of gradations, noting that the form of government of one of the cantons – German-speaking and Catholic Soluthurn (in French Soleure) – 'is entirely aristocratic; being confined to a limited number of families; the people, are almost entirely excluded from any share in the government'. However, the main point in his own analysis of Switzerland's institutions was an awareness that they originated in a common rejection of despotism, though one made within the actualities of history (rather than on the basis of abstract theory) – a victory commemorated in visits to a political shrine near Lucerne, where, in bygone time, a solemn covenant to defend freedom was sworn on the meadows of Rütli: 'On the right ... is a house, in which three persons from the Cantons of Uri, Scheitz [Schwyz] and Unterwalden, swore to overturn the despotic government of the Austrians & to free their country.'

Observing also the revered spot where the Robin Hood of Swiss emancipation, Wilhelm Tell, made a reputed wonderful escape from Austrian bondage, Sir John was shown the tower of Sempach, 'near which the famous battle was fought, in which Leopold was killed, & the liberty of the Swiss secured'.[18]

The legacy of this ancient struggle by free men to retain their liberty was a rough-and-ready equality – though in reality eighteenth-century Switzerland knew little of what we might recognise as modern democracy and human rights. Even so, Throckmorton certainly caught glimpses

---

[18] Brewer, *Pleasures of the Imagination*, p. 207; Burke, *Reflections on the French Revolution*, p. 331 n; *The Farington Diary by Joseph Farington, R.A.*, ed. James Greig (6 vols, London, 1922–28), vol. 1, p. 271; *Throckmorton Journal*, p. 11: 21 August 1792; p. 21: 6 September 1792; p. 22 (b): 9 September 1792.

of a civic republicanism in which, by *tradition*, all played their part in the common defence of hard-won freedoms: in Neuchâtel in western Switzerland, on 17 August

> I assisted at the review of the town guard ... It is composed of all the citizens without distinction of rank or fortune. All are common soldiers, & they chose their own corporals: the serjeants are chosen by the magistrates, then they rise by seniority. I could not help remarking that the magistrates with whom and the other gentlemen of the town I spoke this & the preceding evening, were particularly anxious to extol this system of equality which they assured me, reigned in every department, at the time they were execrating the French revolution, the principal feature of which is the introduction of this equality.

Throckmorton went on to add his interlocutors' commentary on this practical egalitarianism – 'Nous ne connoissons, said they, aucune distinction ni de naissance, ni de richesse' – and, evidently no lover of royal rulers, he further added 'The King of Prussia is sovereign of the country, but he has little power, he can neither levy men nor money.'[19]

All the evidence of these passages – his participation in the militia review, his cordial and carefully recorded conversation with the magistrates and the burghers, his reverence for the historic totems of Swiss freedom – strongly suggest Sir John's admiration for the distinctive Swiss route to liberty and equality. In correspondence, he continued to profess what were for the time radical views – 'I am as great a democrat as ever' – but it was, clearly, the accustomed, non-violent and perhaps the very non-theoretical nature of the Swiss formula that attracted him, as opposed to the then current French model: 'I am convinced the Jacobins have gone too far & and are not to be defended.' There was, indeed, an Anglo-Saxon Whig ideology that saw good institutions as essentially the product of history. As Burke pronounced, 'The very idea of the fabrication of a new government is enough to fill us with disgust and horror. We wished at the period of the [1689] Revolution, and do now wish, to derive all we possess as *an inheritance from our forefathers.*' In other words, as a later nineteenth-century celebrant of the English route to liberty put it, 'England and her institutions have gone though the purifying furnace of time.' Just around the point, in 1792, at which the Throckmorton party crossed the Channel, the *émigré* Swiss artist Henry Fuseli was part of another coterie attempting, in their case without success, to get to the continent. And Fuseli had already painted a heroic depiction of the anti-Austrian oath

---

[19] *Throckmorton Journal*, p. 9: 17 August 1792: in 1707 the Principality of Neuchâtel was successfully claimed by Frederick I of Prussia by right of descent from the first Prince of Orange; Neuchâtel joined the Swiss Confederation in 1856.

that Throckmorton lovingly recorded in the prose of his journal, Fuseli establishing its political significance within a Romantic mythos of freedom grounded in history – a Helvetic Magna Carta. As his animadversions on French, and even more on Swiss, politics show, there was a strong leaning in John Courtenay Throckmorton's political philosophy towards the construct that Burke had already made his own: freedom was won as a bright quartz fetched out of the quarries of time.[20]

Throckmorton had more to say, in his correspondence, about the Swiss political scene – about the conflict, for example, between the small, rural, central 'democratic' cantons and the urbanised 'aristocratic' ones, with particular reference to their sharply opposed attitudes to events in France, these discords now replacing earlier conflicts over religion. But it was in his reflections on the Confederation's religious configurations that Throckmorton could be at his most startling. A hallmark of the Swiss constitution was its federalism, which, indeed, allowed some cantons to maintain oligarchic structures and others relatively more popular systems. In the field of religion, the same insistence on the sovereign right of the individual canton to determine its own arrangements had, following the Reformation, created in Switzerland a chequerboard of confessional statelets, the sometimes slender unity of the Confederation being preserved by recognition of the absolute authority of the cantonal units to adhere either to the old faith or to Protestantism. It was Joseph Berington who commented on the damage done by the Reformation to Switzerland and its former glory, when 'violent commotions were raised by religious disputes, and their effects are sensibly felt at this hour'. The central, Catholic founding-father cantons preserved the 'purest democracy on earth ... whilst the great Protestant cantons have adopted aristocracy, the worst species of despotism.' However, it was not the constitutional differences parting the Catholic from the Protestant sub-divisions of the Confederation that aroused Sir John's interests, but the even wider and deeper differences in religious orientation, cultures, *mores* – and, consequently, in economic practices.[21]

Sir John Courtenay Throckmorton was an acute enough observer to be aware that the central fact of Swiss civic life was inter-provincial diversity. There was no Swiss constitution, only constitutions, and difference was

---

[20] WRO, CR 1998/TLD/fol. 2/2b: Sir John Courtenay Throckmorton to William Throckmorton, 20 September 1792; Burke, *Reflections on the French Revolution*, p. 29; Asa Briggs, *The Age of Improvement* (London, 1967), p. 110; Schama, *History of Britain*, vol. 3, pp. 60–61, 80.

[21] WRO, CR 1998/TLD/fol. 2/2b: Sir John Courtenay Throckmorton to William Throckmorton, 20 September 1792; Berington, *Reflections Addressed to the Rev. John Hawkins*, pp. 241–2; Burke, *Reflections on the French Revolution*, p. 29.

even visually evident in the clothes the people of the cantons wore, for 'It is remarkable that each canton in Switzerland preserves a particular stile of dress, & in entering a different canton the variety is immediately observed.' This observation led the baronet into further reflections on the particularistic Christianities of those quintessentially diverse Swiss cantons, which this rational Catholic of the Enlightenment, who took particular note of a residence once occupied by Rousseau, found ludicrous – an 'absurdity':

> The change [between cantons] is not less sudden in their religion, & that which is compelled to be believed on one side of a hedge, is prohibited on the other ... A rational change however in these matters is, it is to be hoped gradually working in the minds of men.[22]

If there was considerable political heterogeneity, colourful sartorial variety and futile religious diversity between the cantons of the Confederation, Throckmorton seems at first sight to have detected a uniform level of national economic prosperity: 'Among the most striking things to a traveller in Switzerland, are the population and cultivation of the country.' It was a nationally gratifying truism in eighteenth-century England that, just as British freedom meant prosperity, so continental absolutism and its crippling arbitrary taxes led to destitution. Throckmorton subscribed to that kind of analysis of the Swiss affluence that he seems at first sight to have thought was universal across the country: the Switzers' wonderful deliverance from medieval servitude under hereditary monarchs made them all not only free but prosperous, and those benefits 'I am convinced are owing to their having very few taxes, & their great division of property. When the Swiss recovered their [liberty] from the Austrian family, had [the Habsburgs] established a monarchy & the law of primogeniture, their country had now been a desert.'[23]

Closer inspection, though, seems to have revealed not the universality of Swiss prosperity, but its patchiness, the key difference being between Catholic and Protestant districts. In the first place, at Constance, an Austrian possession on the German–Swiss frontier, a city that had only briefly enjoyed the Reformation before being abruptly restored to the old faith by its new overlord Charles V in 1548, Sir John began a series of observations indicating some link in his mind between popery and poverty. The Catholic episcopal city was 'a large unpeopled town with a

---

[22] *Throckmorton Journal*, p. 10: 19 August 1792; p. 23: 9 September 1792.

[23] Ibid., p. 25 (b): 17 September 1792; Raymond D. Tumbleson, *Catholicism in the English Protestant Imagination: Nationalism, Religion, and Literature, 1660–1745* (Cambridge, 1998), p. 193.

melancholy appearance' and 'There appears to be no trade here'. Indeed, it was even as if Habsburg state intervention in order to engraft some donor organs of Genevan Calvinist work-ethic had been rejected by the host, for 'some years past the Emperor Joseph 2d established some Genevese in the suppressed convent of the Dominicans.' This was indeed the kind of action that made 'Josephism' so attractive to Catholic modernists: the substitution for the alleged indolence and inutility of the religious orders by wealth-generating industry, albeit from a firmly Protestant stock. Yet the imperial transplant did not take in that city of churches, and the ingenious, industrious Genevans – 'they make some printed cottons, & and some of them are watchmakers' – 'do not succeed, & I am informed they mean to return to Geneva'.[24]

Within Switzerland itself Throckmorton proceeded to develop further observations that might have been suggested in the first instance by the collapse of the Constance experiment of enterprise-zoning, identifying further evidence of Swiss variability; in this case between solidly Catholic Lucerne, where his party was then staying, and the primary standard-bearer of the Swiss Reformation, Zurich. For Sir John, the differences now seemed to turn on the presence or absence of an air of civic vivacity in a city: 'There is a wonderful difference between this place and Zurich, the latter all alive, this as dead as if a plague has swept the streets; indeed the difference is striking between the Catholic and Protestant cantons in that respect.'[25]

Further observation and reflections encouraged the development and extension of such thoughts:

> The difference is very striking between the capitals of the Protestant, and those of the Catholic cantons: the former are well peopled, clean & handsome, & the people shew a spirit of industry: the latter, on the contrary, are ill peopled & many of them are dirty; the people seem slovenly & idle.

The dirt and the cleanliness, however, were surface manifestations of underlying cultural and attitudinal differences which were induced by the varieties of religious experience between the cantons as a result of confessional polarisations introduced into the Confederation by the Reformation and its divisive sequel. In the familiar Anglo-Saxon Protestant trope, the benign trinity of religious Reformation, political freedom and economic prosperity confronted the alien axis of popish, superstitious religion, arbitrary government and poverty. We have already seen how

---

[24] *Throckmorton Journal*, p. 14 (b): 26 August 1792.

[25] WRO, CR 1998/TCD/fol. 21: Sir John Courtenay Throckmorton, Lucerne, to William Throckmorton, 3 September 1792.

Throckmorton traced the legacy that material well-being owed to political emancipation; now he turned his analysis to the link between what was known to his Protestant compatriots as those inseparable companions in indigence, 'popery and wooden shoes':

> Among other reasons for this difference, I cannot help thinking that it is in some measure to be attributed to the number of priests. Many of these take to the church, as a profession to gain their livelyhood, & not being provided with benefices, which give them a maintenance, are obliged to invent or promote some confrérie, or other method of superstitious devotion, by which they gain profit to themselves, & instil into the minds of the people & particularly children a lazy superstitious inclination which prevents them ever becoming industrious.[26]

Here Throckmorton's delineation of the religious deficiencies that gave rise to impoverishment saw him stepping over well-trodden ground, for the link made, if not between Protestantism and wealth creation, then between Catholicism and economic backwardness, was a cliché long before the appearance in 1904–5 of Max Weber's famous essay on the Protestant ethic and the spirit of capitalism. Part of the set of assumptions that 'popery' was the enemy of wealth-enhancing industry had to do with the sheer length of otherwise employable time that was spent on cultic activities. Thus Throckmorton's co-religionist fellow-squire, the Lancastrian William Blundell (1620–98), bemoaned the sheer number of work days dissipated (in 1683) in an apparently unending cycle of feast-days:

> Christmas began on Tuesday, so that we had at that time eight holydays together, Sunday being included therein. Immediately before that Christmas, we had six days beginning on Wednesday 19th, whereof five were fasting days, one holyday, and one Sunday; so that there were at that time fourteen days altogether, which were all of them either holydays or fasting days.

When joined to Blundell's calculation to the effect that 'if there be four million of working people in a country who are each able to earn 6d per diem, the work of one day will amount to 100,000 *l*.', the economic case against excessive numbers of workless holy days seemed made, for even in Blundell's day, with a recusant population estimated at around 60,000,

---

[26] Colin Haydon, *Anti-Catholicism in Eighteenth-century England, c. 1714–80* (Manchester, 1993), p. 47; *Throckmorton Journal*, p. 26 (b): 17 September 1792 [?] – it might be noted, though, that Throckmorton concluded that 'Nothing can exceed the industry and population' of the 'little territory' of largely Catholic, partly Reformed, German-speaking St Gallen: ibid., p. 15: 27 August 1792.

the loss of earning power to the plebeian Catholic wage-earner if he or she *did* observe all those red-letter days as time off work (but giving them at least Christmas Day free) would be the hefty sum of 6/6d per worker, a dear Christmas for the 'labouring' majority of the English Catholic community.[27]

Yet pious, charitable Squire Blundell was neither an Ebenezer Scrooge before his time nor a godless commercialist bent on wealth accumulation at all costs. In fact, he made nice distinctions between contemporaneous Catholic practices with regard to feast days, distinguishing between indisputably Catholic but industrious, prosperous and festival-rationing Flanders and France on the one hand and, on the other, 'the present state of Spain and the lazy old Irish'. And as the eighteenth-century English Catholic Church shifted its own social base somewhat away from that of gentry-led clusters of peasants and rural artisans into one of an increasingly urbanised and, in part, bourgeois-led community, its great mentors – first John Gother (d. 1704), in *Instructions for Particular States and Conditions of Life* (first published in 1689), then the vicar apostolic Richard Challoner (1691–1781), in the *Garden of the Soul* (first issued in 1740) – provided a persuasive Catholic apologia for the life of endeavour. In 1777, about a century after William Blundell penned his call for a trimming of the English festal programme, Pius VI authorised a drastic reduction in that calendar, the English Catholic community accommodating itself inexorably to what was, for good or ill, the value system of a diligent and acquisitive British world. From his Swiss vantage point, Throckmorton – moderniser, anti-clerical, reformer – was unmistakably placing himself alongside the eighteenth-century advocates of the spirit of progress of the age of the Enlightenment.[28]

Switzerland, with its chequered denominational history and complex patterns of sectarian affiliations, had given Throckmorton opportunities to voice, at least to himself, some of his own religious leanings and prejudices. There was, for example, a fairly mild anti-clerical swipe when he recorded how, from the magnificent library of the Abbey of St Gallen, 'many of the most valuable manuscripts were lost during the councils of Constance [1414–18] & Basle [1431–7], having been borrowed for the use of the bishops & Cardinals & never returned …'. At the municipal library in the same place, though, Sir John was able to display an eirenic-sounding outlook in his appreciation of the library once bequeathed to

---

[27] *Crosby Records: A Cavalier's Notebook. Being Notes, Anecdotes & Observations of William Blundell of Crosby, Lancashire*, ed. T. Ellison Gibson (London, 1880), pp. 121–3.

[28] Michael A. Mullett, 'Catholic and Quaker Attitudes to Work, Rest, and Play in Seventeenth and -Eighteenth-Century England', in R.N. Swanson (ed.), *The Use and Abuse of Time in Christian History*, Studies in Church History, 37 (Woodbridge, 2002), pp. 190–95.

his birthplace by Joachim Vadianus, or Vadian (1483/4–1551), St Gallen's doctor, mayor and Protestant reformer: 'There are twelve volumes of manuscript letters between him & several of the first Reformers.' St Gallen also provided the chance to voice the aesthetic preferences that accompanied Throckmorton's quest for a simplified Catholicism – 'The [Abbey] Church is modern, handsome, but overloaded with ornaments', while in German-speaking and Catholic Lucerne, churches were similarly 'overloaded with meretricious and superstitious ornaments'. In Constance, 'The cathedral is a large building, much adorned in the inside, but in bad taste, as are all the churches I saw in the town.' However, in German-speaking and Catholic Zug ('as well as in the other small cantons') they had a system that was bound to appeal to the recent author of *A Second Letter Addressed to the Catholic Clergy of England on the Appointment of Bishops* (1791). Demanding lay participation in episcopal elections, 'the people elect their own clergy'. That said, in the same way that Throckmorton's political views were at least tested by the convolutions of events in Europe during his tour, so too his ingrained anti-clerical views were undoubtedly softened by the impact on his kindly nature of news of the increasingly violent French Revolutionary campaign against the clergy. So he wrote at Michaelmas 1792:

> The papers mention that a subscription is making in England for the poor priests who are driven from france [*sic*]; if you think it right, subscribe what you think is proper for me; though I do not entirely approve of the conduct of the clergy, they are now much to be pitied, & nothing can justify the treatment they have received.[29]

Throckmorton's Swiss journey seems to have confirmed a number of the tastes and opinions that he would take with him as the vacation ventured down on its next stage, into Italy. However, his party's venture into the country that was purportedly the panting heart of their Catholic faith was far from being pre-ordained by any plan that envisaged the other instalments of the itinerary as merely the prelude to a Roman holiday or Italian grand tour, for, as he wrote to his brother,

---

[29] *Throckmorton Journal*, p. 16: 28 August 1792; p. 16 (b): 28 August 1792; p. 19 (b): 3 September 1792; p. 14 (b) 26 August 1792; p. 19: 2 September 1792; WRO, CR 1998/TCD/fol. 2/4: Sir William Throckmorton, Geneva, to William Throckmorton, 29 September 1792. The crisis in the French Church, ignited by the highly divisive demand by the National Assembly in November 1790 that all clergy swear the oath of allegiance to the Civil Constitution by 4 January 1791, turned into a war of the Revolution against the clergy in the course of 1792, involving massacres and the emigration of 30,000 priests and religious.

When a man sets out to travel, he never knows how far he will go; this is exactly my case. There is no likelihood of Paris being a pleasant sejour for the winter, & Geneva or this place [Lausanne] are not more likely to be so; for there is every prospect of a quarrel between the Swiss & France. In this case, it is very probable we shall go to Italy.[30]

Once in the peninsula, whether by accident or design, Throckmorton once more responded to the conventional expectations that were held of continental locations, for, just as France drew the visitor's attention to its agriculture and Switzerland to its picturesque scenery, so Italy required not so much scenic admiration for the *bel paese* as a connoisseur's eye, and Throckmorton brought it, becoming the model grand tourist, a hungry consumer of the *beaux arts*, knowledgeable, discerning and compulsive, clearly determined to see 'the different objects worthy of notice' in any place.[31]

He also had a historian's perspective, so that when his party made its first stop in Italian territory, at Trent in the north-east, he took note of 'the Cathedral a fine old church, & that in which the council was held'. Perhaps, though, his interest in the great 'ecumenical' synod which had been convened in the city (1545–63) and which had inaugurated within Catholicism the Counter-Reformation phase that witnessed the ascendancy of the Jesuits, the rise of an authoritarian papacy and the profusion of emotive popular cults was less than his admiration during his Alpine journey for the site of the Council of Constance (1414–18). That assembly had incorporated the 'conclave', as Throckmorton called it, which had once struck a blow for constitutional principles in the government of the Church when it 'elected, during the Council Pope Martin 5th, after deposing John 23d'.[32]

Once his Italian tour was properly under way, such notes, focusing on major churches, if not as religious buildings then at least as places of moment in the institutional history of the Church, gave way to a sense of ecclesiastical buildings as, essentially, art galleries. So, in Verona, after noting the repairs to the interior of the immense century Roman amphitheatre, built *c.*290, Throckmorton recorded,

---

[30] WRO, CR 1998/TCD/fol. 21: Sir John Courtenay Throckmorton, Lausanne, to William Throckmorton, 20 September 1792.

[31] *Throckmorton Journal*, p. 33: 24–27 October 1792.

[32] Ibid., p. 32: 22 October, 1792; pp. 14–15: 26 August 1792. In November 1417 at the council called to Constance to heal the wound of the Great Schism, a special conclave of 22 cardinals and 30 prelates representing the six 'nations' into which the council was divided elected Cardinal Oddo Colonna as Martin V (r. 1417–31), following the abdication of the antipope Gregory XII (July 1415) and the depositions (May and July 1417 respectively) of his predecessors, the antipopes John XXIII and Benedict XIII.

In some of the churches are a few good pictures; in San Georgio [sic] is one of P. Veronese, the best.' Roman antiquities, as well as other works by 'the same master', also engaged the traveller's interests in Verona and then, when his little group, proceeding steadily south, arrived in Mantua, the capital of the Duchy of that name, it was all connoisseurship again, when 'We saw the Cathedral, a very handsome church built by Julio [sic] Romano, the colonnades, which divide the aisles have a fine effect … a good picture by Guercino.[33]

Throckmorton's carefully constructed catalogue perfectly encapsulates the tastes and preferences of his nation, period, class and generation: Italian High Renaissance classicism, shading into the early baroque. In Parma, the English party

> Went to see the objects of curiosity … The cathedral, San Giovanni &c in which are some good paintings by Corregio [sic], Parmegianino &c, the cupolas of each church by Corregio … & the famous picture by Corregio, of the Madonna & child, with M. Magdalen, St. Jerom & an Angel.

Linking, via his pupil Parmigiano, the influence of Michelangelo, through mannerism, to the later mainstream of Italian baroque devout art, Correggio employed approaches, including illusionism and kinetic energy, which give his religious works, notably those focused on the Blessed Virgin such as the Parma Dome and the Dresden *Madonna with St George*, the feeling of a kind of sensuous mysticism. By the same token, Parmigiano's mannerist works typically reflect the almost neurotic piety that he developed in his later years. In both his and his master's works, however, such depths of religious emotion seem to be overlooked by Sir John in his brief salesroom-style, 'fine-arts' appraisal of 'some good paintings'.[34]

It was, in other words, Throckmorton's art-for-art's-sake approach that may have been concealing other realities from him, above all the religious passions that had in the first place inspired the 'good painting' he was inspecting. Yet other English visitors were perhaps able to see more fully, and perhaps less superficially, the picture beyond the pictures. Thus the vicar apostolic of the London District, William Poynter (1762–1827), visiting Parma in January 1815, was certainly aware of the great beauty of its churches, but, saying Mass in one of them, though unaware of their exact art history, he was at the same time at least cognisant of their spiritual function and of the aura of the numinous that lay beneath their role as warehouses for 'old masters': 'saw different churches, the Cathedral, ceiling beautifully painted, subterranean chapel, in which the

---

[33] *Throckmorton Journal*, p. 33: 24–27 October 1792.
[34] Ibid, p. 34: 30 October 1792.

Canons celebrate office, 3 monthly in a year'. Poynter – who observed 'Parma a poor town, a great many beggars' – had clearly also retained the eye for social reality that Throckmorton had possessed so acutely in Switzerland, but had perhaps lost to an aficionado's lorgnette in that extended *musée des beaux arts* that made up for him the cities of the *bijou* duchies of northern Italy.[35]

Bishop Poynter was far from immune to the charms of 'good pictures' – the very phrase he used for those he recorded seeing in Modena – but his devotional orientation opened up to him experiences that Throckmorton's outlook seems to have denied him. Thus in Bologna Sir John noted, without comment, a 'Jubilee' issued by the bishop 'on account of the bad situation of ecclesiastical affairs; to be gained by those who visited a famous picture of the Madonna in a church, at a little distance from the town; or, if prevented, any other image of our Lady'. In the same city, by contrast, Poynter was to throw himself enthusiastically into a form of Italian reliquary piety that Throckmorton saw fit not even to notice: 'The church of St Catherine of Bologna, in which we saw and touched her body which is entire, flexible though exposed to the air.'[36]

It was in Rome above all that we can observe the limitations of vision imposed by the combination of Throckmorton's single-minded connoisseurship with his ecclesiological positioning, inducing him to see the Vicar of Christ as little more than the custodian of a particularly fine assemblage of *opere de'arte*. He pointedly refused to satisfy the inquisitive desire of Pius VI, a stickler for court protocol, to meet the English Catholic *proprietario* who had referred to the Holy Father as a 'foreign prelate', though he in fact made undercover contacts, meeting the Pope's unofficial representative in Britain, Monsignor Charles Erskine, whom he may have won over to the Cisalpine case. On the whole, though, he seems to have kept in Rome to a self-denying ordinance imposing silence, if not neutrality, that he had earlier made in Florence: 'I am informed that the Vicars Apostolic have sent C. Plowden to Rome; if they think that I shall trouble myself about their affairs in that quarter, they are mistaken; it is not my intention to open my mouth to any person there on the subject.'

Received into the Society of Jesus in 1759, Charles Plowden, of an old Shropshire recusant gentry family, was a staunch anti-Cisalpine and close associate of Milner. Sir John may have been misinformed about his being sent to Rome by the vicars apostolic during his tenure (1784–94) as

---

[35] *The Diaries of Bishop William Poynter, V.A. (1815–1824)*, ed. Peter Phillips, Catholic Record Society, 79 (London, 2006), p. 25.

[36] Ibid., p. 26; *Throckmorton Journal*, p. 35: 1 November 1792. Catherina de'Vigri was a fifteenth-century Franciscan nun, visionary, artist and devotional writer, canonised in 1712.

chaplain to the Weld family, but if Throckmorton believed that Plowden was bringing an appeal against him to Rome from the English bishops, it would have been perfectly consistent with his ecclesiological stance not to be involved in any way in such an appellate procedure, on one side or the other. However, if he was not in the market for a curial hearing or even a papal *udienza*, he was more than happy to view the papal collections: 'We saw the museum at the Vatican: The additions made to it by the present Pope, with the fine statues formerly belonging to his predecessors, & those collected by the last pope, make it perhaps the finest collections [*sic*] of antique statues in the World.' By the same token, popes were, clearly, to be adjudged primarily in terms of aesthetic criteria: 'In the buildings made by the late & present Popes, there is a great want of taste.'[37]

Once again, Poynter (whose main reason for being in Rome arose from the politics of the quest for full emancipation of the British Catholics) was sensible of the touristic attractions of the Eternal City: 'We went out to see the Vatican, the Capitol, the Tarpeian Rock, Constantine [*sic*] Triumphal Arch, Titus' ditto, the Amphitheatre, the Forum & Column of Trajan.' But at the same time, he appreciated Rome as Catholicism's ritual centre – 'Went to St Peter's, High Mass sung by Card Galeffi, the Pope assisting' – and further remarked on the social condition of Rome, which 'appears miserable' and which Throckmorton overlooked.[38]

It is true, of course, that eighteenth-century Rome was perhaps the world's most important centre for the sale and exchange, as well as the collection, of works of arts, so that, for example, the English Jesuit John Thorpe – in residence in Rome for much of the second half of the eighteenth century, until his death in the years of the Throckmorton party's visit – was taken up with a commission for a copied version of part of Raphael's *Transfiguration*. At the same time, though, Thorpe was fully aware of the city's spiritual pulling power and devotional magnetism: 'The French clergy refugees here behave well, show piety & devotion; several have made the Spi[ritual] Exercises; almost all, who are in town came to say Mass at the Gesu [*sic*] on the feast of St Xaverius; the novena was observed with the usual concourse.'[39]

---

[37] *Throckmorton Journal*, p. 43: January 1793; Scott, 'Throckmorton, Sir John Courtenay'; WRO, 1998/TCD/fol. 2/7: Sir John Courtenay Throckmorton, in Florence, to William Throckmorton, 16 November 1792; Mullett, *English Catholicism 1680–1830*, vol. 5, pp. 1–3; Geoffrey Scott, 'Plowden, Charles, 1743–1821', *ODNB*.

[38] *Poynter Diaries*, p. 29.

[39] Geoffrey Holt, SJ, 'The Letters from Rome of John Thorpe, S.J. to Charles Plowden, S.J., 1784–92', *Recusant History*, 28/3 (2007): 438–40, 446. The Papal States were a major reception area for the many *émigré* French clergy in the early 1790s.

Meanwhile, though, Throckmorton's insistent tourist persona remained firmly in place – 'I went to the top of St. Peter's into the ball' – and indeed he made no apparent distinction between a visit to the Villa Borghese to view works of art and another to the church of Santa Maria del Popolo to see 'a statue of Jonas from the design of Raphael'. Two journal entries, however, evince some widening of his interests. One is an all too brief record of attendance at 'the ceremonies at the Vatican' on 28 March – probably the solemnities of Maundy Thursday, Easter Sunday falling in that year on 31 March. Throckmorton's other distraction from his sightseer's life in Rome was occasioned by lower-class rioting that followed aggressive displays of enthusiasm for the Revolution on the part of French expatriates. Sir John recorded these events quite laconically in the first instance: the 'Trasteverini' – denizens of the low-grade suburb of Trastevere, 'beyond the Tiber' – 'assembled near the quarter of the Jews, & threatened to set fire to it, but they were prevented'. Further details of this incident in which the 'Trasteverini' attacked the ghetto, located around the Via del Portico d'Ottavia, where the Roman Jews had been confined since the anti-Jewish legislation of Paul IV, came in an insightful letter from Sir John to his brother William in January 1793, locating the events within the context of the traditional reactionary papalism, xenophobia and bigotry of the Roman lower orders. The actual attack on the ghetto was preceded by the mob parading

> the street shouting <u>Viva il Papa</u>, <u>non vogliamo Francesi</u> [We don't want the French] &c, & stopped every person till they were ascertained he was not french [sic]; they did the same on Monday & last night, & they have threatened some houses in the Piazza di Spagna, among others the Spanish minister is threatened. On Monday night they assembled to set fire to the quarter of the Jews, but were prevented. In all these transactions, they think they are pleasing the Pope, & they have an idea that he has sent to thank them for what they have done. They took the torches, with which they intended to set fire to the Ghetto, to St Peter's, & expected the Pope would come down to bless them.[40]

Clearly these unsavoury disturbances, which raised expectations in Rome of a French attack (which did not take place until General Louis Berthier entered the city in 1798 and proclaimed the Pope deposed), engaged Throckmorton's considerable interest, even to the extent of dispelling his preoccupation with the fine arts. The Trastevere crowd adopted a collective attitude taken up since the Middle Ages by mobs attacking minorities – the claim that their actions were validated by the highest authorities. It may have been, though, that the ugly scenes around the Roman ghetto

---

[40] *Throckmorton Journal*, pp. 43 ff, 65, 51, 49, 52; WRO, CR 1998/TCD/fol. 2/15: Sir John Courtenay Throckmorton, Rome, to William Throckmorton, 16 January 1793.

confirmed this liberal-minded Whig aristocrat, whose English fellow-Catholics had been exposed to extreme peril in the anti-popish Gordon Riots taking place in London and elsewhere in England in 1780, in a distaste for popular power little less intense than his suspicion of royal despotism and of clerical obscurantism.

In fact, Throckmorton's political attitudes were up for regular review, strongly influenced by the astonishing turn of events, in the course of his party's continental odyssey in 1792–93. In February the Throckmortons were in Naples, hosted by Sir William Forbes of Pitsligo (1734–1806), the Scots banker and writer, staying in Rome for his wife's health over 1792–93, and on 8 February Sir John reported to his brother the reception in the southern city of the execution of Louis XVI, continuing:

> I could not believe they could have perpetuated this crime; there is now I hope an end of all their dreams of liberty, they are not worthy to partake of such a blessing; instead of forwarding they have ruined it's [sic] cause in every part of the world, & are driving all mankind to despotism. Poor Louis! How much have his friends & his enemies to reproach themselves with. That wretch Egalitè [sic] voted for the death of his friend and relative.[41]

The urgent, excited prose glosses over some of the detail of Throckmorton's response to the latest atrocity from France, and in particular whether he thought its 'driving all mankind to despotism' meant that the Jacobins themselves were doing that or that their actions played into the hands of the authoritarian European monarchies that confronted the Revolution in France. That said, the main lines of Sir John's quintessentially Burkean political outlook are present in this reportage and comment.

The Throckmortons' stay in Rome had a stronger flavour of *la dolce vita* than was noticeable in the rest of their continental itinerary. The view of the Roman *beau monde* was that Sir John was 'most polite, most understanding, and, in fine, superior in all respects to any Catholic gentleman they have ever seen in Rome'. They themselves entertained generously, providing a banquet in the English College for all the English lay or clerical residents in the city. At the same time, though, as the Throckmortons' Roman holiday drew towards a close in April 1793, Sir John was moved to offer home thoughts from abroad, both on secular and ecclesiastical politics. First, he reflected on what he viewed as rising divisiveness in the country, along with the reactionary response of William Pitt's administration (1783–1801) to the perceived threat of the spread of French revolutionary notions within

---

[41] Scott, 'Throckmorton, Sir John Courtenay'; John Booker, 'Forbes, Sir William of Pitsligo, the sixth Baronet, 1739–1806)', *ODNB*; WRO, CR 1998/TCD/fol. 2/16a: Sir John Courtenay Throckmorton, Naples, to William Throckmorton, 8 February 1793.

the country: May 1792 saw a government proclamation against subversive literature and the following year Acts were passed enabling the state to deport Irish nationals and ban trade unions. Throckmorton's response was entirely within the constitutionalist Whig stance both of abhorrence of unlicensed violence and detestation of state repression:

> As to politics in England, I am really sick of them, the nation appears to be run mad, & I am sorry to se [sic] so much violence & animosity, when there appears to be so little reason for it; government seems determined to push things to extremities, & if you do not approve of despotic power, you are branded as an enemy of your country: the constitution is held out as the most perfect work of man, yet every act they are doing is a violation of it, inventing new treasons on one hand, & submitting every person to the power & discretion of the magistrate.

At the same time, Throckmorton was now resuming an immediate concern with the affairs and politics of the English Catholic community. He was also involving himself in the prospect of the closure, under revolutionary pressure, and the migration to England of the Liège-based college of the Society of Jesus (itself at that point in time still under the suppression order [1773] of Clement XIV). By 1794 the homeless school was to find a berth at Stonyhurst in Lancashire in the majestic home, and amidst the large estate, of the college's former student Thomas Weld. But, while its future remained uncertain, Throckmorton, who in 1787 had joined other members of the Catholic Committee in backing the setting up of a progressive English Catholic school under lay direction, sought a voice in the outlook for the new school project, though he was torn somewhat between general anti-clericalism and specific anti-Jesuitism on the one hand and, on the other, the opportunity to secure high-quality, low-cost clerically conducted education for English Catholic elites on home ground:

> I am writing to hear from you [William Throckmorton] what you mention of the college at Liege [sic] being dissolved. Although the school they think of setting foot in England, may be begun on Jesuitical principles, every body is affected by those with whom he converses and lives, & I am not much afraid of those principles being inculcated into the minds of boys in England. Do not however relax in your ideas of establishing another; but I doubt if it will succeed with the total exclusion you mention of all ecclesiastics. No master can be had so cheap as them, & I doubt if the idea would take to any great extent; if any fund is raised for the maintenance of the school, the clergy should I think be excluded from the administration of it. At all events I wish you would lose no time in beginning on; take no notice of what the Jesuits do, but pursue your plan steadily. If any money is wanted, you know you have <u>charte</u> [sic] <u>blanche</u> from me.

Throckmorton's own misgivings about the good omens for a lay-led English Catholic school were in fact soundly based and, indeed, the loss without trace of such a scheme should be read as one of the clearest indicators of the mounting triumph of the clericalist party within the English Catholic Church.[42]

By the spring of 1793 the Throckmortons were having to tear themselves away from their Roman art tour: his passion for paintings ('I am very much fascinated with the beaux arts at Rome and leave it with some regret') was fully shared by his wife, as an insertion, evidently from her hand, in a letter home reveals: 'the only thing my head is turned with is pictures'. In fact, their relinquishment of the pleasures of artistic appreciation was not all that abrupt. There was also some recorded contact with the world of *émigré* English Catholicism in Rome: 'I dined at the English College' – the great Roman seminary, known as 'the Venerabile', set up in 1579 by Gregory XIII under the inspiration of William Allen (1532–94) in order to supply priests for the mission to England. The Throckmortons recorded what seems to have been the briefest halt ('We passed by') in Loreto, on the east coast of Italy, south of Ancona. The place was the focus of an extraordinary pilgrimage cult – the holy house, 'Santa Casa', of the family of Jesus, Mary and Joseph, believed to have been removed by angels from the Holy Lands in the late thirteenth century, giving it a refuge from Muslim depredations.[43]

The holy house of Loreto was in fact a dividing rod between Protestant critics of Catholic credulity and the piety of Catholic believers. While one English aristocratic critic took the shrine to task for piling up the donations of pilgrims 'while all the inhabitants of the town almost are starving', Fr Thorpe was only too willing 'to make another visit to that sanctuary', the 'Santuario della Santa Casa' being, strictly speaking the church enclosing the holy house. However, if we were to expect Throckmorton's rationalising Catholicism to explode in the face of pious suspended disbelief in the authenticity of the transported cottage, we would be disappointed, for he recorded, dispassionately enough, only that his party saw the 'Sta Casa, Treasury & c.' Predictably, he was, though, much more interested in the art treasures clustered to the shrine: in the treasury, 'the birth of the Virgin by Annibal Caracci [sic] Madonna & child, said to be by Raphael'. And it was entirely in line with Sir John's aestheticism that, at the party's

---

[42] *Letters and Prose Writings of William Cowper*, p. 375 and n. 1 (citing Bernard Ward, *The Dawn of the Catholic Revival in England, 1781–1803* (2 vols, London, 1909), vol. 2, pp. 39–40); Scott, 'Throckmorton, Sir John Courtenay'; WRO, CR 1998/TCD/fol. 2/20: Sir John Courtenay Throckmorton, Rome, to William Throckmorton, 15 April 1793.

[43] Scott, 'Throckmorton, Sir John Courtenay', p. 693; WRO, CR 1998/TCD/fol. 2/20: Sir John Courtenay Throckmorton, Rome, to William Throckmorton, 15 April 1793; CR 1998/TCD/fol. 2/16a: Sir John (and Lady) Throckmorton, Naples, 8 February 1793; *Throckmorton Journal*, p. 66: 4 April 1793.

re-embarkation from the continent some of the last sights recorded were 'two pictures of Rubens' – the amazing masterpieces, *Descent from the Cross* (1611–14) and *Raising of the Cross* (1610) by Peter Paul Rubens (1577–1640), in the cathedral of Onze Lieve Vrouw in Antwerp.[44]

On his return to England – on 2 August Cowper recorded the recent arrival of 'Sir John and Lady Frog', bringing for him a gift from Lady Spencer of engravings on subjects from the Odyssey – Throckmorton threw himself back into opposition politics. Even if the views on contemporaneous affairs he recorded on the continent reflected a Burkean moderation, he took on the chairmanship of the Foxite Society of Friends of the People, associating closely with Fox himself in his anti-ministerial alliance with George, Prince of Wales (who was to visit Coughton in 1806). The Second Catholic Relief Act, 1791, legalising the opening of Catholic places of worship, allowed Sir John to open an ample new chapel at Coughton, once he and Lady Catherine had taken up residence there (they also spent time at Weston Underwood and Buckland). His love of learning was recognised in the conferment of a doctorate in civil laws by Oxford (1796), his membership of the Society of Dilettanti in 1797 and the dedication to him of a learned scriptural commentary, *Horae biblicae*, by Charles Butler. Following the 1801 Act of Union with Ireland, the Cisalpine Throckmorton, in *Considerations Arising from the Debates in Parliament on the Petition of the Irish Catholics* (1806), applied to his co-religionists in the sister kingdom the same prices of loyalty to the British constitution that had guided him in his work in England. As pressure mounted to extend the earlier relief Acts into a culminating measure of Catholic emancipation, Throckmorton joined the Catholic Board (1808) set up to achieve that goal, though he was never to witness its accomplishment, dying in 1819 at Coughton. Lady Catherine Maria died two years, almost to the day, after him, and the baronet's title was inherited by his brother George.[45]

By turns vivid, reflective, opinionated, peppery, humorous, erudite, inquisitive and absorbed in sights and scenes, the Throckmorton travel journal and letters provide us with an exceptionally deep insight into the thinking and feeling of a central and controversial figure in the story of the English Catholic community at one of the most crucial points in its development.

---

[44] Haydon, *Anti-Catholicism*, p. 27; Holt (ed.), 'Thorpe Letters', p. 434; *Throckmorton Journal*, p. 70: 26 April 1793; p. 90; 10 July 1793. At that point the 'Austrian' Low Countries had not yet fallen to France. This is confusing, as the French won this battle, conquered the Netherlands, but were subsequently driven out in early 1793, before conquering again in 1794.

[45] *Letters and Prose Writings of William Cowper*, pp. 375, 379; Scott, 'Throckmorton, Sir John Courtenay'.

CHAPTER 9

The Throckmortons Come of Age: Political and Social Alignments, 1826–1862

Alban Hood OSB

For half a century the Throckmorton family fortunes rested in the hands of a trio of childless brother baronets. When Sir John Courtenay died in 1819, the title passed to his younger brother George (1754–1826), resident at Weston Underwood, where he lived a quiet life necessitated by his fragile health. He died seven years later and his brother Charles (1757–1840) then inherited the title, which passed on his death to his nephew, Robert George Throckmorton (1800–62). These years saw the Throckmortons come of age, politically and socially, as they became more fully integrated into a new professional class in Georgian and Victorian England. This was a time when English Catholics also came of age in national life, as they gained the political emancipation for which Sir John had worked so tirelessly. These years are also significant for the family as they witnessed the gradual consolidation of Coughton Court and the abandonment of the house at Weston Underwood. The Throckmortons had always enjoyed the pursuits of country gentlefolk, but now these pastimes had to be subordinated to new responsibilities in the locality and nation. Both Charles and Robert Throckmorton succeeded to an inheritance foreseen by Sir John Courtenay. As members of the Catholic lay elite, they were able to take advantage of all the possibilities created for Catholics by the 1829 Catholic Emancipation Act, and thus establish themselves in the centre of English political and social life. They were also among the last representatives of an enduring lay hegemony over the English Catholic Church before that body was subjected to the authority of bishops in 1850.

Dry genealogical data quickly comes to life in the pages of a diary or on the ink-stained parchment of old letters. It has been suggested that whilst the best diarists may not necessarily be the best of men, nonetheless the best diarists usually are men. Like many men of their time, Charles and Robert Throckmorton kept personal journals and maintained a voluminous correspondence, and although they would never have claimed them to be literary masterpieces, nevertheless they provide a premium resource for the historian of the Throckmorton family. Like many of the diaries and letters of the great and good, the journals and missives of the seventh and eighth baronets reveal as much about other people as they do of themselves. Interspersed between everyday events such as meals, journeys and meetings are references to events and figures of the day, such as the coronation of Queen Victoria or audiences with the portly pontiff, Pius IX. The diaries and letters also provide insight into the pastimes and concerns of early nineteenth-century English gentry and sound the familiar family themes of the countryside, travel and concern for the plight of the common man.[1]

Given his medical background,[2] it is hardly surprising that Sir Charles Throckmorton appends the line 'gout of the stomach' to his stark diary entry which announced the death of his brother George in July 1826. The early 'memoranda' of Sir Charles are filled with detailed notes about the animals he shot and dissected, his exploits as a prisoner-of-war in France during the Napoleonic wars and travelogues of his many journeys. The entries in the journal are usually brief and to the point, but reveal a man of passion and energy who was inclined to be grumpy. The diaries mention several family members by name, but there are few references to his wife, Mary, who predeceased him, and it is curious that Sir Charles fails to record her death in his diary in May 1825. His last entry in his journal is simply 'I did not feel myself so well today.' The barren couple appear to have been excellent guardians of their nephews and nieces, William and Frances, who had lost their parents whilst still children.

In contrast to Sir Charles, his nephew and heir Robert was a family man who married the only daughter of Sir John Acton of Aldenham, Elizabeth, with whom he had nine children. Sir Robert's diaries span almost a quarter of a century, but sadly do not cover the years he was in parliament as the first Catholic MP to represent an English constituency since the seventeenth century. Nevertheless, his journals give testament to a busy life of public service and reveal a man keenly interested in the many facets of contemporary society and culture, recording visits to the theatre and to the opera and observing in an entry for May 1858 that 'the new reading room at the British Museum is very handsome and convenient'. Sir Robert's diary, like his uncle's, is peppered with the names of many of the great and good in local and national society, but especially of other Catholic gentry families of the period such as the Eystons, Blounts and the Townleys. Although Sir Robert makes regular reference to his sister Mary, his younger brother Nicholas does not make much of an appearance, and by all accounts 'Nico' (as he was known) was a less steady character than his elder brother.

---

[1] The diaries are WRO, CR 1998/CD/Drawer 8, 7–10 (Sir Charles Throckmorton); Drawer 5, 1–10 (Sir Robert Throckmorton). See also WRO, Z.500 (sm), The Memorandums (1795–1840) of Sir Charles Throckmorton, typescript and MS by Dr William H. McMenemey.

[2] See Geoffrey Scott's chapter in this volume.

Although he 'was clever and good-natured', he had 'an extraordinary flow of animal spirits, and a more than usual love for fun and frolic. He preserved the same character in the world after he had left College. He never took to any profession, and was a well-known character in London and in sporting circles.'[3] Eyebrows must have been raised when Nico took as his wife a 'Miss Chare', the daughter of a farmer in Buckland.

Although the previous three Throckmorton baronets had all had been educated by the Benedictines on the continent at Douai, the eighth baronet, Robert, and his brother Nicholas were educated in England at Oscott College near Birmingham from 1809 to 1815. This was not merely a practical response to the closure of the English Catholic colleges on the continent following the French Revolution, but reflected the Throckmorton family's Cisalpine aspirations, for Oscott was the fulfilment of the Cisalpine vision for English Catholic education. The college had been established in 1794 by the Cisalpines and was unusual in that initially it was under joint lay and clerical management. Sir John Courtenay Throckmorton had been chair of governors for a time, but by the time his nephew arrived at Oscott in 1809, the lay governors had resigned under pressure from John Milner, Vicar Apostolic of the Midland District. In a circular pleading for financial support, Milner wrote that 'when the essential and vital interest in religion in this District lately required that St Mary's College of Oscott should be re-opened as a seminary, it was required of the District to pay off a heavy debt contracted by the former establishment of that place' and that the seminary 'from the character and conduct of its ecclesiastical students, and from the plan of an ecclesiastical life, there adopted, affords the brightest prospect of supplying the District with a succession of truly Apostolical Missionaries'.[4] Despite Milner's aim of turning it into a seminary, Oscott proved to be the main rival of the Jesuit and Benedictine schools, largely because of the breadth of its curriculum and its success during the first half of the nineteenth century in attracting the sons of the Catholic nobility.[5] At Oscott the young Robert Throckmorton fell under the spell of its president, the Rev. Thomas Potts (1754–1819). Despite his habit of referring to his students in his letters as 'the dear boys', Potts was actually a very strict disciplinarian who often wielded the rod. He took particular interest in Robert, whom he noted in 1815 was 'to go to Mr B(erington) ... It is the best place to send him to, as young as he is – not yet 16. Neither London nor Edinburgh will suit him at present. At Buckland he will be safe under

---

[3] *The Oscotian* (1885), p. 147.

[4] Ibid., pp. 140–41.

[5] Alban Hood, 'From Repatriation to Revival: Continuity and Change in the English Benedictine Congregation, 1795–1850', unpublished PhD thesis, University of Liverpool (2006), pp. 203–9.

the eye of his aunt and Mr B.'⁶ Joseph Berington (1743–1827) was an important figure in the English Cisalpine circle as well as the Throckmorton chaplain at Buckland. He had hoped to send the young Robert to Rome to complete his education at the Accademia Ecclesiastica, 'where young men of good family are admitted to study civil and canon law, Church history and Theology. These sciences are taught in the house by some of the ablest men in Rome.'⁷ Most of the students at the Accademia were destined for the priesthood, which probably explained why Throckmorton was not sent there. Oscott remained the favoured place for the education of the male Throckmortons until the middle of the century, for Robert Throckmorton sent his sons Courtenay (1831–53), Herbert (1843–1871) and John (1840–1918) to be educated there. Even after Emancipation, Catholics were not permitted to matriculate at the ancient universities of Oxford and Cambridge without renouncing their faith, but by the 1840s Oscott and other Catholic colleges were able to enrol their students for external degrees of the University of London. The first Throckmorton to matriculate in the nineteenth century was John Throckmorton in 1857. By the late 1840s Downside replaced Oscott as the favoured educational establishment, and the future Throckmorton baronet brothers William (1838–1919) and Richard (1839–1927) were educated there.

For many years the Coughton estate had been neglected in favour of Buckland in Berkshire, but Sir John had opened up the courtyard and built the saloon at the turn of the nineteenth century, which doubled up as a chapel until the building of the Catholic Church at Coughton in 1853. Sir Charles decided to make Coughton his home and handed over Buckland to his nephew and heir, Robert Throckmorton. Both men loved Buckland. Six years after moving to Coughton, Sir Charles confessed to his nephew after a visit to Buckland House that he was still deeply attached to it: 'indeed', he wrote, I never saw it look in greater beauty'.⁸ Charles Throckmorton took pride in the grounds of both these houses and kept a record of the planting undertaken at Buckland and at Coughton by his brothers and himself.⁹ On 9 May 1827, the new baronet left Buckland for Coughton. Arriving at Alcester he was met by a large group of tenants and many of the tradesmen 'with white scarves and decorated with laurel leaves and all mounted on horseback'. They led the new baronet to his seat, where 'over the 1ˢᵗ gate entering, the lawn was inscribed: "may happiness enter with you" and over the tower the motto: "long live Sir Charles".' At

---

⁶ Birmingham City Archives, MS 3101/CD/10/63/16.

⁷ J.P. Chinnici, 'Berington, Joseph (1743–1827)', *ODNB*; Birmingham Archdiocesan Archives, Z5/3/12/6/1.

⁸ WRO, CR 1998/CD/Folder 11/6.

⁹ WRO, CR 1998/CD/Drawer 8/9.

dinner that evening '2 baskets of flowers were served up at dessert with the inscription: "these flowers will fade, not so our gratitude. May your years pass pleasant as the fragrance of these flowers".'[10] Sir Charles's diary for the early months of 1827 is filled with details of improvements being made to the house, from the installation of new fire grates and chimney pieces to the purchase of 'new feather beds and mattresses'. In March he noted that he had been busy planting new shrubs and the following year ordered the construction of a new gateway. Throckmorton then turned his attention to the parish church. It was to be 20 years before a Catholic church was erected on the estate, but Sir Charles took seriously his responsibility to maintain the Anglican church built by his forebears and on 1 May 1828 he proudly declared that he had 'cleaned the monuments in the church, painted the communion rails and rubbed the pews with linseed oil'.[11] Sir Robert also made improvements to both Coughton and Buckland, putting up new buildings in Buckland village and, in February 1845, giving orders for a new arched entrance behind the house at Coughton. Sir Charles preserved much of the furniture, portraits and family heirlooms from Weston Underwood, notably the heraldic stained glass, which he had installed in the Drawing Room at Coughton. Meanwhile, Sir Robert's wife, the former Elizabeth Acton, was responsible, together with her mother, for what is now considered to be 'among the most complete collections of nineteenth century heraldic needlework in England'.[12] Preserving the family heritage meant a great deal to Sir Robert, who announced in his diary for 28 September 1858 that he had 'found an altar stone at the back of the drawing room', which he planned to install in the newly built Catholic church which replaced the chapel in the house.[13]

Both the seventh and eighth baronets are remembered as benevolent landlords. 'Too much praise and commendation', noted an obituarist, 'cannot be given to Sir Charles Throckmorton as a landlord', for 'never had a tenant to complain of anything like harsh or rigorous exactment'. If a tenant was ever down on his luck, 'he experienced at the hand of his landlord the extremity of indulgence'.[14] In January 1827 Sir Charles 'dined with the tenants, including those who paid tithes'. On 'Rent Day' in July 1827 he 'dined with the tenants in the great dining room' at Coughton, and as a special concession 'smoking was allowed in the servants' hall'.[15] In honour of the coronation of Queen Victoria on 28 June 1838, the

---

[10] Ibid.
[11] Ibid.
[12] John M. Robinson, *Heraldry at Coughton Court* (Coughton, 1996), p. 3.
[13] WRO, CR 1998/CD/Drawer 5/9.
[14] *Gentleman's Magazine*, 15 (May 1841), p. 201.
[15] Ibid., p. 201; WRO, CR 1998/CD/Drawer 8/7.

baronet ordered 'medals to be struck at Birmingham' for the children of his servants and tenants, and he hosted a tea party for them at which each child was given an orange. In his will, the baronet left 'a sum of stock sufficient to produce £10 stock yearly in trust, that the vicar and Catholic priest' of Coughton 'should apply the said sum for relief of the poor'.[16] This provision reflected the influential role played by Sir Charles as a member of the parish vestry and therefore an overseer of poor relief, as well as the potential for cooperative action by Anglican and Catholic clergy becoming possible in the nineteenth century. After the death of Sir Robert Throckmorton, the *Faringdon Advertiser* observed that 'in the dispensing of his Charities, he was bountiful impartial and unprejudiced' and that one of his last acts was 'to gather round him in the Park all the children of Buckland village at School Feast, to the number of 140 ... for whose wants and amusements he plentifully provided'.[17]

A recurring Throckmorton family trait in this period is an interest in horticulture and agriculture. During his imprisonment at Verdun in 1805, Sir Charles Throckmorton keenly observed the plants and vegetation around him and noted the technical names for them. He was a keen collector of botanical specimens, many of which he donated in 1836 to the museum attached to the Birmingham Medical School. His flowers and vegetables grown on the Buckland and Coughton estates won many prizes.[18] Agriculture remained a great interest: Sir Charles was a founder of the Warwickshire Agricultural Society on 4 February 1831. He had already demonstrated an interest in new farming experiments. *The Farmers Register* reported: 'During the dry summer of 1826, 34 acres of a siliceous sandy soil on the estate of Sir Charles Throckmorton at Buckland, half of which had been manured with farmyard manure and the remainder with bones' was sown with turnips and 'the portion on which the bones were laid presented a remarkably fine crop, while the part that had been dunged was merely getting into leaf.'[19] His nephew and heir was also involved in agricultural innovation. On 17 August 1853, Sir Robert noted in his diary that he had been 'to see a trial of a reaping machine' at Pusey near Buckland. The following year, on 28 March 1854, he reported: 'I went to Buckland to see the steam engine on my farm start. It works well but the threshing machine is not a good one.' In April 1860 he noted that 'the steam plough seemed to work most admirably'.[20]

---

[16] *VCH Warwickshire*, vol. 3, p. 86.

[17] *Faringdon Advertiser*, 5 July 1862.

[18] *The British and Foreign Medical Review* (1836), p. 207; *The Gardener's Magazine* (May 1832), p. 121; *The Gardener's Magazine and Register of Rural and Domestic Improvement* (1830), p. 518

[19] *The Farmers Register* (1837), p. 322.

[20] WRO, CR 1998/CD/Drawer 5/10.

Sir John's interest in his sheep at Buckland had brought him national notoriety when he made the wager that produced the manufacture of the famous 'Throckmorton coat', which is still displayed at Coughton.[21] His brother, Sir Charles, brought the Buckland sheep to Coughton, and Throckmorton sheep were regular prize-winners at agricultural shows during the century. In 1861, Sir Robert Throckmorton was awarded the first prize of eight sovereigns at the Bath and West of England Society meeting held that year at Truro, and it was noted that his sheep were 'all quality and breeding, the very model of the South Down sheep not now often seen'.[22] These rustic pursuits must have provided a gentle background to other more serious issues which faced the Throckmorton family in the first half of the nineteenth century, beginning with the granting of Catholic Emancipation in 1829.

Sir George's ill-health meant that it was his younger brother Charles who carried on the family involvement in the campaign for Catholic Emancipation in which Sir John had been so deeply involved. During the early 1820s, the prospects of this cause had progressively declined, but by 1824 the newly founded Catholic Association, under the Irish nationalist leader Daniel O'Connell (1775–1847), gave new impetus to the issue. In February 1824 a motion was introduced in the Commons by the radical politician Sir Francis Burdett (1770–1844) to consider the Catholic claims, and although the motion and a subsequent Relief Bill were passed by the Commons, the bill was rejected by the Lords. Various petitions, both supporting and opposing the legislation were presented to parliament in the early part of 1825.[23] Although he proudly declared in his diary that he had signed a petition in favour of Emancipation in February, Charles Throckmorton clearly had little faith in the outcome, for he noted in his diary on 30 May: 'Betted yesterday with Dr Fletcher one guinea that the Catholic Emancipation would not take place in my lifetime.' Despite this fatalism, he expressed his admiration for Daniel O'Connell, who 'spoke for three hours without tiring his hearers'.[24] When the legislation was passed four years later, in March 1829, Throckmorton announced the news in his diary in one brief sentence: 'News arrived that the Catholic question was carried in the House of Commons by a majority of 188.'[25] If Sir Charles lacked enthusiasm for the cause, prominent Cisalpines such as Charles Butler (1750–1832) believed that Sir John's spirit lived on in his nephew, the young

---

[21] See Geoffrey Scott's chapter in this volume.

[22] *The British Farmer's Magazine* (1861), pp. 41, 45.

[23] Philip Hughes, *The Catholic Question 1688–1829: A Study in Political History* (London, 1929), pp. 252–316; G.I.T. Machin, *The Catholic Question in English Politics, 1820 to 1830* (Oxford, 1964), pp. 42–64.

[24] WRO, CR 1998/CD/Drawer 8, no. 7.

[25] WRO, CR 1998/CD/Drawer 8, no. 8.

Figure 9.1   Sir Robert George Throckmorton, eighth baronet (1800–62), Coughton Court.

Robert George Throckmorton, who would be the first Throckmorton to serve in parliament since the sixteenth century (Figure 9.1).[26]

The granting of Catholic Emancipation paved the way for what some historians have termed 'the constitutional revolution', and a decade of parliamentary and social reforms.[27] At the same time, the fall of King Charles X in France caused considerable excitement and brought a revival of interest in England in parliamentary reform. The Reform Bill introduced by Lord John Russell in March 1831 was intended to remove from the electoral system the defects and abuses of which the British public most loudly complained, but its passing by a slim majority of one vote in the Commons was enough to justify the dissolution of parliament and the calling of a general election, which was to be fought on the issue of reform.

Robert George Throckmorton was encouraged to stand as a parliamentary candidate for Berkshire (that then being the county in which Buckland House was situated) by Sir Francis Burdett and Lord Radnor, William Pleydell-Bouverie (1779–1869), a local landowner who had been an MP in the House of Commons for over 20 years. On going to the Lords Radnor devoted his time to issues of the day such as civil rights for dissenters and parliamentary reform. The file of correspondence from Lord Radnor to Robert Throckmorton over 25 years reflects a shared interest in parliamentary reform (and in agricultural experimentation) which transcended their different religious standpoints. Radnor's Anglican Evangelicalism led him to declare the Corn Laws unchristian. He was an astute politician whose radicalism 'was unusual among the great landed magnates of his era' and although he was 'friendly with many whigs', he apparently 'distrusted all who sought power'. Nevertheless, Radnor persuaded influential figures in the local political scene to rally behind Throckmorton, notably John Berkeley Monck (1769–1834), who had been MP for the Borough of Reading from 1820 to 1830 and was very prominent in the local agitation for parliamentary reform.[28] Monck wrote to Radnor a month before the election: 'the cause of reform, to be successful, ought to be fought in the person of Mr. Throckmorton – he has

---

[26] WRO, CR 1998/CD/Drawer 1/Folder 5.

[27] According to J.C.D. Clark, *English Society, 1688–1832* (Cambridge, 1985), p. 412, the effect of the granting of Catholic Emancipation was to open 'the floodgates to a deluge of Whig-radical reform aimed against the characteristic institutions of the ancient regime' during the 1830s, which, apart from targeting the universities, the armed forces and colonial administration, also attacked the Church and thus signalled the break-up of the English confessional state.

[28] Ellis Archer Wasson, 'Bouverie, William Pleydell-, third earl of Radnor (1779–1869), *ODNB*.

everything to recommend him, family, property, a good name, and good principles. I have persuaded my friends here to think so too.'[29]

Although local powerbrokers could not control a county the size of Berkshire in the way they could a pocket borough, titled landowners still exercised considerable influence over deferential county voters. In the early nineteenth century, Lord Craven and Lord Braybrooke were considered the 'patrons' of the Berkshire constituency and could usually persuade the voters to support their favoured candidates. Before the Reform Act it was usual for voters to expect the candidates for whom they voted to meet their expenses in travelling to the poll, and to provide food, liquor and lodgings when they arrived, making the cost of a contested election in some counties prohibitive, though this was less of a factor in a comparatively small county like Berkshire. Since 1794 the county had repeatedly elected Charles Dundas (1751–1832), Baron Amesbury, who, according to a biographer, 'reserved his energy for measures useful to a county: to regulate the sale of corn by weight, to promote planting of potatoes on common land ... and to encourage inland navigation'.[30]

Throckmorton was not the first Catholic MP of modern times (an honour belonging to the Irishman Daniel O'Connell), but he was the first to sit for an English seat, and the first to take the Oath of Allegiance.[31] His election thus represented a momentous symbolic moment in the history of English Catholicism. He entered parliament at a time of crucial political change. The Whigs won a majority of 136 over the Tories, which allowed the passage of the Reform Bill the following year. In the Berkshire election, Throckmorton was supported by John Walter (1776–1847), who lived on the Bearwood estate on the outskirts of Reading. Walter was an influential national figure as owner and editor of *The Times*. He declared that by electing Throckmorton the Berkshire electors would 'show respect and gratitude to the memory of Sir John Throckmorton', and that such an election would be 'the reward long due to the Uncle bestowed upon the nephew'. A Mr Bowles declared at the election meeting that 'Mr Throckmorton is descended from an ancient family ... heir to the virtues of his late uncle which consisted in a love of constitutional freedom and a hatred of all tyranny and oppression.' Although remarking that Throckmorton 'had been lately emancipated from the galling fetters of exclusion', Bowles implied that he was supporting him because Throckmorton was seen to be more of a Whig than a Catholic. Thus, he was 'the friend of an effectual and efficient reform' and his Catholicism was 'not a ground of objection'. In

---

[29] WRO, CR 1998/CD/Drawer 1/Folder 10.

[30] Michael Fry, 'Dundas, Charles, Baron Amesbury (1751–1832)', *ODNB*.

[31] Many Irish MPs elected refused to take the oath and so were not able to take their seats.

his speech to the electors, Throckmorton declared his support for the bill, a 'sweeping measure ... which would sweep away bribery and corruption and ... evils which had so long bowed this suffering country almost to the ground'; for he believed that 'until representation was substituted for nomination, the business of the state could never be properly conducted'. He condemned the 'inefficiency in the conduct of the public business', for 'appointments had been obtained not by merit but by interest'. Going on to criticise the way the country had been governed over the past fifty years, Throckmorton blamed the system of government for 'their weight of debt, their pension-list, and the number of sinecure, useless or extravagantly-paid places', arguing that 'such things would never have occurred if the people had been fairly represented in Parliament'. He promised that if elected, 'the welfare of the people' would be 'the point to which all his exertions would be directed'. He was duly elected, unopposed.[32]

Throckmorton was one of the youngest of the nine Catholics in the Commons in 1831, but all the others represented Irish constituencies. He was to be in parliament for only three-and-a-half years, but what momentous years these proved to be. He presented a petition to the Commons on 20 July 1831, 'praying that the Elective Franchise may be extended to all occupiers of land'.[33] A month later, on 12 August 1831 in the debate on the Reform Bill, he echoed his Berkshire election speech, contesting the attempt of some MPs to 'increase the Representation of their own counties at the expense of their friends'. However, he supported the proposal to grant his own county of Berkshire an extra member, for its 'wealth, population and agricultural importance well entitled it to additional Representative'.[34]

Following the passage of the 1832 Reform Act and related legislation to reform the electoral system, parliament was dissolved on 3 December 1832. Throckmorton was returned to parliament in the subsequent general election, winning 2,774 votes. In the parliament which followed, Throckmorton's name is listed among the 'ayes' in the voting on issues such as the abolition of slavery and military flogging. In his only other speech, on 8 May 1834, he spoke in support of the Enclosure Bill relating to Bucklebury in the county of Berkshire. The local people vigorously contested the bill, believing that it would threaten their rights to collect firewood and graze their animals. In the event the bill was thrown out by 38 noes to 6 ayes.[35] By the summer of 1834, the Whig government had become a focus of disappointment for those who had elected it: too

---

[32] *Berkshire Chronicle and Bucks and Windsor Herald* (14 May 1831), p. 2.
[33] *Hansard's Parliamentary Debates*, Third Series, (London, 1831), vol. 5, p. 80.
[34] Ibid., p. 1325.
[35] *Hansard* (1834), vol. 23, p. 752.

radical for some and not radical enough for others. There were divisions in parliament over Irish Church reform, and an agricultural depression in the country severely dented the popularity of the Whigs among the farming lobby. Lord Grey, the prime minister, resigned in July, and the failure of the king to secure a coalition between Sir Robert Peel and Lords Melbourne and Wellington led to the dissolution of parliament in December and a general election.[36] It was at this point that Robert Throckmorton evidently decided not to stand again as a member for Berkshire. In the subsequent election his seat was taken by Philip Pusey, a neighbourhood friend at Buckland, who had stood for the Tories but been defeated by Throckmorton at the 1832 election. 'I assure you it is with sincere regret,' wrote Pusey, 'that I write to you ... however we may have formerly differed in politics, I always retained the hope that we might become colleagues.' However, Pusey was relieved that when Throckmorton 'decided to retire, I was out of the field as your competitor'. Although Pusey had 'surrendered ... all thoughts of sitting for Berkshire in the new parliament', his 'friends have now been good enough to bring me forward'.[37] Although Throckmorton retired from national politics, he was elected High Sheriff of Berkshire in 1843. He continued to use his influence and political experience until just before his death in June 1862, when he joined 'a deputation to the Home Office to present a memorial concerning the regulation and purification of the waters of the Thames'.[38]

Events in parliament between 1829 and 1834 transformed the political and social status of the Throckmortons, who were now thrust once again into national prominence, and offered them the opportunity to further interests in social issues and social reforms. Both Charles and Robert Throckmorton did much to follow through the reforms enacted by parliamentary legislation. Robert Throckmorton had helped to produce the 1834 Poor Law Amendment Act, which called for parishes to be put into unions so that relief could be provided more easily, principally through the establishment of workhouses. By the early 1830s, Sir Charles had become a benefactor of the Worcester Infirmary and of the Birmingham School of Medicine and Surgery, where he was appointed a governor. He was also a founder member of the Provincial Medical and Surgical Association (later changing its name to the British Medical Association), which played an important part in agitation for medical and social reform in parliament. Throckmorton was a friend and associate of the founder of the association,

---

[36] Norman Gash, *Aristocracy and People: Britain 1815–65* (London, 1979), pp. 159–64.

[37] WRO, CR 1998/CD/Drawer 1/Folder 20/29. See also *Gentleman's Magazine*, 9 (1835), 319.

[38] *Medical Times and Gazette* (7 June 1862), p. 604.

Sir Charles Hastings (1794–1866). Both men were also founder members of the Worcester Natural History Society, and Throckmorton made a number of donations of books, specimens and stuffed animals to each of these societies. On 23 July 1835, Sir Charles noted in his diary that the day before he had been present at a lecture in Oxford given by the renowned geologist William Buckland (1784–1856). The minutes of a meeting of the new Provincial Medical and Surgical Association held that afternoon record the presence of Throckmorton, describing him as 'the father of the profession'.[39] In 1837, Throckmorton provided the stone for the new Alcester workhouse and until his death, three years later, he chaired the meetings of the guardians who supervised the workhouse. His nephew and heir continued the association with the Alcester workhouse and became closely involved also in the building of the new workhouse at Faringdon, near Buckland. One of the last reforms enacted in the decade of reform was the establishment of county police forces in 1839; but it was 1856 before a constabulary was established in Berkshire and in that year Sir Robert Throckmorton took his seat on the county Police Committee.[40] He also continued his uncle's medical involvement by becoming a vice-patron of the Queen's Hospital, Birmingham.

Although the social and political standing of the Throckmortons was enhanced in this period, their status and influence in the English Catholic Church lessened – a reflection of shifting alignments of power within that Church.[41] Until the middle of the nineteenth century, the family had played a leading role in English Catholic affairs through their involvement in bodies such as the Catholic Board. Although Charles and Robert Throckmorton continued to espouse Sir John Throckmorton's Cisalpinist principles, by 1850 the English Catholic ecclesiastical climate had changed and Cisalpinism was effectively dead, as the leadership of the English Catholic community shifted from the laity to the clergy. The shift was most powerfully expressed in the 1850 restoration of the English Catholic hierarchy, which strengthened the authority of the bishops and put an end to the untidy map of ecclesiastical anomalies that had hitherto characterised the Catholic Church in England, anomalies which to a large extent had been exploited by both the Catholic gentry and the regular clergy by establishing their own spheres of influence. John Bossy has argued that English Catholic clergy also shared in the revival of strength and self-confidence that has been detected in other churchmen in the mid-

---

[39] W.H. McMenemey, *The Life and Times of Sir Charles Hastings, Founder of the British Medical Association* (London, 1959), p. 123.
[40] Berkshire Record Office, Q/AC/1, Minutes of the Police Committee, 1856–63.
[41] John Bossy, *The English Catholic Community, 1570–1850* (London, 1975), pp. 323–37.

nineteenth century, a self-confidence that was gained both through seizing the opportunities for leadership that came their way 'by demographic growth, migration and social transformation and by the freedom from external restraint' secured by the Catholic Relief Act of 1791. 'A growing separation from and independence of the laity through the widening range of social functions which fell to them in the age of improvement' accompanied this revival in self-confidence.[42] Whilst the Cisalpinists resisted the influence of papal authority over the English Church, the new breed of English Catholic cleric looked *ultra montes*, across the mountains of the Alps, to take their cue from Rome. However, for a time the aspirations of English Cisalpinists were assisted by Robert Throckmorton's brother-in-law, Charles Januarius Acton (1803–47), who was created a cardinal in 1842. Acton had the ear of Pope Gregory XVI and succeeded in opposing any plans for a restoration of the English hierarchy, for he believed that the English 'throughout their history had been factious, and opposed to authority, and were not to be entrusted with more and more independent power'.[43] Yet by 1847, Acton was dead and a new Pope, Pius IX, encouraged the ultramontane vision of Nicholas Wiseman, whom he created Archbishop of Westminster in September 1850.

A decline in Throckmorton influence in English Catholic affairs was not immediately noticeable until 1855, when the conflicting interests of the family and those of their new local bishop in Birmingham, William Bernard Ullathorne (1806–89) suddenly collided.[44] The dispute centred on the mission at Harvington, which covered a vast area of Worcestershire, and by the early nineteenth century included the rapidly expanding industrial centre of Kidderminster. In 1831, Ullathorne's predecessor as Vicar Apostolic, Thomas Walsh, established a separate mission there, despite the fact that a church at Harvington had been built only six years before by Sir George Throckmorton, principally to accommodate the Kidderminster Catholics.[45] John Brownlow (1795–1875), the chaplain at Harvington, was aggrieved that the foundation of the new mission significantly reduced his congregation, but Robert Throckmorton was more concerned that Bishop Walsh had diverted funds left by the widow of the third Throckmorton baronet, Lady Mary Yate, for the support of the priest at Harvington towards the support of the priest at the new mission

---

[42] Ibid., p. 355.

[43] Nicholas Schofield and Gerard Skinner, *The English Cardinals* (Oxford, 2007), p. 141.

[44] Judith Champ, *William Bernard Ullathorne 1806–1889: A Different Kind of Monk* (Leominster, 2006).

[45] Michael Hodgetts, 'The Throckmortons of Harvington, 1696–1923', *Recusant History*, 26 (2002), 156.

at Kidderminster, and he wrote to Ullathorne to protest. Ullathorne – who famously responded to John Henry Newman's discourse on the need for an educated laity in the Church by asking 'Who are the laity?' – replied to Throckmorton asserting the authority of the bishop to act as he chose, and quoting ecclesiastical laws 'upon which [he had] always acted most vigorously'.[46] Throckmorton replied, declaring angrily that 'my family have been very ill used in this matter', but nonetheless undertook to make up the deficit of Brownlow's income as a result of the diversion of funds. The incident clearly illustrated the increased authority of the bishops and the lessening of the influence of the Catholic gentry.[47] The controversy over Harvington provides a sharp contrast to the foundation a decade earlier of a new mission at Kemerton near Tewkesbury, where the Eyston and Throckmorton families ensured by a trust deed that the property would be conveyed to the Benedictines and not to the local Vicar Apostolic.[48]

Although Robert Throckmorton's relationship with Ullathorne seems to have been strained, he enjoyed an easier relationship with Thomas Grant (1816–70), the first Bishop of Southwark, whom Throckmorton had got to know when Grant had been secretary to Throckmorton's brother-in-law, Cardinal Charles Acton.[49] Although Grant had been one of the architects of the newly restored English Catholic hierarchy, once installed at Southwark, across the Thames from Wiseman's Westminster, he clashed with the cardinal over the latter's refusal to allocate to Grant's diocese a proportion of the funds of the old London district. The already tense situation was made worse by Wiseman's resentment that Grant took upon himself the role of 'the quiet negotiator' between the Catholic Church and the British government, concerning the provision of Catholic chaplains and Catholic education in prisons, the forces and the workhouses. Grant was instrumental in persuading the government in 1859 to allow Catholic education in the workhouses, and he wrote to Throckmorton to enlist his financial support, insisting 'what sad mischief comes' from places 'into which our children are thrown with non-Catholic children'. Grant was also supportive of the introduction of new Reformatory schools, and probably encouraged Sir Robert Throckmorton to chair the committee

---

[46] In reply to Ullathorne's question 'Who are the laity?', Newman quietly remarked that 'the Church would look foolish without them': *The Letters and Diaries of John Henry Newman*, ed. Charles S. Dessain et al. (31 vols, Oxford, 1961–84), vol. 19, p. 141.

[47] David A. Higham, *The Priests and People of Harvington* (Leominster, 2006); Birmingham Archdiocesan Archives, B3326, B3351, B3553.

[48] C. Collins, *St Benet's Church, Kemerton: A History, 1843–2006* (Bredon, 2006), p. 18.

[49] It is perhaps significant that it was Bishop Grant rather than Ullathorne, the local bishop, who was invited to preside at the funeral of Sir Robert Throckmorton at Coughton in the summer of 1862.

set up to establish such a school at the Cistercian abbey of Mount Saint Bernard in Leicestershire.[50]

In the sphere of domestic religion, the Throckmortons maintained chaplains at Buckland, Coughton and Harvington Hall for most of the nineteenth century. At Buckland and Harvington, the chaplains tended to be secular clergy, but the chaplain at Coughton was always Benedictine. The celebrated Cisalpine writer Joseph Berington (1743–1827) was appointed chaplain at Buckland by Sir John Courtenay Throckmorton. Berington's 'exceedingly mild and insinuating manners were such that … there was scarcely a communicant left in the parish church of Buckland, nor standing room in the Catholic chapel'. It was Berington who nurtured the spiritual growth of the young Robert Throckmorton, not only tutoring him but also introducing him to his non-Catholic friends, notably the Galtons, a Birmingham Quaker banking family who lived near Oscott College. Berington has also been credited with forming the Catholic sympathies of a Throckmorton neighbour at Buckland, Edward Bouverie Pusey (1800–82), who went on to be Professor of Hebrew at Oxford and to give his name to a Catholic revival movement within the Church of England. Despite their different sympathies (Edward Pusey's brother Philip stood as a Tory candidate in the 1832 election against Robert Throckmorton), there were strong social ties between the Throckmortons and the Puseys and in his diary Robert Throckmorton notes that in June 1856 he and his daughter 'dined at Dr Pusey's at Christ Church'.[51] Both Sir Charles and Sir Robert fostered close relationships with Anglican clergy, and their diaries often mention that local Anglican bishops were invited to dine at Coughton and Buckland. Nevertheless, the Throckmorton allegiance to the Catholic faith remained strong and often inspired their servants and tenants. Tucked away in their small rural enclaves, the Throckmortons continued to act and be respected as Catholic feudal lords of the manor. Their tenants and servants 'all attended the church services and scrupulously kept all the church's feasts' and, according to an undated newspaper cutting preserved in the family papers, 'at Buckland the tenants and their families continue to this day to divide the churchyard in every case of interment, so that the Protestants all lie on one side and the Catholics on the other'.[52]

The family seem to have had enjoyed a close, almost familial relationship with their priests. The diaries of both Sir Charles and Sir Robert indicate that it was usual for the chaplain to dine and recreate with the family on most evenings. Alexius Pope (1795–1841) was the Benedictine chaplain to

---

[50] Michael Clifton, *The Quiet Negotiator: Bishop Grant, Bishop of Southwark* (Formby, nd), pp. 130–41; WRO, CR 1998/CD/Drawer 2/Folder 39.

[51] WRO, CR 1998/CD/Drawer 5/9; WRO, CR 1998/Box 86/24a.

[52] WRO, CR 1998/Box 86a.

the family from 1823 to 1834 and 'was noted for his great musical talents which he cultivated with unsparing attention and devotion and his society was much courted at Coughton ... being of a lively and jovial disposition'. On 29 September 1827, Sir Charles wrote in his diary that 'Mr Bevington the Organ builder had arrived from London and the organ was installed by 8am.' On 13 November, 'Mr Pope came in the evening and played on the organ.' Pope was still entertaining the Throckmortons and their guests seven years later, even after moving to the nearby mission of Redditch. On 5 August 1834, Sir Charles took his guests to visit Pope, who 'touched the organ and showed its merits with great success. The ladies were in raptures.'[53] The lifestyle of a Benedictine chaplain was very different from the ordered life in the monasteries, and monastic superiors were concerned enough about the potential for scandal to remind their men on the mission 'to say Mass daily and go to Confession weekly', and urging them 'not to be present at races nor to play for great sums at Cards'.[54] Yet such strictures were not needed in the case of Pope's successor as chaplain at Coughton, Francis Davis (1805–89), who stayed for over half a century. Davis was evidently a shy and retiring individual who 'rose at half-past four and paid a visit to the Blessed Sacrament as soon as he came down stairs; then he sat in the vestry saying his prayers, making his meditation, &c, always allowing an hour's preparation for Mass, which he never failed to say'.[55]

In other Catholic houses, the relationship between the family and the chaplain was not always so harmonious. Ambrose Prest, monk of Ampleforth, was appointed chaplain to the Middleton family at Stockeld Park near Wetherby, Yorkshire in 1844. Writing to a confrère, he complained of the squire's interference in pastoral matters: 'The Squire calls from time to time on poor people and induces them to say that they wish to become Catholics ... even when the priest is sent for by poor creatures, he is wanted as the Squire's chaplain and not as God's minister.' The priest also clashed with the lady of the house, who complained that he did not take interest in the family and who, the priest determined, 'shall not wear the priest's cassock'.[56]

At Aldenham, the home of the Actons, Robert Throckmorton's nephew – the young Lord Acton, the future Cambridge historian – complained to the Bishop of Shrewsbury about the chaplain, the Rev. John Morris and 'the

---

[53] Athanasius Allanson, *Biographies of the English Benedictines* (Ampleforth, 1999) p. 362; WRO, CR 1998/Drawer 8/9.
[54] Ampleforth Abbey, Allanson MS, 'History of the English Benedictines', vol. 3, p. 300.
[55] J.A. Morrall, 'The Davis Memorial', *Downside Review*, 11 (1891), 126.
[56] Ampleforth Abbey Archives, MS 243, nos 18 and 18a.

openness and coarseness with which things hardly ever alluded to among Christians were constantly discussed in his sermons'. According to Acton, the priest 'not only awakened the curiosity of young people, and tore away the veil from their imagination but habituated all the congregation to hear the most sacred things, and Our Lady in particular, associated with ideas hardly ever expressed out of a medical school'.[57]

In contrast, the relationship between the Throckmorton family and their chaplains appears to have been marked by a tolerant attitude to clerical shortcomings and weaknesses. Writing to his uncle, Sir Charles, on 24 April 1829, Robert Throckmorton observed of Alexius Pope, 'our good padre is rather complaining'.[58] The apparent ease with which the Throckmortons related to their chaplains can also be contrasted with the tense relationship between Lord Shrewsbury and his chaplain, the ecclesiologist and antiquarian Daniel Rock (1799–1871), whom Shrewsbury recommended to Sir Robert Throckmorton as the new chaplain to Buckland.[59] Writing to Pugin the architect in March 1840 Shrewsbury fulminated:

> I fear it is all up with poor Dr Rock. I wrote him what I thought a very temperate and just reproof ... He tells me my letter was unkind and unjust ... having totally disqualified himself from acting in the Capacity of my domestic chaplain, there is no alternative but to part ... He has some good qualities but a very weak mind ... it will be a great relief to us all to be quit of him for he has long made himself very disagreeable.

However, in his letter of recommendation to Throckmorton a few months later, Shrewsbury adopted quite a different tone: 'Dr Rock would suit you very well,' he enthused. 'He is an excellent creature, a very amiable disposition, a general favourite in society.'[60] Rock often appears as a dining companion in Throckmorton's diary, and in the fourteen years he served as chaplain at Buckland there is no evidence of a conflict between the baronet and the priest.

The expansion of the Catholic community in England by the mid-century was evident in the rural as well as the urban areas. At Coughton itself, the annual number of baptisms had more than doubled from 12 in

---

[57] David Mathew, *Lord Acton and his Times* (London, 1968), p. 70.

[58] WRO, CR 1998/CD/Drawer 1/Folder 16.

[59] Judith Champ, 'Goths and Romans: Daniel Rock, Augustus Welby Pugin and Nineteenth-century English Worship', in R.N. Swanson (ed.), *Continuity and Change in Christian Worship*, Studies in Church History, 35 (Bury St Edmunds, 1999), pp. 289–319; Michael Clifton, 'Rock, Daniel (1799–1871)', *ODNB*.

[60] *The Collected Letters of A.W.N. Pugin*, ed. Margaret Belcher (5 vols, Oxford, 2000) vol. 1, p. 167; WRO, CR 1998/CD/Drawer 1/Folder 12.

1795 to 33 in 1831.⁶¹ On Christmas Day 1826, Sir Charles Throckmorton noted in his diary that 'the chapel was insupportably crowded and hot', but it was another 30 years before a new church was built at Coughton.

By the 1840s, the dominant figure on the landscape of English ecclesiastical architecture in England was unquestionably that of Augustus Welby Northmore Pugin (1812–52). Pugin represented the new generation of English 'Romantic' Catholics, usually converts, who were not popular with those, like the Throckmortons, who had been Catholic for generations. The long-established Catholic families tended to resent this new, brash generation, 'who criticised their chapels and altered their practices, many of which had grown into their own local and rather low-church forms over the centuries that England had been a mission from Rome'.⁶² It was hardly surprising, then, that Sir Charles Throckmorton declared that nothing Pugin made 'would ever enter his house', and that the only subscription he would make for Pugin's cathedral in Birmingham 'would be a barrel full of powder to blow it up'. By a twist of irony, it was Pugin who was commissioned to create the late baronet's memorial brass.⁶³ His nephew Robert, however, admired Pugin's 'very pretty chapel' at Warwick Bridge near Carlisle, but although he engaged Pugin to execute his uncle's memorial brass, he turned to another prominent English Catholic architect of the day, Charles Hansom (1817–88), to build new churches at Buckland, Coughton and Studley.

Until 1848 Mass had been said in Buckland House. According to the 'specifications and conditions' drawn up by Hansom in 1847, the contract for the new building did not include the altars, reredos, pulpit, font, benches, screens, bell, glass for the east windows, the aumbry for the oils, brackets and statues, 'warming apparatus' and the sacristy furniture. The total cost of the finished church was £1,302 and 12 shillings. Sir Robert noted proudly in his diary for 30 April 1848: 'heard mass for first time in Buckland church'.⁶⁴ Throckmorton was theoretically only responsible for providing churches on his estates at Buckland and Coughton, but it was typical of his generosity that he also provided for the needs of the Catholics in Studley, adjacent to Coughton. In June 1851, the Catholics of Studley met in the Barley Mow Inn and 'unanimously resolved' that 'the grateful thanks of the meeting be given and presented' to Sir Robert Throckmorton 'for having generously purchased and piously given, a beautiful piece of land' for the building of a new church, as well as to 'the Trustees to a

---

⁶¹ Birmingham Archdiocesan Archives, P. 127/1/1.
⁶² Rosemary Hill, *God's Architect: Pugin and the Building of Romantic Britain* (London, 2007), p. 206.
⁶³ *Collected Letters of Pugin*, vol. 1, p. 390.
⁶⁴ WRO, CR 1998/LCB/81a; CR 1998/CD/Drawer 5/5.

Fund bequeathed by the late Lady Throckmorton, for having appropriated £1000 from the said Fund towards the intended New Church at Studley'. The foundation stone was laid by Bishop Ullathorne on 6 August 1851.[65] The baronet took special interest in the church at Coughton, and in June 1851 took his son Courtenay to help him select a site on the estate for the building. Work began not long afterwards and on 11 May 1852 Charles Hansom wrote excitedly to Sir Robert: 'I was at Coughton on Friday and was most agreeably surprised and delighted at the appearance of the work which is far beyond all my expectations.' The foundation stone was laid by Bishop Ullathorne in August 1853. The building was a larger and more elaborate edifice than the church at Buckland, and the final cost was £3,500. It is clear that Sir Robert intended the church to be a memorial to his late wife, and this is reflected in its dedication, to Saints Peter and Paul and Saint Elizabeth.[66] The Catholics of Coughton duly wrote to thank Sir Robert 'most gratefully for the New Church and Presbytery' which 'by your and your very kind family's means, has been erected' for their 'spiritual benefit' and the benefit of their 'respective and numerous families'.[67] The new church was built on the estate, in close proximity both to the house and to the Anglican parish church, which now became sandwiched uncomfortably between the two papist bastions of Coughton Court and Saints Peter, Paul and Elizabeth's.

The marriage of Robert Throckmorton and Elizabeth Acton (1806–50) on 16 July 1829 united two Catholic dynasties and underlined the Throckmortons' continuing connections in the nineteenth century with the wider European Catholic world. There is a hint, in a letter from Sir Charles Throckmorton to his nephew on 14 April to congratulate him on his engagement, that not all of the family were initially favourable to the match, but when the wedding came to be solemnised at Aldenham, the seat of the Actons, Sir Charles proudly recorded the events of the day in his diary. 'Breakfasted early,' he wrote, 'after which all attended at chapel where Miss Elizabeth Acton was married to my nephew, Robert, by Mr Charles Acton.' Then, as Catholic priests were not yet licensed by the state to register marriages, the wedding party 'drove down in four shut-up carriages and two open carriages to the Parish Church where Mr Hazelwood … the clergyman of the parish … performed the marriage ceremony with much dignity and propriety'. After the ceremony, 'all retired to the house and sat down to an elegant repast'. Not all the guests, it seemed, behaved in an elegant manner, for one of them reputedly drank no fewer than 23 glasses

---

[65] Coughton Court, Rumpus Room, Box 2, 4.
[66] Coughton Court, Rumpus Room, Box 4, E.
[67] Coughton Court, Rumpus Room, Book 4.

of champagne.[68] The Actons were a colourful, cosmopolitan family, with close connections to Neapolitan nobility as well as to European political figures. Elizabeth Acton's father, Sir John Francis Edward Acton (1736–1811), had been Prime Minister to King Ferdinand IV of Naples from 1780 to 1804, and his intimacy with the Neapolitan royal family sparked rumours that Acton had engaged in an affair with Queen Maria Carolina, the sister of the ill-fated Marie Antoinette of France. Elizabeth's mother, Mary Anne (1786–1873), known as 'Nonna', was aged only 14 when she married Sir John Acton. The fact that her husband was also her uncle, the brother of her father, Joseph Edward Acton (1737–1830), caused considerable scandal.[69] Nonna was to outlive both her daughter, and her son-in-law, dying at the age of 87 in 1873. She had been widowed young, in 1811, when Elizabeth was only five years old. Nonna also scandalised Catholic society when she arrived in London after her husband's death by taking a lover, by whom she had a son. Although she had inherited part of her husband's fortune, Nonna frequently struggled to rescue her legitimate son, the Cardinal, from impecunity. It is even said that she persuaded her daughter to sell some priceless Throckmorton jewellery, to the irritation of Robert Throckmorton, who was then obliged to replace his wife's prized pearls.[70] Nevertheless, marriage into the Acton family did give Throckmorton some useful political and social connections, notably to George Leveson-Gower, the second Earl Granville (1815–91), who was invited by Lord Palmerston in 1840 to become under-secretary at the Foreign Office. Granville married the widow of Elizabeth Acton's brother Richard, and his sister, the contemporary popular novelist Lady Georgiana Fullerton (1812–85), became a Catholic and corresponded with Robert Throckmorton, with whom she shared an interest in philanthropy. Throckmorton's nephew, John Emerich Edward Dalberg Acton (1834–1902), the future Cambridge Regius Professor of Modern History, seems to have relied on his uncle's support and advice in learning to run the family estate at Aldenham. Acton, who himself had been educated in Germany, was instrumental in encouraging Throckmorton to send one of his sons to study in Bonn in 1857.[71]

In other ways, too, both Charles and Robert Throckmorton kept up the family interests in continental Europe. Sir Charles's incarceration in France during the Napoleonic wars did not destroy his love for that country, and after the wars he returned to visit Paris. His nephew was a frequent visitor to

---

[68] Mark Bence-Jones, *The Catholic Families* (London, 1992), pp. 167–8.
[69] The marriage, with papal dispensation, was designed to retain wealth within the family: Stuart Reid, 'Acton, Sir John Francis Edward, sixth baronet (1736–1811)', *ODNB*.
[70] Roland Hill, *Lord Acton* (New Haven, 2000), pp. 287–8.
[71] WRO, CR 1998/CD/Drawer 1/Folder 13.

the continent and his diaries are filled with his travelogues and impressions of the places he visited: Rome and Naples several times, Switzerland in 1836, Bavaria and the Austrian Tyrol in 1841. The winter of 1849–50, spent on Madeira, was planned as a rest cure for his ailing wife, but in the event she died there in the spring of 1850. In 1854 Throckmorton visited Belgium, France and Holland. He was back in Rome and Naples in 1857 and journeyed on into Switzerland and Germany. He instilled a love for continental Europe into his children, several of whom became seasoned travellers. His son John spent some time in Hanover in 1862 and kept a diary of his stay there. His eldest daughter, Mary Elizabeth ('Minny', 1832–1919), became lady-in-waiting to the ill-fated Elizabeth, Empress of Austria (1837–98).

Sir Robert George Throckmorton died of a heart attack at his London home on 28 June 1862. Among the many tributes that were paid to him was a particularly sensitive and poignant one in the local Buckland newspaper, the *Faringdon Advertiser*. This mourned the passing 'of a true Old English Gentleman, and a bright example of a genuine Christian character'.[72] Both Charles and Robert Throckmorton had achieved much for their family and country by the mid-nineteenth century. Most importantly, they had demonstrated that the newly emancipated English Catholic gentry could be trusted and relied upon to make an effective contribution to a society that in many ways still remained suspicious of Catholics and Catholicism.[73] Their story also illustrates a distinct historical irony: just as the Catholic gentry became more integrated into and influential within mainstream English society, their leadership role within the Catholic community – a role they had long taken for granted – was entering a much more uncertain phase.

---

[72] *Faringdon Advertiser* (5 July 1862).
[73] Edward Norman, *Anti-Catholicism in Victorian England* (London, 1968).

APPENDIX: GENEALOGICAL TABLES

Tudor and Early Stuart Throckmortons

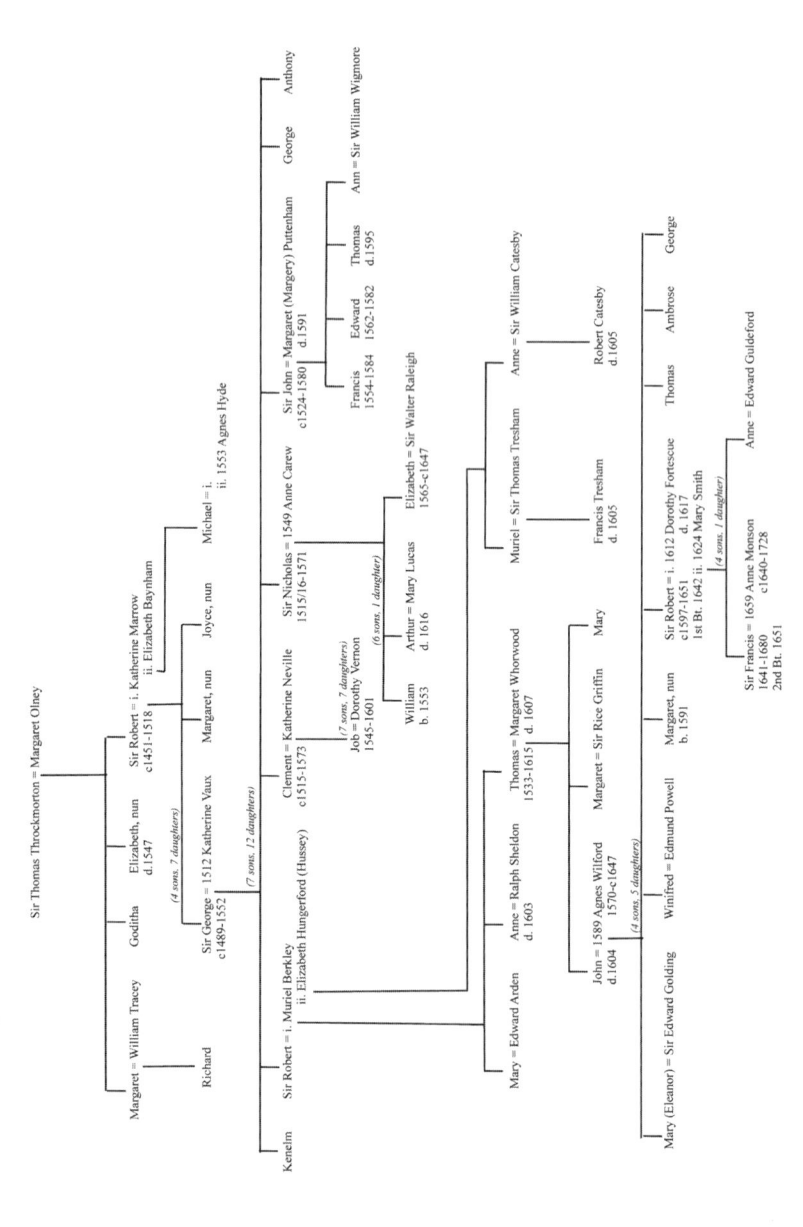

Sir Thomas Throckmorton = Margaret Olney

- Margaret = William Tracey
- Richard
- Goditha
- Sir George = 1512 Katherine Vaux
  c1489-1552
  (7 sons, 12 daughters)
- Elizabeth, nun
  d.1547
  (4 sons, 7 daughters)
- Sir Robert = i. Katherine Marrow
  c1451-1518   ii. Elizabeth Baynham
- Margaret, nun
- Joyce, nun
- Michael = i.
  ii. 1553 Agnes Hyde

Children of Sir George and Katherine Vaux

- Kenelm
- Sir Robert = i. Muriel Berkley
  ii. Elizabeth Hungerford (Hussey)
- Clement = Katherine Neville
  c1515-1573
  (7 sons, 7 daughters)
  Job = Dorothy Vernon
  1545-1601
- Sir Nicholas = 1549 Anne Carew
  1515/16-1571
  (6 sons, 1 daughter)
- Sir John = Margaret (Margery) Puttenham
  c1524-1580   d.1591
- George
- Anthony

Children of Clement and Katherine Neville
- William b. 1553
- Arthur = Mary Lucas
  d. 1616

Children of Sir Nicholas and Anne Carew
- Elizabeth = Sir Walter Raleigh
  1565-c1647
- Muriel = Sir Thomas Tresham
- Anne = Sir William Catesby

Children of Sir John and Margaret Puttenham
- Francis 1554-1584
- Edward 1562-1582
- Thomas d.1595
- Ann = Sir William Wigmore

Children of Sir Robert and Muriel Berkley / Elizabeth Hungerford
- Mary = Edward Arden
- Anne = Ralph Sheldon
  d. 1603
- Thomas = Margaret Whorwood
  1533-1615 d. 1607
- Margaret = Sir Rice Griffin
- Mary

Descendants
- John = 1589 Agnes Wilford
  d.1604   1570-c1647
  (4 sons, 5 daughters)
- Winifred = Edmund Powell
- Margaret, nun
  b. 1591
- Sir Robert = i. 1612 Dorothy Fortescue
  c1597-1651   d. 1617
  1st Bt. 1642 ii. 1624 Mary Smith
  (4 sons, 1 daughter)
- Francis Tresham
  d. 1605
- Robert Catesby
  d. 1605

- Mary (Eleanor) = Sir Edward Golding
- Sir Francis = 1659 Anne Monson
  1641-1680   c1640-1728
  2nd Bt. 1651
- Thomas
- Ambrose
- Anne = Edward Guideford
- George

Late Stuart and Hanoverian Throckmortons

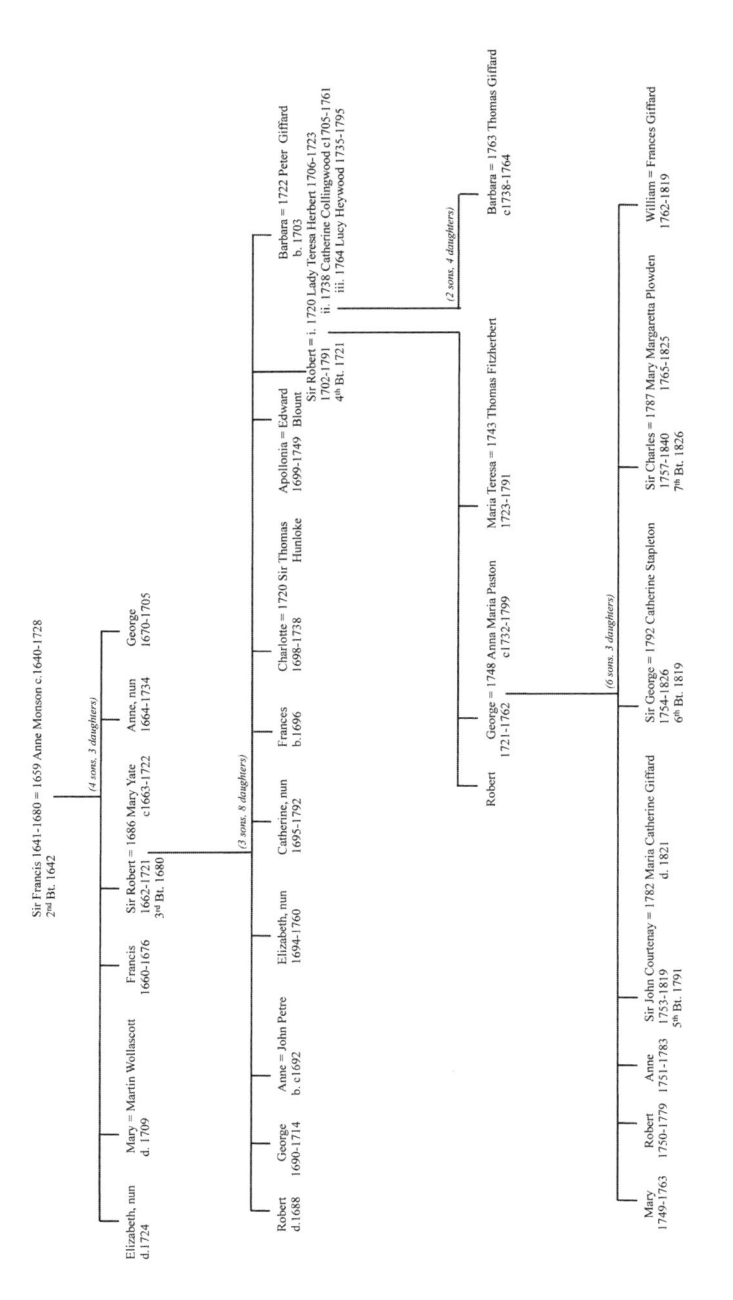

Sir Francis 1641-1680 = 1659 Anne Monson c.1640-1728
2nd Bt. 1642

(4 sons, 3 daughters)

- Elizabeth, nun d.1724
- Mary = Martin Wollascott d. 1709
- Francis 1660-1676
- Sir Robert = 1686 Mary Yate 1662-1721, c1663-1722, 3rd Bt. 1680
- Anne, nun 1664-1734
- George 1670-1705

(3 sons, 8 daughters)

- Robert d.1688
- George 1690-1714
- Anne = John Petre b. c1692
- Elizabeth, nun 1694-1760
- Catherine, nun 1695-1792
- Frances b.1696
- Charlotte = 1720 Sir Thomas Hunloke 1698-1738
- Apollonia = Edward Blount 1699-1749
- Sir Robert: i. 1720 Lady Teresa Herbert 1706-1723; ii. 1738 Catherine Collingwood c1705-1761; iii. 1764 Lucy Heywood 1735-1795
  1702-1791, 4th Bt. 1721
- Barbara = 1722 Peter Giffard b. 1703

Robert

George = 1748 Anna Maria Paston 1721-1762, 1732-1799

Maria Teresa = 1743 Thomas Fitzherbert 1723-1791

Barbara = 1763 Thomas Giffard c1738-1764

(6 sons, 3 daughters)

(2 sons, 4 daughters)

- Mary 1749-1763
- Robert 1750-1779
- Anne 1751-1783
- Sir John Courtenay = 1782 Maria Catherine Giffard 1753-1819, d. 1821, 5th Bt. 1791
- Sir George = 1792 Catherine Stapleton 1754-1826, 1819, 6th Bt. 1819
- Sir Charles = 1787 Mary Margaretta Plowden 1757-1840, 1765-1825, 7th Bt. 1826
- William = Frances Giffard 1762-1819

Victorian Throckmortons

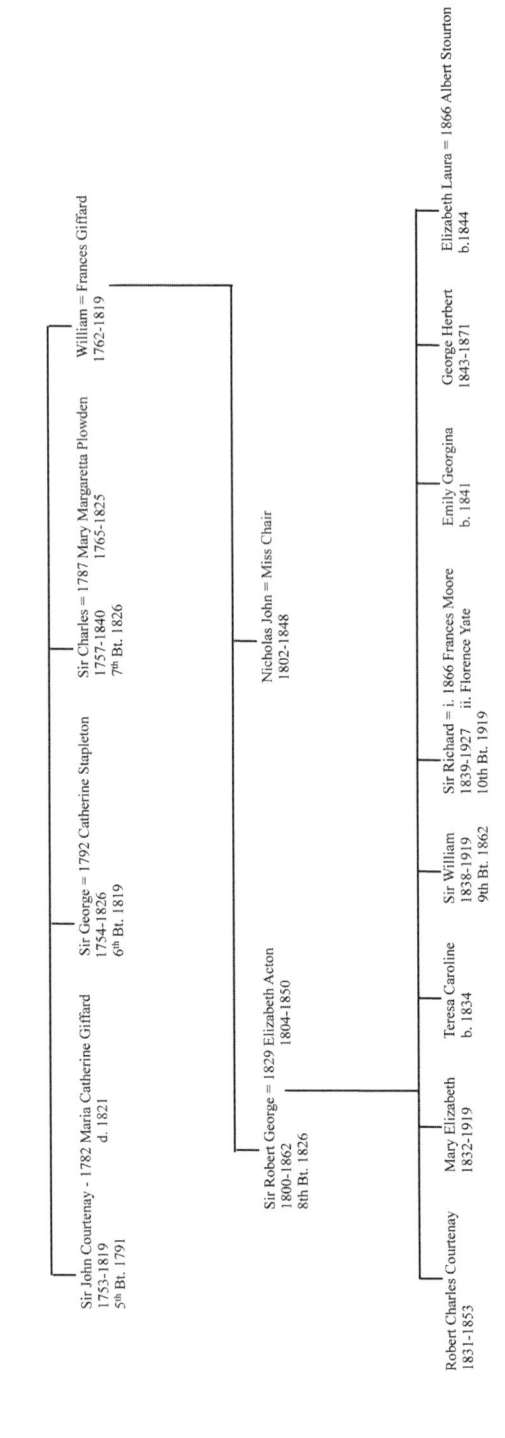

```
Sir John Courtenay - 1782 Maria Catherine Giffard         Sir George = 1792 Catherine Stapleton         Sir Charles = 1787 Mary Margaretta Plowden         William = Frances Giffard
1753-1819                  d. 1821                        1754-1826                                     1757-1840                1765-1825                1762-1819
5th Bt. 1791                                              6th Bt. 1819                                  7th Bt. 1826
                                                                                                                                                          │
                                                                                                                                                          │
                                                                                                        Nicholas John = Miss Chair
                                                                                                        1802-1848

Sir Robert George = 1829 Elizabeth Acton
1800-1862                 1804-1850
8th Bt. 1826
        │
   ┌────┴──────┬──────────────┬──────────────┬──────────────────────────────┐                                              ┌──────────────┬──────────────┬──────────────┐
Robert Charles Courtenay   Mary Elizabeth   Teresa Caroline   Sir William         Sir Richard = i. 1866 Frances Moore      Emily Georgina   George Herbert   Elizabeth Laura = 1866 Albert Stourton
1831-1853                  1832-1919        b. 1834           1838-1919           1839-1927       ii. Florence Yate        b. 1841          1843-1871        b. 1844
                                                              9th Bt. 1862        10th Bt. 1919
```

Index

References to illustrations in bold type

Abbots Salford 181, 202
Act of Union (Ireland) 27
Acton, Charles Januarius 29, 260–61, 266
Acton, Lord John Emerich Edward
    Dalberg 29–30 263–4, 267
Acton family 267
Adams, Simon 86
Agazzari, Alfonso 11
Alcester 18, 250
    abbey 57
    recusants' list 112
    workhouse 259
Aldenham 266
Aldington 57
Allen, William 110
Ampthill 44
Andrews, Sir Francis 192
Anne of Cleves 52, 57
Appellant Controversy 25, 96
Archer, Maude 59
Archer, Richard 59
Arden, Mary (Throckmorton) 79, 103
Arundel, Lady 79
Ashby St Ledgers 99, 101, 113
Ashley, Ralph 93, 118
Askew, Anne 61
Aston Cantlow 44
Audley, Sir Thomas 37
Aveling, Hugh 4–5

Bagshaw, Christopher 96
Baker, Augustine 178
Balsall 35–6, 52
Banbury Castle, 12, 88
Barantyne, Sir William 38, 42
Barnard, Etwell 5, 161, 166–7
Barnes, William 97
Bassett family 108–9
Bates, Thomas 103–4, 113
Bath 19, 205

Catholic chapel 27
Batoni, Pompeo 197–8
Batty, Matthew 106
Bayly, William 167
Beauchamp Court 57
Beeston, Robert 199
Berden, Nicholas 118
Berington, Joseph 20–23, 26, 28, 209,
    215, 217, 231, 250, 262
Betham, Richard 14
Bevington, Mr 263
Bigland, Ralph 204
Bilson, Thomas 119
Birmingham
    Catholic chapel 172
Blanchardists 27
Blount, Apollonia (Throckmorton) 178,
    187
Blount, Mr 132
Blount, Sir Christopher 110
Blount family of Mawsley 178
Blundell, William 234–5
Bodenham, Sir Roger 120
Boleyn, Anne 41–2
Bolt, John 108–9, 132
Bonde, William 53
Bordesley Abbey 56
Bossy, John 1–2, 4–5, 16, 17–19, 28, 259
Boughton, Edward 97
Bowles, Mr 256
Braddocks 108
Brewer, John 220
British Museum 25, 248
Broadway, Jan 12, 14
Brokesby, Robert 90
Bromley, Sir Edward 110
Bromley, Sir Henry 101, 110
Brooks, Harold F. 119
Brooksby, Eleanor 101, 103, 114
Broughton Castle, 12

Broune, Ralph 72
Brown, John 79
Browne family of Cowdray and Battle 4
Browne, Anthony, 1st Viscount Montague 70
Browne, Henry, 5th Viscount Montague 202
Brownlow, John 260–61
Bruges 184
Bryan, Sir Francis 43, 66
Buckland, William 259
Buckland House 213, 262
    chapel 20, 21, 28, 204, 214, 216, 262, 264–5
    estate 24, 173, 207, 209, 221, 250–53
    house 174, 194, 195, 205–7
    missal 176
Bucklebury 257
Buckmaster, William 38
Burdett, Sir Francis 255
Burdett, Robert 72
Burdett, Thomas 46
Burke, Edmund 27, 224
Burghley, Lord 88, 90
Burrell, Mrs 187
Bushel, Sir Edward 113
Bushwood Hall 111, 114
Butler, Charles 27–8, 245, 253
Butler, John 72
Buxton 116
Byres, James 198

Cambridge 165, 167–8
    Dominican friars 33
    Franciscan friars 33
Campion, Edmund 102
Canning, Francis 202
Canning family 27
'Capability' Brown 207
Carew, Lady 113
Carew, Sir George 112
Carrington, Lord 175
Carrington, Mr 195
Caryll, John 161
Cassey, Cassandra 109
Catesby, Lady
Catesby, Richard 59

Catesby, Robert 88, 93–4, 96–7, 100, 103, 106, 111, 113, 114, 116, 118–19, 131
Catholic Board 245
Catholic Emancipation Act 28, 214, 247, 253
Catholic Relief Acts 21, 23, 26, 27, 204, 209, 213–14, 219, 245, 260
Cecil, Robert 14, 86, 89, 90
Cecil, Thomas 88
Chaddesley Corbett 205
Challoner, Richard 204, 235
Chare, Miss 249
Chesterton 62
Chichester, John 194
Church Honeybourne 57
Cisalpinism 21–3, 25, 27–8, 199, 201, 208, 214–18, 226, 243, 245, 249, 259
Clarke, Sir John 45
Clifford family 201
Clopton, William 112
Clopton House 100, 111–13
Cogan, Susan 13, 14
Cole, William 54, 181, 183, 188, 189
Combe Abbey 52
Concordat of 1801 23, 28
Constable, Augustine 181
Constable, Sir Henry 116
Constable, Sir Marmaduke 38
Constable, Sir Marmaduke II 72
Coombe Abbey 94
Corker, James Maurus 215, 218
Coughton Court
    chapel 18, 20, 24, 28–9, 148, 172, 175, 176–177, 202, 206, 214, 245, 250, 251, 262–3, 265–6
Coughton
    parish church 34, 74, 176, 206, 251
    recusants' list 112
Collinson, Patrick 6
Compton, Sir William 35
Cope, Sir Anthony 37
Cowper, William 181, 183–4, 202, 208, 214–15, 224, 245
Crawford, Patricia 70
Cromwell, Oliver 156

INDEX

Cromwell, Thomas 36–7, 41–4, 46, 48–50, 57–8, 60, 71
Cust, Richard 12, 84

Davis, Francis 263
Deerhurst 109
Denny Abbey 53–4, 55–6
Devizes 60
Dieulouard 185
Digby family of Gayhurst 99
Digby, Lady 93, 97, 99, 100, 103, 104, 109
Digby, Sir Everard 93–4, 97, 99, 100, 101, 103, 130
Digby, Sir Robert 94, 111
Digby, Venetia 136
Dingley, Thomas 36, 42, 47–9
Docwra, Martin 36
Docwra, Thomas 35
Dormer, Charles 219
Dormer, Sir Robert 107, 116
Douai
  English College 15, 16, 110, 139, 176
  St Gregory's 188–9, 213
Douglass, John 20–21
Downside 250
Dudley, Ambrose 86
Dudley, Richard 104
Dudley, Sir Robert 94–97
Dudley, Thomas 86
Duffy, Eamon 217
Dugdale, William 31
Dunsmore Heath 94, 110
Dupuy, Jacques and Pierre 22
Dyos, Roger 72–3

East, Alban, alias West, alias Jerningham 121
East, Mr 141
Edward VI xiv, 9, 10
Edwards, Francis 110
Egerton, Lady 89
Egerton, Sir Thomas 117–18
Elizabeth I xiii, 6, 9, 10
Elizabeth, Empress of Austria 268
Ellington, Connecticut xiv
Elrington, Edward 54

Elton, Sir Geoffrey 40
Ely 88
Englefield, Sir Thomas 42
Erasmus 53, 171
Erskine, Charles 239
Espen, Bernard van 26
Essex, Sir William 38, 42, 45–7
Essex Rebellion 94, 110
Evesham Abbey 33, 52, 57, 60
Eyston, Robert 200
Eyston family 27, 261

Faringdon 259
Faringdon Advertiser 268
Farington 107
Farmer, Henry 161
Fawkes, Guy 95, 111
Feckenham, John 60, 65
Fenwick, Francis 184, 192
Ferrers, Edward 72
Fisher, John 39–40, 44
Fisher, Robert 44
Fitzherbert, Maria-Teresa (Throckmorton) 188, 201
Fladbury 7, 62
Fletcher, Dr. 253
Fleury, Claude 26
Flower, John 113
Fontainebleau 192
Forbes, Sir William, of Pitsligo 242
Fortescue, Adrian 104
Fortescue, Sir Francis 104, 106, 110, 136–8
Fox, Charles James 27–8, 209, 216, 245
Foxcote 181, 202
Fraser, a priest 96
Fraser, Lady Antonia 116
Fulke Greville 86, 111, 113
Fullerton, Lady Georgiana 267
Fulwood, Richard 105

Gage, Margaret 89
Gage, Thomas 185
Gallicanism 22–6, 180, 182, 185, 187, 209, 215
Galton family 262
Garnet, Henry 93, 97, 98–103, 105–8, 110

Garnet, Thomas 100
Gayhurst 109
George, Prince of Wales 245
Gerard, John 100, 104, 106–9, 136
Gerard, Thomas 119
Giffard, Barbara (daughter of 3rd bart.) 201
Giffard, Barbara (daughter of 4th bart.) 188, 201
Giffard family 201
Giffard, Thomas 214
Gifford, Sir John 38
Gifford, William 16
Golding, Eleanor (Throckmorton) 139
Gother, John 235
Graham, Sir James 24
Grant, John 113
Grant, Thomas 161
Grant family of Norbrook 99
Grattan, Henry 23
Gray, Lady 108
Greenwood, Gregory 182–3
Gregson, Gregory 26, 183–4, 208–9
Greville, Sir Edward 72, 114–15
Greville, Sir Giles 35
Grey, Frances 204
Grey, Lady Jane, 10
Grey, Thomas 53
Griffin, Rice 77–8
Griffin, Margaret (Throckmorton) 77
Grove Park 107
Guildford, Richard 33
Guldeford family 164
Gunpowder Plot xiii, 93–121, 169
Gunter, Geoffrey 46

Habington, John 101
Habington, Thomas 104, 107, 118
Haigh, Christopher 16
Hall, Hugh 79
Handford family 27
Hanover 268
Hansom, Charles 28, 265–6
Harrington, Sir John 86
Harris, a priest 116
Harrowden 106, 108, 109
Hart, Nicholas 109

Harvington 20, 172–3, 175, 176, 181, 260, 262
Haseley 43, 73
Haselor 137
Hasstings, Sir Charles 259
Hatton, Christopher 90
Hawkes, Thomas 9
Heal, Felicity 5, 73
Hearne, Thomas 200, 207
Henry VIII xiii, 4, 9, 31, 41–2, 48, 57
Herbert, Lady Mary 195
Hibbard, Caroline 15
Hindlip 93, 101, 104, 107, 110
Hoare, William 207
Hodgetts, Michael 13
Holbeach House 93
Holmes, Clive 73
Holte, Sir Thomas 72, 115
Holywell 16, 99, 166, 169, 178
Hood, Alban 21, 24, 27
Hopton, Sir Owen 80
Hornilow, Thomas 155
Hoskins, Anthony 104
Houlbrooke, Ralph 78
Howard, Anne, Countess of Arundel 89–90
Howard, Joseph 195
Howard, Lady Katherine 87–8
Howard, Philip, Earl of Arundel 90
Huddington Court 93, 99, 100, 104, 109, 112
Huddlestone, Dorothy, 106, 107
Huddlestone, Henry 106, 107
Hughes, Anne 151, 153
Hunloke, Charlotte (Throckmorton) 187
Huntington, earls of 90
Husee, John 45, 47
Hussey, Giles 194

Irlam, Peter 44
Irthlingborough 106

Jacobitism 187, 191, 194, 195, 200, 202
James II 18
Jansenism 181–3, 185, 187, 192–4
Johnson, priest 17, 116
Jones, Norman 70

INDEX

Katherine of Aragon 59, 178
Kemerton 27, 261
Kempson, George 137–8
Kempson, Richard 160
Kenilworth Castle 94–6, 107
Kenilworth, abbot of 42
Keyes, Robert 113
Kidderminster 260–61
Kinlet 99, 112, 113
Knapton, George 207
Knightley, Edmund and Richard 37
Knollys, Lettice 110

Lacon family of Kinlet 99, 100, 151
Laithwaite, Thomas 106, 107–8
Lambech, John 90
Largillière, Nicolas de 191, 195, 196
Latimer, Hugh 42
La Vallière, Louise de 193
Legh, Thomas 53
Leveson-Gore, George, Earl Granville 267
Leicester, 60
  abbot of 43
  earl of 86
Leigh, Alice (Dudley) 94, 96–8
Leigh, Catherine 94
Leigh, Sir Thomas 111, 115–16
Le Tourneux, Nicolas, 194
Liège, English Jesuit college 243
Lincoln 44
Lindley, Keith 150
Lingard, John 28
Lisle, Lord 50
Little, Agnes 52
London
  Warwick Street chapel 27
Louth, John 61
Louvain
  St Monica's 15–16, 109, 112, 131–2, 138
Luke, Sir Samuel 156
Lyttelton, Humphrey 118

Maldon 60
Malvern 167
Manners, Francis and George 110

Manners, Lord John 28
Mannock, Anselm 202
Marprelate Tracts 5, 74
Marshall, Peter 5, 9
Mary Queen of Scots, xiii, 9, 10, 79
Mary I 10–11, 178
Mathew, David 215
Maxstoke 52
Mayes, Lawrence 200
Maynooth Grant 24
Mendelson, Sarah 70
Metfoote, John 164
Meysey family of Shakenhurst Park and Hartley Court 100
Middle Littleton 57
Milner, John 20, 21, 216–17, 219, 239, 249
Molland 205
Monck, John Berkeley 255
Monmouth, Humphrey 53
Montague, Viscounts 4, 19
Moore, Robert 96
Moor Hall 102, 103, 126, 130, 132, 135, 156, 161, 165
Mordaunt, Lewis 164
More, Sir Thomas 39–40, 58
Morgan, Henry 111
Morgan, Thomas 146
Morgan family of Heyford 132
Morison, Richard 50
Morgan, Thomas 15
Mounteagle, Lady 87
Mount St Bernard Abbey 262
Mullett, Michael 24, 27

Newenham, William 72
Newman, Peter 150
Nicole, Pierre 193
Northampton 44

O'Connell, Daniel, 253, 256
Oldcorne, Edward 93, 98, 101–2, 110, 116
Ombersley 56, 137, 160
Oscott College 209, 249–50, 262
Oversley 57, 58, 161, 184
Owen, Nicholas 93, 100, 103, 105

Oxford 165
    Dominican friars 33
    Franciscan friars 33

Packington, Robert 45
Paget, Charles 15
Pakington, Humphrey 102, 112, 118
Palmer, Sir Thomas 47
Panemore, Richard 42
Pantin, W. A. 7
Paris
    Conceptionist nuns, 'Blue nuns' 176, 179, 184, 190
    English Augustinian canonesses 22, 184, 187, 189, 190, 192, 194
    English Benedictine monks 176, 183
    Port-Royal 183, 189–90
    St Gregory's 192
Park Hall 79
Parr, Queen Katherine 51, 60–61
Parr, Sir William 37, 51, 60
Paston, James 198, 220
Peel, Sir Robert 24
Pendarves, Mary Delany 19, 202
Percy, John 101, 103, 109
Percy, Thomas 94, 106
Perkins family of Ufton Court 100
Persons, Robert 96, 100
Peto, Goditha (Throckmorton) 39, 54
Peto, Joanna 54
Peto (Peyto), John 62
Peto, William 38–41, 54
Petre, Anne (Throckmorton) 187, 201
Pevsner, Nikolas 207
Phillips, Thomas 209–10
Pigott, Nathaniel 199
Pilgrimage of Grace 44–8, 127
Pitt, William 242
Pius IX, Pope 29
Pleydell-Bouverie, William, Lord Radnor 255
Plowden, Charles 239–40
Plowden family 201
Plumerden, Thomas 193
Pole, Geoffrey 49
Pole, Reginald 48–9, 59
Pope, Alexius 262–4

Porter, William 32
Portland, Duchess 202
Potts, Thomas 249
Powell, Winifred (Throckmorton) 139
Poynter, William 238–40
Princenhoff, Bruges 190
Pugin, Augustus Welby 28, 265
Pusey, Edward Bouverie 262
Pusey, Philip 258, 262
Puttenham, Margaret 14
Pye, Henry 207

Quebec Act 26
Questier, Michael 4, 70, 123

Ralegh (Raleigh), Sir Walter xiv, 5, 86
Ravenstone 52, 172, 206
Reading Abbey 52
Reynolds, Richard 40–41, 53
Rheims 16
Rich, Lady Penelope 108
Rich, Richard 56, 57–8, 60, 61
Ridcall, Francis 116
Roanoke, Virginia xiv
Rock, Daniel 28–9, 264
Rome
    Accademia Ecclesiastica 250
    artists 24, 197–8
    English College 16, 244
Rookwood family of Coldham 100
Rookwood, Ambrose 99–100, 112, 113
Rookwood, Elizabeth 100
Rookwood, Robert 99
Rookwood, Thomas 113
Roper, Anne 138
Roper, Sir Francis 96
Roper, Sir William 138
Ross Williamson, Hugh 103, 110, 116
Rouen 190
Rowington 52
Rowlands, Marie 70
Rowse, A. L. 5, 6, 10, 17
Russell, Elizabeth 102, 109, 112
Rutland, Earl of 110
Rutland, 3rd earl of 86

Salwey, Anthony 162–3

INDEX 279

Salwey, Humphrey 169
Salwey, Richard 161–2, 166, 169
Salwey, Thomas 141, 163–6, 169–170
Sambourne 112, 126, 160, 161, 205
Sandys, Lord 110
Sandys family 146
Scarborough 19
Scott, Geoffrey 24
Scudamore, John 56
Segneri, Paolo 193
Shakespeare, William 104
Sheldon, Anne (Throckmorton) 105
Sheldon, Hugh 105
Sheldon, William 155, 161
Sheldon family 146, 199
Short, Richard 193
Shrewsbury, Lord 264
Sidney, Sir Robert 97
Simeon, Sir George 107
Simpson, Benedict 183
Singleton, William 105–7
Smith, Charles 146
Smith, Francis 110, 138
Smith, James 164–5, 167, 169
Smith, Sir John 149, 175
Society of Dilettanti 245
Society of Friends of the People 245
Solihull 43, 60
Sommerville, John 79
Southampton, Earl of 110
Southcott, Thomas 195
Southwell, Catherine 97
Southwell, Elizabeth 96–7
Southwell, Robert 11, 14, 121
Spencer, Alice 117–19
Spencer, Anne 117, 119
Spencer, Elizabeth 117
Spencer, Lady 245
Spencer, Sir John 116
Spenser, Sir William 37
Spernall 126, 206
Squiers, Granville 120
Standon Lordship 188
Stapleton family 201
Starkey, David 6
Stonor, John Talbot 20, 200
Stonyhurst 243

Stanford, William 202
Strange, Thomas 105, 106–7
Stratford-upon-Avon 72, 74
   Holy Cross guild 33
Straunge, Lady Anne 118
Strickland, Thomas 200
Stubbs, Justinian 109
Studley
   Augustinian canons 33, 52, 57
   church 28, 57, 265–6
Sugar, John, alias Cocks 115
Swetman, Francis 106

Tabula Eliensis 12, 176
Tanner, Katheryn 54
Tanworth 59, 128
Tate, William 109
Tattenhoe 43
Taylor, Mr 109
Tempest, Thomas 113
Terringham, Lady 75
Terringham, Thomas 76
Tesimond, Oswald 95, 99, 103–4, 106,
   109, 111, 119
Tewkesbury Abbey 57
Thorpe, John 198, 240
Throckmorton, Agnes (Wilford) 15, 76–7,
   82, 84–5, 102, 123ff.
Throckmorton, Agnes, of Temple Grafton
   112
Throckmorton, Ambrose (son of John)
   139, 157, **158**
Throckmorton, Anna Maria (Paston) 19,
   27, 182, 188–9, 202, **203**, 204–5
Throckmorton, Anne (daughter of Sir
   Robert, 1st bart.) 152, 161
Throckmorton, Anne (d. 1734) 184–5,
   187, 190–92, **196**
Throckmorton, Anne (d.1728) 165, 170,
   178, 179, 192
Throckmorton, Anne (d. 1783) 189–90
Throckmorton, Anthony 10, 32, 65
Throckmorton, Arthur 13–14, 87
Throckmorton, Catherine (d. 1792) 187
Throckmorton, Catherine (Collingwood)
   19, 201–2
Throckmorton, Catherine (Stapleton) 202

Throckmorton, Sir Charles (7th baronet) 183, 188–189, 194, 198, 208, 247–8, 250–53, 258–9, 262–3, 265–8
Throckmorton, Clement (d. 1573) 9, 60–61, 65, 73–4
Throckmorton, Clement (son of Job) 74
Throckmorton, Courtenay (d.1853) 250, 266
Throckmorton, Dorothy (Fortescue) 104, 135, 137–8
Throckmorton, Edward 110
Throckmorton, Edward (d. 1582) 11, 14, 15, 121
Throckmorton, Elizabeth (d. 1547) 53–4, 56
Throckmorton, Elizabeth (d. 1724) 179, 190, 191
Throckmorton, Elizabeth (d. 1760) 187, 190–91, **196**
Throckmorton, Elizabeth ['Bess'] xiv
Throckmorton, Elizabeth (Acton) 29, 248, 251, 266–8
Throckmorton, Elizabeth (Baynham) 48
Throckmorton, Frances (daughter of Sir Robert, 3rd bart.) 187
Throckmorton, Francis (d. 1584) xiii, 5, 11, 14, 15, 79–80, 127
Throckmorton, Francis (d.1676) 184
Throckmorton, Sir Francis (2nd baronet) 5, 16, 17, 141, 152, 161–170, 171–2, 176, 179, 184, 190
Throckmorton, Francis (s. of George) 189
Throckmorton, George (son of Sir George) 32, 60–61
Throckmorton, George (son of John) 139
Throckmorton, George (d. 1705) 192–4
Throckmorton, George (d. 1714) 185,
Throckmorton, George (d. 1762) 54, 183, 188, 195
Throckmorton, George (6th bart) 188–9, 198, 204, 208, 220, 247–8, 260
Throckmorton, George, of Chisfield 172
Throckmorton, George, of Temple Grafton 103, 112
Throckmorton, Sir George xiii, xiv, 5, 6, 9, 15, 16, 31–67, 71–2

Throckmorton, Herbert (d. 1871) 250
Throckmorton, Job (died 1601) 5, 74, 86, 87
Throckmorton, John (d. 1445) 7
Throckmorton, John (d.1604) 12, 15, 73, 81, 87–8, 123–5, 130–31
Throckmorton, John 79
Throckmorton, John (d. 1918) 250, 268
Throckmorton, Sir John (d.1580) xiii, 10–11, 32, 60, 65
Throckmorton, Sir John Courtenay (5th baronet) 6, 20–29, 180, 183, 188–9, 194, 198–200, 205–9, **210**, 211, 213–45, 247, 250, 253, 256, 262
Throckmorton, Joyce (daughter of Sir Robert) 54
Throckmorton, Katherine (Marrow) 33
Throckmorton, Katherine (Vaux) 32, 51, 63, **64**
Throckmorton, Kenelm 9, 32, 37, 43, 56, 60–61, 65
Throckmorton, Margaret (b. 1591) 109, 125, 138
Throckmorton, Margaret (wife of William Tracy) 53
Throckmorton, Margaret (daughter of Sir Robert) 54
Throckmorton, Margaret or Margery (Puttenham) 14–15, 79–80
Throckmorton, Margaret (Whorwood) 78, 89
Throckmorton, Maria Catherine (Giffard) 202, 208, 213–14, 219, 224
Throckmorton, Mary (Smith) 17, 138, 141, 152, 156, 161, 162, 164, 168
Throckmorton, Mary (Yate) 173, 260
Throckmorton, Mary (d. of Thomas) 75–6, 78, 83, 91, 140
Throckmorton, Mary (d. 1709) 176
Throckmorton, Mary (d. 1763) 189
Throckmorton, Mary (daughter of William) 248
Throckmorton, Mary Elizabeth (d.1919) 268
Throckmorton, Mary Margaretta (Plowden) 248

Throckmorton, Michael 15, 48–50, 59–60
Throckmorton, Muriel, Lady Tresham 14
Throckmorton, Sir Nicholas (d. 1571) xiv, 9, 10, 13, 32, 51, 60–63, 65
Throckmorton, Nicholas (d. 1848) 248–9
Throckmorton, Sir Richard (10th baronet) 250
Throckmorton, Sir Robert (died 1518) 7, 32, 33–4, 36, 52, 63, 65, 176
Throckmorton, Robert (son of Sir George) 9, 10, 15, 32, 51, 61, 62, 72
Throckmorton, Sir Robert (1st baronet) 12, 73, 81–4, 123, 128–38, 140–41, 143–61, 175
Throckmorton, Sir Robert (3rd baronet) 18, 172, 178–9, 181, 184, 198–9, 206–7
Throckmorton, Sir Robert (4th baronet) 20, 24, 34, 176, 178, 182, **186**, 187–9, 191, 194–5, **196**, 202, 204–7
Throckmorton, Robert (d. 1779) 189, **197**, 198
Throckmorton, Sir Robert George (8th baronet) xiii, 7, 28–9, 247–8, 250, 252–3, **254**, 255–62, 264–8
Throckmorton, Teresa (Herbert) 195, 200
Throckmorton, Thomas (d. 1414) 7
Throckmorton, Thomas (d. 1595) 11, 13–14, 15, 79
Throckmorton, Thomas (d. 1615) 10, 12, 73, 75, 76–8, 81–3, 86, 89, 93, 97, 99, 101, 102, 123–4, 127–8, 130–39
Throckmorton, Thomas (son of John) 84, 139, 141, 143, 154, 157, 159
Throckmorton, Thomas, of Tortworth 14
Throckmorton, William (Uncle of Sir George Throckmorton) 35
Throckmorton, William (marriage 1714) 20
Throckmorton, Sir William 172
Throckmorton, William (d.1819) 188–9, 194, 208, 237, 241, 243
Throckmorton, Sir William (9th baronet) 250
Throckmorton, Worcs. 152, 161, 205

Throckmorton Plot 14, 15, 96
Throgmerton, Richard 60
Tootell, Hugh, alias Charles Dodd 181–2
Topcliffe, Richard 108, 116
Tracy, Richard, 53
Tracy (Tracey), William 53
Trent, Council of 26
Tresham, Francis 87–8, 93, 119, 131
Tresham, Muriel (Throckmorton) 85, 88–90
Tresham, Sir Thomas 12, 73, 87–9, 127, 128
Trimble, William 3
Troy, François du 195
Tyldesley, Bridget 179
Tyndale, William 53
Tyringham, Lady 156

Uckington 56
Udall, William 99
Ullathorne, William Bernard 21, 260–61, 266
Underhill, Edward 9

Vaux, Anne 100, 101, 103
Vaux, Elizabeth 106–9
Vaux, Lord 1, 85
Vaux, Mary 107
Vaux, Sir Nicholas 32
Verney, Greville 97
Verney, Sir Richard 13, 97, 107–9, 111, 112
Versailles 195

Walker, Augustine 24, 197, 198, 220
Wall, John 168, 175
Wallop, Sir John 50
Walpole, Horace 183
Walsh, Thomas 260
Walsham. Alexandra 16
Walsingham, Sir Francis 80, 89, 90
Walter, John 256
Wanklyn, Malcolm 5, 16
Warren, Robert 113
Warwick 60, 146
    castle 10, 72
    countess of 89

earl of 62, 86
Franciscan friars 33
Warwick Bridge 265
Waters, Francis 160
Waters, Robert 175
Westminster Abbey 65
West, Thomas 228
Weston, William 36–7, 52
Weston Underwood 7, **8**, 14, 17, 18, 22, 26, 75–6, 99, 103, 123, 130, 133, 135, 140, 141, 146–7, 152, 154, 156, 159, 164, 165, 168, 172, 173, 175, 178, 179, 181–4, 202, 204–6, 208, 213–14, 247, 251
White Webbs 100, 108
Wickhamford 57
Wigston 52
Wilford, Thomas 81–3
Wilks, Joseph Cuthbert 20, 209, 219
Willis, Browne 204
Wilson, Nicholas 40–41
Wintour, Thomas 106
Wintour family of Huddington 99, 113
Witham, Thomas 192–4

Wollascott, Frances 190–92, 195, **196**
Wollascott, Mary (Throckmorton) 184
Wollascott, Mary 190
Wolsey, Thomas 35–7, 52
Wood, John 195, 206
Woods, Richard 207
Worcester
    earl of 109, 120
    Throckmorton almshouse 34
Wotton, Nicholas 49
Wright family 111, 113, 114
Wright, Christopher 106
Wright, John 94, 106
Wriothesley, Chancellor 61
Wroxall Priory 52
Wyatt's rebellion 9
Wythie, Bernard 182

Yate, ?James 102
Yate, Sir John 178
Yate, Lady Mary 175
Yate family 175–6
Young England 28